Business, Industry, and Trade in the Tropics

The tropics is an area of enormous opportunity and potential. The countries situated between the Tropics of Cancer and Capricorn are largely developing in nature. There is huge interest in the types of business investments made in Southeast Asia, Central Africa, and the Amazonian tropical belts. These tropical regions continue to face opportunities and challenges in attracting foreign direct investments as well as the need to complement and/or compete with larger economies external to the tropics.

This book provides an empirical assessment of the key sociocultural, economic, environmental, and political factors that influence the business dynamics of organizations operating within the tropics. It will address but is not limited to topics such as attracting businesses to the tropics, facilitating smooth, stable conditions for business operations and sustainability, national institutions, and regulations that shape the way business is done, and the increasing deployment of new technologies and entrepreneurial innovations which are defining the global tropics as a distinct business region. It will offer readers a key focus for developing a deeper understanding of the factors and frameworks that influence and shape business activity in the area.

While the primary audience for the book consists of academics and students from the fields of economics (environmental economics, developmental economics), business, international trade, tourism, and area studies, it will also provide a practical resource for government policy analysts wanting to fully appreciate some of the key economic and business issues facing the region.

Jacob Wood is an Associate Professor of Business at James Cook University (JCU), Singapore.

Taha Chaiechi is an Associate Professor of Economics in the College of Business, Law, and Governance at James Cook University (JCU), Cairns, Australia.

K Thirumaran is the Academic Head for JCUS Business School, James Cook University (JCU), Singapore.

Routledge Advances in Business, Industry and Trade in the Tropics

Series editors: **Jacob Wood, K Thirumaran and Taha Chaiechi**

Situated between the Tropics of Cancer and Capricorn the countries that make up the Tropics are largely developing in nature.

The *Routledge Advances in Business and Industry in the Tropics* series provides a detailed appraisal of the Tropics. With a focus on economic development, business, governance, tourism, and international trade, this series captures the complexities and heterogeneous nature of one of the fastest growing regions in the world. The series uncovers the economies, political institutions, and socio-economic conditions of the region and the growing pains that many countries face.

Each of the books in the series, investigate the ongoing structural changes associated with economic development that takes into account evolving industry compositions and the emergence of new competitive advantages and explore transformative growth and fundamental reorientation of economic resources as part of the solution through a post-Keynesian lens.

The series provides critical, theoretical and practical policy-based content for academics, business leaders, and institutional bodies alike.

Business, Industry, and Trade in the Tropics
Edited by Jacob Wood, Taha Chaiechi and K Thirumaran

For more information in this series, please visit: https://www.routledge.com/Routledge-Advances-in-Business-Industry-and-Trade-in-the-Tropics/book-series/RABAIT

Business, Industry, and Trade in the Tropics

Edited by Jacob Wood, Taha Chaiechi and K Thirumaran

Routledge
Taylor & Francis Group
LONDON AND NEW YORK

First published 2022
by Routledge
4 Park Square, Milton Park, Abingdon, Oxon OX14 4RN

and by Routledge
605 Third Avenue, New York, NY 10158

Routledge is an imprint of the Taylor & Francis Group, an informa business

British Library Cataloguing-in-Publication Data
A catalogue record for this book is available from the British Library

Library of Congress Cataloging-in-Publication Data
Names: Wood, Jacob, editor. | Chaiechi, Taha, 1977-editor. |
Thirumaran, K. (Tourism and hospitality scholar), editor.
Title: Business, industry and trade in the Tropics/edited by Jacob Wood, Taha Chaiechi and K. Thirumaran.
Description: Abingdon, Oxon; New York, NY: Routledge, 2022. |
Series: Routledge advances in business, industry and trade in the Tropics |
Includes bibliographical references and index.
Identifiers: LCCN 2021048120 (print) | LCCN 2021048121 (ebook) |
ISBN 9780367721213 (hbk) | ISBN 9780367721350 (pbk) |
ISBN 9781003153580 (ebk)
Subjects: LCSH: Business enterprises–Tropics. | Organizational change–Tropics. | Tropics–Economic conditions. | Sustainability–Tropics.
Classification: LCC HF1008 .B865 2022 (print) | LCC HF1008 (ebook) |
DDC 658.4/060913–dc23/eng/20211202
LC record available at https://lccn.loc.gov/2021048120
LC ebook record available at https://lccn.loc.gov/2021048121

ISBN: 978-0-367-72121-3 (hbk)
ISBN: 978-0-367-72135-0 (pbk)
ISBN: 978-1-003-15358-0 (ebk)

DOI: 10.4324/9781003153580

Typeset in Bembo
by Deanta Global Publishing Services, Chennai, India

Contents

Figures

Tables

Contributors

Benedict Atkinson is a Senior Lecturer at JCU Singapore Business School, James Cook University, Singapore.

Akhmad Bayhaqi is a Senior Analyst at the APEC Policy Support Unit.

Vahid Biglari is a Lecturer at the University of Newcastle, Singapore.

Taha Chaiechi is an Associate Professor of Economics at the College of Business, Law, and Governance, James Cook University, Australia.

Wai-Mun Chia is an Associate Professor at the Department of Economics, School of Social Science, Nanyang Technological University, Singapore.

Emiel L. Eijdenberg is a Senior Lecturer of Business at JCU Singapore Business School, James Cook University, Singapore.

Gohar Feroz Khan is an Associate Professor at the School of Management and Marketing, University of Waikato, Hamilton, New Zealand.

Reetika Gupta is an Associate Professor of Marketing at ESSEC Business School, Singapore.

Haejin Jang is a Learning Advisor at James Cook University, Singapore.

Yenee Kim is an Assistant Professor of Marketing at EDHEC Business School, France.

Enno Masurel is a Professor in Sustainable Entrepreneurship at the Department of Management and Organization Studies, School of Business and Economics Vrije Universiteit, Amsterdam, the Netherlands.

Malobi Mukherjee is a Lecturer of Business at James Cook University, Singapore.

Nelson Obange is a Senior Lecturer at the Department of Economics School of Business and Economics Maseno University, Kenya.

Rael A. Onyango is a Researcher at the Department of Management and Organization Studies, School of Business and Economics Vrije Universiteit Amsterdam, the Netherlands.

Zahra Pourabedin is a Lecturer in Business at JCU Singapore Business School, James Cook University, Singapore.

Josephine Pryce is an Associate Professor, College of Business, Law and Governance, James Cook University, Australia.

Omary Swallehe is a Senior lecturer at Mzumbe University Dar es Salaam Campus College, Tanzania.

Sook-Rei Tan is a Lecturer at JCU Business School, James Cook University, Singapore.

K Thirumaran is a Senior Lecturer at JCU Business School, James Cook University, Singapore.

Pengji Wang is an Associate Professor at JCU Singapore Business School, James Cook University, Singapore.

Jacob Wood is an Associate Professor at JCU Singapore Business School, James Cook University, Singapore.

Yohannes Workeaferahu Elifneh is an Assistant Professor at the Department of Management, Addis Ababa University, Ethiopia.

Jie Wu is an Associate Professor at the Department of International Economics and Trade, College of Economics, Zhejiang University of Technology, China; and Adjunct Research Fellow at JCU Singapore Business School, James Cook University, Singapore.

Huiping Zhang is an Associate Professor at JCU Singapore Business School, James Cook University, Singapore.

1 Business-financing options' effects on micro-enterprise performance in the tropics

The case of Kisumu County, Kenya

Rael A. Onyango[1], Emiel L. Eijdenberg[2], Enno Masurel[3] and Nelson Obange[4]

Introduction

Entrepreneurs are economic actors, and their activities (i.e., starting, managing, owning, and exiting their enterprises) are fundamental factors in economic development (Acs et al., 2008; Kirzner, 1974, 1997; Szirmai et al., 2011). The creation of organizations (referred to as *enterprises* in this chapter) is known as 'entrepreneurship', and the individuals who create them are 'entrepreneurs' (Gartner, 1988). Entrepreneurship occurs worldwide, in many different forms. Particularly in emerging economies, such ventures are known as 'micro-enterprises', which will be defined and discussed in the next section, as they are crucial because they create jobs and are one way to get people out of extreme poverty (Bruton et al., 2013; Sutter et al., 2019). Many emerging economies are located in the world's tropical region, between latitudes 23°26'11.5' North and 23°26'11.5' South (Feeley & Stroud, 2018).

One may ask, 'Why do the tropics matter?' This region matters because: (1) it is where most people on the planet live in general, and most children specifically; (2) it has the greatest biodiversity; and (3) it is where most cultures, which are based on linguistic diversity, live. Fuelled by rapid population growth, the tropics are becoming wealthier rapidly, which goes hand in hand with increased trade and investment. However, these upward socioeconomic trends are jeopardized by challenges and effects from climate change and humanity's heavy ecological footprint (State of the Tropics, 2020). Within this socioeconomically challenged region, most of the emerging economies lie in Africa, including the nation examined in our study: Kenya.

Apart from poverty, many emerging economies are defined by malfunctioning infrastructure, low life expectancy, and government and market failure (Cohen & Winn, 2007; African Development Bank Organisation for Economic Cooperation and Development/United Nations Development Programme, 2016). For some people, these issues may sound like factors that would discourage people from investing in entrepreneurial ventures, but others see investment opportunities, as long as effective and creative responses to environmental and institutional challenges are undertaken (Eijdenberg & Thompson, 2020a). The

DOI: 10.4324/9781003153580-1

millions of micro-entrepreneurs who call the tropics home try to seize opportunities on a daily basis. As a result, opportunity exploitation makes their micro-enterprises perform in a particular way, as they either fail, stabilize, or grow.

Micro-enterprises' performance, particularly in the tropical context, is receiving increasing attention from the academic community (Adekunle, 2011; Al Mamun & Fazal, 2018; Engström & McKelvie, 2017). Determinants of micro-enterprise performance in particular have been studied frequently (Al Mamun & Ekpe, 2016; Al Mamun & Fazal, 2018; Gebreeyesus, 2011). One of the most notable and persistent challenges that micro-enterprises face in emerging economies, compared with industrialized economies, appears to be business financing (Beck et al., 2015; Fatoki, 2014a; Isaga & Musabila, 2017). It has been noted that in emerging economies, financial systems have failed to generate savings to invest in micro-enterprises and thereby stimulating them (Dupas & Robinson, 2013). Lending institutions are known to be sluggish and sometimes unwilling to provide loans for micro-enterprises (Ezeoha & Ituma, 2017).

While considering the interplay between micro-enterprise financing and performance, we perceived a literature gap. While most studies on financing systems have focussed more often than not on corporate financing and small and medium-size enterprises' capital (Osei-Assibey et al., 2012), these studies have not taken into account the complexities involved in financing micro-enterprises (Alkire & Foster, 2011), particularly in tropical emerging economies. Moreover, considering this study's context, i.e., Kenya, little is known about the effects from different business-financing options that micro-enterprises use. What is known are the effects from some types of business finance, including micro-finance (Rotich et al., 2015; Simeyo et al., 2013); debt financing, such as trade credit and equity financing (Githaigo & Kabiru, 2015; Raude et al., 2015); and factors that influence micro-enterprises' financial access (Bunyasi et al., 2014) in Kenya. What is not known are the effects from (combinations of) different business-financing options. With this in mind, an empirical approach that can identify which business-financing combinations and options could be useful to boost micro-enterprises' performance represents an obvious literature gap. More specifically, a need exists to examine how micro-enterprises choose to balance personal financing (i.e., contributions from micro-entrepreneurs, such as personal savings), internal financing (i.e., use of retained business earnings) and external financing (e.g., funding from family and friends, angel finance, venture capital, crowdfunding and commercial banks), as this balancing act can affect their performance. This considered, the following research question will be answered in this chapter: *to what extent does the use of different business-financing options affect micro-enterprises' performance in an emerging economy?* To answer the research question, primary data from 326 micro-enterprises in Kenya were collected and analyzed. The next section examines the relevant literature. Subsequently, the study's methodology is laid out, followed by the study's findings. Finally, the chapter closes with a concluding discussion.

Literature review

In this section, we start by drawing a picture of micro-enterprises and their performance. Subsequently, different forms of business financing of micro-enterprises are discussed.

Micro-enterprises and their performance

The concept of micro-enterprises varies across the world depending on region, industry, and subsector. Thus, a uniform way to define *micro-enterprise* may not exist. Normally, a thin line exists when differentiating a micro-enterprise from a small business. This study defines a *micro-enterprise* based on number of employees, i.e., a micro-enterprise is a business with less than ten employees, as this is the main standard in Kenya (Berisha & Pula, 2015; Ministry of Industrialisation, Trade and Enterprise Development, 2021). Micro-enterprises are prototypical businesses found in many emerging economies in the tropics (Mead & Liedholm, 1998): 'Hundreds of millions of poor people in developing countries make their living as micro-entrepreneurs: As farmers, street vendors and home workers, and in a range of other occupations, a large share of them [are] women' (World Bank, 2004, p. 33). Men often are unable to take home sufficient income from their paid, regular jobs to sustain their families, and this shortage in family income often pushes women to start micro-enterprises themselves, although some men operate micro-enterprises on the side to generate additional income for their families.

Micro-enterprises often are involved in food preparation and vending activities, e.g., selling *ugali, chapatti*, or fish on the streets in Kenya. Other items sold include sandals, handicrafts, airtime cellphone cards, clothes, and utensils. Micro-entrepreneurs start, operate, and own (often informal) 'one-person operations [that are] poorly managed, sometimes temporary, less-productive and undercapitalised' (Kiggundu, 2002, p. 248). These characteristics result in 'limited ability to compete on price and quality' (Kristiansen et al., 2005, p. 366). As a consequence, this elicits large numbers of micro-entrepreneurs exercising copycat behaviour, selling basically identical products everywhere across emerging economies.

Although different types of entrepreneurial motivations exist and they even may change over time (Eijdenberg et al., 2021), micro-entrepreneurs are typically necessity-motivated, i.e., they launch their enterprises for survival or other needs-driven reasons (Eijdenberg, 2016; Eijdenberg & Masurel, 2013). In rapidly urbanizing regions in the tropics, micro-enterprises more often than not are located in urban areas, near large prospective customer bases and infrastructural facilities that these regions offer (Choongo et al., 2020). Furthermore, micro-enterprises often operate in the informal economy, which 'consists of economic activities that occur outside of formal institutional boundaries, but which remain within informal institutional boundaries for large segments of society' (Webb et al., 2013, p. 598). Considering that many micro-enterprises are informal (for an extensive discussion, see Abdallah & Eijdenberg, 2019;

Abdallah et al., 2020), a hide-and-seek game is played between micro-entrepreneurs and local authorities, i.e., debt collectors chase after micro-entrepreneurs to pay taxes and bills, so they often relocate quickly in and around urban areas with their 'mobile' self-built premises (e.g., wooden or carton boxes) to avoid local authorities' reach (Choongo et al., 2020). This hints at another typical characteristic of micro-enterprises: they may start today, then may be gone tomorrow (i.e., either they move to other sites or they close down business operations entirely). Nevertheless, their informal and fluid character does not necessarily mean that micro-enterprises always aim to exit the informal economy by any means. Instead, the sense of freedom from the government, few procedures, and low capital requirements are attractive attributes, motivating micro-entrepreneurs to remain in the informal economy (Abdallah et al., 2020; Abdallah & Eijdenberg, 2019). Capturing micro-enterprises' performance in emerging economies is often difficult. In emerging economies, many micro-enterprises either do not maintain their bookkeeping (Frese et al., 2007), or in the event that they do, their bookkeeping is often of poor quality, making it challenging to assess their enterprise performance (Batana, 2013; Young, 2012). As a consequence, more and more entrepreneurship scholars (e.g., Eijdenberg, 2016; Eijdenberg & van Montfort, 2017) have adopted alternative yardsticks to measure enterprise performance, e.g., development of personal wealth. These gauges usually are more contextualized and often are viewed as proxies, e.g., possessing a TV or refrigerator, or having electricity, running water, or high-quality materials used at home (Booysen et al., 2008; Pouw & Elbers, 2012). In the present study, we used a similar contextualized and adaptive approach, i.e., items identified with development of personal wealth aside from prototypical firm growth items (e.g., sales, assets, number of employed people, and supplies). Thus, considering our analyses, micro-enterprises' performance is a combination of: a) firm growth; and b) development of personal wealth.

Business-financing options

Although business financing ideally supports micro-enterprises (Fakudze & Machethe, 2015; Nukpezah & Blankson, 2017), 'if you ask entrepreneurs what is the most important bottleneck that they experience, they would probably not start with knowledge, but with finance' (Dana et al., 2018, p. 122). Most micro-enterprises do not have a reliable and credible way to prove their creditworthiness to overcome informational asymmetry problems that arise while seeking business financing. Or else they have difficulties accessing or are unaware of available business-financing options (Fatoki, 2014b; Ssendi & Anderson, 2009). These issues force micro-enterprises to depend on different business-financing options, and examples of such options identified in the academic literature can be categorized broadly into three groups: personal financing; internal financing; and external financing, as depicted in Table 1.1. In this table, the most prominent examples of each category are provided. Note that combinations of these business-financing options are also possible.

Table 1.1 Business-financing options at a glance*

Option	*Examples*	*Selection of references*
Personal financing	Micro-entrepreneur's contributions, such as personal savings	Abor (2017)
Internal financing	Retained business earnings	Abor (2017)
External financing	Family, friends, and relatives	Abor (2017) Kotha and George (2012)
	Angel finance, venture capital, crowdfunding	Abor (2017) Berger and Udell (1988)
	Commercial banks, mobile money**	Berger and Udell (1988) Hughes and Lonie (2007)
	Non-bank financial institutions (NBFIs) such as micro-finance institutions (MFIs) and savings and credit cooperatives (SACCOs)	Abor (2017) Johnson (2004)
	Savings and credit groups, such as rotating savings and credit associations (ROSCAs)	Abor (2017) Gichuki et al. (2014)
	Government funds and enterprise grants	Abor (2017) Daskalakis et al. (2013)
	Trade credit	Berger and Udell (1988)
	Loan sharks, pawn financing, moneylenders	Abor (2017) Ayyagari et al. (2010)

Note: * The references in this table are not collectively exhaustive. ** Mobile money 'is a payment system (storing of value, payment instrument and channel) that enables financial services (payments, savings, credit and insurance) using ubiquitous mobile technology' (David-West et al., 2019, p. 277).

Although it may be perceived as a risk and, therefore, a hindrance to performance (Ukanwa et al., 2018), external financing generally elicits positive effects on micro-entrepreneurs' performance, albeit with some reservations (Ferdousi, 2015; Nukpezah & Blankson, 2017). Several studies have demonstrated that younger and less-educated entrepreneurs actively use external financing, while older and more educated entrepreneurs are less likely to seek or use external financing (Vos et al., 2007). Also worth noting are the arguments advanced about constrained micro-enterprises turning to trade credit and informal finance, particularly when it is difficult to obtain external financing via credit institutions (Casey & O'Toole, 2014).

Furthermore, reactions have been mixed and inconsistent concerning informal finance and trade credit's role in managing enterprises' growth (Ferrando & Mulier, 2013). That is, evidence indicates that industries which use more trade credit grow relatively faster in economies with poorly developed financial markets (Fisman & Love, 2003), mainly because a micro-enterprise can finance production more easily if its suppliers provide working capital, or the micro-enterprise can sell more if it can alleviate financial constraints on its customers (Ferrando & Mulier, 2013). Therefore, business-financing options are a matter of great concern for many micro-entrepreneurs and policy-makers due to their various effects, which this study seeks to discover.

Methodology

The study's tropical context: Kenya

This research was conducted in Kenya, East Africa. Although viewed as one of the most stable economies in Africa (Voigt, 2020), Kenya typically is still viewed as 'emerging', a quality defined by socioeconomic indicators. In 2019, gross domestic product (GDP) growth was 5.4%, while the average GDP per capita was USD 4,330. Kenya's main economic sector is agriculture, which contributes about one-third to the national GDP. About three-quarters of the population works at least part-time in the agricultural sector (Central Intelligence Agency, 2021). However, like other African countries, Kenya is urbanizing rapidly: cities and towns are major magnets for younger residents (e.g., 40% of Kenyans are below 15 years old, and the median age is 20 years old). Kenya's population totals 53 million, with highly populated areas including Kenya's capital and largest city, Nairobi; coastal areas of the Indian Ocean (which include the City of Mombasa); and the shores of Lake Victoria (which include the City of Kisumu) (Central Intelligence Agency, 2021).

Kenya's land mass comprises 580,367 square kilometres. The nation has low plains at the coast and highlands, and plateaus in the centre. Due to altitude differences, the climate varies from humid tropical along the ocean coast to arid in the hinterlands (Central Intelligence Agency, 2021). The equator runs through the middle of the country, and the Great Rift Valley runs from north to south across the country. Mount Kenya is the country's highest peak, at 5,199 metres. Like other places in the tropics, Kenya faces increasing climate challenges, such as desertification, deforestation, drought, and floods, which all are impacting local biodiversity and natural resources greatly (State of the Tropics, 2020).

Data collection

We chose a quantitative research design based on the administration of a pen-and-paper questionnaire (Saunders et al., 2009). This type of research design frequently has been used in other emerging economies in the tropics (cf. Eijdenberg & Borner, 2017; Eijdenberg & Ehmann, 2019). Data collection took place in Kisumu County during the August–September 2018 period. Kisumu is the fifth-largest city in Kenya, located in the western part of the country. Kisumu lies on the shores of Lake Victoria, the world's second-largest freshwater lake, shared with neighbouring countries Tanzania and Uganda. Lake Victoria's presence has enabled the rise and dominance of micro-enterprises entailing fish sales in the area. This is one reason why this research focussed on micro-enterprises in the fishing industry.

The questionnaire was established based on *a priori* conversations with key players in the fishing industry, a literature review, and team discussions. The final questionnaire was created based on these individual insights' iterative processes and the literature: in this chapter, part of the fully anonymous questionnaire is presented as a 'measurement instrument': for comprehensibility and consistency purposes, this measurement instrument was limited, reworded, and recoded using dummy variables different from the original questionnaire (e.g., the items 'gender' and 'age' reflect the original 'What is your gender?' and 'When were you born?' questions). See Table 1.2. The original questionnaire is available upon request.

Convenience and snowball sampling were used to choose respondents. Within this sampling technique, the so-called 'random walk procedure' (Frese et al., 2007, p. 1486) was followed, a common sampling method that often is applied in other tropical and economically emerging areas (see, e.g., Eijdenberg & Ostertag, 2021; Eijdenberg & Thompson, 2020b). With this procedure in mind, the respondents were selected based on these inclusion criteria: 1) their enterprises had less than ten employees (i.e., a qualification to be a micro-enterprise; Ministry of Industrialisation, Trade and Enterprise Development, 2021), and 2) the respondents were fish vendors, who pay a fixed amount of money daily (i.e., market fees) to the county authorities, in Kisumu County. Therefore, all the areas where fish are sold in Kisumu's central business district and its surrounding residential areas were visited, and fish vendors were surveyed face-to-face on their business premises. The sites (i.e., areas, landmarks, neighbourhoods, and districts) where the respondents were found included: Jubilee Fish Market; Kibuye Market, Vunduba, Dunga, Nyalenda, Nyamasaria, Manyatta, Kondele, Migosi, Mamboleo, Car Wash, Kona-lejo, Kona Mbaya, Koyango, Obunga, Bandani, Riat, Nyawita, Kodongo, and next to Tuskys. Note that the fish vendors may have moved from these areas since they participated in this study due to displacement from demolitions and infrastructural developments that the county government instituted. Furthermore, using a sample threshold of $N > 50 + 8m$, in which m represents the number of independent variables in the study (Tabachnick et al., 2007), the 'random walk procedure' in Kisumu County eventually resulted in $N = 326$ completed questionnaires.

Out of the 326 micro-entrepreneurs, 98% were females and 2% were males. A high percentage of female micro-entrepreneurs is consistent with much empirical evidence from other emerging economies in Africa (Adom, 2015; Amine & Staub, 2009). Despite this prevalence of females in the sample, female entrepreneurs are more disadvantaged when it comes to securing financial capital for their micro-enterprises than their male counterparts (Adom, 2015; Kiggundu, 2002). In addition, the micro-entrepreneurs' average age was 42, while the median was 40. Furthermore, the youngest respondent was 19, and the oldest 76. The micro-entrepreneurs' average years of experience with these

Table 1.2 Measurement instrument

#	*Item*	*Scale*
Micro-entrepreneur's characteristics		
1	Gender	Male; female
2	Age	Ratio? Number?
3	People working in the micro-enterprise	Micro-entrepreneurs who work alone; micro-entrepreneurs who employ people
Firm growth★		
4	Sales	Greatly decreased; decreased; neither increased nor decreased; increased; greatly increased
5	Assets (e.g., motorcycle, business premises)	
6	Number of employed people	
7	Supplies (i.e., inventory)	
Development of personal wealth★		
8	The amount I spent on housing (i.e., built or bought a home [home ownership], etc.)	Greatly decreased; decreased; neither increased nor decreased; increased; greatly increased
9	The amount spent on educating dependents	
10	The amount spent on acquiring prestigious items (e.g., car, satellite TV, motorcycle)	
11	The amount spent on insurance (e.g., on life insurance and other types, such as health insurance)	
12	The amount spent on acquiring financial assets (e.g., stocks, treasury bills and bonds, commodity derivatives, savings bonds and accounts, trusts)	
Business-financing options★★		
13	Personal financing (i.e., micro-entrepreneur's own contributions, such as personal savings)	No; yes
14	Internal financing (i.e., use of retained business earnings)	
15	External financing (e.g., family and friends, angel finance, venture capital crowdfunding, commercial banks, etc.)	

Note: ★ In the original pen-and-paper questionnaire, the items in these sections were preceded by the question, 'Considering your yearly business performance, how did the following indicators change in 2017 compared with 2016?' ★★ Reference years: 2016 and 2017.

Table 1.3 Descriptive statistics for firm growth and development of personal wealth

Item	*Mean*	*Standard deviation*
Firm growth		
Sales	2.56	1.13
Assets	3.22	.69
Number of employed people	3.03	.40
Supplies	2.87	.81
All	2.91	.53
Development of personal wealth		
Amount spent on housing	3.53	.91
Amount spent on educating dependents	4.13	.63
Amount spent on acquiring prestigious items	3.47	.74
Amount spent on insurance	3.19	.72
Amount spent on acquiring financial assets	3.17	.83
All	3.51	.50

enterprises was 14.5, while the median was 13. Out of all the micro-entrepreneurs in the study, 92% were operating their micro-enterprises alone, while the other 8% employed staff. Moreover, the descriptive statistics for the firm growth items and the development of personal wealth items are summarized in Table 1.3. From this table, it can be concluded that asset growth registers the highest score for firm growth items, whereas the amount spent on education dependents registers the highest score for the development of personal wealth items. It also can be observed that the standard deviations are rather low, i.e., there was not much spread between the respondents.

The business-financing options were divided into three major categories in the measurement instrument (see Table 1.1 for a more comprehensive overview that includes references): personal financing (i.e., contributions from the micro-entrepreneur, such as personal savings); internal financing (i.e., retained business earnings); and external financing (e.g., funds from family and friends, angel finance, venture capital, crowdfunding, and commercial banks). Not being mutually exclusive, we observed eight combinations of business-financing options (see Table 1.4). Table 1.4 indicates that a majority of the micro-entrepreneurs, i.e., 24.2%, used a combination of internal and external financing.

Results

Considering the firm growth items, our ANOVA revealed a statistically significant difference, at the $p < .05$ level, in sales based on business-financing options used [F (7,318) = 2.28, p = .03] (see Table 1.5). The other items did not yield any significant differences – namely assets [F (7,306) = 1.25, p = .28], number of employed people [F (7,310) = 1.01, p =.42] and supplies [F (7,313) = .82,

Table 1.4 Combinations of business-financing options

Business-financing options	*Frequency (N)*	*Percentage*
Internal financing and external financing	79	24.2
Internal financing	53	16.3
External financing	51	15.6
Personal financing and internal financing and external financing	51	15.6
Personal financing and external financing	35	10.8
Personal financing and internal financing	23	7.1
Personal financing	21	6.4
None of these financing options	13	4.0
Total	326	100

Table 1.5 ANOVA for firm growth

Firm growth items	*ANOVA groups*	*Sum of squares*	*df*	*Mean square*	F	*Significance*
Sales	Between sub-groups	19.81	7	2.83	2.28	.03**
	Within groups	394.70	318	1.24		
	Total	414.51	325			
Assets	Between groups	4.11	7	.59	1.25	.28
	Within groups	144.28	306	.47		
	Total	148.40	313			
Number of employed people	Between groups	1.16	7	.17	1.01	.42
	Within groups	50.64	310	.16		
	Total	51.80	317			
Supplies	Between groups	3.83	7	.55	.82	.57
	Within groups	207.93	313	.66		
	Total	211.76	320			
All items	Between groups	1.99	7	.28	1.03	.41
	Within groups	88.12	318	.28		
	Total	90.11	325			

Note: ** Significant at 5% level.

p = .57], nor was there a statistically significant effect for all firm growth items together [F (7,318) = 1.03, p = .41] (see Table 1.5 for all details).

Moving forward from the significant value of sales in Table 1.5, the business-financing options are ranked on their descending means of sales in Table 1.6. We observed a limited significant difference between the eight sub-groups of micro-enterprises: only the micro-enterprises that combined internal and external financing and those that used external financing only scored lower in terms of sales growth than the other six sub-groups of micro-enterprises (with personal financing only, the combination of personal, internal, and external financing, the combination of personal and internal financing, the combination

Table 1.6 T-test results for business-financing options and sales

Combinations of business-financing options	*Mean*	*Standard deviation*	*1*	*2*	*3*	*4*	*5*	*6*	*7*	*8*
1. Personal financing	3.00	1.14	–							
2. Personal financing and internal financing and external financing	2.84	1.29	.629	–						
3. Personal financing and internal financing	2.78	1.00	.504	.827	–					
4. Personal financing and external financing	2.69	1.16	.327	.563	.743	–				
5. Internal financing	2.58	1.05	.138	.265	.445	.673	–			
6. None of these financing options	2.54	0.97	.234	.355	.481	.685	.885	–		
7. Internal financing and external financing	2.30	1.02	.008***	.013**	.049**	.097*	.126	.440	–	
8. External financing	2.25	1.18	.016**	.018**	.067*	.098*	.134	.427	.802	–

Note: *** Significant at 1% level; ** significant at 5% level; * significant at 10% level.

of personal and external financing, internal financing only, and none of the business-financing options at all). With some reservations, it can be concluded that a positive relationship exists between personal financing and sales growth.

Considering the development of personal wealth items, our ANOVA demonstrated a statistically significant effect only on the amount spent on housing [F (7,311) = 2.41, p = .02] (see Table 1.7). No statistically significant effects were revealed for the other four items concerning development of personal wealth, viz. the amounts spent on education of dependents [F (7,317) = 1.40, p = .21], acquisition of prestigious household items [F (7,313) = .93, p = .49], life insurance and other forms of insurance [F (7,311) = .33, p = .94], and financial assets [F (7,307) = .81, p = .58], nor was there a statistically significant effect for all items together [F (7,318) = 1.49, p = .17] (see Table 1.7 for all details).

The business-financing options are ranked in descending order based on amount spent on housing in Table 1.8. Again, we observed only a limited significant difference between the eight groups of micro-enterprises. This table's major revelation is that the combination of personal and internal financing, personal financing only, and the combination of personal, internal, and external financing did not show significant differences with each other in terms of the amount spent on housing, and that they scored higher than the other five

Table 1.7 ANOVA for development of personal wealth

Development of personal wealth items		*Sum of squares*	*df*	*Mean square*	F	*Significance*
Amount spent on housing	Between groups	13.44	7	1.92	2.41	.02**
	Within groups	248.03	311	.80		
	Total	261.47	318			
Amount spent on educating dependents	Between groups	3.81	7	.54	1.40	.21
	Within groups	123.50	317	.39		
	Total	127.31	324			
Amount spent on acquiring prestigious household items	Between groups	3.58	7	.51	.93	.49
	Within groups	172.39	313	.55		
	Total	175.97	320			
Amount spent on insurance	Between groups	1.20	7	.17	.33	.94
	Within groups	162.75	311	.52		
	Total	163.95	318			
Amount spent on financial assets	Between groups	3.88	7	.55	.81	.58
	Within groups	210.21	307	.69		
	Total	214.08	314			
All items	Between groups	2.55	7	.36	1.49	.17
	Within groups	77.81	318	.25		
	Total	80.36	325			

Note: ** Significant at 5% level.

Table 1.8 T-test results for business-financing options and amount spent on housing

Combinations of business-financing options	*Mean*	*Standard deviation*	*1*	*2*	*3*	*4*	*5*	*6*	*7*	*8*
1. Personal financing and internal financing	3.95	.84	–							
2. Personal financing	3.79	.71	.507	–						
3. Personal financing and internal and external financing	3.67	.86	.193	.582	–					
4. Internal and external financing	3.56	.94	.077*	.317	.505	–				
5. Internal financing	3.53	1.01	.087*	.306	.462	.874	–			
6. External financing	3.38	.81	.008***	.056*	.088*	.275	.413	–		
7. None of these financing options	3.38	.87	.065*	.159	.298	.539	.673	.986	–	
8. Personal financing and external financing	3.12	.88	.001***	.006***	.006***	.022**	.056**	.162	.356	–

Note: *** Significant at 1% level; ** Significant at 5% level; * Significant at 10% level.

forms of business financing (the combination of internal and external financing, internal financing only, external financing only, none of the business-financing options at all, and the combination of personal and external financing). Again with some reservations, it can be noted that a positive relationship exists between personal financing and the amount that micro-entrepreneurs spent on housing.

Concluding discussion

With respect to the research question, the findings suggest that only limited evidence exists that different business-financing options affect micro-enterprises' performance in Kenya's tropical emerging economy. Only with some reservations can it be stated that a positive relationship exists between personal financing and sales growth (as a firm growth item) and between personal financing and increased spending on housing (as development of a personal wealth item), compared with internal and external financing. No relationship was found between the other firm growth items (i.e., assets, number of employed people, and supplies) and business-financing options. As for development concerning personal wealth development items (i.e., the amount spent on education dependents, prestigious household items, insurance, and financial assets), no relationships with the business-financing options were found.

Business financing's limited effect on micro-enterprises' performance may derive from the idea that different forms of financing are hardly different in terms of availability and costs in practice. However, external financing may not be easily accessible to micro-entrepreneurs, possibly due to a lack of collateral. Furthermore, micro-enterprises' profits may be low; thus, retained earnings will be low, thereby limiting options for internal and personal financing (the latter due to a limited transfer of business income to the micro-entrepreneur's household). The rather prominent role of personal financing, above internal and external financing, may have to do with the overlap between the micro-enterprise and the household, i.e., income from the micro-enterprise is transferred to the household rapidly.

This chapter's main contributions can be broken down into two levels. On a general level, this chapter boosts understanding of entrepreneurship contexts worldwide (Eijdenberg & Thompson, 2020a; Lepeley et al., 2019). On a specific level, it contributes to the understanding of the micro-enterprises' domain and their business financing (Manini et al., 2016; Nukpezah & Blankson, 2017) by finding only a limited effect from business-financing options on micro-enterprises' performance and that a positive relationship exists between personal financing and micro-enterprises' performance, with some reservations. Nonetheless, we identified two major limitations in our study: we only surveyed a relatively small sample, in a specific tropical area (i.e., Kenya's Kisumu County). From this, we formulated recommendations for future research. First, these findings should be applied to other tropical regions, both inside Kenya and in other emerging economies. Second, qualitative research (e.g., focus groups, interviews, observations) should be conducted to complement this study's quantitative approach.

Regarding the practical implications, we refer to our granular findings. Practitioners such as educators and trainers are encouraged to focus on factors that *do* elicit an effect on micro-enterprises' performance, i.e., personal financing, as opposed to those that *do not* elicit an effect, i.e. internal and external financing. Our findings indicate that personal financing, defined as own contributions by the micro-entrepreneur, do pay off. This is what educators and trainers should emphasize to students and nascent micro-entrepreneurs as the takeaway from these findings. Teaching students and nascent micro-entrepreneurs who are self-sustainable financially (e.g., through education in contextualized financial management, bookkeeping, and business planning in primary and secondary school, as well as higher and vocational education) are more independent and reliant on their inner strength and, therefore, are more resilient in the event of future financial setbacks and challenges, such as economic crises, rising competition and unexpected extraneous shocks, such as the current COVID-19 pandemic. However, micro-entrepreneurs in the tropics should understand and rely on what has been suggested to educators and trainers, i.e., that personal financing is the route to better micro-enterprise performance. This is probably the safest way to establish and structure a micro-enterprise because debt and/or external capital is avoided. We also concluded that only with some reservations is there a positive relationship between personal financing and sales growth, and between personal financing and increased spending on housing, compared with internal and external financing. Turning to personal financing (i.e., from the household to the firm) *may* have to do with saving money. Therefore, encouraging micro-entrepreneurs to save money through savings accounts and other such measures would be conducive to better micro-enterprise performance.

Acknowledgements

This book chapter is part of Rael A. Onyango's PhD dissertation. The authors acknowledge the support by SPADE which stands for 'Building Stronger Capacities to link Spatial Planning to Agribusiness and Public Policy Development in Greater Western Kenya'. SPADE is a NICHE project which is funded by the Dutch Ministry of Foreign Affairs and managed by NUFFIC. The project is coordinated by the Centre of International Cooperation of Vrije Universiteit Amsterdam. The project is implemented in Kenya through a joint collaboration with Maseno University. The financial support from the SPADE project was fundamental for the study design, data collection, and write-up of this book chapter. The authors declare that no competing interests exist.

Notes

1 School of Business and Economics, Vrije Universiteit Amsterdam, the Netherlands.
2 Corresponding author: JCU Singapore Business School, James Cook University, Singapore. Email: emiel.eijdenberg@jcu.edu.au.
3 School of Business and Economics, Vrije Universiteit Amsterdam, the Netherlands.
4 Department of Economics, Maseno University, Kenya.

References

Abdallah, G. K., & Eijdenberg, E. L. (2019). Entry and stay in the informal economy: Qualitative findings from a least-developed country. *Journal of Enterprising Culture, 27*(2), 115–145.

Abdallah, G. K., Masurel, E., Naudé, W. A., & Eijdenberg, E. L. (2020). Unboxing entrepreneurial motivations in Tanzania: Business-related and personal-related factors. *Journal of African Business. Early Cite:* https://doi.org/10.1080/15228916.2020.1785236.

Abor, J. Y. (2017). *Entrepreneurial finance for MSMEs: A managerial approach for developing markets*. Springer International Publishing.

Acs, Z. J., Desai, S., & Hessels, J. (2008). Entrepreneurship, economic development and institutions. *Small Business Economics, 31*(3), 219–234.

Adekunle, B. (2011). Determinants of microenterprise performance in Nigeria. *International Small Business Journal, 29*(4), 360–373.

Adom, K. (2015). Recognising the contribution of female entrepreneurs in economic development in sub-Saharan Africa: Some evidence from Ghana. *Journal of Developmental Entrepreneurship, 20*(1), 1550003.

Al Mamun, A., & Ekpe, I. (2016). Entrepreneurial traits and micro-enterprise performance: A study among women micro-entrepreneurs in Malaysia. *Development in Practice, 26*(2), 193–202.

Al Mamun, A., & Fazal, S. A. (2018). Effect of entrepreneurial orientation on competency and micro-enterprise performance. *Asia Pacific Journal of Innovation and Entrepreneurship, 13*(3), 379–398.

Alkire, S., & Foster, J. (2011). Understandings and misunderstandings of multidimensional poverty measurement. *Journal of Economic Inequality, 9*(2), 289–314.

Amine, L. S., & Staub, K. M. (2009). Women entrepreneurs in sub-Saharan Africa: An institutional theory analysis from a social marketing point of view. *Entrepreneurship & Regional Development, 21*(2), 183–211.

Ayyagari, M., Demirgüç-Kunt, A., & Maksimovic, V. (2010). Formal versus informal finance: Evidence from China. *Review of Financial Studies, 23*(8), 3048–3097.

Batana, Y. M. (2013). Multidimensional measurement of poverty among women in Sub-Saharan Africa. *Social Indicators Research, 112*(2), 337–362.

Beck, T., Lu, L., & Yang, R. (2015). Finance and growth for microenterprises: Evidence from rural China. *World Development, 67*, 38–56.

Berger, A. N., & Udell, B. F. (1988). The economics of small business finance: Roles of private equity and debt markets in the financial growth cycle. *Journal of Banking & Finance, 22*(6–7), 613–673.

Berisha, G., & Pula, J. S. (2015). Defining small and medium enterprises: A critical review. *Academic Journal of Business, Administration, Law and Social Sciences, 1*(1), 17–28.

Booysen, F., van der Berg, S., Burger, R., Maltitz, M. von, & Du Rand, G. (2008). Using an asset index to assess trends in poverty in seven Sub-Saharan African countries. *World Development, 36*(6), 1113–1130.

Bruton, G. D., Ketchen Jr, D. J., & Ireland, R. D. (2013). Entrepreneurship as a solution to poverty. *Journal of Business Venturing, 28*(6), 683–689.

Bunyasi, G., Bwisa, H., & Namusonge, G. (2014). Effects of entrepreneurial finance on growth of small and medium enterprises in Kenya. *European Journal of Business and Management, 6*(31), 113–123.

Casey, E., & O'Toole, C. M. (2014). Bank lending constraints, trade credit and alternative financing during the financial crisis: Evidence from European SMEs. *Journal of Corporate Finance, 27*, 173–193.

Central Intelligence Agency (2021). The World factbook: Kenya. https://www.cia.gov/the-world-factbook/countries/kenya/

Choongo, P., Eijdenberg, E. L., Chabala, M., Lungu, J., & Taylor, T. K. (2020). The evolution of urban entrepreneurship in Zambia. In: M. N. Iftikhar, J. B. Justice, & D. B. Audretsch (Eds.), *Urban studies and entrepreneurship* (pp. 249–269). Springer.

Cohen, B., & Winn, M. I. (2007). Market imperfections, opportunity and sustainable entrepreneurship. *Journal of Business Venturing, 22*(1), 29–49.

Dana, L.-P., Ratten, V., & Honyenuga, B. Q. (2018). *African entrepreneurship: Challanges and opportunities for doing business. Palgrave studies of entrepreneurship in Africa.* Palgrave Macmillan.

Daskalakis, N., Jarvis, R., & Schizas, E. (2013). Financing practices and preferences for micro and small firms. *Journal of Small Business and Enterprise Development, 20*(1), 80–101.

David-West, O., Iheanachor, N., & Umukoro, I. O. (2019). Mobile money as a frugal innovation for the bottom of the pyramid: Cases of selected African countries. *Africa Journal of Management, 5*(3), 274–302.

Dupas, P., & Robinson, J. (2013). Savings constraints and microenterprise development: Evidence from a field experiment in Kenya. *American Economic Journal: Applied Economics, 5*(1), 163–192.

Eijdenberg, E. L. (2016). Does one size fit all? A look at entrepreneurial motivation and entrepreneurial orientation in the informal economy of Tanzania. *International Journal of Entrepreneurial Behaviour & Research, 22*(6), 804–834.

Eijdenberg, E. L., & Borner, K. (2017). The performance of subsistence entrepreneurs in Tanzania's informal economy. *Journal of Developmental Entrepreneurship, 22*(1), 1–22.

Eijdenberg, E. L., & Ehmann, L. (2019). Exploring well-being indicators of women micro-entrepreneurs in Zambia. In: M.-T. Lepeley, K. Kuschel, N. Beutell, N. Pouw, & E. L. Eijdenberg (Eds.), *Well-being of women in entrepreneurship: A global perspective* (pp. 359–373). Routledge.

Eijdenberg, E. L., & Masurel, E. (2013). Entrepreneurial motivation in a least-developed country: Push factors and pull factors among MSEs. *Journal of Enterprising Culture, 21*(1), 19–43.

Eijdenberg, E. L., & Ostertag, F. (2021). Resource-conserving entrepreneurial behaviour of micro-entrepreneurs: Evidence from a Tanzanian community. In: S. Azzali & K. Thirumaran (Eds.), *Tropical constrained environments and sustainable adaptations* (pp. 27–44). Springer.

Eijdenberg, E. L., & Thompson, N. A. (2020a). *Entrepreneurs' creative responses to institutional challenges: Insider perspectives from Sub-Saharan Africa.* Emerald Group Publishing.

Eijdenberg, E. L., & Thompson, N. A. (2020b). Jump for joy: Happiness as the route to increased living standards of entrepreneurs in Zambia. *Small Enterprise Research, 27*(2), 240–257.

Eijdenberg, E. L., & van Montfort, K. (2017). Explaining firm performance in African least-countries: Evidence from Burundi and Tanzania. *International Review of Entrepreneurship, 15*(3), 375–394.

Eijdenberg, E. L., Isaga, N. M., Paas, L. J., & Masurel, E. (2021). Fluid entrepreneurial motivations in Tanzania. *Journal of African Business, 22*(2), 171–189.

Engström, P., & McKelvie, A. (2017). Financial literacy, role models and micro-enterprise performance in the informal economy. *International Small Business Journal, 35*(7), 855–875.

Ezeoha, A., & Ituma, A. (2017). An institutional analysis of entrepreneurship development in Nigeria. In: A. Akinyoade, T. Dietz, & C. U. Uche (Eds.), *African dynamics: Vol. 15. Entrepreneurship in Africa* (pp. 147–171). Brill.

Fakudze, C. D., & Machethe, C. L. (2015). Improving smallholder livestock farmers' incomes through value chain financing in South Africa. *Development in Practice, 25*(5), 728–736.

Fatoki, O. (2014a). Enhancing access to external finance for new micro-enterprises in South Africa. *Journal of Economics, 5*(1), 1–6.

Fatoki, O. (2014b). The financing options for new small and medium enterprises in South Africa. *Mediterranean Journal of Social Sciences, 5*(20), 748–755.

Feeley, K. J., & Stroud, J. T. (2018). Where on Earth are the 'tropics'? *Frontiers of Biogeography, 10*(1–2), e38649

Ferdousi, F. (2015). Impact of microfinance on sustainable entrepreneurship development. *Development Studies Research, 2*(1), 51–63.

Ferrando, A., & Mulier, K. (2013). Do firms use the trade credit channel to manage growth? *Journal of Banking & Finance, 37*(8), 3035–3046.

Fisman, R., & Love, I. (2003). Trade credit, financial intermediary development and industry growth. *Journal of Finance, 58*(1), 353–374.

Frese, M., Krauss, S. I., Keith, N., Escher, S., Grabarkiewicz, R., Luneng, S. T., Friedrich, C. (2007). Business owners' action planning and its relationship to business success in three African countries. *Journal of Applied Psychology, 92*(6), 1481–1498.

Gartner, W. B. (1988). 'Who is an entrepreneur?' is the wrong question. *American Journal of Small Business, 12*(4), 11–32.

Gebreeyesus, M. (2011). Innovation and microenterprises growth in Ethiopia. In: A. Szirmai, W. Naudé & M. Goedhuys (Eds.), *Entrepreneurship, innovation and economic development* (pp. 122–146). Oxford University Press.

Gichuki, C. N., Mulu-Mutuku, M., & Kinuthia, L. N. (2014). Performance of women-owned enterprises accessing credit from village credit and savings associations in Kenya. *Journal of Global Entrepreneurship Research, 4*(1), 1–13.

Githaigo, P. N., & Kabiru, C. G. (2015). Debt financing and financial performance of small and medium size enterprises: Evidence from Kenya. *Journal of Economics Finance and Accounting, 2*(3), 473–481.

Hughes, N., & Lonie, S. (2007). M-PESA: Mobile money for the 'unbanked' turning cell phones into 24-hour tellers in Kenya. *Innovations: Technology, Governance, Globalisation, 2*(1–2), 63–81.

Isaga, N., & Musabila, A. (2017). Challenges to entrepreneurship development in Tanzania. In: A. Akinyoade, T. Dietz, & C. U. Uche (Eds.), *African dynamics: Vol. 15. Entrepreneurship in Africa* (pp. 232–254). Brill.

Johnson, S. (2004). The impact of microfinance institutions in local financial markets: A case study from Kenya. *Journal of International Development, 16*(3), 501–517.

Kiggundu, M. N. (2002). Entrepreneurs and entrepreneurship in Africa: What is known and what needs to be done. *Journal of Developmental Entrepreneurship*, 7(3), 239–258.

Kirzner, I. M. (1974). *Competition and entrepreneurship.* University of Chicago Press.

Kirzner, I. M. (1997). Entrepreneurial discovery and the competitive market process: An Austrian approach. *Journal of Economic Literature, 35*(1), 60–85.

Kotha, R., & George, G. (2012). Friends, family or fools: Entrepreneur experience and its implications for equity distribution and resource mobilisation. *Journal of Business Venturing, 27*(5), 525–543.

Kristiansen, S., Kimeme, J., Mbwambo, A., & Wahid, F. (2005). Information flows and adaptation in Tanzanian cottage industries. *Entrepreneurship & Regional Development, 17*(5), 365–388.

Lepeley, M.-T., Kuschel, K., Beutell, N., Pouw, N., & Eijdenberg, E. L. (Eds.) (2019). *Wellbeing of women in entrepreneurship: A global perspective.* Routledge.

Manini, M. M., Abdillahi, U. A., Wanyama, K., & Simiyu, J. (2016). Effect of business financing on the small and medium enterprises in Lurambi Sub-County, Kenya. *European Journal of Business and Management, 8*(2), 1–21.

Mead, D. C., & Liedholm, C. (1998). The dynamics of micro and small enterprises in developing countries. *World Development, 26*(1), 61–74.

Ministry of Industrialisation, Trade and Enterprise Development (2021). Micro and small enterprises act, 2012. https://www.industrialization.go.ke/index.php/policies/99-micro-and-small-enterprises-act-2012

Nukpezah, J. A., & Blankson, C. (2017). Microfinance intervention in poverty reduction: A study of women farmer-entrepreneurs in rural Ghana. *Journal of African Business, 18*(4), 457–475.

African Development Bank/Organisation for Economic Cooperation and Development/ United Nations Development Programme (2016). *African Economic Outlook 2016: Sustainable Cities and Structural Transformation.* OECD Publishing.

Osei-Assibey, E., Bokpin, G. A., & Twerefou, D. K. (2012). Microenterprise financing preference. *Journal of Economic Studies, 39*(1), 84–105.

Pouw, N., & Elbers, C. (2012). Modelling priority patterns in asset acquisition: The case of smallholder farmers in three rural districts in Uganda. *Journal of Development Studies, 48*(9), 1360–1374.

Raude, J. M., Wesonga, W., & Wawire, P. (2015). Equity financing strategy and the performance of small and medium enterprises in Kenya. *International Journal of Business and Management, 10*(4), 193–202.

Rotich, I., Lagat, C., & Kogei, J. (2015). Effects of microfinance services on the performance of small and medium enterprises in Kenya. *African Journal of Business Management, 9*(5), 206–211.

Saunders, M., Lewis, P., & Thornhill, A. (2009). *Research methods for business students.* Pearson Education.

Simeyo, O., Martin, L., Nyamao, N. R., Patrick, O., & Odondo, A. J. (2013). Effect of provision of micro-finance on the performance of micro-enterprises: A study of youth micro-enterprises under Kenya Rural Enterprise Programme (K-REP), Kisii County, Kenya. *African Journal of Business Management, 5*(20), 8290–8300.

Ssendi, L., & Anderson, A. R. (2009). Tanzanian micro-enterprises and micro-finance: The role and impact for poor rural women. *Journal of Entrepreneurship, 18*(1), 1–19.

State of the Tropics (2020). 2020 report. https://www.jcu.edu.au/state-of-the-tropics/publications/2020

Sutter, C., Bruton, G. D., & Chen, J. (2019). Entrepreneurship as a solution to extreme poverty: A review and future research directions. *Journal of Business Venturing, 34*(1), 197–214.

Szirmai, A., Naudé, W. A., & Goedhuys, M. (2011). *Entrepreneurship, innovation and economic development: WIDER studies in development economics.* Oxford University Press.

Tabachnick, B. G., Fidell, L. S., & Ullman, J. B. (2007). *Using multivariate statistics* (Vol. 5). Pearson Education.

Ukanwa, I., Xiong, L., & Anderson, A. (2018). Experiencing microfinance: Effects on poor women entrepreneurs' livelihood strategies. *Journal of Small Business and Enterprise Development, 25*(3), 428–446.

Voigt, M. (2020). Entrepreneurship in times of post-election riots: A case study of small business owners in Kisumu, Western Kenya. *African Identities, 18*(3), 313–328.

Vos, E., Yeh, A. J.-Y., Carter, S., & Tagg, S. (2007). The happy story of small business financing. *Journal of Banking & Finance, 31*(9), 2648–2672.

Webb, J. W., Bruton, G. D., Tihanyi, L., & Ireland, R. D. (2013). Research on entrepreneurship in the informal economy: Framing a research agenda. *Journal of Business Venturing, 28*(5), 598–614.

World Bank (2004). *World development report 2005: A better investment climate for everyone.* World Bank and Oxford University Press.

Young, A. (2012). The African growth miracle. *Journal of Political Economy, 120*(4), 696–739.

2 Profiling the tropical entrepreneur

Emiel L. Eijdenberg[1] *and Taha Chaiechi*[2]

Entrepreneurship in general

Entrepreneurship is probably one of the oldest human undertakings. From early hunter-gatherers to the ancient Greeks and Romans, people came together to trade products and goods. Based on scarcity, products and goods gained economic value. Fast-forward to the Industrial Revolution in the 18th and 19th centuries, a time of greater added value to products and services that could cater to large consumer markets, e.g., apparel, automobiles, and home appliances. During this time (1755), Richard Cantillon, an Irish banker and businessman based in Paris, outlined the principles in his *Essai sur la nature du commerce en general*, viewed today as the earliest notion of (scientific) entrepreneurship written on paper (Cantillon, 1755/1999).

Today, *entrepreneurship* is understood as the discovery of value-added opportunities, often in the form of creative, innovation-driven products and services that destroy or disrupt established markets and even societies (Kirzner, 1974, 1997; Schumpeter, 1934). Contemporary examples of the most successful entrepreneurial ventures include Apple, Facebook, and Microsoft. These companies' products and services have radically changed how people communicate, live, and work in the past few decades. Another example is Airbnb, which is viewed as the largest platform for non-hotel accommodations, as the organization does not own or rent any real estate, unlike conventional hotel chains. An important aspect is that many entrepreneurial ventures are based in the West, i.e., developed, industrialized countries in the Northern Hemisphere, sometimes referred to socioeconomically as the Global North.

However, entrepreneurship is happening not only in the Western context, but also worldwide. Increasingly, scholars have been researching entrepreneurship in many emerging economies (Bruton et al., 2008; Bruton et al., 2013; Kiss et al., 2012), where it is on the rise and often viewed as either a necessity to make a living due to a lack of alternative opportunities, or as a means to escape from meaningless, unsatisfying, and/or low-paying jobs at established organizations (Eijdenberg & Masurel, 2013; Eijdenberg et al., 2015; Kiggundu, 2002). From an academic perspective, the challenging institutional contexts are interesting settings to study because entrepreneurs are forced to think and

DOI: 10.4324/9781003153580-2

act in creative ways to respond to the constraints they face (Eijdenberg et al., 2019). For example, a sub-optimal education system in Tanzania persuaded entrepreneurs to homeschool their children. In Zambia, badly governed waste management prompted entrepreneurs to take matters into their own hands and come up with their own garbage-collection systems (Eijdenberg & Thompson, 2020). Although various entrepreneurial forms, activities, and types in emerging economies have been studied extensively, all these aspects of entrepreneurship have been overlooked in terms of the common denominator in most of these economies: their climatological and geographical context. This observed gap leads to the following research question (RQ) to be answered in this chapter: *what is the profile of a tropical entrepreneur?*

To answer the RQ, we constructed a profile based on sociodemographics (i.e., age, gender, and education), conducting business in the tropics (i.e., in terms of coastal proximity, prevalence of infectious diseases, and low agricultural productivity) and a broad range of stipulations concerning the particular business's industry and location. The primary data were sourced from entrepreneurs in different tropical countries. This global region is delimited in latitude by the Tropic of Cancer in the Northern Hemisphere, at 23°26′11.5′ N, and the Tropic of Capricorn in the Southern Hemisphere, at 23°26′11.5′ S (Feeley & Stroud, 2018), a region comprising 40% of the world's population. The tropics are depicted in Figure 2.1.

Entrepreneurship in the tropics

The tropics are typically a warm region that experiences little seasonal change in day-to-day temperatures. Due to growing populations, rapid migration, and urbanization, it is expected that by 2025, the tropics will be home to most of the world's population and two-thirds of its children (State of the Tropics, 2020; United Nations, 2020). Most of these people live in emerging economies that all face significant challenges (Azzali & Thirumaran, 2021), such as climate change, deforestation, logging, and desertification. These developments go hand in hand with increasing poverty and hunger (United Nations, 2020). Furthermore, environmental pollution exerts a negative effect on entrepreneurs' life satisfaction in the tropics, resulting in less-profitable ventures (Choongo et al., 2021). To combat these effects in tropical emerging economies, local entrepreneurs have responded differently, including resource-conserving entrepreneurial behaviour contextualized in a resource-scarce environment (Eijdenberg & Ostertag, 2021), e.g., using improvised and locally sourced, environmentally friendly alternatives for single-use plastics (Chawla et al., 2021), amongst other measures.

Amongst tropical economies, only Hong Kong and Singapore are viewed as high-income industrialized countries (ranked third and second in the world, respectively, in terms of ease of doing business; see Ease of Doing Business, 2021). Notwithstanding, some tropical countries have experienced heavy entrepreneurship activity. According to the recent Global Report from Global

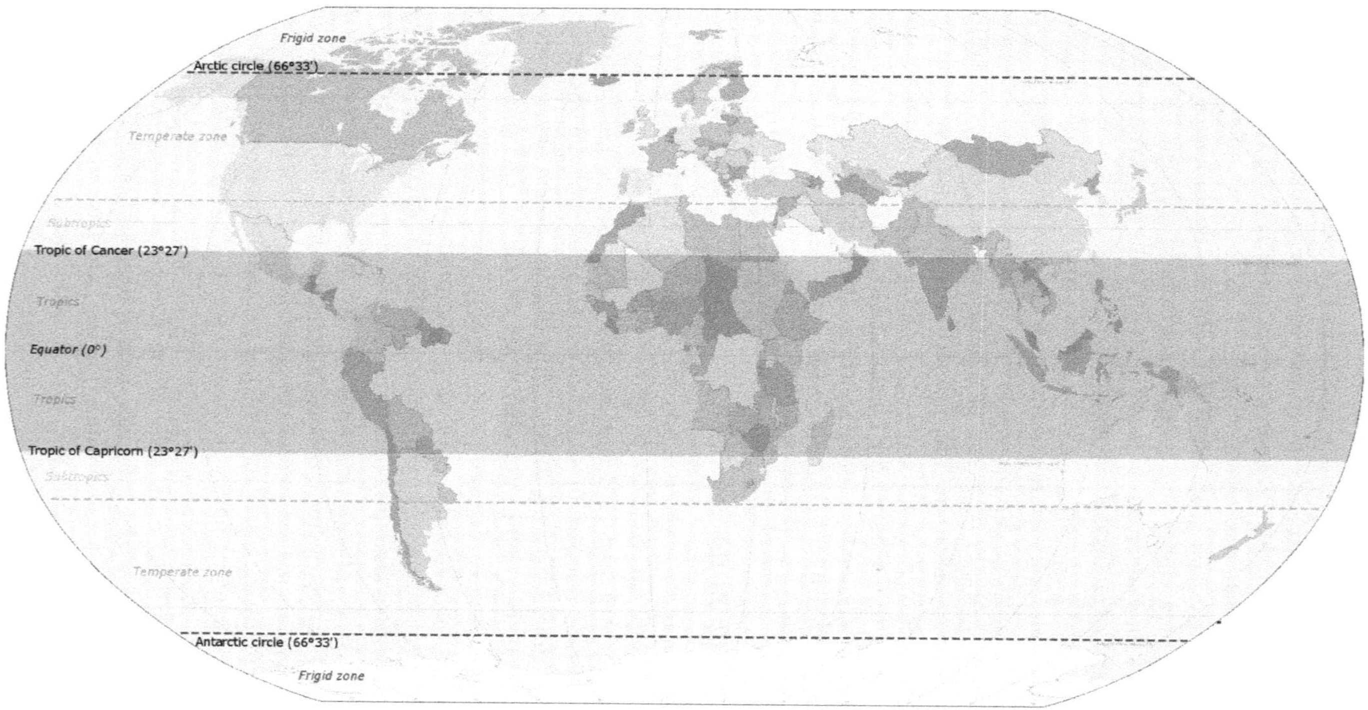

Figure 2.1 The world map. The tropics is highlighted in crimson. Note: This is a Creative Common License map (CC BY-SA 3.0), author "KVDP". Source: https://en.wikipedia.org/wiki/Tropics#/media/File:World_map_indicating_tropics_and_subtropics.png

Entrepreneurship Monitor (GEM), more than 30% of all adults ages 18–64 in Angola, Colombia, Panama, and Togo are active in total early-stage entrepreneurial activities (TEA) (Global Entrepreneurship Monitor, 2021). Back in 2012, countries like Ghana, Malawi, Nigeria, and Uganda all ranked high on the same measure, with values above 35% (Global Entrepreneurship Monitor, 2012). Furthermore, ten years before that, around the time of GEM's inception, India and Thailand had the highest TEA scores of all countries measured (Global Entrepreneurship Monitor, 2002). Simultaneously, several tropical countries are among the least performing in terms of ease of doing business (e.g., South Sudan, Venezuela) (Ease of Doing Business, 2021) or TEA in GEM reports for 2002 and 2012 (e.g., Taiwan in 2002, Malaysia in 2012) (Global Entrepreneurship Monitor, 2002, 2012).

Thinking along the lines of climatological and geographical context, apart from other factors, such as technological development and culture, Sachs et al. (2001) contended that three factors define economic success for tropical countries (see Sachs et al.'s [2001] paper for a complete and detailed overview):

1. *Coastal proximity*. According to Sachs et al. (2001), transportation of goods, services, and people is less costly by sea than by land or air. Thus, economies near coastlines, particularly those with strategic water connections to the hinterlands (e.g., the Danube and Rhine Rivers in Europe), have a great advantage over landlocked and hinterland economies (e.g., Congo, Rwanda, and Uganda).
2. *Prevalence of infectious diseases*. Unlike temperate climates, the tropics are characterized by many infectious diseases, such as Chagas' disease, dengue fever, malaria, and rabies (Sachs et al., 2001).
3. *Agricultural productivity*. Cultivating soils in the tropics, such as rainforests and other fragile soils in warm and humid areas, is less productive than in temperate climates. Of the world's major food grains (i.e., wheat, maize [corn], and rice), only wheat grows well in temperate climates. Maize and rice crops can grow in the tropics, but are usually more productive in temperate and subtropical climates. Apart from these factors identified by Sachs et al. (2001), it is commonly known that the tropics' hot and humid climate is viewed as more challenging to work in and be productive than in cooler, less humid, and more temperate climates.

Regarding entrepreneurship, we know that the entrepreneur – viewed as the creator of organizations – has received much scholarly attention since Gartner's and colleagues seminal work in the late 1980s and 1990s (Gartner, 1988, 1990; Gartner et al., 1989; Gartner et al., 1994). Most of this work involves who an entrepreneur is and what defines these individuals, e.g., in terms of decision-making (cf. Busenitz & Barney, 1997; Kitching & Rouse, 2020; Sarasvathy, 2001), motivation (cf. Shane et al., 2003; Barba-Sánchez & Atienza-Sahuquillo, 2017; Naffziger et al., 1994), and orientation (cf. Covin & Wales, 2012; Lumpkin & Dess, 1996; Wales et al., 2020). These definitions all are derived from and based in a Western context, but entrepreneurs in emerging economies have received increasing attention for the same reasons (e.g., for decision-making, see Eijdenberg et al., 2017; for motivation, see Eijdenberg et al., 2015; for orientation, see Eijdenberg, 2016). However, of all these studies, emerging economies in the tropics were chosen for their underdeveloped and challenging socioeconomic conditions (e.g., poor education systems, low incomes, lack of employment), not for their climatological and geographical context. All things considered, we can conclude that a comprehensive profile can be drawn of the entrepreneur in the Western context and emerging economies in the tropics based on socioeconomic conditions, but a profile of *the tropical entrepreneur* based on climatological and geographical context is missing. In fact, a keyword search of 'tropical entrepreneur' through Google Scholar (as of 30 June 2021) elicited zero hits.

Methods in brief

We used a quantitative research design, with data collected between October 2020 and March 2021. Qualtrics was used as the online survey platform. Following a purposive sampling approach, this chapter's authors used their professional networks (e.g., contacts from entrepreneurship and incubation centres and LinkedIn connections) to reach out to respondents. Through the critical first question of the survey, the respondents *identified themselves as entrepreneurs*. Based on this purposive sampling (Saunders et al., 2009), we reached $N = 203$ respondents. After clearing the data set, $n = 81$, only fully completed responses were considered for further analyses. Table 2.1 presents the measurement instrument and the source from the literature.

Results

To construct the profile, we performed frequency, descriptive, and correlation calculations. Table 2.2 presents the frequencies of Items 1–5, and Table 2.3 presents the same statistics for Items 6–9.

From Table 2.2, it can be concluded that most of our entrepreneurs are male (70.4%), age 45 or younger (65.4%), have university educations (79%), and did (past)/do (present) not have parents as entrepreneurs (56.8%). Table 2.3 indicates that basing business operations in coastal proximity does not matter to these entrepreneurs, viz. the tendency is towards the unimportant (i.e., should be understood as 'does not matter') side of the scale, measured from the midpoint value of 4 (71.6%). However, basing business operations in an area with a relatively wide variety of infectious diseases seems to be important (i.e., should be understood as 'matters') to the entrepreneurs, as shown by a tendency towards the important side of the scale, measured from the midpoint value of 4 (64.2%). Moreover, entrepreneurs believe that basing business operations in an area of relatively low agricultural productivity does not matter or is unimportant to a different degree, i.e., 72.8% is at the midpoint value of 4 or below. Finally, the same applies to basing business operations in

Table 2.1 Measurement instrument

Item #	*Item*	*Scale*
1	My business is based in the tropical urban area	1 = No; 2 = Yes, in the city
2	What is your gender?	1 = Male; 2 = Female
3	What is your age?	1 = 30 years or younger; 2 = 31–45 years; 3 = 46–60 years; 4 = 61–75 years; 5 = 76 years or older
4	What is your highest educational degree?	1 = No degree; 2 = Primary school; 3 = Lower secondary school; 4 = Higher secondary school; 5 = Diploma, polytechnic, vocational or applied sciences; 6 = University bachelor's degree; 7 = University master's degree; 8 = PhD
5	Were, or are, your parents entrepreneurs?	1 = No; 2 = Yes, my father; 3 = Yes, my mother; 4 = Yes, both
6	Business operations in coastal proximity is to me …	1 = Extremely unimportant; 2 = Unimportant; 3 = Rather unimportant; 4 = Neither unimportant, nor important; 5 = Rather important; 6 = Important; 7 = Extremely important
7	Business operations in an area of relatively many kinds of infectious diseases is to me …	
8	Business operations in an area of relatively low agricultural productivity is to me …	
9	Business operations in the tropics is to me generally speaking …	

Note: Items 6–9 are based on Sachs et al. (2001)'s three economic success factors of tropical countries. The scale including 'extremely unimportant' to 'extremely important' should be understood as the extent to whether it matters or is a concern to the respondent. Thus, the scale reflects a degree of relevance to the individual.

the tropics in general (74%). All things considered, it can be concluded that entrepreneurs based in the tropics do not view their location, as measured by Sachs et al.'s (2001) factors of economic success, as problematic. This is confirmed in Table 2.4, which presents the correlation coefficients, including mean (*M*), median (*Mdn*), and standard deviation (*SD*) for all items. The table indicates that Items 6, 7, and 8 in particular form a strongly correlated cluster.

We conducted additional cross-tabulations to examine how the responses are distributed among all items in terms of percentages. We measured how the percentages for Items 2–5 (i.e., sociodemographic statistics) are distributed in Items 6–9 (i.e., business operations in the tropics). From cross-tabulations, we concluded the following:

1. Unlike female entrepreneurs, male entrepreneurs have stronger sentiment in terms of not viewing coastal proximity as important.

Table 2.2 Frequencies (percentages) of items 1–5

Scale	*1*	*2*	*3*	*4*	*5*
No	7.4				
Yes	92.6				
Male		70.4			
Female		29.6			
30 years or younger			21		
31–45 years			44.4		
46–60 years			32.1		
61–75 years			2.5		
76 years or older			0		
No degree				1.2	
Primary school				0	
Lower secondary school				0	
Higher secondary school				1.2	
Diploma, polytechnic, vocational, or applied sciences				11.2	
University bachelor's degree				35.8	
University master's degree				43.2	
PhD				7.4	
No					56.8
Yes, my father					21.0
Yes, my mother					11.1
Yes, both					11.1
Total	100	100	100	100	100

Table 2.3 Frequencies (percentages) of items 6–9

Scale	*6*	*7*	*8*	*9*
Extremely unimportant	11.1	11.1	19.8	14.8
Unimportant	24.7	16.1	18.5	13.6
Rather unimportant	8.6	8.6	8.6	7.4
Neither unimportant, nor important	27.2	19.8	25.9	38.2
Rather important	6.2	8.6	6.2	6.2
Important	11.1	24.7	12.4	13.6
Extremely important	11.1	11.1	8.6	6.2
Total	100	100	100	100

2. Both male and female entrepreneurs indicated that basing business operations in an area with a relatively wide variety of infectious diseases is important to them.
3. Male entrepreneurs typically view basing business operations in an area of relatively low agricultural productivity as being far less (i.e., 'extremely') unimportant compared with their female counterparts.

Table 2.4 *M*, *Mdn*, *SD*, and Pearson's correlation coefficients

Item #	*M*	*Mdn*	*SD*	*1*	*2*	*3*	*4*	*5*	*6*	*7*	*8*	*9*
1	1.93	2.00	.26	1								
2	1.30	1.00	.46	−.13	1							
3	2.16	2.00	.78	.24*	−.34**	1						
4	6.38	7.00	1.03	−.03	.10	−.14	1					
5	1.77	1.00	1.04	.16	.07	−.15	.13	1				
6	3.70	4.00	1.88	−.07	.09	−.14	−.05	.06	1			
7	4.17	4.00	1.95	.07	.07	−.002	.02	.06	.40**	1		
8	3.52	4.00	1.94	−.10	−.02	.07	−.16	.24*	.55**	.20	1	
9	3.73	4.00	1.75	−.02	−.05	.01	.02	.17	.58**	.33**	.56**	1

Note: * Correlation is significant at .05 level (2-tailed); ** Correlation is significant at .01 level (2-tailed).

4. Respondents from the 46–60 age group generally seemed undecided on basing business operations in coastal proximity (i.e., they view it as neither unimportant, nor important) compared with all other age groups, but coastal proximity is clearly more important to the 31–45 age group.
5. Entrepreneurs in the 31–45 age group typically find basing business operations in an area of relatively low agricultural productivity to be more important than do the other age groups.
6. Basing business operations in coastal proximity seems to be less important for university master's degree-educated entrepreneurs, compared with their bachelor's degree-educated counterparts.
7. Basing business operations in an area with a relatively wide variety of infectious diseases is viewed as most important for master's degree-educated entrepreneurs.
8. Entrepreneurs who did not have or do not have parents as entrepreneurs found basing operations in coastal proximity or in an area of relatively low agricultural productivity to be relatively unimportant, while basing operations in an area with a relatively wide variety of infectious diseases is important to them.

Recommendations for future research

This chapter's findings contribute to many calls for research on contextualization of entrepreneurship in terms of different shapes, times, and environments (Welter, 2011; Welter et al., 2019; Zahra et al., 2014). As noted earlier, entrepreneurship is not a static, but rather a dynamic phenomenon that evolves over time and spans different regions of the planet, one of which is the tropics, and how entrepreneurs perceive this is largely unknown. Going forward, our findings may serve as the first steps that cut a path through this unexplored realm.

These findings could be explored further through future research, which can be conducted in various ways. To explore more about the tropical entrepreneur and the underlying factors that define this type of individual, we set the agenda for future research as follows:

1. Researchers are encouraged to conduct more quantitative studies on the individual entrepreneur (i.e., micro-level), the enterprise (i.e., meso-level) and the environment (i.e., macro-level) in the tropical context. For instance, entrepreneurial motivation (see, e.g., Murnieks et al., 2020; Naffziger et al., 1994; Shane et al., 2003), decision-making under uncertainty and bricolage (e.g., Sarasvathy, 2001; Chandler et al., 2011; Fisher, 2012; Servantie & Rispal, 2018) are possible future avenues for research on individual entrepreneurs in the tropics. Moreover, enterprise performance (Bouquet et al., 2009; Teece, 2007) and (access to) financing and other resources (Fang et al., 2013) in the tropics are other possibilities for future research. Finally, typical natural resources of the tropical environment such as food and staples (e.g., cane sugar, coffee, cocoa, many fruits and spices), rubbers, oils, and woods (e.g., mahogany, teak), amongst many others, that may cater to local entrepreneurs, are factors to consider for future research. Alternatively, cross-country, cross-economic and cross-institutional context comparisons can be made to assess differences and similarities between multiple countries within the tropics (e.g., Nigeria vs. Kenya; Hong Kong vs. Taiwan).
2. From a methodological perspective, we recommend that researchers engage in inferential statistical analysis to elicit richer findings. For example, future qualitative research on the tropical entrepreneur could be based on grounded theory development (Corbin & Strauss, 1990; Corbin & Strauss, 2015) or case study research (Eisenhardt, 1989; Eisenhardt & Graebner, 2007) to unravel deeper and more meaningful understandings that could not have been captured otherwise with quantitative research. In tandem with solely qualitative research as a way of 'taking a step back' from the solely quantitative approach, mixed-methods studies (for different types in entrepreneurship research methods, see Molina-Azorín et al., 2012) would triangulate the findings, thereby providing greater, more comprehensive and holistic perspectives on the tropical entrepreneur himself or herself and in context.

Concluding remarks

Following the RQ, the chapter aimed to profile the tropical entrepreneur. Based on our analyses of primary data, we can declare a few main takeaways. We relied on Sachs et al.'s (2001) determinants of economic success in tropical countries, i.e., perceived coastal proximity, prevalence of infectious diseases, and agricultural productivity. For profiling purposes (refer to the statistics in Tables 2.2–4), we can conclude with great certainty that the perception or the entrepreneur's awareness of his or her tropical context is generally low, i.e., basing a start-up in a tropical location does not seem to matter to the entrepreneur. However, on a granular level, we refer to Points 1–8 in the Methods and Results section. These points demonstrate how the tropical entrepreneurs – in terms of gender, age, and education – perceive their context differently.

Explanations for these differences could be found in many socioeconomic, cultural, and contextual circumstances. For example, the reason why those in the 46–60 age group are rather undecided on basing business operations in coastal proximity, while the 31–45 age group finds this important, possibly because the latter age group is keener on leisure activities and lifestyles conducive to living near bodies of water, compared with the former age group. Furthermore, master's degree-educated entrepreneurs perceive business operations in an area with a relatively wide variety of infectious diseases as being a more important issue than their differently educated counterparts, possibly because of their education, upbringing, or conditions (e.g., the feeling of having much to lose on a personal or professional level).

Finally, in terms of practical implications, this chapter's findings may serve as a (preliminary) strategic outline for practitioners (e.g., educators, trainers) and entrepreneurs in the tropics. For example, when the relevance of the tropical context for entrepreneurship concerns being educated and trained, instructors should focus not only on master's degree students, but even more so on other educational levels (refer to Point 7 in the Methods and Results section). Moreover, context-conscious entrepreneurs could help others become more aware of their climatological and geographical context by taking inclusive action, e.g., involving other gender, age, and education groups that either perceive their context as unimportant or are indifferent. In so doing, opportunities may increase in the local context.

Notes

1 Corresponding author: JCU Singapore Business School, James Cook University, Singapore. Email: emiel.eijdenberg@jcu.edu.au.
2 College of Business, Law and Governance, James Cook University, Australia.

References

Azzali, S., & Thirumaran, K. (Eds.) (2021). *Tropical constrained environments and sustainable adaptations. Managing the Asian century*. Springer.

Barba-Sánchez, V., & Atienza-Sahuquillo, C. (2017). Entrepreneurial motivation and self-employment: Evidence from expectancy theory. *International Entrepreneurship and Management Journal, 13*(4), 1097–1115.

Bouquet, C., Morrison, A., & Birkinshaw, J. (2009). International attention and multinational enterprise performance. *Journal of International Business Studies, 40*(1), 108–131.

Bruton, G. D., Ahlstrom, D., & Obloj, K. (2008). Entrepreneurship in emerging economies: Where are we today and where should the research go in the future. *Entrepreneurship Theory and Practice, 32*(1), 1–14.

Bruton, G. D., Filatotchev, I., Si, S., & Wright, M. (2013). Entrepreneurship and strategy in emerging economies. *Strategic Entrepreneurship Journal*, 7(3), 169–180.

Busenitz, L. W., & Barney, J. B. (1997). Differences between entrepreneurs and managers in large organizations: Biases and heuristics in strategic decision-making. *Journal of Business Venturing, 12*(1), 9–30.

Cantillon, R. (1755/1999). *Essai sur la nature du commerce en général*. MacMillan.

Chandler, G. N., DeTienne, D. R., McKelvie, A., & Mumford, T. V. (2011). Causation and effectuation processes: A validation study. *Journal of Business Venturing, 26*(3), 375–390.

Chawla, T., Eijdenberg, E. L., & Wood, J. (2021). Environmental resilience of Bottom of the Pyramid strategies toward single-use plastics: A recipe from an emerging economy. In T. Chaiechi (Ed.), *Economic effects of natural disasters* (pp. 161–178). Elsevier.

Choongo, P., Eijdenberg, E. L., Lungu, J., Chabala, M., Taylor, T. K., & Masurel, E. (2021). The influence of environmental pollution and drought on the satisfaction with life of entrepreneurs in Zambia's mining sector. In T. Chaiechi (Ed.), *Economic effects of natural disasters* (pp. 147–160). Elsevier.

Corbin, J. M., & Strauss, A. (1990). Grounded theory research: Procedures, canons, and evaluative criteria. *Qualitative Sociology, 13*(1), 3–21.

Corbin, J., & Strauss, A. (2015). *Basics of qualitative research: Techniques and procedures for developing grounded theory*. Sage Publications.

Covin, J. G., & Wales, W. J. (2012). The measurement of entrepreneurial orientation. *Entrepreneurship Theory and Practice, 36*(4), 677–702.

Ease of Doing Business (2021). Ease of doing business rankings. Retrieved from https://www.doingbusiness.org/en/rankings

Eijdenberg, E. L. (2016). Does one size fit all? A look at entrepreneurial motivation and entrepreneurial orientation in the informal economy of Tanzania. *International Journal of Entrepreneurial Behavior & Research, 22*(6), 804–834.

Eijdenberg, E. L., & Masurel, E. (2013). Entrepreneurial motivation in a least developed country: Push factors and pull factors among MSEs in Uganda. *Journal of Enterprising Culture, 21*(01), 19–43.

Eijdenberg, E.L. & Ostertag, F. (2021). Resource-conserving entrepreneurial behaviour of micro-entrepreneurs: Evidence from a Tanzanian community. In: S. Azzali & K. Thirumaran (Eds.), *Tropical constrained environments, sustainable adaptations: Businesses and communities* (pp. 27—44). Springer.

Eijdenberg, E. L., Paas, L. J., & Masurel, E. (2015). Entrepreneurial motivation and small business growth in Rwanda. *Journal of Entrepreneurship in Emerging Economies*, 7(3), 212–240.

Eijdenberg, E. L., Paas, L. J., & Masurel, E. (2017). Decision-making and small business growth in Burundi. *Journal of Entrepreneurship in Emerging Economies, 9*(1), 35–64.

Eijdenberg, E. L., & Thompson, N. A. (2020). *Entrepreneurs' creative responses to institutional challenges: Insider perspectives from sub-Saharan Africa*. Emerald Group Publishing.

Eijdenberg, E. L., Thompson, N. A., Verduijn, K., & Essers, C. (2019). Entrepreneurial activities in a developing country: An institutional theory perspective. *International Journal of Entrepreneurial Behavior & Research, 25*(3), 414–432.

Eisenhardt, K. M. (1989). Building theories from case study research. *Academy of Management Review, 14*(4), 532–550.

Eisenhardt, K. M., & Graebner, M. E. (2007). Theory building from cases: Opportunities and challenges. *Academy of Management Journal, 50*(1), 25–32.

Fang, Y., Wade, M., Delios, A., & Beamish, P. W. (2013). An exploration of multinational enterprise knowledge resources and foreign subsidiary performance. *Journal of World Business, 48*(1), 30–38.

Feeley, K. J., & Stroud, J. T. (2018). Where on Earth are the 'tropics'? *Frontiers of Biogeography, 10*(1–2), e38649.

Fisher, G. (2012). Effectuation, causation, and bricolage: A behavioral comparison of emerging theories in entrepreneurship research. *Entrepreneurship Theory and Practice, 36*(5), 1019–1051.

Gartner, W. B. (1988). 'Who is an entrepreneur?' is the wrong question. *American Journal of Small Business, 12*(4), 11–32.

Gartner, W. B. (1990). What are we talking about when we talk about entrepreneurship? *Journal of Business Venturing, 5*(1), 15–28.

Gartner, W. B., Mitchell, T. R., & Vesper, K. H. (1989). A taxonomy of new business ventures. *Journal of Business Venturing, 4*(3), 169–186.

Gartner, W. B., Shaver, K. G., Gatewood, E., & Katz, J. A. (1994). Finding the entrepreneur in entrepreneurship. *Entrepreneurship Theory and Practice, 18*(3), 5–9.

Global Entrepreneurship Monitor (2002). *Global Report 2002.* Global Entrepreneurship Research Association, London Business School.

Global Entrepreneurship Monitor (2012). Global Report 2012. Global Entrepreneurship Research Association, London Business School.

Global Entrepreneurship Monitor (2021). *Global Report 2020/2021.* Global Entrepreneurship Research Association, London Business School.

Kiggundu, M. N. (2002). Entrepreneurs and entrepreneurship in Africa: What is known and what needs to be done. *Journal of Developmental Entrepreneurship,* 7(3), 239–258.

Kirzner, I. M. (1974). *Competition and entrepreneurship.* University of Chicago Press.

Kirzner, I. M. (1997). Entrepreneurial discovery and the competitive market process: An Austrian approach. *Journal of Economic Literature, 35*(1), 60–85.

Kiss, A. N., Danis, W. M., & Cavusgil, S. T. (2012). International entrepreneurship research in emerging economies: A critical review and research agenda. *Journal of Business Venturing, 27*(2), 266–290.

Kitching, J., & Rouse, J. (2020). Contesting effectuation theory: Why it does not explain new venture creation. *International Small Business Journal, 38*(6), 515–535.

Lumpkin, G. T., & Dess, G. G. (1996). Clarifying the entrepreneurial orientation construct and linking it to performance. *Academy of Management Review, 21*(1), 135–172.

Molina-Azorín, J. F., López-Gamero, M. D., Pereira-Moliner, J., & Pertusa-Ortega, E. M. (2012). Mixed methods studies in entrepreneurship research: Applications and contributions. *Entrepreneurship & Regional Development, 24*(5–6), 425–456.

Murnieks, C. Y., Klotz, A. C., & Shepherd, D. A. (2020). Entrepreneurial motivation: A review of the literature and an agenda for future research. *Journal of Organizational Behavior, 41*(2), 115–143.

Naffziger, D. W., Hornsby, J. S., & Kuratko, D. F. (1994). A proposed research model of entrepreneurial motivation. *Entrepreneurship Theory and Practice, 18*(3), 29–42.

Sachs, J. D., Mellinger, A. D., & Gallup, J. L. (2001). The geography of poverty and wealth. *Scientific American, 284*(3), 70–75.

Sarasvathy, S. D. (2001). Causation and effectuation: Toward a theoretical shift from economic inevitability to entrepreneurial contingency. *Academy of Management Review, 26*(2), 243–263.

Saunders, M., Lewis, P., & Thornhill, A. (2009). *Research methods for business students* (5th ed.). Pearson Education Limited.

Schumpeter, J. A. (1934). *The theory of economic development.* Harvard University Press.

Servantie, V., & Rispal, M. H. (2018). Bricolage, effectuation, and causation shifts over time in the context of social entrepreneurship. *Entrepreneurship & Regional Development, 30*(3–4), 310–335.

Shane, S., Locke, E. A., & Collins, C. J. (2003). Entrepreneurial motivation. *Human Resource Management Review, 13*(2), 257–279.

State of the Tropics (2020). State of the Tropics Report 2020. Retrieved from https://www.jcu.edu.au/state-of-the-tropics/events/past-events/international-day-of-the-tropics

Teece, D. J. (2007). Explicating dynamic capabilities: The nature and microfoundations of (sustainable) enterprise performance. *Strategic Management Journal, 28*(13), 1319–1350.

United Nations (2020). The future belongs to the tropics. Retrieved from https://www.un.org/en/observances/tropics-day

Wales, W. J., Covin, J. G., & Monsen, E. (2020). Entrepreneurial orientation: The necessity of a multilevel conceptualization. *Strategic Entrepreneurship Journal, 14*(4), 639–660.

Welter, F. (2011). Contextualizing entrepreneurship: Conceptual challenges and ways forward. *Entrepreneurship Theory and Practice, 35*(1), 165–184.

Welter, F., Baker, T., & Wirsching, K. (2019). Three waves and counting: The rising tide of contextualization in entrepreneurship research. *Small Business Economics, 52*(2), 319–330.

Zahra, S. A., Wright, M., & Abdelgawad, S. G. (2014). Contextualization and the advancement of entrepreneurship research. *International Small Business Journal, 32*(5), 479–500.

3 Does institutional quality matter for the nexus between environmental quality and economic growth?

A tropics perspective

Huiping Zhang[1], *Pengji Wang*[2], *and Jacob Wood*[3]

Introduction

For many years, economic development has been the main driver of social progress and hence a key focus for governments in many countries around the world. Accompanying these economic activities are, unfortunately, higher levels of energy consumption and the degradation of our environment. Therefore, developing economies in the tropics face the challenging burden of balancing the pursuits of economic development and environmental sustainability (Persadie and Ramlogan, 2007). Over the past two decades, the deterioration of our environment and the subsequent demands of climate change have become one of the world's most pressing problems. Many countries have called for a global effort to protect the environment by creating the UN Framework Convention on Climate Change (UNFCCC). Within this framework lie further international negotiations such as the Paris Agreement, which mark some of the most significant actions addressing climate change since the 1990s.

Echoing the increased importance of environmental protection, a sizable set of studies (see Grossman and Krueger, 1993; Friedl and Getzner, 2003; Plassmann and Khanna, 2006; Jalil and Feridun, 2011, among others) examine the nexus between economic growth and environmental quality. The seminal work of Grossman and Krueger (1993) proposes an environmental Kuznets curve (EKC, henceforth) to represent the relationship between the two variables of interest. It postulates an inverted U-shaped relationship between a country's level of economic development and its environmental quality. Initially, environmental quality decreases with economic development before improving again as incomes rise above a certain threshold. Grossman and Krueger (1995) further show three contributing causes behind the shape of the EKC; namely, the scale effect (the environment gradually deteriorates as sustained economic growth requires more resources and as such generates more waste and pollution), the composition effect (the structure of the economy changes from one that includes energy-intensive industries through to one which is driven by services and technology-intensive industries), and the

DOI: 10.4324/9781003153580-3

technique effect (obsolete technologies are replaced by upgraded, new, cleaner technologies).

Over recent decades, the EKC hypothesis has been tested extensively using various indicators of environmental quality across different countries. For instance, Markandya et al. (2006) and Fodha and Zaghdoud (2010) focus on air pollutants, such as carbon dioxide and sulfur dioxide, Paudel et al. (2005) and Orubu and Omotor (2011) examine water pollution, while Gui et al. (2019) concentrate on solid wastes. However, no real consensus has been formed around the results. Further, the possible reasons for the EKC remain divided, ranging from progress in economic development levels, moving from a clean agrarian economy to a highly polluting industrialized economy to a clean service economy, through to finalizing the creation of high-income environmentally aware economies (Dinda, 2004).

Another strand of the literature investigates the relationship between environmental quality and economic growth that is conditional on institutional developments, which are related to both variables through the reactions of different parties including policymakers, businesses, and other market participants involved with economic growth and its side effects (Dasgupta et al., 2002). In particular, Wawrzyniak and Doryn (2020) revisit the economic growth–environmental quality relationship against the background of institutional quality, using a sample of 93 emerging and developing countries from 1995 to 2014. They argue that it is the institutional factors that accompany economic growth enhancing environmental quality. Other studies explore the impact of foreign direct investment (FDI) on the EKC hypothesis as it could affect both economic growth and the environmental degradation of the host country (Jensen, 1996; Frankel and Romer, 1999). However, evidence in this field is mixed (see List and Co, 2000; Cole and Elliot, 2005, among others).

In this chapter, we extend the literature by testing the EKC hypothesis and examining the impact of institutional quality and FDI on the environmental quality–economic growth relationship using a sample of 46 tropical countries from 1971 to 2014. According to the World Population Review, the tropics make up about 40% of the planet's surface area and are home to approximately 40% of the world's population.[4] However, despite varied economic, political, and social histories, almost all of the tropical countries remain underdeveloped with the exception of Singapore. Sachs (2001) shows that GNP per capita in the tropical regions was 25% of that in the temperate zone in 1992. On the other hand, the tropics are extremely important because they help to conserve and balance the ecosystem of the earth. Environmental protection is not just an issue of an individual tropical country, as it determines the sustainability of the whole world. In this chapter, we aim to uncover the intricate relationship among economic growth, environmental protection, and institution quality in the universe of tropical countries.

Focusing on CO_2 emissions, which are the most common indicator of climate change and environmental quality, we confirm the existence of the EKC in these countries and the significance of institutional quality in improving the environmental quality in tropics. FDI is found to have a very limited impact on the nexus between growth and environmental quality. These findings help to broaden our understanding of the deeper forces driving the global environmental quality – economic growth nexus. The policy implication is that higher economic growth alone does not warrant a better living environment. Growth needs to be accompanied by better institutional quality, particularly higher levels of political stability and better accountability, to promote a country's environmental quality.

The remainder of this chapter proceeds as follows. The second part assesses the literature on testing the EKC hypothesis and the impact of institutional quality and FDI on the relationship between growth and environmental quality. The third part presents our data, measures, and methodology. The main findings are shown in the fourth section. The fifth part concludes.

Literature review

Empirical testing of the EKC hypothesis

Built on the work of Kuznets (1955), which uncovered an inverted U-shape curve between income per capita and income inequality, Grossman and Krueger (1993) found the same trajectory for the relationship between environmental degradation and income per capita, therefore proving a basis from which the EKC hypothesis can emerge. Ever since then, a significant number of studies have conducted empirical analyses to test this hypothesis, some are focusing on country-specific tests while others are exploring this nexus in a multi-country context.

Examples of country-level testing for the EKC hypothesis include Friedl and Getzner (2003) for Australia, Jalil and Feridun (2011) and Du et al. (2012) for China, Day and Grafton (2003) and Hamit-Haggar (2012) for Canada, Ghosh (2010) and Kanjilal and Ghosh (2013) for India, Saboori et al. (2012) for Malaysia, Akbostanci et al. (2009) and Ozturk and Acaravci (2010) for Turkey, Plassmann and Khanna (2006) and Franklin and Matthias (2012) for the United States, and Giovanis (2013), and Sephton and Mann (2016) for the United Kingdom. Across countries, Stern and Common (2001) studied the EKC hypothesis for 73 developed and developing countries, Vollebergh et al. (2009) for 24 OECD countries, Zhu et al. (2012) for 20 emerging countries, Markandya et al. (2006), and Acaravci and Ozturk (2010) for European countries, Jaunky (2011) for 36 high-income countries, and Wawrzyniak and Doryn (2020) for a sample of 93 emerging and developing countries. A summary of the EKC literature can be found from Tiba and Omri (2017), Moutinho et al. (2017), and Sarkodie and Strezov (2019). Overall, the evidence of the EKC hypothesis is still divided, primarily due to different environmental variables, methodologies, and data sets. Focuses have been drawn in these studies from various environmental aspects: air pollutants (such as carbon dioxide and sulfur dioxide), water pollution, solid waste, oil, gas, or coal.

Institutional developments and the EKC hypothesis

There has been a strand of literature focusing on the impact of institutional developments on environmental quality, showing that certain institutional qualities such as political stability, government effectiveness, and corruption control contribute to a reduction in pollution (see Gani, 2012; Apergis and Ozturk, 2015; Abid, 2016; Gholipour and Farzanegan, 2018). Related to these studies, Dasgupta et al. (2002), among others, suggest that the relationship between income and environmental quality is not static but determined by reactions to economic growth and its side effects of different parties, including citizens, businesses, policymakers, regulators, and other market participants. With a sample of 30 developed and developing countries from 1982 to 1994, Panayotou (1997) incorporates policy considerations into the income–environment relationship and found that effective policies and institutions can significantly reduce environmental degradation at lower income levels and accelerate improvements at higher income levels. Cropper and Griffiths (1994) and Jones and Manuelli (2001) show that among poor countries with weak political institutions, pollution increases with growth, while it decreases with growth in wealthy countries with strong institutions, as countries with strong institutional frameworks are typically wealthier and are therefore better able to regulate emissions. Tamazian and Rao (2010) concentrate on 24 transition economies for the period of 1993–2004 and confirm the importance of institutional quality for environmental performance. Using a sample of 58 Middle Eastern and African and 41 EU countries for the period 1990 to 2011, Abid (2017) find a monotonically increasing relationship between CO_2 emissions and GDP in both regions and highlight policymakers should regulate and enhance the role and efficiency of domestic institutions in order to have sustainable positive economic performance and to reduce carbon dioxide emission simultaneously. Wawrzyniak and Doryn (2020) find government effectiveness modifies the economic growth–emissions relationship within 93 emerging and developing countries over the 1995–2014 period.

FDI and the EKC hypothesis

Over the past several decades, many emerging and developing countries have liberalized their economies by removing barriers to trade and investment. Such measures help attract FDI to these transitional countries, which can stimulate economic growth (Frankel and Romer, 1999). However, Jensen (1996) and the World Bank (2000) find that FDI may also result in more industrial pollution and environmental degradation. As such, FDI becomes relevant to the EKC debate.

There have been several studies examining the interplay of FDI, institutional quality, and the EKC hypothesis. Studies by Cole and Elliot (2005) and Feridun (2006) show that FDI inflows lead to increased environmental degradation, while others (List and Co, 2000; De Soysa and Neumayer, 2005, among others) find that higher FDI inflows are associated with lower levels of per capita CO_2 emissions. Another strand of research explores the channels through which FDI could affect environmental quality. For instance, Tamazian et al. (2009) find an increase in FDI inflows improves research and development (R & R&D) expenditure and, therefore, higher energy efficiency, leading to improved environmental quality in BRIC countries. Claessens and Feijen (2007) show that financial liberalization and development can spur greater environmental improvements through improved governance. Pao and Tsai (2011) find FDI leads to increased CO_2 emissions in BRIC countries and urge developing countries to strictly examine foreign investment qualifications or promote environmental protection through the coordinated know-how and technological transfer with foreign companies to avoid environmental damage.

Despite the aforementioned intensive research in this field, to the best of our knowledge, little has been done to explore the existence of the nexus between income and environment quality in tropical countries exclusively. Moreover, little is known regarding whether institutional quality and FDI significantly affects this nexus within this region. We aim to fill this gap by conducting the analyses below.

Data and methodology

Data

Our sample covers all tropical countries.[5] The data on CO_2 emission and economic growth are downloaded from the World Development Indicators (WDI) database while the data on institutional quality are obtained from the World Governance Indicators (WGI) database, both of which are created and maintained by the World Bank. Based on the data availability, our final sample consists of 46 tropical countries.

Data and variables from WDI

The summary statistics of the variables from the WDI are tabulated in Table 3.1. The data series of CO_2 emissions start from 1971 and end mostly by 2014, although some countries (i.e., Angola, Myanmar, and Niger) have no such data before 1990. On average, there are 31 annual observations in each country. The average CO_2 emission is 1.9 metric tons per capita, while the average GDP per capita is about 4,200 in constant 2010 USD. As a comparison, the median GDP per capita of all countries in the world over the same period is 7,192 in constant 2010 USD, indicating that most tropical countries belong to emerging or developing countries, except for only a few developed countries such as Singapore.

As indicated by the literature, environmental quality is closely related to the country's economic growth and development. Figure 3.1 plots the country-level average CO_2 emissions (kg) per 2010 USD of GDP. Countries such as

Table 3.1 Summary statistics

Country	*Start year*	*Number of years*	CO_2	*GDP*
Angola	1996	11	1.21	3.40
Benin	1974	41	0.25	0.90
Bolivia	1976	39	1.12	1.63
Brazil	1975	40	1.70	8.86
Cambodia	1995	20	0.24	0.61
Cameroon	1979	36	0.30	1.33
Colombia	1971	44	1.60	4.74
Congo, Dem. Rep.	2005	10	0.04	0.34
Congo, Rep.	1978	37	0.47	2.89
Costa Rica	1977	38	1.31	6.02
Dominican Republic	1971	44	1.68	3.51
Ecuador	1976	30	1.97	4.10
El Salvador	1976	37	0.77	2.61
Eritrea	1998	3	0.27	0.66
Ethiopia	1981	34	0.06	0.24
Gabon	1978	37	4.93	10.67
Guatemala	1977	38	0.70	2.54
Haiti	1971	36	0.17	1.39
Honduras	1974	41	0.72	1.64
India	1975	40	0.87	0.78
Indonesia	1983	32	1.27	2.28
Jamaica	1976	39	3.25	4.44
Kenya	1971	44	0.28	0.87
Malaysia	1975	33	5.13	6.43
Mauritius	1994	21	2.53	6.54
Mexico	1979	36	4.03	8.57
Mozambique	1991	24	0.10	0.35
Myanmar	2000	15	0.24	0.76
Nicaragua	1977	26	0.73	1.45
Niger	2000	15	0.07	0.46
Nigeria	1977	38	0.65	1.71
Panama	1977	38	1.82	5.65
Paraguay	1975	40	0.62	3.53
Peru	1990	25	1.24	3.84
Philippines	1977	38	0.80	1.78
Senegal	1974	41	0.47	1.16
Singapore	2005	10	8.83	46.46
Sudan	1977	38	0.28	1.04
Suriname	2000	15	3.79	7.45
Tanzania	1995	20	0.13	0.63
Thailand	1975	40	2.24	3.10
Togo	1974	41	0.25	0.58
Trinidad and Tobago	1975	40	20.54	9.94
Venezuela, RB	1985	29	6.28	12.77
Vietnam	2000	14	1.24	1.12
Zambia	2003	11	0.20	1.33
Average		31	1.90	4.20

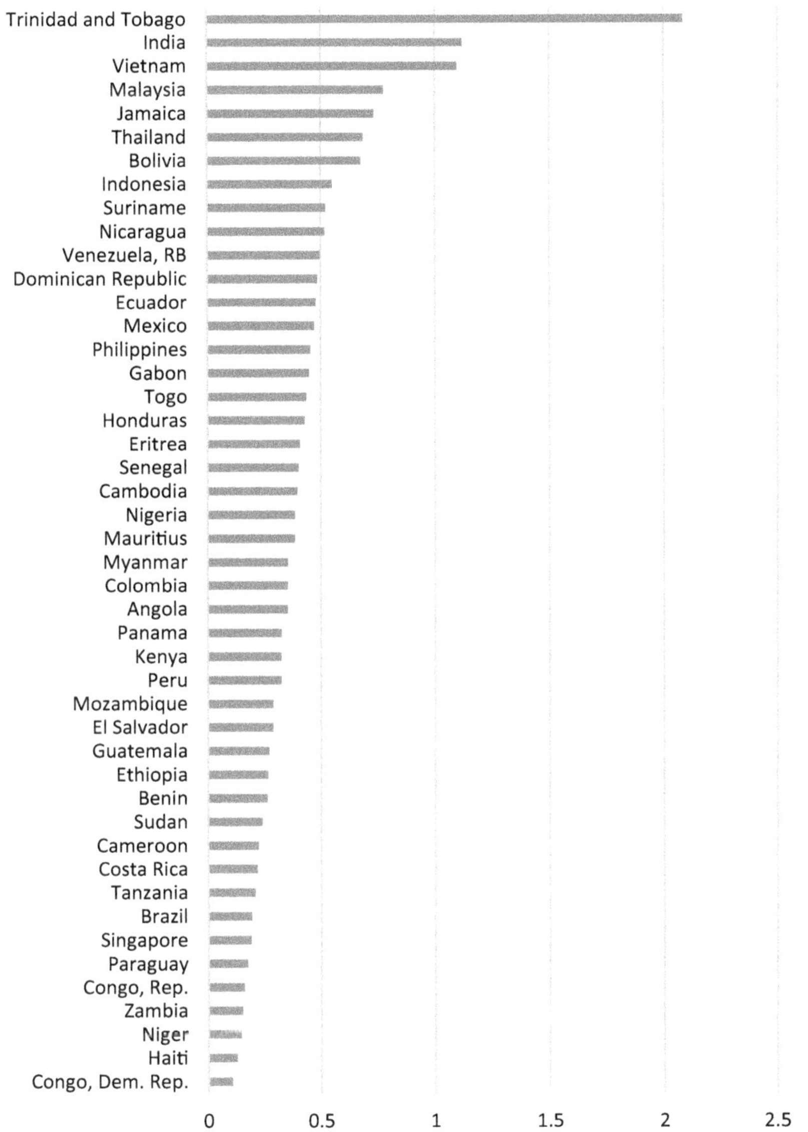

Figure 3.1 CO_2/GDP across countries. Note: This figure is generated using the World Development Indicators (WDI) database of the World Bank

Trinidad and Tobago, India, Vietnam, and Malaysia have sub-optimum environmental quality compared to their GDP per capita, while countries such as Singapore, Haiti, and the Democratic Republic of the Congo display better levels of environmental quality.

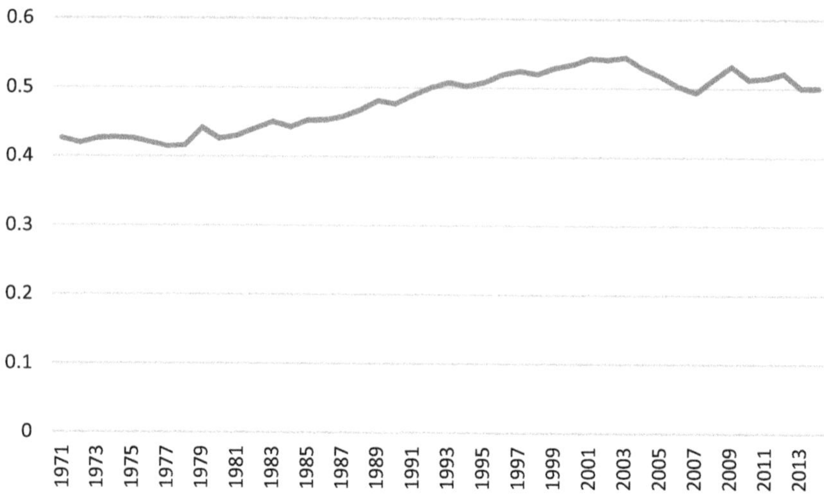

Figure 3.2 Global average CO_2. Note: This figure is generated using the World Development Indicators (WDI) database of the World Bank

The global average of GDP-weighted CO_2 emission per 2010 USD of GDP over the 1971 to 2014 period is plotted in Figure 3.2. It is evident that the ratio has been increasing, from about 0.4 in the early 1970s to its peak of 0.54 in the early 2000s, followed by a slight decline to 0.5 in 2014. This trend is consistent with both the negative correlation between economic growth and environmental quality at an earlier stage and the positive impact of environment protection from the joint efforts of various organizations, institutions, and governments, as suggested by the literature described above.

Additionally, based on the related literature, we also construct the following variables from the WDI database: (1) Fossil fuel energy consumption per capita (Arminen and Menegaki, 2019), *FFEC*, calculated as energy use (in kg of oil equivalent per capita) multiplied by the share of fossil fuel energy consumption; (2) Renewable energy consumption per capita (Bilgili et al., 2016), *RNEC*, which is a product of energy use (in kg of oil equivalent per capita) and the share of combustible renewables and waste in total energy; (3) Personal remittances received per capita (Pradhan et al., 2017), *PREM*, which is converted to constant 2010 USD using the GDP deflator; and (4) Foreign direct investment net inflows (List and Co, 2000; De Soysa and Neumayer, 2005), *FDI*, measured in constant 2010 USD with the GDP deflator.

Data and variables from WGI

The data from the WGI starts from 1996; however, they are systematically unavailable for all countries in the years 1997, 1999, and 2001. There are six individual variables of institutional quality: control of corruption, government effectiveness, political stability and absence of violence/terrorism, regulatory quality, the rule of law, and voice and accountability. We retrieve their estimates from WGI, which give the country's score on the aggregate indicators and are measured in units of standard normal distribution, ranging from approximately -2.5 to 2.5. Higher values indicate better institutional quality.

To reduce the error and noise associated with individual proxies, we construct a composite index (IQIndex) to capture the overall institutional quality of a country based on its rank of the six measures. In particular, for each year, we rank each of the six institutional quality measures among the 46 countries and every country is assigned its rank in each of these measures. The rank value is from 1 to 10 and a higher rank value signifies better institutional quality. Next, we define the $IQIndex_{c,y}$ as the simple average of the six ranking variables for country *c* in year *y*. If a country has missing data for one or two measures, we average the remaining measures.

The time-series average of the IQIndex is calculated for each country and then plotted in Figure 3.3. Tropical countries such as Trinidad and Tobago, Singapore, Costa Rica, and Mauritius are in the top deciles of institutional quality. Countries including the Democratic Republic of the Congo, Sudan, Myanmar, and Haiti have been disorderly administered.

Methodology

Armoured with annual data at the country level, we follow the literature (Ang, 2007; Apergis and Payne, 2010; Kasman and Duman, 2015, among others) by adopting the quadratic form of the relationship between environmental quality and per capita income to test the EKC hypothesis:

$$\begin{aligned} \mathrm{CO2}_{c,y} &= a + b1 \times GDP_{c,y} + b2 \times GDP^2_{c,y} \\ &+ b3 \times CO2_{c,y-1} + b4 \times FFEC_{c,y} + b5 \times RNEC_{c,y} \\ &+ b6 \times PREM_{c,y} + b7 \times FDI_{c,y} + e_{c,y} \end{aligned} \tag{1}$$

$CO2_{c,y}$ stands for carbon dioxide emissions, measured in metric tons per capita, and $GDP_{c,y}$ denotes the per capita GDP in constant 2010 USD, both for country *c* in year *y*. The control variables are as defined in the part above 'Data and variables from WDI'. The logarithm of all variables in the regressions is used to mitigate the impact of extreme values. The ordinary least squares (OLS) method is employed to estimate the unknown parameters. Both country and year fixed effects are considered to control for any omitted variables related to different countries and periods. If the EKC hypothesis holds, we should find the coefficient of $GDP_{c,y}$, $b1$, is significantly positive while that of $GDP^2_{c,y}$, $b2$, is significantly negative.

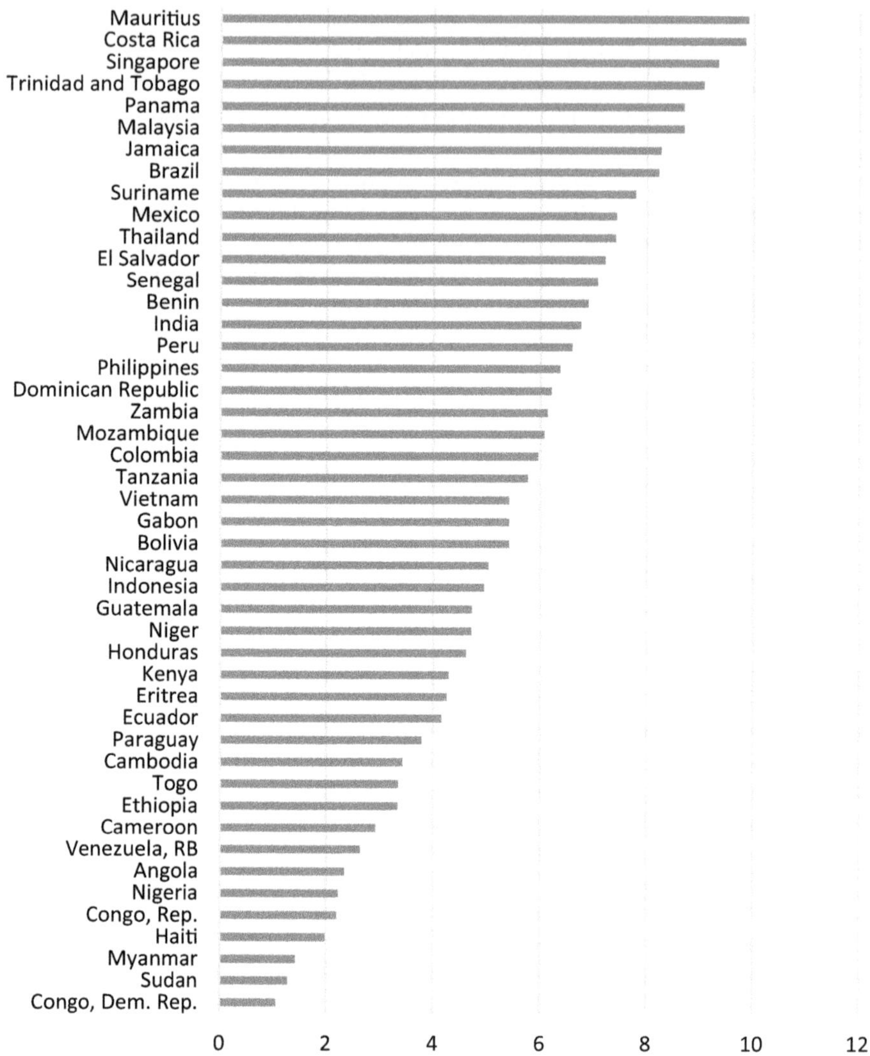

Figure 3.3 Country-level institutional quality index. Note: This figure is generated using the World Governance Indicators (WDI) database of the World Bank

Key results

In this section, we present our main findings from the regression analyses. We firstly verify the existence of the EKC hypothesis in which an inverted U-shaped relationship between environmental quality and per capita income is supported in the tropics. Subsequently, we illustrate the impact of institutional quality on the nexus between environmental quality and economic development. Lastly, the channel effect of foreign direct investment is explored.

The EKC hypothesis

The estimation results of Model (1) are tabulated in Table 3.2. For the full sample period of 1971 to 2014, the estimated coefficients of GDP per capita and its square are 0.544 and -0.026, respectively, both are significant at the 1% level and in a sign consistent with the EKC hypothesis. This finding confirms the inverted U-shape relationship between economic development and environmental quality across 46 tropical countries. Additionally, the coefficient of lagged CO_2 emissions is significantly positive, suggesting a strong momentum in environmental quality. Fossil fuel is found to significantly contribute to air pollution, as expected. On the other hand, factors such as renewable energy consumption, personal remittances, and foreign direct investments do not significantly affect CO_2 emissions, possibly because their values are relatively low with smaller variations across these tropical countries.

We also estimate Model (1) for the two 22-year sub-periods, 1971–1992 and 1993–2014 and report these results in the last two columns of Table 3.2. It is evident that the inverted U-shape relationship between per capita GDP and CO_2 emissions mainly comes from the more recent sample years. One possible reason is the smaller number of observations in the first sub-period, which only accounts for one-third of total observations. Additionally, the growth rates of both per capita GDP and CO_2 emissions are different in the two sub-periods. They are 1.2% and 7.2% in 1971–1992 but 2.5% and 3.3% in 1993–2014. With a sluggish economic growth rate during an earlier stage, environmental quality is less of priority for institutions and governments.

Table 3.2 Testing results of the EKC hypothesis

	1971–2014	*1971–1992*	*1993–2014*
$GDP_{c,y}$	0.544***	-0.582	0.500***
	(0.129)	(0.824)	(0.116)
$GDP^2_{c,y}$	-0.026***	0.058	-0.021***
	(0.008)	(0.053)	(0.008)
$CO2_{c,y-1}$	0.506***	0.386***	0.581***
	(0.018)	(0.031)	(0.024)
$FFEC_{c,y}$	0.377***	0.275***	0.354***
	(0.021)	(0.050)	(0.026)
$RNEC_{c,y}$	-0.009	0.009	-0.011
	(0.016)	(0.049)	(0.017)
$PREM_{c,y}$	-0.001	-0.016	0.006
	(0.004)	(0.010)	(0.004)
$FDI_{c,y}$	0.001	-0.006	-0.001
	(0.004)	(0.008)	(0.004)
OBS	1419	514	905
Adj. R^2	0.991	0.983	0.995

Note: Standard errors are reported in brackets. Both country and year fixed effects are included. The *, **, and *** denote significance level at 10%, 5%, and 1%, respectively. Coefficients of intercepts are not reported for simplicity.

The impact of institutional quality on the per capita GDP–CO_2 emissions relationship

There have been several explanations for the existence of an inverted U-shape relationship between income and CO_2 emissions, one of which is institutional quality. As Dinda (2004) and Ghalwash (2008) suggest, people's preference for good environmental quality increases with their income. Put it differently, an above-threshold level of economic development alone does not necessarily mean a country's environment will be better; it is their institutional quality that contributes to the improved environmental quality. To examine the impact of institutional quality, in each year, we divide sample countries into low- and high-institutional groups based on the median value of the IQIndex and estimate Model (1) within each group. The results reported in Table 3.3 indicate that the inverted U-shape of the income–CO_2 emissions relationship holds only for the group with high institutional quality, indicating that institutional features indeed matter for the relationship of interest.

To examine the impact of institutional quality more directly, we add the various proxies of institutional quality and their interaction terms with $GDP_{c,y}$ and $GDP^2_{c,y}$ into Model (1) in order to moderate the impact of per capita GDP on CO_2 emissions by institutional quality. The new estimation results are presented in Table 3.4.

Focusing on the estimation results using the IQIndex as the institutional quality measure (reported in last column of Table 3.4), we find the effect of

Table 3.3 Testing the EKC hypothesis in different groups of institutional quality

	Low IQ	*High IQ*
$GDP_{c,y}$	0.081	0.485***
	(0.289)	(0.186)
$GDP^2_{c,y}$	0.006	-0.022**
	(0.022)	(0.011)
$CO2_{c,y-1}$	0.553***	0.411***
	(0.041)	(0.042)
$FFEC_{c,y}$	0.402**	0.503***
	(0.041)	(0.046)
$RNEC_{c,y}$	0.006	-0.011
	(0.042)	(0.017)
$PREM_{c,y}$	0.021**	0.004
	(0.009)	(0.005)
$FDI_{c,y}$	0.005	0.001
	(0.007)	(0.006)
OBS	335	353
Adj. R^2	0.994	0.997

Note: 'IQ' stands for institutional quality. Standard errors are reported in brackets. Both country and year fixed effects are included. The *, **, and *** denote significance level at 10%, 5%, and 1%, respectively. Coefficients of intercepts are not reported for simplicity.

Table 3.4 Estimation results with institutional quality proxies

	CC	*GE*	*PV*	*RQ*	*RL*	*VA*	*IQIndex*
$GDP_{c,y}$	0.189	0.268	-0.030	0.453**	0.581***	0.003	0.035
	(0.255)	(0.246)	(0.242)	(0.212)	(0.226)	(0.238)	(0.276)
$GDP^2_{c,y}$	-0.003	-0.007	0.013	-0.023	-0.030*	0.010	0.004
	(0.018)	(0.018)	(0.017)	(0.015)	(0.016)	(0.017)	(0.020)
$IQ_{c,y}$	-0.225	-0.219*	-0.392***	-0.158	-0.084	-0.454***	-0.645***
	(0.144)	(0.133)	(0.143)	(0.140)	(0.147)	(0.166)	(0.200)
$GDP_{c,y}$ *$IQ_{c,y}$	0.054	0.053	0.096***	0.033	0.012	0.113***	0.147***
	(0.038)	(0.036)	(0.038)	(0.036)	(0.038)	(0.043)	(0.051)
$GDP^2_{c,y}$ *$IQ_{c,y}$	-0.003	-0.003	-0.006***	-0.002	0.000	-0.007***	-0.008***
	(0.002)	(0.002)	(0.002)	(0.002)	(0.002)	(0.003)	(0.003)
$CO2_{c,y-1}$	0.521***	0.525***	0.525***	0.519***	0.520***	0.521***	0.522***
	(0.029)	(0.029)	(0.029)	(0.029)	(0.029)	(0.029)	(0.029)
$FFEC_{c,y}$	0.423***	0.417***	0.414***	0.423***	0.418***	0.429***	0.416***
	(0.029)	(0.029)	(0.028)	(0.029)	(0.029)	(0.029)	(0.028)
$RNEC_{c,y}$	-0.014	-0.015	-0.014	-0.008	-0.016	-0.011	-0.008
	(0.018)	(0.018)	(0.018)	(0.018)	(0.018)	(0.018)	(0.018)
$PREM_{c,y}$	0.010**	0.010**	0.011**	0.010**	0.010**	0.008*	0.010**
	(0.005)	(0.005)	(0.005)	(0.005)	(0.005)	(0.005)	(0.005)
$FDI_{c,y}$	0.006	0.005	0.004	0.004	0.005	0.003	0.002
	(0.004)	(0.004)	(0.004)	(0.005)	(0.005)	(0.005)	(0.004)
Adj. R^2	0.996	0.996	0.996	0.996	0.996	0.996	0.996

Note: 'IQ' stands for institutional quality. Standard errors are reported in brackets. Both country and year fixed effects are included. The *, **, and *** denote significance level at 10%, 5%, and 1%, respectively. Coefficients of intercepts are not reported for simplicity.

institutional quality subsumes the impact of per capita GDP and its square on CO2 emissions: the estimated coefficients of $GDP_{c,y}$ and $GDP_{c,y}^2$ become statistically indifferent from zero, while those of the two interaction terms are significant and in an expected sign. This finding is consistent with the results of Table 3.3; that is, the significance of the relationship between income and CO_2 emissions depends on countries' institutional quality and it exists in countries with above-average institutional quality only. Additionally, the significantly negative coefficient of the IQIndex suggests countries with better institutional quality on average have less pollution.

On the other hand, we find mixed results for individual proxy of institutional quality (reported in columns 1 to 6 of Table 3.4). The prominent impact of the IQIndex primarily comes from two proxies: political stability and absence of violence/terrorism (PV) and voice and accountability (VA), whereas the other five institutional quality proxies do not have a significant conditional effect. These findings justify our construction of the composite index, the IQIndex, which removes noises and biases related to any single proxy and explains some different findings in the related literature on the conditional effect of institutional quality. For instance, Wawrzyniak and Doryn (2020) find increments of CO_2 emissions decrease with per capita GDP among 93 emerging and developing countries with low government effectiveness. Aside from different sample countries, using one single proxy of institutional quality is an important reason for their different conclusions on the moderating effect of institutional quality.

FDI, institutional quality, and the per capita GDP–CO_2 emissions relationship

As an important contributor to the local economy, FDI has been shown to affect environmental quality as well as being the nexus between GDP and environment quality in some countries (List and Co, 2000; De Soysa and Neumayer, 2005). Meanwhile, some studies also find that FDI is related to a country's institutional quality. For instance, Buchanan et al. (2012) provide evidence that institutional quality has a positive and significant effect on FDI using a sample of 164 countries from 1996 to 2006. In this sub-section, we explore the moderating impact of FDI within the tropical countries by adding interaction terms involving FDI into our Model (1).

We tabulate these new results in Table 3.5 and summarize them as follows. First, when institutional quality is not included, as shown in column (1), FDI does not significantly affect CO_2 emissions. Nor does it have any impact on the nexus between per capita GDP and CO_2 emissions. Second, FDI marginally affects CO_2 emissions when the effect of institutional quality is controlled, as reported in columns (2) and (3). More FDIs are associated with higher level of CO_2 emissions. In these two model specifications, we also find very limited impact of FDI on the relationship between per capita GDP and CO_2 emissions, evidenced by the mostly nonsignificant estimated coefficients of $GDP_{c,y} \times FDI_{c,y}$

Table 3.5 Estimation results with more interaction terms involving FDI

	(1)	*(2)*	*(3)*
$GDP_{c,y}$	1.492*	1.345	1.176
	(0.846)	(0.838)	(0.996)
$GDP^2_{c,y}$	-0.077	-0.071	-0.057
	(0.055)	(0.055)	(0.073)
$IQ_{c,y}$		-0.683***	-0.739***
		(0.203)	(0.220)
$GDP_{c,y}$*$IQ_{c,y}$		0.157***	0.189***
		(0.052)	(0.075)
$GDP^2_{c,y}$*$IQ_{c,y}$		-0.009***	-0.012*
		(0.003)	(0.006)
$CO2_{c,y-1}$	0.517***	0.515***	0.515***
	(0.029)	(0.029)	(0.029)
$FFEC_{c,y}$	0.420***	0.416***	0.416***
	(0.029)	(0.028)	(0.028)
$RNEC_{c,y}$	-0.012	-0.004	-0.004
	(0.018)	(0.018)	(0.018)
$PREM_{c,y}$	0.010**	0.010**	0.010**
	(0.005)	(0.005)	(0.005)
$FDI_{c,y}$	0.249	0.302*	0.291*
	(0.158)	(0.159)	(0.168)
$GDP_{c,y}$*$FDI_{c,y}$	-0.058	-0.073*	-0.066
	(0.042)	(0.042)	(0.048)
$GDP^2_{c,y}$*$FDI_{c,y}$	0.003	0.004	0.004
	(0.003)	(0.003)	(0.003)
$GDP_{c,y}$* $IQ_{c,y}$*$FDI_{c,y}$			-0.001
			(0.002)
$GDP^2_{c,y}$*$IQ_{c,y}$*$FDI_{c,y}$			0.000
			(0.000)
Adj. R^2	0.996	0.996	0.996

Note: Standard errors are reported in brackets. Both country and year fixed effects are included. The *, **, and *** denote significance level at 10%, 5%, and 1%, respectively. Coefficients of intercepts are not reported for simplicity.

and $GDP^2_{c,y} \times FDI_{c,y}$. Third, FDI does not change the impact of institutional quality on CO_2 emissions as well as on the nexus between per capita GDP and CO_2 emissions, which suggests the dominant impact of institutional quality in this context. Overall, we show that, while FDI may lead to environmental degradation, it does not significantly affect the nexus between per capita GDP and CO_2 emissions or the conditional impact of institutional quality. Put it differently, while countries with better institutional quality tend to attract more FDI, the increased FDI in these countries does not significantly change the relationship between economic development and environmental quality in these countries.

Conclusions

While many studies have tested the EKC hypothesis, none of them concentrates exclusively on countries located in the tropics, a region that makes up around 40% of the planet's surface area and approximately 40% of the world's population.[6] This chapter seeks to fill the gap by not only testing EKC hypothesis but also examining the impact of important factors including institutional quality and FDI on the nexus between economic growth and environmental quality. These issues are particularly crucial for the tropics as most countries in this region are developing and emerging markets with below average GDP per capita. As such, driving higher levels of economic growth is a key priority; however, in seeking to achieve this aim they also have to deal with the side effects as well, one of which is environmental degradation. How to spur economic growth while maintaining a relatively good living environment challenges many governments in tropical countries.

Our study found evidence to support the EKC hypothesis using a sample of 46 countries from the tropics and data from the 1971 to 2014 period. Similar to many other countries, environmental quality deteriorates as economic activities increase before economic growth reaches a threshold, after which environmental quality improves with economic growth. However, this pattern does not occur automatically. Further analysis shows that a country's institutional quality matters for the nexus between growth and the environment. With a composite institutional quality index measure constructed using six proxies of institutional quality from World Bank, we find the EKC hypothesis is evident only in tropical countries with better institutional quality. In particular, institutional quality such as political stability, absence of violence/terrorism, and voice and accountability significantly moderate the effect of per capita GDP on CO_2 emissions. While prior studies have found that FDI has been related to economic growth, environmental quality, and institutional quality, we find its impact on the nexus between economic growth and environmental quality very weak and limited. Hence, we suggest governments and policymakers in tropical countries commit more effort to improve the quality of their institutions to reduce the negative impact of economic growth on environmental quality.

Notes

1 Corresponding author: JCU Singapore Business School, JCU Singapore, Singapore. Email. huiping.zhang@jcu.edu.au.
2 JCU Singapore Business School, JCU Singapore, Singapore.
3 JCU Singapore Business School, JCU Singapore, Singapore, and Department of International Trade, Chungnam National University, Daejeon, South Korea.
4 From https://worldpopulationreview.com/country-rankings/tropical-countries.
5 The list of tropical countries can be found from https://worldpopulationreview.com/country-rankings/tropical-countries.
6 From World Population Review, https://worldpopulationreview.com/country-rankings/tropical-countries.

References

Abid, M. (2016). Impact of economic, financial and institutional factors on CO2 emissions: Evidence from Sub-Saharan Africa economies. *Utilities Policy*, *41*, 85–94. doi:10.1016/j.jup.2016.06.009

Abid, M. (2017). Does economic, financial and institutional developments matter for environmental quality? A comparative analysis of EU and MEA countries. *Journal of Environmental Management*, *188*,183–194. doi:10.1016/j.jenvman.2016.12.007

Acaravci, A., and Ozturk, I. (2010). On the relationship between energy consumption, CO2 emissions and economic growth in Europe. *Energy*, *35*(12), 5412–5420. doi:10.1016/j.energy.2010.07.009

Akbostanci, E., Turut-Asik, S., and Tunc, G. I. (2009). The relationship between income and environment in Turkey: Is there an environmental Kuznets curve?. *Energy Policy*, *37*, 861–7.

Ang, J. B. (2007). CO2 emissions, energy consumption, and output in France. *Energy Policy*, *35*(10), 4772–4778. doi:10.1016/j.enpol.2007.03.032

Apergis, N., and Ozturk, I. (2015). Testing environmental Kuznets curve hypothesis in Asian countries. *Ecological Indicators*, *52*, 16–22. doi:10.1016/j.ecolind.2014.11.026

Apergis, N., and Payne, J. E. (2010). The emissions, energy consumption, and growth nexus: Evidence from the commonwealth of independent states. *Energy Policy*, *38*(1), 650–655. doi:10.1016/j.enpol.2009.08.029

Arminen, H., and Menegaki, A. N. (2019). Corruption, climate and the energy-environment growth nexus. *Energy Economics*, *80*, 621–634. doi:10.1016/j.eneco.2019.02.009

Bilgili, F., Kocak, E., and Bulut, U. (2016). The dynamic impact of renewable energy consumption on CO2 emissions: A revisited environmental Kuznets curve approach. *Renewable and Sustainable Energy Reviews*, *54*, 838–845. doi:10.1016/j.rser.2015.10.080

Buchanan, B. G., Le, Q. V., and Rishi, M. (2012). Foreign direct investment and institutional quality: Some empirical evidence. *International Review of Financial Analysis*, *21*. 81–89.

Claessens, S., and Feijen, E. (2007). *Financial sector development and the millennium development goals* (Vol. 89). World Bank Working Paper. World Bank.

Cole, M. A., and Elliot, R. J. R. (2005). FDI and the capital intensity of 'dirty' sectors: A missing piece of the pollution haven puzzle. *Review of Development Economics*, *9*(4), 530–548.

Cropper, M., and Griffiths, C. (1994). The interaction of populations, growth, and environmental quality. *American Economic Review*, *84*(2), 250–254.

Dasgupta, S., Laplante, B., Wang, H., and Wheeler, D. (2002). Confronting the environmental Kuznets curve. *Journal of Economic Perspectives*, *16*(1), 147–168. doi:10.1257/0895330027157

Day, K. M., and Grafton, Q. (2003). Growth and the environment in Canada: An empirical analysis. *Journal of Agricultural Economics*, *51*, 197–216.

De Soysa, I., and Neumayer, E. (2005). False prophet or genuine savior? Assessing the effects of economic openness on sustainable development, 1980–1999. *International Organization*, *59*(3), 731–772.

Dinda, S. (2004). Environment Kuznets curve hypothesis: A survey. *Ecological Economics*, *49*(4), 431–455. doi:10.1016/j.ecolecon.2004.02.011

Du, L., Chu, W., and Cai, S. (2012). Economic development and carbon dioxide emissions in China: Provincial panel data analysis. *China Economic Review*, *23*, 371–84.

Feridun, M. (2006). Impact of trade liberalization on the environment in developing countries: The case of Nigeria. *MPRA Paper*, *731*, 39–56.

Fodha, M., and Zaghdoud, O. (2010). Economic growth and environmental degradation in Tunisia: An empirical analysis of the Environmental Kuznets Curve. *Energy Policy, 38*, 1150–6.

Frankel, J. A., and D. Romer (1999), Does trade cause growth? *American Economic Review, 89*, 379–399.

Franklin, R., and Matthias, R. (2012). Growing up and cleaning up: The environmental Kuznets curve redux. *Applied Geography, 32*(1), 29–39.

Friedl, B. M., and Getzner, M. (2003). Determinants of CO2 emissions in a small open economy. *Ecology Economics, 45*, 133–148.

Gani, A. (2012). The relationship between good governance and carbon dioxide emissions: Evidence from developing economies. *Journal of Economic Development, 37*, 77–93.

Ghalwash, T. (2008). Demand for environmental quality: An empirical analysis of consumer behavior in Sweden. *Environmental Resource Economics, 41*(1), 71–87.

Gholipour, H. F., and Farzanegan, M. R. (2018). Institutions and the effectiveness of expenditures on environmental protection: Evidence from Middle Eastern countries. *Constitutional Political Economy, 29*(1), 20–39. doi:10.1007/s10602-017-9246-x

Ghosh, S. (2010). Examining carbon emissions economic growth nexus for India: A multivariate cointegration approach. *Energy Policy, 38*, 3008–14.

Giovanis, E. (2013). Environmental Kuznets curve: Evidence from the British Household Panel Survey. *Economic Modelling, 30*, 602–11.

Grossman, G. M., and Krueger, A. B. (1993). Environmental impacts of a north American free trade agreement. In P. Garber (Eds.), *The U. S.-Mexico free trade agreement*. MIT Press.

Grossman, G. M., and Krueger, A. B. (1995). Economic growth and the environment. *Quarterly Journal of Economics, 110*(2), 352–377.

Gui, S., Zhao, L., and Zhang, Z. (2019). Does municipal solid waste generation in China support the Environmental Kuznets Curve? New evidence from spatial linkage analysis. *Waste Management, 84*, 310–319.

Hamit-Haggar M. (2012). Greenhouse gas emissions, energy consumption and economic growth: A panel cointegration analysis from Canadian industrial sector perspective. *Energy Economics, 34*, 358–64.

Jalil A., and Feridun, M. (2011). The impact of growth, energy and financial development on the environment in China: A cointegration analysis. *Energy Economics, 33*, 284–91.

Jaunky, V. C. (2011). The CO2 emissions-income nexus: Evidence from rich countries, *Energy Policy, 39*(3), 1228–1240.

Jensen, V. (1996). The pollution haven hypothesis and the industrial flight hypothesis: Some perspectives on theory and empirics. CDE Working Paper, Vol. 1996.5. Centre for Development and the Environment, University of Oslo.

Jones, L., and Manuelli, R. (2001). Endogenous policy choice: The case of pollution and growth. *Review of Economic Dynamics, 4*(2), 369–405.

Kanjilal, K., and Ghosh, S. (2013). Environmental Kuznets curve for India: Evidence from tests for co-integration with unknown structural breaks. *Energy Policy, 56*(C), 509–515.

Kasman, A., and Duman, Y. S. (2015). CO2 emissions, economic growth, energy consumption, trade and urbanization in new EU member and candidate countries: A panel data analysis. *Economic Modelling, 44*, 97–103. doi:10.1016/j.econmod.2014.10.022

Kuznets, S. (1955). Economic Growth and Income Inequality. *American Economic Review, 45*(1), 1–28.

List, J. A., and Co, C. Y. (2000). The effect of environmental regulation on foreign direct investment. *Journal of Environmental Economics and Management*, *40*(1), 1–20.

Markandya, A., Golub, A., and Pedroso-Galinato, S. (2006). Empirical analysis of National Income and SO2 emissions in selected European countries. *Environmental Resource Economics*, *35*(3), 221–257. doi:10.1007/s10640-006-9014-2

Moutinho, V., Varum, C., and Madaleno, M. (2017). How economic growth affects emissions? An investigation of the environmental Kuznets curve in Portuguese and Spanish economic activity sectors. *Energy Policy*, *106*, 326–344. doi:10.1016/j.enpol.2017.03.069.

Orubu, O., and Omotor, D. G. (2011). Environmental quality and economic growth: Searching for environmental Kuznets curves for air and water pollutants in Africa. *Energy Policy*, *39*, 4178–88.

Ozturk, I., and Acaravci, A. (2010). CO2 emissions, energy consumption, and economic growth in Turkey. *Renewable and Sustainable Energy Reviews*, *14*, 3220–5.

Panayotou, T. (1997). Demystifying the Environmental Kuznets Curve: Turning a Black Box into a Policy Tool. *Environment and Development Economics*, *2*(4), 465–84.

Pao, H. T., and Tsai, C. M. (2011). Multivariate Granger causality between CO2 emissions, energy consumption, FDI (foreign direct investment) and GDP (gross domestic product): Evidence from a panel of BRIC (Brazil, Russian Federation, India, and China) countries. *Energy*, *36*, 685–93.

Paudel, K. P., Zapata, H., and Susanto, D. (2005). An empirical test of environmental Kuznets curve for water pollution. *Environmental and Resource Economics*, *31*, 325–348.

Persadie, N., and Ramlogan, R. (2007). Pursuing development and protecting the environment: Dilemma of the developing world. In K. R. Gupta, M. Jankowska, and P. Maiti (Eds.), *Global environment: Problems and policies* (pp. 58–106). Atlantic.

Plassmann, F., and Khanna, K. (2006). Household income and pollution implications for the debate about the environmental Kuznets curve hypothesis. *Journal of Environmental Development*, *14*, 22–41.

Pradhan, R. P., Arvin, M. B., Hall, J. H., and Nair, M. (2017). Trade openness, foreign direct investment, and finance-growth nexus in the Eurozone countries. *The Journal of International Trade and Economic Development*, *26*, 336–360. doi:10.1080/09638199.2016.1249392

Saboori, B., Sulaiman, J., and Mohd, S. (2012). Economic growth and CO2 emissions in Malaysia: A co-integration analysis of the Environmental Kuznets Curve. *Energy Policy*, *51*, 184–91.

Sachs, J. D. (2001). Tropical underdevelopment. National Bureau of Economic Research Working paper 8119.

Sarkodie, S. A., and Strezov, V. (2019). A review on Environmental Kuznets Curve hypothesis using bibliometric and meta-analysis. *Science of the Total Environment*, *649*, 128–145. doi:10.1016/j.scitotenv.2018.08.276.

Sephton, P., and Mann, J. (2016). Compelling evidence of an environmental Kuznets curve in the United Kingdom. *Environmental & Resource Economics*, *64*(2), 301–315.

Stern, D. I. (2001). Common MS. Is there an Environmental Kuznets Curve for sulfur? *Journal of Environmental Economic Management*, *41*(2), 162–78.

Tamazian A., and Rao B. (2010). Do economic, financial and institutional developments matter for environmental degradation? Evidence from transitional economies. *Energy Economics*, *32*, 137–45.

Tamazian, A., Piñeiro, J., and Vadlamannati, K. C. (2009). Does higher economic and financial development lead to environmental degradation: Evidence from BRIC countries. *Energy Policy*, *37*(1), 246–253.

Tiba, S., and Omri, A. (2017). Literature survey on the relationships between energy, environment and economic growth. *Renewable and Sustainable Energy Reviews*, *69*, 1129–1146. doi:10.1016/j.rser.2016.09.113.

Vollebergh, H. R. J., Melenberg, B., and Dijkgraaf, E. (2009). Identifying reduced-form relations with panel data: The case of pollution and income. *Journal of Environmental Economic Management*, *58*, 27–42.

Wawrzyniak, D., and Doryn, W. (2020). Does the quality of institutions modify the economic growth-carbon dioxide emissions nexus? Evidence from a group of emerging and developing countries. *Economic Research-Ekonomska Istraživanja*, *33*(1), 124–144. doi:10.1080/1331677X.2019.1708770

World Bank (2000). Is globalization causing a 'race to the bottom' in environmental standards? In *PREM economic policy group and development economics group*. World Bank.

Zhu, H. M., You, W. H., and Zeng, Z. F. (2012). Urbanization and CO2 emissions: A semi- parametric panel data analysis. *Economic Letters*, *117*, 848–50.

4 A bottom of pyramid perspective on quality education in the tropics

Yenee Kim[1], *Malobi Mukherjee*[2], *and Reetika Gupta*[3]

Introduction and background

An initial look at progress in quality education, the fourth goal in the United Nation's Sustainability agenda (2019), shows that despite the 91% enrolment in primary education in developing countries, more than 50% of the young people in 58 out of 133 countries had not completed upper secondary school. Access to quality education for all people is central to achieving the SGDs. According to the latest State of the Tropics (2020) reports published by James Cook University, the tropics lag behind the rest of the world in education outcomes and this is the key focus for the region especially to reduce inequalities in society. Education is essential for economic growth, health and well-being, gender inequality, and almost all aspects of sustainable development (State of the Tropics, 2020). In all societies, education and income are correlated, yet a number of regions in the tropics have lower than average educational attainment. As per the United Nation's Sustainability agenda (2019), one in ten young people (out of just under one billion global youth) lacked basic reading, writing, and numeracy skills. Youth literacy remained a significant problem in many nations, particularly among the poorest youth in some regions of the tropics which are also home to 85% of the world's poorest people (State of the Tropics, 2020). UNESCO (2019) reports highlight an average of 92% of the poorest youth (aged 20–29) across sub-Saharan Africa, Central and Southern Asia had not completed upper secondary school, compared to 22% in Oceania. To examine the reasons behind these low completion rates, the authors conducted a study that uncovered the psychological mechanisms that drive education goals for the Bottom of Pyramid (BoP)[4] population in Tropical Eastern India[5] where only 50% of the urban/rural poorest young adults had completed their upper secondary education (UNESCO 2019). We chose the state of West Bengal because the upper secondary school completion rates were below the national average of 43% for those with a middle and low income (UNESCO 2019), suggesting the dropout rates from school were quite high.

The overall findings show an interactional effect between campaign framing and financial deprivation on attitudes towards the campaign. Specifically, BoP consumers with higher levels of financial deprivation prefer education

DOI: 10.4324/9781003153580-4

campaigns with a desirability framing of obtaining education (e.g., successful future) compared to a feasibility framing of obtaining education (e.g., easy access to education). Conversely, BoP consumers with lower levels of income prefer education campaigns with a feasibility framing compared to a desirability framing of obtaining education.

The chapter is organized as follows. First, we present a brief review of the education circumstances in Tropical Eastern India and differences in financial deprivation levels among the BoP sector. Then we discuss construal level theory to develop our theoretical framework and hypothesis. Next, we present our study and findings showing support for our hypothesis. Lastly, we conclude with theoretical and managerial implications along with suggestions for implementing quality education in Tropical Eastern India and its limitations.

Education at the bottom of pyramid in India's tropical regions

According to Naveed and Sutoris (2020), there is a dialectical relationship between poverty and education. Poverty shapes (and often limits) children's educational aspirations, opportunities, and experiences, yet the attainment of education is often the first step towards poverty alleviation. However, the vicious cycle of poverty and resultant prioritization of expenses often results in families curtailing education expenses thereby impeding opportunities for economic development, distribution of national income, and social mobility (Becker 1967). Naveed and Sutoris (2020) explain that a combination of poverty-related factors such as early childhood development, childhood poverty, intergenerational mobility, and the distribution of public resources on education impact access to quality and relevant education amongst the poorest in the world.

According to UNDP (2018) reports, there has been an unprecedented expansion of mass schooling in South Asia over the recent decades resulting in widened access to education for women, the socially disadvantaged poor, and the poor. In the case of India, improved access to schools has contributed to a reduction in education poverty with a lower percentage (11.6 %) of households where no members have been in school for more than six years. The comparative figures for India's neighbouring countries, namely Bangladesh, Bhutan, Nepal, and Pakistan are higher. While the UNDP (2018) report concludes that educational deprivation is not a primary contributor to the multidimensional poverty index India, UNESCO (2019) highlights that the persistent problem in India lies in the non-completion of school among the poorest young adults with only 8% completing upper secondary school.

Academics in the field have highlighted a number of socioeconomic and technological factors as the key antecedents of non-completion of upper secondary schooling in India. The issues with non-completion continue to persist even though recent research by Vishwanathan et al (2021) highlights the prevalence of vocational market place literacy among subsistence communities or Nedugadi et al (2018) and Pal et al (2009)'s research underscoring the significant impact of mobile technology on improving teachers' effectiveness and reducing student absenteeism. According to Sriprakash (2016), one of the causes of this problem of non-completion is the prevalence of an education system inspired by the Euro-American model of society building which has resulted in the poorest in India perceiving the classrooms as an alien context that is not reflective of their lived experience. Studies in the context of rural West Bengal (Maji and Sarkar 2017) have highlighted that economic backwardness and physical bottlenecks are a fundamental impediment to uptake of education among the BoP population. Researchers (Chaudhri and Jha, 2013; Banki and Neogi, 2014) suggest that a lack of parental awareness of the importance of education, additional pressures on children to contribute to household income, and daily chores are key contributors to school dropouts in India. Kabeer and Mahmud (2009) have also added that often families are reluctant to take risks in making education investments, given the uncertain returns on education in the future. More recently, Patra et al. (2021) have highlighted from their research in the state of West Bengal that a lack of basic awareness about the importance of education has also contributed to the educational backwardness in the state. Several research articles on the state of education in West Bengal (Ramesh, 2013; Samanta and Bajpai, 2015; Guha and Das, 2014; Daripa, 2017) have focused on regulations, political unrest, lack of facilities, access, infrastructure as the fundamental challenges to progress in education uptake by the economically and socially backward population in the region. The BoP consumer perspective on education is rather scant in the literature: a few studies (Patra and Panigrahi, 2018; Chakraborty, 2019) in a West Bengal context have focused on psychological barriers of pupils, parents' unwillingness, and language and cultural barriers to the uptake of education. The uncertainties and priorities around education (or the lack thereof) can be addressed through a deeper understanding of what good and relevant education might mean for those living in poverty (Naveed and Sutoris, 2020).

Academic research on BoP consumers highlights that the BoP's lack of hope and financial constraints determine their consumption choices (Naveed and Sutoris, 2020; Dembek et al., 2020, 2018). Accordingly, in this chapter, we seek to shed light on the psychological factors determining preference towards education campaigns. We apply construal level theory to understand if and why BoP consumers with varying levels of financial deprivation can have different preferences when it comes to education campaigns for children. In doing so, we contribute to the BoP literature by providing a consumer-based understanding of the antecedents driving adoption and completion of education among the bottom of pyramid population in Tropical Eastern India with a specific focus on the state of West Bengal.

Financial deprivation and BoP consumers

The level of financial deprivation increases when consumers evaluate their financial well-being, a state that conveys how people perceive their financial situation which can range from being worse off to better off (Diener et al., 1999; Sharma and Alter, 2012), as negative or damaging. Past research has shown that consumers with varying levels of financial deprivation can show differences in their decision-making such as compromising moral decisions (Sharma et al., 2014) and preferring myopic choices and scarce goods (Johar et al., 2015; Sharma and Alter, 2012) when financial deprivation levels are high. Researchers suggest that this is because financial deprivation prompts consumers to react in certain ways due to their deficient situation.

Due to almost non-existent stable employment and income, BoP consumers have a lack of regular access to necessities such as food as well as education, leading to limited literacy and numeracy skills (Hart, 2007; Prahalad, 2004; Prahalad and Hart, 2002). Thus, using education campaigns developed for non-BoP consumers may not be effective in generating responses from the BoP consumers. For example, BoP consumers tend to prefer visual stimuli because of the low literacy rate (Hasan et al., 2017) and prefer specific products matched to their circumstances such as fridge-free products (Chikweche and Fletcher 2010). This necessitates the framing of education campaigns aligned with the comprehensive ability of BoP consumers.

Building on previous research, we investigate how BoP consumers who constantly have high levels of financial deprivation react to different types of campaign framing, particularly related to the education of their children. We further examine the differences in the effectiveness of education campaign framings among BoP consumers as the overall BoP sector is extensive, consisting of 85% of the poorest people living in the tropics (State of the Tropics, 2020), and thus, it is difficult to speculate that financial deprivation levels are constant within the sector (Rangan et al., 2011). For example, the BoP sector consists of consumers who may earn semi-regular incomes and can sparingly afford consumer goods such as a television, bicycles, and mobile phones. However, there are also consumers who rely solely on aid from nonprofit organizations or government programmes to obtain basic necessities like food, clean water, and shelter. Consequently, we examine how BoP consumers across income levels react differently towards the same framing of campaigns due to varying levels of financial deprivation. In the next section, we examine this phenomenon more deeply using the lens of construal level theory.

Construal level and BoP consumers

Construal level theory proposes that individuals construe stimuli in their environment abstractly (high construal level) or concretely (low construal level) prompted by how close or far individuals subjectively feel from an object or event (Liberman and Trope, 1998). In other words, as customers' construal levels are shifted due to differences in the psychological distance towards an object or event, they will naturally adopt different mindsets. A customer in a low construal level mindset tends to focus on the specific attributes of products in a contextualized perspective, and how these specific attributes will help achieve the end goal (feasibility aspects) (Liberman and Trope, 1998; Fujita et al., 2008). On the other hand, a customer in a high construal level mindset tends to focus on the values and reasons for the purchase in a holistic perspective, and the desired higher-order end goals (desirability aspects) (Liberman and Trope 1998; Fujita et al., 2008). In other words, when individuals perceive an object or event to be distant, they generally focus on the desirability factors and construe their thoughts in a more general, abstract manner. Compared to this, when individuals perceive the same object or event to be closer, they focus on the feasibility factors and construe their thoughts in a more detailed, concrete manner (Trope and Liberman, 2011; Vallacher and Wegner, 1989).

We argue that financial deprivation plays a key role in influencing BoP consumers' reactions to education campaigns as the varying levels of financial deprivation are likely to trigger different construal levels. For example, fewer financial constraints can shape how probable an event can be and consumers tend to perceive events with higher probability and less psychological distance (Trope and Liberman, 2011; Wakslak et al., 2008). We posit that BoP consumers with lower levels of financial deprivation perceive education to be psychologically closer at a lower construal level due to the higher probability of their children being able to obtain the education. In the case of BoP consumers with higher levels of financial deprivation lacking basic necessities, education is perceived to be psychologically further, at a higher construal level, due to the lower probability of their children being able to obtain the education. We, therefore, contend that BoP consumers with higher financial deprivation will place more emphasis on the desirability (vs. feasibility) aspects of the education such as 'a successful future' due to the higher construal level. On the other hand, BoP consumers with lower financial deprivation will place more emphasis on the feasibility (vs. desirability) aspects of the education such as 'ease of access to the education' due to the lower construal level.

Accordingly, we hypothesize that BoP consumers with higher levels of financial deprivation prefer desirability-framed education campaigns (vs. feasibility-framed education campaigns), whereas those with lower levels of financial deprivation prefer feasibility-framed education campaigns (vs. desirability-framed education campaigns).

Study

We conducted a study with BoP respondents in a West Bengal village in Tropical Eastern India to determine the relative preference for the two different framing types of computer education – feasibility framing (i.e., ease of access) and the desirability framing (i.e., successful future). Institutional Review Board (IRB) clearance for ethical research was taken by the co-author from Essec Business School who designed and collected the data and was waived as exempt by HREC, JCU, as the data was collected when the second author was not an employee of JCU Singapore. We conducted fieldwork in the state of West Bengal where the upper secondary completion rates were below the national average (43%) for middle-income groups at 38% and at 25% for the poor and 13% for poorest sections of the population as per the UNESCO 2019 database. The state of West Bengal was a convenient choice logistically as two of the authors of the book chapter hailed from the state of West Bengal and their familiarity with the local language simplified the questionnaire administration as well. The authors were able to administer the questionnaires through local researchers who belonged to the community and had prior experience in administering questionnaires which established trust and comfort among the respondents.

The objective of this study is to examine the interaction between financial deprivation and campaign framing on liking of the campaign. We predicted that liking of the campaign would be higher for the desirability-framed campaign compared to the feasibility-framed campaign as financial deprivation increases, whereas liking of the campaign would be higher for the feasibility-framed campaign compared to the desirability-framed campaign as financial deprivation decreases.

Method

Administration. Before conducting the study, we strived to adapt the study and procedure to BoP consumers who have low literacy levels (Viswanathan et al., 2009). Specifically, we conducted the study through face-to-face interactions in which the research assistants verbally asked each question and recorded each response. Further, we used visual stimuli that presented the level of agreement instead of using numerical values which are commonly used to non-BoP consumers for the scales (e.g., Hasan et al., 2020; Viswanathan et al., 2005; Viswanathan et al., 2009). Lastly, the research assistant gave a short explanation regarding the message in the campaign to each respondent when presenting the education campaign. Responses for each respondent took an average of 45 minutes.

Participants and design. A total of 80 BoP consumers (40.0% female; $M_{age} = 44.3$ years) were recruited in West Bengal, Tropical Eastern India for this study. The experiment employed a two-level (Campaign Framing: Desirability vs. Feasibility) between-subjects design where campaign framing was manipulated between-subjects and financial deprivation, a continuous independent variable, was measured. We manipulated campaign framing by emphasizing either desirability or feasibility aspects of computer education for the child of the participants (see Figure 4.1).

Procedure. First, each participant indicated their level of financial deprivation on a three-item seven-point scale adopted from Prawitz et al. (2006) (Financial Well-Being Scale, $\alpha = .61$). Next, the participants viewed one of two randomly determined healthcare campaigns framed on either desirability or feasibility aspects of computer education for one's child along with a verbal explanation of the message. Following this, participants indicated their liking of the campaign on a two-item seven-point bipolar scale (dislike very much/like very much, not at all favourable/very favourable; $\alpha = .61$). The manipulation check question involved participants indicating the aspects that were emphasized in

Education Campaign with Desirability Framing	Education Campaign with Feasibility Framing
Computer Education	Computer Education
Secure your child's successful future through computer education!	**Your child can have simple and easy access to computer education.**
Every child has the right to be educated.	**Every child has the right to be educated.**
Computer education can bring an end to poverty and provide a better life. Let your children obtain computer education to enhance employment opportunities and enjoy a quality life.	**Getting the right computer education is simple and easy. Computer education centers are accessible easily by feet or local transportation. Interested children can also receive discounts to reduce the financial burden on parents and families.**
For a successful and fulfilling future for your children, make computer education priority for your beloved children.	**Take advantage pf the easily accessible computer education and enrol your child at one of the neighbouring computer centers.**

Figure 4.1 Education campaign stimuli

the education campaign (how simple it is to receive computer education/the benefits of receiving computer education) on a 7-point bipolar scale. Finally, participants answered questions regarding their demographic information such as gender and age.

Results

Manipulation check. Participants focused more on the desirability factors of obtaining computer education in the desirability condition ($M = 5.75$) versus the feasibility condition (M = 5.10, $F(1, 78) = 4.671$, $p < .05$), showing that the manipulation of campaign framings was successful.

Interaction. Consistent with our prediction, there was a significant interaction between campaign framing and financial deprivation on liking of the campaign ($b = -.83$, $t = -2.81$, $p < .001$; see Figure 4.2). We found a significant main effect of campaign framing ($b = 5.29$, $t = 2.78$, $p < .01$) and a significant main effect of financial deprivation ($b = 1.48$, $t = 2.96$, $p < .01$) as well. This indicates that the participants had higher liking of the campaign for the desirability-framed campaign and when financial deprivation was higher. We conducted a floodlight analysis (Spiller et al., 2013) to examine the simple effects of campaign framing (desirability vs. feasibility) on liking of the campaign across financial deprivation levels. The results revealed two significant Johnson-Neyman regions ($p < .05$) when participants' financial deprivation levels were 6.77 or above ($b = -.32$, $t = -1.99$, $p = .05$) and 5.89 or below ($b = .41$, $t = 1.99$, $p = .05$). This demonstrates that participants had significantly higher liking for the desirability-framed campaign compared to the feasibility-framed campaign when financial deprivation levels were 6.77 or higher. On the other hand, participants had significantly higher liking for the feasibility-framed campaign compared to the desirability-framed campaign when financial deprivation levels were 5.89 or lower. Overall, the results of the study demonstrated a significant interaction between financial deprivation and campaign framing on liking of the campaign supporting our theoretical framework.

Theoretical and managerial implications

This research contributes to the literature in several ways. First, we employ construal level theory to better understand the effectiveness of framing of

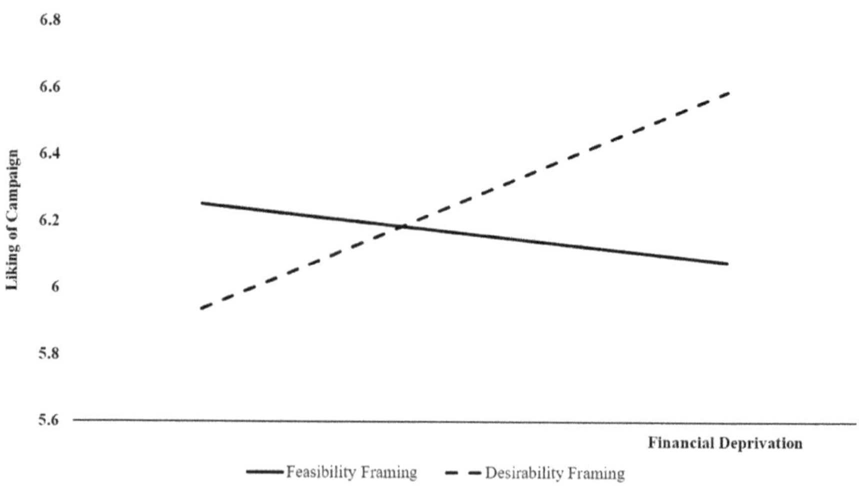

Figure 4.2 Interaction between financial deprivation and campaign type on liking of campaign

education campaigns among BoP consumers. Construal level theory has been widely used in non-BoP contexts (Fujita et al., 2008; Trope and Liberman, 2011), but not extensively examined in the BoP literature and thus, can contribute to enhancing our understanding of why BoP consumers prefer different types of education framing based on their financial deprivation levels.

Second, we respond to calls for more empirical and quantitative research on BoP consumers providing strategic implications to elicit long-lasting, positive outcomes (Dembek et al., 2020; Kolk et al., 2014). Specifically, we take a bottom-up approach for a deep dive into underlying psychological mechanisms underlying BoP consumers' preferences for educational campaigns to improve our understanding of factors driving long-term, sustainable influence on BoP education.

Third, with some notable exceptions (e.g., Hasan et al., 2020; Rangan et al., 2011), we do not treat the extensive BoP sector as a whole but rather recognize the differences across income levels. Accordingly, we examine our predicted effect across financial deprivation levels upholding that the different income levels are characterized by stark differences in basic living standards and can impact variances in decision-making among BoP consumers (Rangan et al., 2011). Specifically, we show how financial deprivation levels influence BoP consumers' unique preferences for differently framed education campaigns.

Implications for implementation of quality education in Tropical Eastern India

The State of the Tropics report published by James Cook University in 2020 underscored the significance of education for the attainment of economic growth, health and well-being, gender equality, and all aspects of sustainable development stated in the UN sustainable development goals (State of the Tropics, 2020). This report also stated that creating opportunities for students to stay in school longer would enable them to acquire greater literacy, numeracy and the ability to engage with technology. Motivating students to continue with their education would therefore be fundamental for societal and economic development in the tropics. In this context, our findings highlight the need for a differentiated strategy in communicating the benefits of education among the BoP population in emerging tropical countries. This differentiated approach could entail the adoption of skills-based vocational education campaigns for BoP with higher levels of financial deprivation since they expressed greater liking for education campaigns focusing on benefits of computer education in our research findings. For the BoP with lower levels of financial deprivation, the educational campaigns would need to focus on convenience and ease of access to education centres. The ramifications of these findings are threefold for policymakers, businesses, and educational institutions involved in the delivery of education to BoP in emerging tropical markets.

First, policymakers would need to rethink their education curriculum to include skills-based vocational programmes especially in areas of skills shortage.

A major step in this direction was taken by the Central Government when it set up a skills development programme in 2015 to train over 40 crore (crore: ten million) people in a variety of skills by the year 2022. As a part of this programme, the national skill development mission was set up to give school dropouts the opportunity to undertake vocational training in order to improve their employability options. This scheme had the objective of enabling a large number of Indian youth to take up industry-relevant skills training to help them secure a better livelihood (MSDE 2021). Despite these initiatives, the recently published India Skills Report (2021) highlights that the employability of the Indian youth stood at 45.9% in 2020, the lowest in a number of years. West Bengal (the state where the authors conducted fieldwork for this research project) provided the nineth highest employability opportunity in the country despite having the second highest computer literacy in the country. Moreover, the data in this report pertained to employability in Tier 1–3 cities and lacked any information on employability opportunities for rural BoP. Tiwari (2020) highlights that the penetration of vocational training in rural India was abysmally low and during the 2017–2018 period 93.7% of youth had not received any vocational training. Noting that 70% of the Indian population living in rural areas were predominantly agrarian-based communities, Ramasamy et al. (2020) recommend that vocational training in these areas should be context-specific, responsive to the needs of individuals and learners while being relevant and flexible. The authors are also of the view that vocational education could be relevant to a predominantly agrarian rural BoP if the training focused on areas of immediate economic development for the communities, such as reskilling for the digitalization of agriculture. The need for digital agriculture in India has been well accepted but at a very nascent stage of development (Confederation of Indian Industries 2020). Policymakers could therefore rethink the vocational education curriculum for rural agrarian BoP in India especially since India is the largest exporter of rice in the world, holding 32.5% of the total rice export worth USD 1.7 billion (Worlds Top Export 2020).

Second, the existing skills development programmes are designed to offer opportunities to school dropouts and not necessarily to motivate students at the risk of drop out to continue with a relevant vocational training. A more proactive approach towards preventing high rates of school dropouts would require policymakers to reevaluate the existing curriculum offered in public schools and embed a parallel vocational training option at the beginning of secondary/higher secondary school. Such an approach would require an educational ecosystem comprising community leaders, educators, and industry partners collaborating to create a curriculum aligned to the skilling and upskilling needs of the communities. Industry partners would have to liaise with government departments to redesign the educational curriculum and provide initial training to rural educators. Within this ecosystem, students would also be given the opportunity to engage in practical training by way of industry internship with the final objective of applying the skill sets to improve local community production of goods and services unique to those communities. The policymaker, educator, industry nexus would aim at providing a circular vocational training where students would go through the entire circular process and end up using the experience gained along the way to improve their local production capabilities. Industry partners could also gain from this process by setting up a more sustainable and transparent supply chain network for trade of goods in the future.

Third, the policymakers would have to rethink the implementation strategy for education to make vocational training easily accessible to the rural BoP. Technology could be used to disseminate relevant theoretical information via online platforms specially tailored to suit ease of access on remote villages with low Internet speed. Educational institutions could collaborate with rural schools to provide blended learning to rural BoP students whereby training centres in cities could video stream lectures to students in remote villages. The inherent flexibility of an online vocational education supplemented by occasional travel to training centres for practical training could alleviate issues with accessing vocational education from remote rural areas. A mutually beneficial and collaborative relationship between urban-rural education centres mediated by effective utilisation of tech-enabled online learning, together with government investments to support the collaboration would therefore be a first step in creating relevant and conveniently accessible vocational education for rural BoP.

Limitations

This research specifically investigated the interaction effect in an education context, particularly education for the children of the BoP consumers. Though we show that higher-order desirability-oriented framing is more effective amongst more financially deprived BoP consumers, the results may be reversed in other contexts (e.g., healthcare) or even when the target of the education is oneself and not the children. Further, this study was conducted on BoP consumers in Tropical Eastern India, and different perspectives on education may generate diverging results in other cultures or geographical regions of the tropics.

Conclusion

This research was conducted to ascertain the psychological mechanisms influencing preferences for varied education campaigns in order to improve our understanding of the factors contributing to high dropout rates in schools in Eastern Tropical India. Our findings highlighted that education which was easily accessible and linked to improved employment was viewed favourably by BoP consumers. Based on these findings, the authors recommend that relevant vocational training addressing the unique requirements of rural BoP communities would be an initial step in improving quality of education in the poorest regions of Tropical Eastern India. However, the implementation of such education would require an ecosystem of policymakers, educators, industry stakeholders, and representatives of the rural BoP collaborating in the design, delivery, impact, and measurement of socioeconomic improvement of such quality education. The authors are of the view that attainment of the UN Sustainable Goal of quality education would be dependent on making education relevant to communities living below the poverty line in emerging tropical countries.

Notes

1 EDHEC Business School, France, 24 Avenue Gustave Delory, CS50411, 59057 Roubaix Cedex 1- France.
2 Corresponding author: James Cook University, Singapore, 149 Sims Drive, Singapore Email: malobi.mukherjee@jcu.edu.au.
3 ESSEC Business School. Singapore, Essec Asia-Pacific Campus. 5 Nepal Park, Singapore.
4 According to Prahlad (2019), the global population of the Bottom of Pyramid or BoP (with daily earnings of \$1.90–\$3.20 as per the World Bank's classification in 2018) had reduced from 4 billion in 2007 to 3.5 billion in 2017.
5 India in Southern Asia lies mostly in the tropics (Jammu Kashmir and North East India being the only two exceptions) (Morgan, R.F. 2011). The study was undertaken in rural West Bengal on the outskirts of Calcutta, situated less than 100 km south of the Tropic of Cancer.

References

Banki, A., & Neogi, D. (2014). Poverty and earning compulsions for the family have pushed children out of schools: A study in dropouts in basic education level in North-East India. *International Journal of Social Economics, 42*(10), 946–958.

Becker, H. S. (1967). Whose side are we on? *Social Problems, 14*(3), 239–247.

Chakraborty, P. (2019). Educational status of the tribal West Bengal: Special reference to the Paschim Medinipur District. *Global Journal of Sociology and Anthropology, 9*(1), 1–14.

Chaudhri, D. P., & Jha, R. (2013). India's gender bias in child population, female education and growing prosperity: 1951–2011. *International Review of Applied Economics, 27*(1), 23–43.

Chikweche, T., & Fletcher, R. (2010). Understanding factors that influence purchases in subsistence markets. *Journal of Business Research, 63*(6), 643–650.

Daripa, S. K. (2017) A comparative study of the educational status of tribals in West Bengal: With special reference to the district of Purulia. *International Journal of Research in Social Sciences*, 7(10), 658–670.

Dembek, K., Sivasubramaniam, N., & Chmielewski, D. A. (2020). A systematic review of the bottom/base of the pyramid literature: Cumulative evidence and future directions. *Journal of Business Ethics, 165*(3), 365–382.

Dembek, K., York, J., & Singh, P. J. (2018). Creating value for multiple stakeholders: Sustainable business models at the Base of the Pyramid. *Journal of Cleaner Production, 196*, 1600–1612.

Diener, E., Suh, E. M., Lucas, R. E., & Smith, H. L. (1999). Subjective well-being: Three decades of progress. *Psychological Bulletin, 125*(2), 276.

Fujita, K., Eyal, T., Chaiken, S., Trope, Y., & Liberman, N. (2008). Influencing attitudes toward near and distant objects. *Journal of Experimental Social Psychology, 44*(3), 562–572.

Guha, N., & Das, P. (2014). Educational advancement of schedule tribes in West Bengal (1947–2011). *Vidyasagar University Journal of Economics, XVIII*, 2013–14. ISSN – 0975-8003.

Hart, S. L. (2007). *Capitalism at the crossroads: Aligning business, earth, and humanity* (2nd ed., pp. 18–23). Wharton School Publishing.

Hasan, R., Lowe, B., & Petrovici, D. (2020). Consumer adoption of pro-poor service innovations in subsistence marketplaces. *Journal of Business Research, 121*, 461–475.

Hasan, M. R., Lowe, B., & Rahman, M. (2017). Visual cues and innovation adoption among bottom of the pyramid consumers. *Qualitative Market Research: An International Journal, 20*(2), 147–157.

James Cook University. (2020). *State of the tropics 2020 report*. James Cook University. https://www.jcu.edu.au/state-of-the-tropics.

Johar, G., Meng, R., & Wilcox, K. (2015). Thinking about financial deprivation: Rumination and decision making among the poor. *ACR North American Advances, 43*, 209–210.

Kabeer, N., & Mahmud, S. (2009). Imagining the future: Children, education and intergenerational transmission of poverty in urban Bangladesh. *IDS Bulletin, 40*(1), 10–21.

Kolk, A., Rivera-Santos, M., & Rufin, C. (2014). Reviewing a decade of research on the 'base/bottom of the pyramid' (BOP) concept. *Business & Society, 53*, 338–377.

Liberman, N., & Trope, Y. (1998). The role of feasibility and desirability considerations in near and distant future decisions: A test of temporal construal theory. *Journal of Personality and Social Psychology, 75*(1), 5.

Maji, K., & Sarkar, S. (2017). Intra-district disparities in primary education: A case study of Bankura District, West Bengal. *Space and Culture, India, 4*(3), 77–92.

Morgan R. F. (2011) A new journal for the torrid zone. *Journal of Tropical Psychology, 1*(1), 1–1

Naveed, A., & Sutoris, P. (2020). *Poverty and education in South Asia. Handbook of education systems in South Asia* (pp. 1–23). Springer.

Nedungadi, P., Mulki, K., & Raman, R. (2018). Improving educational outcomes & reducing absenteeism at remote villages with mobile technology and WhatsAPP: Findings from rural India. *Education and Information Technologies, 23*(1), 113–127.

Pal, J., Lakshmanan, M., & Toyama, K. (2009). My child will be respected: Parental perspectives on computers and education in Rural India. *Information Systems Frontiers, 11*(2), 129–144.

Patra, S., & Panigrahi, N. (2018). Educational status of the marginalized: A study among the Santals of Paschim Medinipur District, West Bengal. *Journal of Social Sciences, 57*(1–3), 22–28.

Patra, S., Dutta, A. K., & Karnojora, U. D (2021). An analysis on the educational awareness of marginalized communities of Nayagram Block, Jhargram District, West Bengal. *NSOU-Open Journal, 4*(1), 36–44.

Prahalad, C. K. (2004). *The fortune at the bottom of the pyramid: Eradicating poverty through profits* (pp. 9–14). Wharton School Publishing.

Prahalad, C. K., & Hart, S. L. (2002). Strategy+ business. *The Fortune at the Bottom of the Pyramid, 26*, 2–14.

Prahlad, D. (2019) The new fortune at the bottom of the pyramid. *Consumer & Retail*, 2 January 2019/Spring 2019, Issue 94.

Prawitz, A., Garman, E. T., Sorhaindo, B., O'Neill, B., Kim, J., & Drentea, P. (2006). InCharge financial distress/financial well-being scale: Development, administration, and score interpretation. *Journal of Financial Counselling and Planning, 17*(1), 34–49

Ramasamy, M., & Pilz, M. (2020). Vocational training for rural populations: A demand-driven approach and its implications in India, *International Journal for Research in Vocational Education and Training (IJRVET)*. ISSN 2197-8646. https://www.econstor.eu/bitstream/10419/227468/1/1741926521.pdf

Ramesh, K. (2013). Levels of education of the marginalised people in India. *IJSSIR*, *2*(3), 168–176.

Rangan, V., Kasturi, M. C., & Petkoski, D. (2011). 'Segmenting the base of the pyramid'. *Harvard Business Review*, *89*(6). https://hbr.org/2011/06/the-globe-segmenting-the-base-ofthe-pyramid [Last accessed 28 June 2021].

Samanta, R., & Bajpai, R. (2015) Regional disparity in primary and upper primary level of education of Paschim Medinipur: A block level analysis. *International Journal of Science and Research (IJSR)*, *4*(5), 17–24.

Sharma, E., & Alter, A. L. (2012). Financial deprivation prompts consumers to seek scarce goods. *Journal of Consumer Research*, *39*(3), 545–560.

Sharma, E., Mazar, N., Alter, A. L., & Ariely, D. (2014). Financial deprivation selectively shifts moral standards and compromises moral decisions. *Organizational Behavior and Human Decision Processes*, *123*(2), 90–100.

Spiller, S. A., Fitzsimons, G. J., Lynch Jr, J. G., & McClelland, G. H. (2013). Spotlights, floodlights, and the magic number zero: Simple effects tests in moderated regression. *Journal of Marketing Research*, *50*(2), 277–288.

Sriprakash, A. (2016). Modernity and multiple childhoods: Interrogating the education of the rural poor in global India. *The 'Poor Child': The cultural politics of education, development and childhood* (pp. 151–167). Routledge.

Tiwari, P. (2020). Importance of skilling and re-skilling in rural India. *Times of India*, 8th September 2020. https://timesofindia.indiatimes.com/blogs/developing-contemporary-india/importance-of-skilling-and-re-skilling-in-rural-india/ [Last Accessed 28 June 2021].

Trope, Y., & Liberman, N. (2011). Construal level theory. *Handbook of Theories of Social Psychology*, *1*, 118–134.

UNDP. (2018). *UNDP Annual Report 2018*. UNDP. https://annualreport.undp.org/2018/#

UNESCO. (2019). *World Inequality Database on Education*. UNESCO. https://www.education-inequalities.org/ [Last Accessed 27 June 2021].

United Nations. (2019). *United Nationals Sustainable Development Goals Report*. United Nations. https://www.undp.org/content/undp/en/home/sustainable-developmentgoals.html#:~:text=The%20Sustainable%20Development%20Goals%20(SDGs,peace%20and%20prosperity%20by%202030) [Last Accessed June 26 2021].

Vallacher, R. R., & Wegner, D. M. (1989). Levels of personal agency: Individual variation in action identification. *Journal of Personality and Social Psychology*, *57*(4), 660.

Viswanathan, M., Rosa, J. A., & Harris, J. E. (2005). Decision making and coping of functionally illiterate consumers and some implications for marketing management. *Journal of Marketing*, *69*(1), 15–31.

Viswanathan, M., Umashankar, N., Sreekumar, A., & Goreczny, A. (2021). Marketplace Literacy as a Pathway to a Better World: Evidence from Field Experiments in Low-Access Subsistence Marketplaces. *Journal of Marketing*, *85*(3), 113–129.

Wakslak, C. J., Nussbaum, S., Liberman, N., & Trope, Y. (2008). Representations of the self in the near and distant future. *Journal of Personality and Social Psychology*, *95*(4), 757.

Other sources

https://msde.gov.in/en/schemes-initiatives/schemes-initiatives-through-nsdc [Last accessed 3 April 2021].

Confederation of Indian Industry (2020) India Skills Reports 2020: Reimagining India's talent landscape for a $5T economy. Available from https://www.skillreporter.com/2020/02/editorial/india-is-facing-acute-shortage-of-skilled-workforce/ [Last accessed 3 April 2021].

https://www.worldstopexports.com/rice-exports-country/ [Last accessed 4 April 2021].

5 Achieving the Sustainable Development Goals (SDGs)

A tropical region perspective

Pengji Wang[1], Huiping Zhang[2], and Jacob Wood[3]

Introduction

The Sustainable Development Goals (SDGs) are a universal call to action to end poverty, protect the planet, and improve the lives and prospects of people all around the world. The 17 Goals were adopted by all UN member states in 2015, as part of the '2030 Agenda for Sustainable Development', which sets out a 15-year plan to achieve the Goals (UN, n.d.). These goals cover the three dimensions of sustainable development: economic growth, social inclusion, and environmental protection.

The United Nations and its member states are currently engaged in extensive discussions about how best to support countries achieve their Sustainable Development Goals (SDG) by 2030. However, according to the latest progress report, unless the rate of progress increases, many countries will struggle to achieve their SDGs by 2030 (United Nations, 2018). A process that will be made all the more challenging, given the complex interlinkages that exist among the 17 SDGs (Fu, Wang, Zhang, Hou, and Li, 2019; Gao and Bryan, 2017).

Noting the complex interrelationships that exist across the SDGs, scholars have adopted a range of methodological approaches, including a nexus approach (Liu et al., 2018), network analysis (Moinuddin, 2017), as well as a series of analyses that examine the interactions, synergies, and trade-offs that exist among the goals (Nilsson, Griggs, and Visbeck, 2016). Such synergies, or positive interactions, exist when two or more of the goals enjoy symbiotic relationships with each other, while trade-offs, or negative interactions, exist when two or more of the goals ultimately work against or clash with each other (Pradhan, Costa, Rybski, Lucht, and Kropp, 2017). However, do these synergies or trade-offs always apply to certain goals for all countries? Nilsson, Griggs, and Visbeck (2016) posited that countries should interpret the SDGs according to their national circumstances and levels of development. Differences in geography, governance, and technology make it inappropriate to rely on generalized knowledge.

In this chapter, we focus on the tropical region. The tropics lie between the latitude lines of the Tropic of Cancer and the Tropic of Capricorn, including

DOI: 10.4324/9781003153580-5

the equator and parts of North America, South America, Africa, Asia, and Australia, and account for 36% of the Earth's landmass and is home to about a third of the world's people (National Geographic, n.d.). The majority of the world's most vulnerable communities are also in the tropics, and will be most affected by environmental threats (UN, 2017). To have a better understanding of challenges in meeting global development goals for the tropics, this chapter examines the tropical countries' efforts towards achieving the sustainable goals from 2000 to 2019, using the SDG database compiled by the United Nations. The big range of economic development levels that exists for countries in tropical regions also allows us to assess how and to what extent the SDGs interact in countries of different economic growth trajectories. This will in turn shed further light on what governments can do to shape better sustainable development policies.

An overview of the SDGs

The SDGs contain 17 goals, 169 targets, and 232 indicators. These 17 SDGs address the 'triple bottom line approach to human wellbeing' (Sachs, 2012, p. 2206), i.e., people's wellbeing, environmental sustainability, and economy sustainability. Among the 17 goals, four goals are related to economy, i.e., *SDG 8 Promote Sustained, Inclusive, and Sustainable Economic Growth*, *SDG 9 Build Resilient Infrastructure and Sustainable Industrialization*, and *SDG 17 Global Partnership*. They are concerned with sustainable economic development.

Seven goals relate to ***people***. Three of these goals set the target for people's basic standard of living and health, including *SDG 1 No Poverty*, *SDG 2 Zero Hunger*, and *SDG 3 Good Health and Well-being*. Another four, i.e., *SDG 4 Quality Education*, *SDG 5 Gender Equality*, *SDG 10 Reduce Inequality*, *SDG 16 Peace, Justice, and Strong Institutions*, are concerned with people's social well-being in terms of inclusiveness and equality. Other than these goals that are specifically dedicated to people, other SDGs address people at the target and indicator levels. For example, one indicator under *SDG 7 Affordable and Clean Energy*, states 'By 2030, ensure universal access to affordable, reliable and modern energy services', which establishes a target of access for basic electricity services.

Five goals are related to the ***planet***, i.e., *SDG 6 Clean Water and Sanitation*, *SDG 7 Affordable and Clean Energy*, *SDG 11 Sustainable Cities and Communities*, *SDG 12 Responsible Production and Consumption*, *SDG 13 Climate Action*, *SGD 14 Life below Water*, and *SGD 15 Life on Land*. These goals are concerned with the sustainable use and development of marine, forest, energy, and other resources of our planet.

Based on the above rationale, we have designated each SDG in Table A5.1 in the Appendix as primarily focusing on one of the systems: people, environment/planet, and economic growth. Such rearrangement allows us to analyze further the UN SDGs using the systems approach to sustainability.

Table 5.1 Economic growth from 2000 to 2019

	HI			*UMI*			*LMI*			*LI*		
	2000	2018/2019	Average growth rate	2000	2018/2019	Average growth rate	2000	2018/2019	Average growth rate	2000	2018/2019	Average growth rate
C080101: Annual growth rate of RGDP per capita (> =7% for least developed countries)			+1.40			+2.18			+2.95			+2.02
	2000	2018/2019	Change	2000	2018/2019	Change	2000	2018/2019	Change	2000	2018/2019	Change
C090201: Manufacturing value added as a proportion of GDP	8.42	6.39	**–24.0%**	15.94	13.55	–15.0%	12.34	11.57	–6.3%	8.84	9.01	**+1.9%**

Relationship between the SDGs

The holistic nature of the SDG framework implies that a large number of potential interactions across the 169 targets have to be considered by poli cymakers. Such interactions have been termed 'synergies' (where progress in one goal favours progress in another) or trade-offs (where progress in one goal hinders progress in another), and vice versa (Pradhan et al., 2017). In recent years, scholars have made efforts to figure out to what extent the SDGs synergize or have some form of trade-off with each other. A group of studies provided evidence that synergies among SDGs outweigh the trade-offs. For instance, in a systematic analysis of trade-offs and synergies among and within SDGs across all countries, Pradhan et al. (2017) find that synergies (indicated by positive correlations of at least 0.60 among indicators) among SDGs largely outweigh trade-offs (indicated by negative correlations of lower than –0.60) in many countries; however, negative and non-classified correlations are also observed in all SDGs. Based on a team of scientists' expert judgement on the level of interaction between four entry-level SDGs (2 Zero Hunger, 3 Good Health and Well-being, 7 Affordable and Clean Energy, and 14 Life Below Water) and all others, moreover, the Griggs et al. (2017) study identifies 238 positive and only 66 negative interactions. Zhao et al. (2021), using the examples of tourism and panda loans between the globally important Wolong Nature Reserve for panda conservation and the rest of the world, uncover a total of 17 synergies and two trade-offs. Specifically, SDGs 1 (no poverty), 2 (zero hunger), 9 (industry, innovation, and infrastructure), and 17 synergized with SDG 8 in Wolong, mainly through the development of the tourism industry which enhances the infrastructure and provides important employment opportunities. In summary, synergies exist mainly across SDGs related to people's wellbeing and economic growth. With regard to planet goals, the above SDGs have both synergy and trade-offs with SDG 15: synergy is demonstrated by favouring forest recovery projects (SDG indicator 15.2.1), while trade-offs exist because of human's intervention into local ecosystems (panda habitat).

On the other hand, studies also provide evidence of the trade-off between economic growth and sustainable resource use, through two groups of SDGs (Eisenmenger et al., 2020). For instance, it is found that FDIs (an indicator for economic growth SDG) in food production usually favours large-scale and export-oriented agricultural output that increases national economic growth but makes local communities more vulnerable to the loss of land and external price shocks with more destructive effects on livelihoods than small-scale improvements in access to land and water in local farming communities (De Schutter, 2011). Meanwhile, SDG 12 (responsible consumption and production) is associated with trade-offs, especially regarding economic progress (Pradhan et al., 2017). Lusseau and Mancini (2019) reported the trade-off between 'limiting climate change, reducing inequalities and responsible consumption' and poverty alleviation and reducing inequalities.

The complexity of the SDGs is further compounded when countries of different growth trajectories are categorized under one grouping. Though the SDGs are intended to be universal, in the sense of embodying a universally shared common global vision of progress, that achieves a safe, just, and sustainable space for all human beings to thrive on the planet, countries at different growth trajectories are facing different challenges in order to achieve more sustainable development. For example, developing countries might be currently undergoing the highly contradictive process of driving economic growth and while also ensuring sustainable resource use for industrialization processes. Duflo et al. (2008) found that in the short term, productivity increases in Kenya may be achieved most cost-effectively through the use of inorganic fertilizers, but this can adversely affect ecosystems and, in the long term, the sustainability of the agricultural sector and its productive capacity. This might not be a big concern for developed countries. Studies suggested that the ecological dimension of the SDGs is identified as the main area for development in industrialized countries (Biermann et al., 2017).

Accordingly, the objective of our study is to provide a review and assessment of tropical countries' SDG achievement and the interactions among the SDGs. By doing so, we highlight the area to improve, as well as the synergies and trade-offs for each group of tropical countries, which could shed light on the transformational action required to overcome past trends and deliver the largest benefits possible. In the next section, we will introduce the data. Following that we report the main findings.

Methodology

Country selection

This chapter focuses on tropical countries. A tropical country list was obtained from https://worldpopulationreview.com/country-rankings/tropical-countries. Such a list encompasses a wide range of countries at different economic development stages. As a result, we refer to the country classifications provided by the World Bank in which each tropical country is referred to as high income (HI), upper middle income (UMI), lower middle income (LMI), and low income (LI) country categories, and then examine their SGDs. In total, there are 19 HI countries, 27 UMI countries, 23 LMI countries, 25 LI countries, and 2 countries do not have a category based on the World Bank categorization scheme. A complete list of the countries with their categories is presented in Table A5.2 in the Appendix.

Sustainable Development Goals

The UN (2015) lists several possible indicators for each SDG. Most of the data for the indicators are from the World Bank Sustainable Development Goals and World Development Indicators databases, three are from the Millennium

Table 5.2 People SDG indicators from 2000 to 2019

	Desired change	*HI*			*UMI*			*LMI*			*LI*		
		2000	*2018/2019*	*Change*	*2000*	*2018/2019*	*Change*	*2000*	*2018/2019*	*Change*	*2000*	*2018/2019*	*Change*
Living condition													
C010101: Proportion of the population living below the international poverty line (0 poverty)	↓	3.49	0.30	**−91.4%**	9.82	3.03	−69.2%	34.16	21.97	−35.7%	66.01	42.16	−36.1%
C010401: Proportion of population with access to basic services	↑	92.51	96.40	+4.2%	79.52	88.52	+11.3%	52.33	64.82	+23.9%	36.11	45.61	**+26.3%**
C020203: Prevalence of anaemia in women aged 15 to 49 years (0 hunger)	↓	22.57	19.15	−15.2%	30.69	24.13	**−21.4%**	43.28	37.99	−12.2%	48.59	43.46	−10.5%
C030101: Maternal mortality ratio (<less than 70 per 100,000 live births)	↓	58.25	47.50	−18.5%	130.91	90.96	−30.5%	505.74	284.11	**−43.8%**	971.27	545.73	**−43.8%**
C030201: Under-5 mortality rate (<25 per 1,000 live births)	↓	16.64	11.68	−29.8%	31.84	19.16	−39.8%	86.74	43.39	−50.0%	125.44	61.55	**−50.9%**
c030202: Neonatal mortality rate (<12 per 1,000 live births)	↓	11.14	7.64	−31.4%	16.63	11.67	−29.8%	33.74	21.60	**−36.0%**	41.29	27.11	−34.3%
C030301: Number of new HIV infections per 1,000 uninfected population	↓	0.58	0.21	−64.2%	0.87	0.52	−40.4%	1.75	0.55	**−68.3%**	2.53	0.87	−65.6%
C030302: Tuberculosis incidence per 100,000 population	↓	18.68	12.66	−32.2%	84.32	75.93	−10.0%	311.22	209.42	**−32.7%**	242.00	182.95	−24.4%
C030303: Malaria incidence per 1,000 population	↓	24.74	0.89	**−96.4%**	74.27	28.29	−61.9%	169.15	84.84	−49.8%	330.25	212.99	−35.5%
C030b01: Proportion of the target population covered by all vaccines included in their national programme	↑	94.72	82.73	−12.7%	85.00	74.39	−12.5%	67.17	75.45	+12.3%	54.41	72.82	**+33.8%**
C070101: Proportion of population with access to electricity (all have access)	↑	95.57	99.62	+4.2%	84.93	95.51	+12.5%	46.05	74.37	+61.5%	20.23	40.36	**+99.6%**
Social wellbeing													
C040501: Education parity indices	Closer to 1	0.99	**1.05**	6.3%	0.83	0.93	12.2%	0.75	0.94	24.9%	0.54	1.12	**108.6%**
C050501: Proportion of seats held by women in (a) national parliaments and (b) local governments	↑	11.17	20.61	84.5%	12.45	24.82	99.4%	8.74	22.57	**158.1%**	8.95	21.09	135.6%

Development Goal Indicators, and one is from the Credit Suisse Global Wealth Report 2016. However, many data points are missing. Among the 17 goals, a few goals, such as the SDGs 10, 11, and 13 do not have sufficient observations for the indicators and hence we did not consider them in this chapter. In the end, we focus on 14 goals. In addition, some of the indicator time-series are not available for all time steps and countries. To cover a sufficient number of countries and time periods, under each goal, we only selected a few primary indicators with at least 1000 observations, given that the complete data points should be 1920. In the next section, we firstly review the SDG of the four groups of tropical countries and then examine to what extent the synergies and trade-offs exist among the different SDGs.

Results

An overview of the SGDs of tropical countries

We examine the achievement of the SGDs for the four groups of tropical countries in Tables 5.1, 5.2, and 5.3. In those tables, we report the average index of four groups of tropical countries in 2000 and 2019 and show the change in percentage terms.

SDGs related to economic growth

We focus on two key indicators for economic growth. The first indicator examines the annual growth rate of real GDP per capita (C080101), which is an indicator for sustainable economic growth. The UN sets the target for this indicator for the least developed countries as at least 7%. Table 5.1 shows the average economic growth rate for the tropical countries in four income groups has been around 1.4% to 2.95%. The economic growth rate for LI countries is still far from the target (7%). More measures have to be taken to boost LI countries' economic growth to achieve the target.

The second indicator examines the manufacturing value added as a proportion of GDP (C090201), which is an indicator of the industry's share of employment and gross domestic product and helps evaluate the industrialization process. Only LI countries show an increase for this indicator. The rising share of value-added in manufacturing in the industrialization stage represents a significant movement in employment levels from the agricultural to the industrial sectors. However, the target set for this indicator is to double the share of manufacturing value for the least developed countries by 2030. LI countries still have to work harder to achieve such a goal.

Interestingly, our data shows a declining trend for this indicator for HI, UMI, and LMI tropical countries; such a decline is particularly pronounced in HI and UMI countries. This may suggest that the occurrence of de-industrialization (Rowthorn and Ramaswamy, 1997), which is a phenomenon in which the share of manufacturing employment declines in an economy.

Table 5.3 Planet SDG indicators from 2000 to 2019

	Desired change	*HI*			*UMI*			*LMI*			*LI*		
		2000	*2018/2019*	*change*	*2000*	*2018/2019*	*change*	*2000*	*2018/2019*	*change*	*2000*	*2018/2019*	*change*
C060401: Change in water-use efficiency over time value added in USD / m3 of water withdrawn	↑	87.83	65.54	**–25.4%**	17.41	19.88	+14.2%	14.34	21.75	+51.7%	4.58	9.10	+98.7%
C060402: Level of water stress Water withdraw as a proportion of available freshwater resources	↓	16.38	36.90	+125.3%	3.97	11.36	+186.2%	7.38	13.09	+77.4%	6.73	8.86	+31.7%
C070102: Proportion of population with primary reliance on clean fuels and technology	↑	95.00	95.00	0.0%	68.73	82.05	19.4%	+18.84	28.89	53.4%	5.14	7.55	**+46.9%**
C070201: Renewable energy share in the total final energy consumption	↑	7.16	3.45	**–51.7%**	28.78	23.69	–17.7%	58.16	48.40	–16.8%	85.93	78.03	–9.2%
C200208: Installed renewable energy-generating capacity (in watts per capita)	↑	68.15	187.79	**+175.6%**	155.86	227.23	+45.8%	+29.83	62.75	+110.4%	11.72	15.76	+34.5%
C140101: marine pollution	↓	3.21	1.83	–42.9%	4.37	2.40	**–45.0%**	3.45	4.01	+16.4%	2.44	3.12	**+27.9%**

(*Continued*)

Table 5.3 (Continued)

	Desired change	*HI*			*UMI*			*LMI*			*LI*		
		2000	*2018/2019*	*change*	*2000*	*2018/2019*	*change*	*2000*	*2018/2019*	*change*	*2000*	*2018/2019*	*change*
C140501: Coverage of protected areas in relation to marine areas	↑	20.62	32.65	+58.4%	29.74	47.65	+60.2%	20.95	30.39	+45.0%	20.05	39.10	**+95.0%**
C150102: proportion of important sites for terrestrial and freshwater biodiversity that are covered by protected areas	↑	29.35	40.07	+36.5%	32.03	48.87	**+52.6%**	26.49	39.26	+48.2%	37.60	41.54	+10.5%
C150401: Coverage by protected areas of important sites for mountain biodiversity	↑	57.68	66.58	+15.4%	36.04	50.86	+41.1%	26.71	38.19	**+43.0%**	45.41	48.09	+5.9%
C200203: Domestic material consumption, domestic material consumption per capita, and domestic material consumption per GDP	↓	22.57	18.91	–16.2%	30.69	24.04	**–21.7%**	43.28	37.93	–12.4%	48.59	43.49	**–10.5%**
C070301: Energy intensity measured in terms of primary energy and GDP	↓	5.15	4.15	–19.3%	3.79	3.48	–8.4%	5.92	4.22	–28.8%	9.87	6.92	**–29.9%**

De-industrialization is a result of multiple factors, two of which are the rise of service industry (in our HI tropical countries, particularly those small island states) and the globalization of markets – more production activities are shifted to lower income countries (Rowthorn and Ramaswamy, 1997). For the industrialized countries (HI and UMI countries), de-industrialization is the natural outcome of successful economic development and is generally associated with rising living standards (Rowthorn and Ramaswamy, 1997). However, for LMI countries, it could mean that manufacturing jobs are lost, which could hurt people's living standards.

SDGs related to people

Table 5.2 shows the achievement of people-related SDGs from 2010 to 2019. The first group of indices show the living condition of tropical countries. All groups of tropical countries have improved along the years in all the indices. HI and UMI countries have achieved all or most of the targets set for *SDG1 No Poverty* (C010101 and C010401), *SDG 2 Zero Hunger* (C020203), and *SDG3 Healthy Lives* (C030101, C030201, C030202, C030301, and C030302), while LMI and LI countries are still far from the desired target.

Moving on to social wellbeing, with regard to *SDG 4 Quality Education* (C040501) all tropical countries demonstrate improvement, with HI countries receiving the best score. Regarding *SDG 5 Gender Equality* (C50501), all four groups of tropical countries have a similar proportion of women holding seats in government.

SDGs related to the planet

Table 5.3 shows the achievement of planet-related SDGs from 2010 to 2019. Goal 6 aims to substantially increase water-use efficiency across all sectors and ensure sustainable withdrawals and the supply of freshwater to address water scarcity and substantially reduce the number of people suffering from water scarcity by 2030. The first indicator is the level of water stress (C060402). HI tropical countries are facing higher level water stress as compared with those in other categories. This could be explained by the fact that most of the HI countries in the tropical regions are small island states (as shown in the Appendix), which have limited options when developing their freshwater resources and hence lack fresh water (IGRAC, n.d.). In fact, 71% of small island states face a risk of a water shortage, a figure that goes up to 91% in small island states with the lowest altitude (UNESCO, 2019). Some small island states are working in this area. For example, Singapore is internationally recognized as a model city for integrated water management and an emerging Global Hydrohub – a leading centre for business opportunities and expertise in water technologies (PUB, n.d.). In addition, UMI tropical countries experienced the highest increase in the level of water stress. This could be due to the fact that the UMI countries have experienced fast economic growth over the last 20 years; moreover, the development of industrial sectors, urbanization, improvements in the standard of living (entailing a change in dietary patterns) also boosts the water use (Duarte et al. 2013).

Another indicator examines water-use efficiency (WUE) (C060401), which is defined as the value added of a given major sector divided by the volume of water used by the sector. Such sectors include agriculture, forestry, fishing, mining, and quarrying; manufacturing; electricity, gas, steam and air conditioning supply, constructions; and all the service sectors. A closer look at the WUE suggests that tropical countries in the UMI, LMI, and LI groups are improving in terms of their WUE; the improvement is particularly prominent in LMI and LI tropical countries. This could be attributed to the fact that in these countries, technical, managerial, and institutional developments associated with economic growth result in an increase in water-use efficiency (Duarte et al. 2013). However, for HI tropical countries, the WUE was high in 2000 and 2001 (87.83 and 81.46), then declined substantially to 57.15 in 2003. This again could be attributed to the economic structure of many small island states. Studies have shown that the higher the proportion of high-consumption industry, the lower the water-use efficiency (Lopez-Gunn et al., 2012; Cao et al., 2018). The tourism industry, which is well known for its heavy water consumption (Pérez et al. 2020), represents more than 30% of small island states' total exports (UN, n.d.).

In terms of energy use, we find that all tropical countries have seen an increase in the proportion of clean fuels (C070102) and the amount of renewable energy-generating capacity being installed (C200208), with the most pronounced improvement being recorded in HI tropical countries. However, the share of renewable energy in the total energy consumption declines for all tropical countries; the decline is also most significant in HI tropical countries. Such results suggest that though renewable energy is being promoted worldwide, current economic models mainly rely on fuel energy, given its advantage in cost and availability.

In terms of protecting marine resource, all four groups of tropical countries have improved in conserving more coastal and marine areas (C140501), with LI countries experiencing the most significant improvement. However, when looking into the marine pollution (C140101), we find though HI and UMI tropical countries see a decline in such pollution, the level of marine pollution has increased in LI and LMI countries. Such findings seem to align with the conclusions drawn in previous academic works. For example, Barnes (2019) suggests that as income per capita increases in a country, environmental pollution such as mismanaged plastic waste per capita increases (as in LMI and LI countries). After some tipping point, mismanaged plastic waste per capita will decrease (as in HI and UMI countries) due to an increase in environmental improvement efforts, because growing economies have stronger financial means from which to development and implement new technological innovations that reduce pollution (Barnes, 2019).

The last two indices examine the use of input (resource and energy) as compared with output (GDP). Generally all tropical country groups are reducing their use of materials (C200203) and energy (C070301), indicating they place less pressure on the environment, which aligns with the SDGs of improving global resource efficiency in consumption and production and decoupling economic growth from environmental degradation. This might be attributed to the fact that economic growth and technology improvement provide a means for further reducing the amount of materials used in the production process (Lindmark, 2002).

Trade-off or synergies?

Analytical approach

Next, we put the selected indicators together and assess to what extent the three groups of SDGs synergize or are traded off with each other. Following Pradhan et al. (2017), we capture the synergies and trade-offs in a statistical sense; that is, as the existence of a significant positive and negative correlation, respectively. A significant positive correlation between a pair of SDG indicators is classified as a synergy while a significant negative correlation is classified as a trade-off.

The correlation analysis is carried out between unique pairs of a selected indicator time-series, considering country group data. For example, we analyze the correlation between available data on 'maternal mortality ratio' (indicator of SDG 3 Good health and wellbeing) and 'Real GDP per capita growth rate' (indicator of SDG 8 Sustainable economic growth) for each country. This is done in order to capture both synergies and trade-offs between different goals.

Given the nature of an indicator, an increase or a decrease of its value in time carries different meanings for attaining the SDGs. For example, SDG 3 needs to be achieved by declining the 'maternal mortality ratio' and by increasing the 'portion of births attended by skilled health personnel'. We assign a positive sign to indicators that are desirable to increase and a negative sign to those indicators that need a reduction to meet the SDGs. This avoids false results like a trade-off in case of decreasing maternal mortality and increasing income. A similar rationale would apply in cases of synergies.

The nonparametric Spearman's rank correlation (ρ) analysis is used to assess monotonic relationships between all possible combinations of the unique indicator data pairs for each country group. Spearman's correlation coefficient (ρ) provides a measure to evaluate the strength of an association between two variables (Spearman, 1904). Unlike Pearson's correlation analysis, Spearman's analysis is able to capture nonlinear correlation between the variables and is less sensible to outliers (Hauke and Kossowski, 2011). Spearman's analysis is widely used to identify a general relation beyond the linear correlation between two variables in various disciplines (e.g., Kellner and Hubbart, 2017; Pradhan et al., 2017; Sesnie et al., 2017).

The correlation with a ρ value of less than 0.05 is considered as statistically significant. For those correlation coefficients showing significance, we decide synergy or trade-off based on a Spearman's ρ. A Spearman's ρ value greater than 0.5 is considered to indicate a strong synergy (positive association) between the two indicators. A ρ between 0.3 and 0.5 indicates a moderate synergy, and a ρ greater than 0 and smaller than 0.3 indicates a weak or negligible synergy. Similarly, a ρ less than -0.5 is considered to indicate a strong trade-off (negative association). A ρ between –0.5 and –0.3 indicates a moderate trade-off, and a ρ smaller than 0 and greater than –0.3 indicates a weak or negligible trade-off. For those correlation coefficients not showing significance, we categorize the relationship between two targets as 'no relation'.

We then tally the results of the correlations between indicator pairs and then present them for each country cluster (similar economic development level). Interactions of SDG indicators across two goals are quantified by the percentage of synergies, trade-offs, and no relation of indicator pairs that fall into two distinct goals. We choose the percentage value to represent the interactions among the SDGs to avoid any bias that may arise from variation in the amount of available indicator data among the SDGs.

Table 5.4 shows the percentages of synergies and trade-offs that exist between the goals for four groups of tropical countries. The percentage is obtained based on the correlation matrix of four groups of tropical countries shown in Tables 5.5, 5.6, 5.7, and 5.8, respectively.

Economic growth vs. people

When looking into the correlation between economic indicators and indicators about people's wellbeing, we find synergies exist mostly for people's economic wellbeing, instead of social wellbeing. With regard to people's economic wellbeing, data shows more synergies exist for UMI, LMI, and LI countries than for HI countries. In UMI, LMI, and LI countries, strong synergies exist between the economic growth rate and the achievement of no poverty, zero hunger, and almost all healthy lives targets for UMI and LMI countries (as shown in Tables 5.6, 5.7, and 5.8). For LI countries, the economic growth rate shows strong synergies with the achievement of no poverty, zero hunger, and limited healthy lives targets (lower maternal mortality rate), but only have a weak or moderate synergy with the reduction of tropical diseases (Table 5.8). Such results suggest that the level of economic growth needs to be sustained for a longer time for LI countries to accumulate sufficient resources to substantially improve their hygiene conditions and public health service, as UMI and LMI have achieved.

In the HI country group in Table 5.5, when looking into the correlation between economic indicators and people indicators, we find that economic growth indicators have a moderately positive correlation, or no correlation with most of the indicators related to living standards. The industrialization indicator on one hand, has a strong negative correlation with economic growth; while on the other hand, it has a moderate and negative relationship with various health lives' goal indicators. Such results support previous

Table 5.4 Percentage of synergies and trade-offs between SDGs in four groups of tropical countries

		Strong synergy > 0.5	*Moderate synergy .3 – .5*	*Weak or negligible synergy 0 ~ 0.3*	*Strong trade-off < –0.5*	*Moderate trade-off –0.5 – –0.3*	*Weak or negligible trade-off –0.3~0*	*No correlation Not significant*
Economic growth and people (26 links for HI, UMI, LMI, and LI)	HI	3.8	19.2	19.2	7.7	3.8	11.5	34.6
	UMI	30.8	15.4	23.1	0.0	3.8	11.5	15.4
	LMI	23.1	26.9	34.6	0.0	0.0	0.0	15.4
	LI	15.4	7.7	19.2	0.0	3.8	19.2	34.6
Economic growth and planet (20 correlations for HI, 22 links for UMI, LMI, and LI)	HI	5.0	40.0	5.0	15.0	5.0	20.0	10.0
	UMI	0.0	18.2	22.7	0.0	4.5	31.8	22.7
	LMI	13.6	22.7	22.7	0.0	9.1	13.6	18.2
	LI	0.0	27.3	22.7	0.0	4.5	9.1	36.4
People and planet (130 correlations for HI, 140 links for UMI, LMI, and LI)	HI	7.7	10.0	10.0	11.5	12.3	13.1	35.4
	UMI	6.4	16.4	24.3	2.1	5.7	27.1	17.9
	LMI	10.7	15.7	32.1	2.1	4.3	13.6	21.4
	LI	1.4	15.0	23.6	0.7	9.3	19.3	30.7

Table 5.5 Correlation matrix of HI countries

		1	2	3	4	5	6	7	8	9	10	11	12	13	14	15
RGDP growth rate	C080101															
Industrialization	c090201	–0.600*														
Less poverty	c010101rev	**–0.615***	**0.660***													
Access to basic service	c010401	–0.040	0.481*													
Less anaemia in women	c020203rev	0.177*	–0.079													
Low maternal mortality	c030101rev	–0.118	0.150													
Low under-5 mortality	c030201rev	0.202*	–0.104													
Low neonatal mortality	c030202rev	0.302*	–0.214*													
Less HIV infections	c030301rev	0.281*	0.340*													
Less tuberculosis	c030302rev	0.163*	–0.431*													
Less malaria	c030303rev	0.099	**–0.621***													
More vaccination	c030b01	0.340*	–0.084													
Access to electricity	c070101	0.091	–0.197*													
Equal and quality education	c040501_1abs	–0.108	0.007													
Gender equity	c050501	–0.300*	0.314*													
Water-use efficiency	c060401	0.490*	–0.539*	**0.392***	–0.228*	0.281*	0.315*	0.473*	**0.506***	**0.744***	0.207*	–0.25	0.238*	0.274*	0.002	0.076
Lower water stress level	c060402rev	0.469*	–0.298*	**–0.624***	**–0.544***	–0.450*	**–0.584***	–0.262*	–0.239*	–0.099	–0.310*	**–0.730***	0.352*	**–0.562***	0.217*	0.133
Reply on clean fuels	c070102	.	.	.	.	.	.	.	.	.	.	.	.	.	.	.
Renewable energy share	c070201	–0.023	0.384*	**–0.887***	–0.108	–0.388*	–0.344*	–0.367*	–0.372*	**–0.720***	–0.179*	–0.340*	–0.090	–0.373*	0.303*	–0.143
Renewable energy capacity	c200208	–0.037	0.370*	**–0.718***	0.170*	–0.151*	–0.071	–0.049	–0.108	–0.237*	–0.230*	**–0.624***	–0.317*	–0.074	0.166*	–0.076
Less marine pollution	c140101rev	0.412*	**–0.571***	–0.211	–0.164*	–0.002	–0.148	0.396*	**0.539***	–0.392*	–0.010	**0.811***	0.152	0.099	–0.223*	0.091
Conserving marine areas	c140501	0.373*	–0.392*	**–0.831***	0.097	–0.469*	–0.457*	0.069	0.092	–0.472*	–0.197*	**–0.648***	0.106	–0.121*	–0.127	0.273*
Conserving terrestrial and inland ecosystem	c150102	0.242*	–0.175*	**–0.541***	0.094	–0.319*	–0.172*	0.016	–0.037	**0.541***	–0.272*	**–0.662***	0.141	–0.115	–0.169*	0.335*
Conserving mountain ecosystem	c150401	0.343*	–0.289*	0.253	**0.508***	–0.251*	0.158	0.245*	0.267*	**0.702***	–0.191	**–0.716***	0.263*	0.114	–0.048	**0.777***
Material consumption	c200203rev	**0.563***	**–0.680***	–0.103	0.120	0.492*	0.266*	0.401*	**0.561***	0.422*	0.373*	**0.709***	0.011	0.446*	0.064	–0.078
Energy intensity	c070301rev	0.356*	–0.244*	**–0.671***	–0.311*	–0.017	–0.344*	–0.020	0.148	–0.053	–0.217*	**0.696***	–0.048	–0.210*	0.157*	–0.086

Table 5.6 Correlation matrix of UMI countries

		1	*2*	*3*	*4*	*5*	*6*	*7*	*8*	*9*	*10*	*11*	*12*	*13*	*14*	*15*
RGDP growth rate	C080101															
Industrialization	c090201															
Less poverty	c010101rev	0.423★	0.159★													
Access to basic service	c010401	**0.622★**	0.016													
Less anaemia in women	c020203rev	**0.593★**	–0.236★													
Low maternal mortality	c030101rev	**0.684★**	0.219★													
Low under-5 mortality	c030201rev	**0.664★**	0.074													
Low neonatal mortality	c030202rev	**0.661★**	0.189★													
Less HIV infections	c030301rev	**0.592★**	0.245★													
Less tuberculosis	c030302rev	0.352★	–0.376★													
Less malaria	c030303rev	**0.621★**	0.314★													
More vaccination	c030b01	0.274★	0.001													
Access to electricity	c070101	**0.551★**	0.260★													
Equal and quality education	c040501_1abs	–0.163★	–0.040													
Gender equity	c050501	0.112★	–0.150★													
Water-use efficiency	c060401	**0.285★**	–0.115	0.360★	0.199★	0.180★	0.368★	0.278★	**0.300★**	0.142★	0.217★	0.140★	0.061	0.156★	–0.232★	–0.203★
Lower water stress level	c060402rev	–0.112	–0.181★	–0.058	–0.231★	–0.155★	–0.296★	–0.103	–0.066	–0.168★	–0.287★	–0.233★	–0.230★	–0.254★	0.230★	–0.028
Reply on clean fuels	c070102	0.479★	–0.257★	**0.506★**	**0.647★**	**0.507★**	**0.700★**	**0.689★**	**0.624★**	0.299★	0.505★	**0.437★**	**0.308★**	0.565★	**–0.306★**	0.259★
Renewable energy share	c070201	–0.181★	0.057	–0.468★	**–0.541★**	–0.235★	**–0.567★**	–0.392★	–0.282★	0.103	**–0.511★**	–0.236★	–0.295★	–0.440★	0.238★	–0.158★
Renewable energy capacity	c200208	**0.192★**	0.361★	0.1647★	–0.041	0.185★	0.095	0.214★	0.292★	0.355★	–0.240★	0.320★	–0.010	0.271★	0.133★	0.048
Less marine pollution	c140101rev	**0.168★**	**0.202★**	**0.525★**	0.305★	0.022	0.311★	0.281★	0.243★	0.079	0.130★	0.440★	0.139★	0.347★	–0.239★	0.025
Conserving marine areas	c140501	–0.255★	0.308★	–0.145★	–0.290★	–0.112★	–0.335★	–0.209★	–0.123★	–0.307★	–0.392★	–0.156★	–0.336★	–0.067	–0.090	0.229★
Conserving terrestrial and inland ecosystem	c150102	–0.234★	0.087	0.199★	–0.051	–0.279★	–0.110★	–0.086	–0.168★	–0.429★	–0.227★	–0.188★	–0.105★	–0.032	–0.268★	0.169★
Conserving mountain ecosystem	c150401	–0.167★	–0.225★	0.204★	0.107★	–0.195★	–0.079	–0.105★	–0.173★	**–0.497★**	–0.068	–0.138★	0.011	–0.097★	–0.081	–0.157★
Material consumption	c200203rev	0.374★	–0.340★	0.378★	0.305★	0.300★	0.398★	0.278★	0.201★	–0.039	0.4156★	0.241★	0.017	0.399★	–0.101	0.253★
Energy intensity	c070301rev	**0.247★**	–0.036	0.048	0.170★	0.379★	0.320★	0.240★	0.192★	0.349★	0.4739★	0.251★	–0.135★	0.304★	0.069	0.345★

Table 5.7 Correlation matrix of LMI countries

		1	*2*	*3*	*4*	*5*	*6*	*7*	*8*	*9*	*10*	*11*	*12*	*13*	*14*	*15*
RGDP growth rate	C080101															
Industrialization	c090201	0.165*														
Less poverty	c010101rev	0.472*	0.229*													
Access to basic service	c010401	**0.567***	0.441*													
Less anaemia in women	c020203rev	0.416*	0.084													
Low maternal mortality	c030101rev	**0.719***	0.271*													
Low under-5 mortality	c030201rev	**0.734***	0.370*													
Low neonatal mortality	c030202rev	**0.699***	0.390*													
Less HIV infections	c030301rev	0.225*	0.161*													
Less tuberculosis	c030302rev	0.380*	0.132*													
Less malaria	c030303rev	**0.547***	0.216*													
More vaccination	c030b01	0.200*	0.224*													
Access to electricity	c070101	**0.668***	0.368*													
Equal and quality education	c040501_1abs	−0.102	0.087													
Gender equity	c050501	0.170*	0.044													
Water-use efficiency	c060401	0.070	−0.322*	−0.111	−0.227*	−0.035	−0.133*	−0.232*	−0.123*	−0.224*	0.356*	−0.364*	−0.088	−0.115*	0.247*	−0.256*
Lower water stress level	c060402rev	−0.161*	−0.114*	−0.108	−0.123*	−0.024	0.007	−0.090	−0.004	0.154*	0.111	−0.176*	0.179*	−0.115*	0.018	−0.037
Reply on clean fuels	c070102	**0.629***	0.394*	**0.630***	**0.530***	0.446*	**0.535***	**0.575***	**0.532***	0.151*	0.333*	0.499*	0.159*	**0.579***	−0.045	0.372*
Renewable energy share	c070201	−0.378*	0.043	**−0.601***	−0.473*	−0.285*	−0.410*	−0.407*	−0.253*	**−0.604***	−0.178*	**−0.618***	−0.082	−0.439*	0.197*	−0.318*
Renewable energy capacity	c200208	**0.610***	0.437*	0.374*	**0.514***	**0.544***	**0.634***	**0.618***	**0.695***	−0.081	0.190*	0.364*	0.297*	**0.536***	0.059	0.107*
Less marine pollution	c140101rev	0.239*	0.130*	0.207*	0.315*	0.215*	0.323*	0.323*	0.338*	0.445*	0.143*	0.237*	0.178*	0.335*	−0.106	−0.112*
Conserving marine areas	c140501	**0.521***	0.126*	0.296*	0.229*	0.363*	0.438*	0.495*	**0.503***	−0.011	0.023	0.260*	0.216*	0.294*	−0.032	0.325*
Conserving terrestrial ecosystem	c150102	0.383*	0.255*	−0.183*	0.110*	0.174*	0.221*	0.300*	0.453*	0.009	0.046	0.054	0.174*	0.171*	0.167*	0.244*
Conserving mountain ecosystem	c150401	0.432*	0.161*	−0.048	0.253*	0.282*	0.373*	0.410*	**0.510***	−0.054	−0.008	0.165*	0.181*	0.292*	0.030	−0.022
Material consumption	c200203rev	0.326*	0.027	0.297*	0.350*	0.218*	0.182*	0.129*	0.162*	0.224*	0.178*	0.162*	−0.153*	0.383*	0.126	0.064
Energy intensity	c070301rev	0.030	−0.190*	**0.556***	0.211*	0.208*	0.185*	0.144*	0.066	**0.584***	0.188*	0.278*	−0.021	0.209*	−0.242*	0.355*

Table 5.8 Correlation matrix of LI countries

		1	*2*	*3*	*4*	*5*	*6*	*7*	*8*	*9*	*10*	*11*	*12*	*13*	*14*	*15*
RGDP growth rate	C080101															
Industrialization	c090201	−0.050														
Less poverty	c010101rev	0.252*	−0.196*													
Access to basic service	c010401	**0.522***	0.203*													
Less anaemia in women	c020203rev	0.040	−0.245*													
Low maternal mortality	c030101rev	**0.657***	0.150*													
Low under-5 mortality	c030201rev	**0.630***	−0.064													
Low neonatal mortality	c030202rev	0.470*	−0.040													
Less HIV infections	c030301rev	−0.161*	−0.334*													
Less tuberculosis	c030302rev	0.252*	0.010													
Less malaria	c030303rev	0.055	−0.208*													
More vaccination	c030b01	0.448*	0.034													
Access to electricity	c070101	**0.516***	−0.090													
Equal and quality education	c040501_1abs	−0 203*	0.063													
Gender equity	c050501	0.197*	−0.017													
Water-use efficiency	c060401	0.139*	0.192*	0.309*	0.162*	−0.085	0.046	0.168*	0.176*	−0.318*	0.154*	−0.234*	0.193*	0.093	−0.216*	0.208*
Lower water stress level	c060402rev	0.007	0.137*	0.083	0.070	−0.395*	−0.289*	−0.204*	−0.238*	−0.263*	−0.122*	−0.376*	−0.045	−0.175*	−0.123	−0.021
Reply on clean fuels	c070102	0.199*	−0.014	0.409*	0.067	0.207*	0.322*	0.397*	0.316*	0.407*	0.243*	0.381*	0.307*	0.451*	−0.169*	0.220*
Renewable energy share	c070201	−0.390*	−0.124*	−0.462*	−0.346*	0.352*	−0.295*	−0.367*	−0.320*	−0.136*	−0.329*	−0.126*	−0.299*	−0.476*	0.180*	0.220*
Renewable energy capacity	c200208	0.381*	0.191*	0.118*	0.105*	0.285*	0.483*	0.235*	0.232*	−0.242*	0.071	−0.245*	0.176*	0.274*	0.025	0.383*
Less marine pollution	c140101rev	0.121	−0.024	−0.083	0.021	0.283*	0.329*	0.051	0.221*	0.112	−0.180*	0.173*	−0.160*	−0.013	0.033	−0.080
Conserving marine areas	c140501	0.010	0.457*	−0.191*	0.391*	−0.363*	0.111	−0.029	−0.113	**−0.504***	−0.306*	−0.340*	−0.069	−0.212*	−0.106	0.037
Conserving terrestrial and inland ecosystem	c150102	−0.204*	0.354*	−0.081	0.109*	−0.168*	−0.175*	−0.073	−0.032	−0.428*	−0.075	−0.375*	0.037	−0.215*	0.051	−0.018
Conserving mountain ecosystem	c150401	−0.090	0.400*	−0.062	0.146*	−0.306*	0.061	−0.015	0.184*	−0.178*	0.188*	−0.411*	0.051	−0.025	0.047	−0.148*
Material consumption	c200203rev	0.372*	0.099	0.345*	0.222*	0.119*	0.486*	**0.568***	**0.576***	−0.006	0.242*	0.377*	0.360*	0.411*	−0.205*	0.088
Energy intensity	c070301rev	0.025	0.055	0.241*	0.356*	−0.198*	−0.065	0.110*	0.080	0.343*	0.294*	0.132*	0.110*	0.086	−0.120	−0.103

studies that show that for high-income countries in the tropics, de-industrialization seems to be correlated with successful economic development and is generally associated with rising living standards (Rowthorn and Ramaswamy, 1997).

On the other hand, we find little or no synergies for people's social wellbeing. The only moderate synergy is found for HI countries between industrialization and gender equity (measured by the proportion of women taking leadership roles in government). It is probably attributed to the fact that industrialization may be associated with a higher level of participation of women in the workforce and hence a greater representation of women in leadership roles. However, a moderate trade-off also exists between economic growth rate and gender equity (proportion of women taking leadership roles in government). Such a negative relationship is found in Altuzarra et al. (2021), though contrary to most of the literature (e.g. Bertay, Dordevic, and Server, 2020). In Altuzarra et al. (2021), they interpret that matters that are on the agendas of female parliamentarians in these countries may have an impact on women's wellbeing, but these developments are not yet reflected in economic growth.

Economic growth vs. the planet

With regard to the correlation between economic indicators and planet indicators, in all four groups of tropical countries, synergies outweigh trade-offs. HI and LMI countries have more synergies than those in UMI and LI groups. For example, in the HI country group, the economic growth rate shows a moderate to strong positive correlation with water-use efficiency, lower water stress level, less marine pollution, conserving the marine and mountain ecosystem, and less material and energy consumption. Such results further support the Environmental Kuznets Curve (EKC) (Mazzanti, Montini, and Zoboli, 2009; Stern, 2004), which suggests a decoupling between economic growth and environmental pressure when an economy grows to a certain stage, due to an increase in environmental improvement effort.

LMI countries also show high levels of synergy between economic growth and planet sustainability. Strong synergies exist between economic growth and use of clean fuels, installation of renewable energy capacity, conserving marine areas. Moderate synergies are found between economic growth and conserving the terrestrial and inland ecosystem, mountain ecosystem, and material consumption.

In contrast, for UMI counties, synergies seem to only exist between economic growth rates and the use of clean fuels and lower material consumption. Furthermore, industrialization shows a positive correlation with renewable energy capacity installation and conserving marine areas.

For LI countries, GDP growth seems to only synergize with less material consumption and more renewable energy capacity building. Industrialization has more synergies with conserving the marine ecosystem, the terrestrial and inland ecosystem, and the mountain ecosystem.

On another note, in HI countries, some strong trade-offs exist between economic growth and the planet. Trade-offs occur between industrialization and marine pollution, water-use efficiency, and material consumption. Such results provide a good reason for those HI countries to upgrade their economic growth model to balance the sustainable economic growth and environment sustainability. At the same time, de-industrialization, as evidenced by the negative relationship between GDP growth rate and industrialization, could be the effort made by these HI countries to upgrade their economic growth model (transiting from an economic model dominated by manufacturing industries to one dominated by service-based industries) and alleviate such trade-offs.

People vs. the planet

When referring to the people vs. the planet debate, the UMI and LMI countries have more synergies than HI and LI countries. HI countries experience more trade-offs than UMI, LMI, and LI countries, as shown in Table 5.4.

In UMI and LMI countries, most of the synergies exist between the use of clean fuels and the people's economic wellbeing indicators (no poverty, zero hunger, and healthy lives). However, such a positive correlation could be more attributed to that 'use of clean fuels', other than being a planet indicator, also indicates a better economic status of the country. Ultimately, it is the economic growth that leads to such a spurious correlation.

In HI countries, trade-offs mainly exist between people's economic wellbeing (no poverty) and conserving planet resources. Such a trade-off may be attributed to the fact that many high-income tropical countries are small island states. On the first note, they rely heavily on the tourism industry and focus primarily on fragile biotic systems like beaches, reefs, and other coastal resources; the fragile land and marine ecosystems make these small island states particularly vulnerable to biodiversity loss and climate change. At the same time, they are of a small economic size and have limited natural resources and domestic market, which makes them vulnerable to exogenous economic shocks and a lack of economic alternatives. Therefore, they face the tension of allocating national funds to improve people's economic wellbeing and environment problem (UN, n.d.). The ultimate solution is probably to maintain sustainable economic growth.

Conclusion

In this chapter, we review the tropical countries' sustainable development and assess the synergies and trade-offs of different SDGs, based on the SDG framework developed by the UN. An overview of countries' SDG achievements suggests that though all four groups of tropical countries have made an improvement in the three categories of SDGs, LMI and LI countries still have a long way to achieve the SDGs related to economic growth and people's economic wellbeing. HI and UMI countries are facing additional pressures around the sustainable use of water resources.

In terms of interactions between three categories of SDGs, overall, data from the most recent 20 years suggests that in tropical countries, synergies dominate trade-offs. Economic growth shows synergies with people's economic wellbeing, particularly in UMI, LMI, and LI countries, though little synergy was found with social wellbeing. Economic growth also does more good than harm to the environment in tropical countries. Such synergy is a result of more financial resources coupled with better technology brought by economic growth being committed to alleviating the pressure on environment. Industrialization, on the other hand, has a different impact on the environment for countries at different economic growth trajectories. With regard to the interaction between people-related and planet SDGs, special attention should be given to HI countries, most of which are small island states and experience a trade-off between people's economic wellbeing (no poverty) and conserving planet resources, due to their unique and particular vulnerabilities linked to their small size and lack of natural resources.

Notes

1 Corresponding author: JCU Singapore Business School, JCU Singapore, Singapore. Email: pengji.wang@jcu.edu.au.
2 JCU Singapore Business School, JCU Singapore, Singapore.
3 JCU Singapore Business School, JCU Singapore, Singapore, and Department of International Trade, Chungnam National University, Daejeon, South Korea.

References

Altuzarra, A., Gálvez-Gálvez, C., and González-Flores, A. (2021). Is gender inequality a barrier to economic growth? A panel data analysis of developing countries. *Sustainability, 13*(1), 367.

Barnes, S. J. (2019). Understanding plastics pollution: The role of economic development and technological research. *Environmental Pollution, 249*, 812–821.

Bertay, A. C., Dordevic, L., and Sever, C. (2020). *Gender inequality and economic growth: Evidence from industry-level data.* International Monetary Fund.

Biermann, F., Kanie, N., and Kim, R. E. (2017). Global governance by goal-setting: The novel approach of the UN Sustainable Development Goals. *Current Opinion in Environmental Sustainability, 26*, 26–31.

Cao, X., Ren, J., Wu, M., Guo, X., Wang, Z., & Wang, W. (2018). Effective use rate of generalized water resources assessment and to improve agricultural water use efficiency evaluation index system. *Ecological Indicators, 86*, 58–66.

De Schutter, O. (2011). How not to think of land-grabbing: Three critiques of large-scale investments in farmland. *The Journal of Peasant Studies, 38*(2), 249–279.

Duarte, C. M., Losada, I. J., Hendriks, I. E., Mazarrasa, I., and Marbà, N. (2013). The role of coastal plant communities for climate change mitigation and adaptation. *Nature Climate Change, 3*(11), 961–968.

Duflo, E., Kremer, M., and Robinson, J. (2008). How high are rates of return to fertilizer? Evidence from field experiments in Kenya. *American Economic Review, 98*(2), 482–88.

Eisenmenger, N., Pichler, M., Krenmayr, N., Noll, D., Plank, B., Schalmann, E., Wandl, M. T., and Gingrich, S. (2020). The Sustainable Development Goals prioritize economic growth over sustainable resource use: A critical reflection on the SDGs from a socio-ecological perspective. *Sustainability Science*, *15*, 1101–1110.

Fu, B., Wang, S., Zhang, J., Hou, Z., and Li, J. (2019). Unravelling the complexity in achieving the 17 sustainable-development goals. *National Science Review*, *6*(3), 386–388.

Gao, L., and Bryan, B. A. (2017). Finding pathways to national-scale land-sector sustainability. *Nature*, *544*(7649), 217–222.

Griggs, D. J., Nilsson, M., Stevance, A., and McCollum, D. (2017). *A guide to SDG interactions: From science to implementation*. International Council for Science.

Hauke, J., and Kossowski, T. (2011). Comparison of values of Pearson's and Spearman's correlation coefficients on the same sets of data. *Quaestiones Geographicae*, *30*(2), 87–93.

International Groundwater Resources Assessment Centre (IGRCA). (n.d.). Small Island Developing States (SIDS). https://www.un-igrac.org/areas-expertise/small-island-developing-states-sids

Kellner, E., and Hubbart, J. A. (2017). Improving understanding of mixed-land-use watershed suspended sediment regimes: Mechanistic progress through high-frequency sampling. *Science of the Total Environment*, *598*, 228–238.

Lindmark, M. (2002). An EKC-pattern in historical perspective: Carbon dioxide emissions, technology, fuel prices and growth in Sweden 1870–1997. *Ecological Economics*, *42*(1–2), 333–347.

Liu, J., Hull, V., Godfray, H. C. J., Tilman, D., Gleick, P., Hoff, H., and Li, S. (2018). Nexus approaches to global sustainable development. *Nature Sustainability*, *1*(9), 466–476.

Lopez-Gunn, E., Zorrilla, P., Prieto, F., & Llamas, M. R. (2012). Lost in translation? Water efficiency in Spanish agriculture. *Agricultural Water Management*, *108*, 83–95.

Lusseau, D., and Mancini, F. (2019). Income-based variation in Sustainable Development Goal interaction networks. *Nature Sustainability*, *2*(3), 242–247.

Mazzanti, M., Montini, A., and Zoboli, R. (2009). Municipal waste generation and the EKC hypothesis new evidence exploiting province-based panel data. *Applied Economics Letters*, *16*(7), 719–725.

Moinuddin, M. (Ed.). (2017). *Sustainable Development Goals interlinkages and network analysis: A practical tool for SDG integration and policy coherence*. Institute for Global Environmental Strategies.

National Geographic. (n.d.). https://www.nationalgeographic.org/encyclopedia/tropics/

Nilsson, M., Griggs, D., and Visbeck, M. (2016). Policy: Map the interactions between Sustainable Development Goals. *Nature*, *534*(7607), 320–322.

Pérez, D. M. G., Martín, J. M. M., Martínez, J. M. G., and Sáez-Fernández, F. J. (2020). An analysis of the cost of water supply linked to the tourism industry. An application to the case of the Island of Ibiza in Spain. *Water*, *12*(7), 2006.

Pradhan, P., Costa, L., Rybski, D., Lucht, W., and Kropp, J. P. (2017). A systematic study of Sustainable Development Goal (SDG) interactions. *Earth's Future*, *5*(11), 1169–1179.

PUB. (n.d.) Singapore water story. https://www.pub.gov.sg/watersupply/singaporewaterstory

Rowthorn, R. E., and Ramaswamy, R. (1997). Deindustrialization: Causes and implications. (April 1997). Available at SSRN: https://ssrn.com/abstract=882291 or http://dx.doi.org/10.2139/ssrn.882291

Sachs, J. D. (2012). From millennium development goals to sustainable development goals. *The Lancet, 379*(9832), 2206–2211.

Sesnie, S. E., Tellman, B., Wrathall, D., McSweeney, K., Nielsen, E., Benessaiah, K., ... and Rey, L. (2017). A spatio-temporal analysis of forest loss related to cocaine trafficking in Central America. *Environmental Research Letters, 12*(5), 054015.

Spearman, C. (1904). The proof and measurement of association between two things. *The American journal of psychology 15*(1), 72–101

Stern, D. I. (2004). The rise and fall of the environmental Kuznets curve. *World Development, 32*(8), 1419–1439.

UNESCO. (2019). Small islands: Meeting the challenges of freshwater resilience. https://en.unesco.org/news/small-islands-meeting-challenges-freshwater-resilience

United Nations (2018). *The Sustainable Development Goals report 2018.* United Nations.

United Nations. (n.d.a). About small island developing states. https://www.un.org/ohrlls/content/about-small-island-developing-states

United Nations. (n.d.b). UN marks day of the tropics with focus on region's vulnerability. https://www.un.org/sustainabledevelopment/blog/2017/06/un-marks-day-of-the-tropics-with-focus-on-regions-vulnerability/

Zhao, Z., Cai, M., Wang, F., Winkler, J. A., Connor, T., Chung, M. G., and Liu, J. (2021). Synergies and tradeoffs among Sustainable Development Goals across boundaries in a metacoupled world. *Science of the Total Environment, 751*, 141749.

Appendix

Table A5.1 SDGs and indicators covered in this chapter

	Goal	*Indicator*	*Measure*	*Goal*
Economy growth	**G8**	C080101	8.1.1 Annual growth rate of real GDP per capita	8.1 Sustain per capita economic growth in accordance with national circumstances and, in particular, at least **7%** gross domestic product growth per annum in the least developed countries
	G8	C080201	8.2.1 Annual growth rate of real GDP per employed person	8.1 Sustain per capita economic growth in accordance with national circumstances and, in particular, at least **7%** gross domestic product growth per annum in the least developed countries
	G9	C090201	9.2.1 Manufacturing value added as a proportion of GDP and per capita	9.2 Promote inclusive and sustainable industrialization and, by 2030, significantly raise industry's share of employment and gross domestic product, in line with national circumstances, and **double** its share in the least developed countries
People				
Living condition	Goal 1 No poverty	C010101 (rev)	1.1 Proportion of the population living below the international poverty line	1.1 By 2030, eradicate extreme poverty for all people everywhere, currently measured as people living on less than $1.25 a day
		C010401	1.4.1 Proportion of population living in households with access to basic services	1.4 By 2030, ensure that all men and women have equal rights to economic resources, as well as access to basic services
	Goal 2 Zero Hunger	C020203 (rev)	2.2.3 Prevalence of anaemia in women aged 15 to 49 years	2.2 By 2030, end all forms of malnutrition
	Goal 3. Healthy lives	C030101 (rev)	3.1.1 Maternal mortality ratio	3.1 By 2030, reduce the global maternal mortality ratio to less than 70 per 100,000 live births
		C030201 (rev)	3.2.1 Under-5 mortality rate	3.2 By 2030, reduce under-5 mortality to at least as low as 25 per 1,000 live births

(*Continued*)

Table A5.1 (Continued)

	Goal	*Indicator*	*Measure*	*Goal*
		C030202 (rev)	3.2.2 Neonatal mortality rate	3.2 By 2030, reduce neonatal mortality to at least as low as 12 per 1,000 live births
		C030301 (rev)	3.3.1 Number of new HIV infections per 1,000 uninfected population	3.3 By 2030, end the epidemics of AIDS
		C030302 (rev)	3.3.2 Tuberculosis incidence per 100,000 population	3.3 By 2030, end the epidemics of tuberculosis
		C030303 (rev)	3.3.3 Malaria incidence per 1,000 population	3.3 By 2030, end the epidemics of malaria
		C030b01	3.b.1 Proportion of the target population covered by all vaccines included in their national programme	3.b Provide access to medicines for all
		C070101	7.1.1 Proportion of population with access to electricity	**7.1 By 2030, ensure universal access to affordable, reliable and modern energy services**
Social wellbeing, inclusiveness, and equity	**Goal 4. Inclusive and equitable education**	C040501 (closer to 1) –1: smaller, the	4.5.1 Parity indices	4.5 By 2030, ensure equal access to all levels of education
	Goal 5. Gender equality	C050501	5.5.1 Proportion of seats held by women in (*a*) national parliaments and (*b*) local governments	5.5 Ensure women's equal opportunities for leadership at all levels of decision-making in political, economic, and public life
Planet				
Water resources	**Goal 6. Sustainable management of water and sanitation**	C060401	6.4.1 Change in water-use efficiency over time	6.4 By 2030, ensure sustainable withdrawals and supply of freshwater to address water scarcity
		C060402 (rev)	6.4.2 Level of water stress: freshwater withdrawal as a proportion of available freshwater resources	
		C060601	6.6.1 Change in the extent of water-related ecosystems over time	6.6 By 2020, protect and restore water-related ecosystems, including mountains, forests, wetlands, rivers, aquifers, and lakes

Energy	**Goal 7 Affordable and clean energy**	**C070102**	7.1.2 Proportion of population with primary reliance on clean fuels and technology	
		C070201	7.2.1 Renewable energy share in the total final energy consumption	7.2 By 2030, increase substantially the share of renewable energy in the global energy mix
		C200208	7.b.1 Installed renewable energy-generating capacity in developing countries (in watts per capita)	7.b By 2030, expand infrastructure and upgrade technology for supplying modern and sustainable energy services for all in developing countries, in particular least developed countries, small island developing States, and landlocked developing countries, in accordance with their respective programmes of support
Marine resource	**Goal 14**	C140101 (rev)	14.1.1 (*a*) Index of coastal eutrophication; and (*b*) plastic debris density	14.1 By 2025, prevent and significantly reduce marine pollution
		C140501	14.5.1 Coverage of protected areas in relation to marine areas	14.5 By 2020, conserve at least 10% of coastal and marine areas
Terrestrial and inland ecosystem	**Goal 15**	C150102	15.1.2 Proportion of important sites for terrestrial and freshwater biodiversity that are covered by protected areas, by ecosystem type	15.1 By 2020, ensure the conservation, restoration and sustainable use of terrestrial and inland freshwater ecosystems
		C150401	15.4.1 Coverage by protected areas of important sites for mountain biodiversity	15.4 By 2030, ensure the conservation of mountain ecosystems
		C150501 (rev)	15.5.1 Red List Index	15.5 Take urgent and significant action to reduce the degradation of natural habitats, halt the loss of biodiversity and, by 2020, protect and prevent the extinction of threatened species
Use of resources	**G7**	C070301——rev	7.3.1 Energy intensity measured in terms of primary energy and GDP	7.3 By 2030, double the global rate of improvement in energy efficiency
	G12	C200203 (rev)	12.2.2 Domestic material consumption, domestic material consumption per capita, and domestic material consumption per GDP	12.2 By 2030, achieve the sustainable management and efficient use of natural resources

Note: SDGs are re-categorized based on UN SDG database (https://unstats.un.org/sdgs/indicators/database/).

Table A5.2 Tropical country economy classification

Country	*Category*		
Saint Martin	HI	Small island developing States	
Anguilla	NA	Small island developing States	
Antigua and Barbuda	HI	Small island developing States	
Aruba	HI	Small island developing States	
Bahamas	HI	Small island developing States	
Barbados	HI	Small island developing States	
British Virgin Islands	HI	Small island developing States	
Cayman Islands	HI	Small island developing States	
French Guiana	HI		
Guadeloupe	HI	Small island developing States	
Martinique	HI	Small island developing States	
Mauritius	HI	Small island developing States	Southern Africa
Panama	HI		Latin America and the Caribbean: Mexico and Central America
Reunion	HI		
Saint Kitts and Nevis	HI	Small island developing States	
Seychelles	HI	Small island developing States	
Singapore	HI	Small island developing States	Asia
Trinidad and Tobago	HI	Small island developing States	Latin America and the Caribbean: Caribbean
Turks and Caicos Islands	HI	Small island developing States	
United States Virgin Islands	HI	Small island developing States	
Burkina Faso	LI	Heavily indebted poor countries	West Africa
Burundi	LI	Heavily indebted poor countries	East Africa
Central African Republic	LI	Heavily indebted poor countries	Central Africa
Chad	LI	Heavily indebted poor countries	Central Africa
DR Congo	LI	Heavily indebted poor countries	East Africa
Eritrea	LI	Heavily indebted poor countries	East Africa
Ethiopia	LI	Heavily indebted poor countries	East Africa
Gambia	LI	Heavily indebted poor countries	West Africa
Guinea	LI	Heavily indebted poor countries	West Africa
Guinea–Bissau	LI	Heavily indebted poor countries	Central Africa
Haiti	LI	Heavily indebted poor countries	Caribbean
Liberia	LI	Heavily indebted poor countries	West Africa
Madagascar	LI	Heavily indebted poor countries	East Africa
Malawi	LI	Heavily indebted poor countries	Southern Africa
Mali	LI	Heavily indebted poor countries	West Africa
Mozambique	LI	Heavily indebted poor countries	Southern Africa
Niger	LI	Heavily indebted poor countries	West Africa
Republic of the Congo	LI	Heavily indebted poor countries	Central Africa
Rwanda	LI	Heavily indebted poor countries	East Africa
Sierra Leone	LI	Heavily indebted poor countries	West Africa
Somalia	LI	Heavily indebted poor countries	East Africa
Sudan	LI	Heavily indebted poor countries	North Africa

(*Continued*)

Table A5.2 (Continued)

Country	*Category*		
Togo	LI	Heavily indebted poor countries	West Africa
Uganda	LI	Heavily indebted poor countries	East Africa
Vietnam	LMI		Asia
Angola	LMI		South Africa
Benin	LMI	Heavily indebted poor countries	West Africa
Bolivia	LMI	Heavily indebted poor countries	South Africa
Cambodia	LMI		East Asia
Cameroon	LMI	Heavily indebted poor countries	Central Africa
Comoros	LMI	Heavily indebted poor countries	East Africa
Djibouti	LMI		East Africa
El Salvador	LMI		Latin America and the Caribbean Mexico and Central America
Honduras	LMI	Heavily indebted poor countries	Latin America and the Caribbean Mexico and Central America
India	LMI		South Asia
Ivory Coast (Côte d'Ivoire)	LMI	Heavily indebted poor countries	West Africa
Kenya	LMI		East Africa
Laos	LMI	Landlocked developing countries	East Asia
Mauritania	LMI	Heavily indebted poor countries	North Africa
Myanmar	LMI		East Asia
Nicaragua	LMI	Heavily indebted poor countries	Latin America and the Caribbean Mexico and Central America
Nigeria	LMI		West Africa
Philippines	LMI		East Asia
Sao Tome and Principe	LMI	Heavily indebted poor countries	Central Africa
Senegal	LMI		West Africa
Tanzania	LMI		East Africa
Timor–Leste	LMI		East Asia
Zambia	LMI	Heavily indebted poor countries	Southern Africa
Montserrat	NA	Small island developing States	
Belize	UMI	Small island developing States	
Brazil	UMI		Latin America and the Caribbean South America
Brunei	UMI		East Asia
Colombia	UMI		Latin America and the Caribbean South America
Costa Rica	UMI		Latin America and the Caribbean Mexico and Central America
Cuba	UMI		Latin America and the Caribbean: Caribbean
Dominica	UMI	Small island developing States	
Dominican Republic	UMI	Small island developing States	Latin America and the Caribbean: Caribbean
Ecuador	UMI		Latin America and the Caribbean South America
Equatorial Guinea	UMI		Central Africa
Gabon	UMI		Central Africa
Grenada	UMI	Small island developing States	

(Continued)

Table A5.2 (Continued)

Country	*Category*		
Guatemala	UMI		Latin America and the Caribbean Mexico and Central America
Guyana	UMI	Heavily indebted poor countries	Latin America and the Caribbean: Caribbean
Indonesia	UMI		East Asia
Jamaica	UMI	Small island developing States	Latin America and the Caribbean: Caribbean
Malaysia	UMI		East Asia
Mayotte	UMI		
Mexico	UMI		Latin America and the Caribbean Mexico and Central America
Paraguay	UMI		Latin America and the Caribbean South America
Peru	UMI		Latin America and the Caribbean South America
Puerto Rico	UMI	Small island developing States	
Saint Lucia	UMI	Small island developing States	
Saint Vincent and the Grenadines	UMI	Small island developing States	
Suriname	UMI	Small island developing States	
Thailand	UMI		East Asia
Venezuela	UMI		Latin America and the Caribbean South America

Note: The categorization is based on World Bank country classification.

6 An assessment of trade facilitation impacts on China's outward foreign direct investment to ASEAN countries

Jie Wu[1], Jacob Wood[2], and Haejin Jang[3]

Introduction

As a global manufacturing powerhouse that engages in activities that occupy the middle of the value chain, China has done much to grow its global standing. In this regard, China's 'Going Global' strategy in the late 1990s (Fu et al., 2020), and arguably, the recent Belt and Road Initiative (BRI, hereafter) in 2013 have been key in driving new economic development opportunities through outward foreign direct investment (OFDI). They also represent China's changing ideological perception towards multinational corporations and policy environment for Chinese firms' transnational operations. As such, these developments have allowed China to cement itself as the hegemonic power in Asia, with its trade and investment activities playing a key role in driving the development of nations throughout the region and the wider global economy (Wu et al., 2021). The economic powerhouse is now a key assembling hub in many Asian supply chains and has been instrumental in making sure that exports manufactured in Asia remain cost-competitive globally. Furthermore, China's OFDI has had a significant positive impact on economic growth in these host countries as it has helped to fill in their local resource and technology gaps and in doing so overcome some of their major internal constraints to growth (Fu et al., 2020).

China's level of OFDI makes it an important global foreign investor, ranking second behind the US in 2018 (Ramasamy and Yeung, 2020). Since 2000, China's OFDI stock has increased from a mere USD 28 billion in 2000 to nearly USD 1.5 trillion in 2017 (Ramasamy and Yeung, 2020). Of this, two-thirds of Chinese OFDI stock went to Asia, with Hong Kong topping the list (MOFCOM, 2017). This growth meant that by the end of 2018, China was found to be actively investing in more than 43,000 overseas organizations across 188 countries (MOFCOM, 2018). Of the top ten countries that receive FDI from China, only Singapore is from the ASEAN region (see Table 6.1).

The vast majority, some 90%, of China's global foreign direct investment companies, are export companies. As such, the issue of trade facilitation is concerned particularly in being able to attract foreign investment. It is therefore important that countries remove unnecessary bureaucratic red tape which can

DOI: 10.4324/9781003153580-6

Table 6.1 Top ten countries/regions receiving China's OFDI as at 2016

Ranking	*Country*	*Stock (in 100 million USD)*	*Weight (%)*
1	Hong Kong	7807.45	57.5
2	Cayman Islands	1042.09	7.7
3	British Virgin Islands	887.66	6.5
4	USA	605.8	4.4
5	Singapore	334.46	2.5
6	Australia	333.51	2.5
7	Netherlands	205.88	1.5
8	UK	176.12	1.3
9	Russia	129.8	1
10	Canada	127.26	0.9

Source: MOFCOM, 2017.

lead to delays in the movement of goods across borders. Trade facilitation is the process by which the export and import process is simplified, modernized, and harmonized. In order to make these kind of changes possible, the World Trade Organization (WTO) set about a series of negotiations which concluded at the 2013 Bali Ministerial Conference on the landmark Trade Facilitation Agreement (TFA), which entered into force on 22 February 2017 (WTO, 2021). Important provisions within the TFA refer specifically to mechanisms from which the movement, release, and clearance of goods can be expedited. Moreover, it contains additional provisions for technical assistance and capacity building (WTO, 2021).

With China looking to further its OFDI objectives, the issue of trade facilitation and the need to simplify and expedite to movement of goods across borders is therefore very important. However, at present little has been done to measure the impact of trade facilitation on outward FDI. As such, this study looks to break new ground in two key ways. Firstly, using four key areas: (1) logistics and infrastructure environment; (2) customs environment; (3) regulatory environment; and (4) finance and e-commerce to measure the investment facilitation index of the ASEAN countries through the principal component analysis method. Secondly, using an extended gravity model, we then conduct an empirical study on the impact of trade facilitation on China's OFDI.

Literature review

This study focuses on two key areas of research. Firstly, the issue of OFDI, and the way in which China has used it as an increasingly important developmental tool. Secondly, the notion of trade facilitation and the important role it plays in today's increasingly interconnected global economy.

In the context of OFDI from China, much of the recent literature has focused on its key determinants (see Cui and Jiang, 2009; Wang et al., 2012; Lu et al., 2014; Hong et al., 2015; Shi et al., 2017; Gaur et al., 2018; Luo and Tung, 2018). These studies highlight a wide range of factors, although inflation rate, export, import, corruption, infrastructure, and geographic distance are the significant determinants of China's investment in Asia. Other studies have highlighted how these factors affect China's behaviour, in particular its entry mode and capability development (Driffield et al., 2014; Liu and Giroud, 2016; Buckley and Munjal, 2017). These studies also laid the foundation for future studies on the role that OFDI plays in upgrading the capabilities of China's MNEs (Li et al., 2016; Li et al., 2017), in particular the role of the state in this process (see Gaur et al., 2018; Deng et al., 2018). In addition to this, there has been a focus in recent times on China's overseas investments in developing marketplaces. In this regard, Fu et al. (2020) show that China's OFDI impact is greater than that of the US. In particular, they show that while both countries have a significant positive impact on capital accumulation in developing countries, Chinese OFDI has a stronger effect on employment and productivity growth than US OFDI. Moreover, the growth impact of Chinese OFDI is stronger in low-income countries, while US OFDI demonstrates significant effects mainly in middle-income countries (Fu et al., 2020). In other research, Shi and Hu (2019), also showed that the BRI was a key factor in promoting Chinese OFDI in developing ASEAN economies through increased senior leader visits and enhanced diplomatic relations. Despite these efforts, little has been done to specifically assess and measure the impact of trade facilitation on outward FDI.

The issue of trade facilitation has become an increasingly important issue in recent times. Apart from the WTO, trade facilitation is a subject of great importance for many international organizations including several United Nations (UN)-type bodies, the World Customs Organization (WCO), and those involved with supply chain security and international trade and logistics (Grainger, 2011). The topic of trade facilitation is very much focused on the operational aspects of international trade. More specifically, trade facilitation examines the quality of the trade environment and how it impacts on efficient trade operations. Despite such assertions, there is, however, no internationally recognized standard definition of trade facilitation, and the scope of its coverage tends to expand. According to the WTO's 'Trade Facilitation Agreement' on the obligations of members, trade facilitation should include at least the following aspects: publication and availability of information; opportunity to comment, information before entry into force, and consultations; advance rulings; procedures for appeal or review; other measures to enhance impartiality, non-discrimination and transparency; disciplines on fees and charges imposed on or in connection with importation and exportation and penalties; release and clearance of goods; border agency cooperation; formalities connected with importation, exportation and transit; freedom of transit; customs cooperation. As such, trade facilitation is the simplification and coordination of the behaviours, procedures, and practices involved in the process of international trade to ensure that all related behaviours occur in an effective, transparent, and predictable way.

Measuring trade facilitation

Construction of a trade facilitation index measurement system

Scholars generally follow the basic ideas of Wilson et al. (2003) in order to construct a national trade facilitation index, namely through the use of four indicators, which include: port efficiency, customs environment, institutional environment, and e-commerce. However, with developments in science and technology, the field of international trade has continuously improved, while the factors that influence trade facilitation have also changed greatly. By combining the latest provisions of the 'Trade Facilitation Agreement' and the characteristics of the economic development of ASEAN countries, this study defines the primary indicators as being port efficiency (P), customs environment (C), regulatory environment (R), and finance and e-commerce (F). However, we build on this basic structure by taking into consideration a further 21 secondary indicators, making the measurement of trade facilitation more scientific and relevant to today's trading environment. Of the primary indicators, regulatory environment (R), and finance and e-commerce (F) mainly reflect domestic obstacles in a country's international trade, while port efficiency (P) and customs environment (C) mainly reflect border barriers. These indicators comprehensively evaluate the level of trade facilitation of ASEAN[4] countries from different perspectives, see Table 6.2 for specific indicators.

There are 21 secondary indicators used in this study. These data are derived from the Global Competitiveness Report (GCR), the Global Information Technology Development Report (GITR), and Transparency International (TI), with the scores obtained being between 1 and 7 points, or 0 and 100 points. The scores are also positively correlated with the level of trade facilitation: the higher the score, the higher the level of facilitation.

Taking into account the difference in the value range of each secondary index, this study standardizes all secondary indicators to eliminate the influence of dimensions. The transformation method is used to divide the original value of each secondary indicator by the maximum value of the indicator in order to obtain the normalized value between 0 and 1.

Calculation of the trade facilitation level of ASEAN countries

To calculate the trade facilitation level of ASEAN countries, the first step is to determine the weight of each indicator. For the determination of the weight of each indicator in the trade facilitation indicator system, the current research literature uses generally one of three methods. First, the simple average method, which takes the average of each indicator score as the final score

Table 6.2 Index composition of trade facilitation measurement system

Primary indicator	*Secondary indicator*	*Score range*	*Data source*
Logistics and infrastructure environment (L)	Quality of highway infrastructure (L1)	1–7	GCR
	Quality of railway infrastructure (L2)	1–7	GCR
	Quality of port infrastructure (L3)	1–7	GCR
	Quality of aviation infrastructure (L4)	1–7	GCR
	Quality of communication and power infrastructure (L5)	1–7	GCR
Customs environment (C)	Irregular payments and bribes (C1)	1–7	GCR
	Burden of customs procedure (C2)	1–7	GCR
	Prevalence of non-tariff barriers (C3)	1–7	GCR
	Corruption Perceptions Index (C4)	0–100	TR
Regulatory environment (R)	Transparency of government policymaking (R1)	1–7	GCR
	Burden of government regulation (R2)	1–7	GCR
	Efficiency of legal framework in settling disputes (R3)	1–7	GCR
	Efficiency of legal framework in challenging regulations (R4)	1–7	GCR
	Judicial independence (R5)	1–7	GCR
	Favouritism in decisions of government officials (R6)	1-7	GCR
Finance and e-commerce (F)	Availability of financial services (F1)	1–7	GCR
	Affordability of financial services (F2)	1–7	GCR
	Government online service index (F3)	0–1	GITR
	E-Participation Index (F4)	0-1	GITR
	Availability of latest technologies (F5)	1–7	GCR
	Firm-level technology absorption (F6)	1–7	GCR

of trade facilitation level. Second, the assignment method. Some scholars draw on the conclusions made by Wilson et al. (2003), by using the weights of the first-level indicators to calculate the facilitation level of each country. Third, the principal component analysis (PCA) method, which reduces the number of complex factors down to a few independent principal components while retaining most of the information of the original data; that is, a few variables are used to explain the majority of variables. Compared with other methods, this method is more scientific and objective and does not rely on subjective judgement for empowerment. Therefore, it is widely used in the field of trade facilitation. In summary, this study uses the PCA method to calculate the weight of each indicator.

In order to verify the feasibility of the principal component extraction of the obtained data, the KMO test was first performed on the data. KMO statistics are used to compare the relationship between simple correlation coefficients and partial correlation coefficients between secondary indicator variables, with a value range of 0 to 1. The closer the statistic is to 1, the stronger the correlation between the variables and the more suitable for PCA. The test results are shown in Table 6.3. The results from this table show that as the overall KMO statistics reaches 0.9192, each secondary indicator is highly correlated with other indicators, indicating that the selected secondary indicator data is suitable for PCA. For the 21 secondary indicators, the PCA is performed using Stata 16.0 software. The results show that there are two principal components extracted with eigenvalues greater than 1, and the cumulative variance contribution rate is 85.69%. This means that the extracted principal components have a strong explanatory power for the original indicators. The coefficient of the secondary indicators of each principal component in the output result is shown in Table 6.4.

In this study, the coefficients of the secondary indicators of each principal component in the output result are multiplied by the variance contribution rate of the principal component, and then divided by the cumulative variance contribution rate of all the principal components extracted. Finally, the comprehensive evaluation model of trade facilitation is obtained by summation of each principal component.

$$\begin{aligned} \mathrm{Comp} = {} & 0.214\mathrm{L}_1 + 0.207\mathrm{L}_2 + 0.195\mathrm{L}_3 + 0.202\mathrm{L}_4 \\ & + 0.214\mathrm{L}_5 + 0.224\mathrm{C}_1 + 0.228\mathrm{C}_2 + 0.198\mathrm{C}_3 + 0.223\mathrm{C}_4 \\ & + 0.189\mathrm{R}_1 + 0.207\mathrm{R}_2 + 0.220\mathrm{R}_3 + 0.158\mathrm{R}_4 + 0.221\mathrm{R}_5 \\ & + 0.211\mathrm{R}_6 + 0.174\mathrm{F}_1 + 0.190\mathrm{F}_2 + 0.211\mathrm{F}_3 + 0.204\mathrm{F}_4 \\ & + 0.192\mathrm{F}_5 + 0.182\mathrm{F}_6 \end{aligned} \tag{1}$$

In order to fix the value range of the final score between 0 and 1, the coefficients are further normalized to obtain the weight of each secondary indicator.

Table 6.3 KMO test

Variable	*KMO*	*Variable*	*KMO*
L1	0.8951	R3	0.9572
L2	0.9181	R4	0.9174
L3	0.9122	R5	0.9293
L4	0.9249	R6	0.8897
L5	0.9098	F1	0.858
C1	0.9011	F2	0.912
C2	0.9299	F3	0.9265
C3	0.9401	F4	0.9309
C4	0.9504	F5	0.9309
R1	0.9415	F6	0.9033
R2	0.9299	Overall	0.9192

Table 6.4 The coefficient of the secondary indicators of each principal component

Variable	*Comp1*	*Comp2*
Quality of highway infrastructure (L1)	0.2284	0.0187
Quality of railway infrastructure (L2)	0.1988	0.3149
Quality of port infrastructure (L3)	0.221	-0.1643
Quality of aviation infrastructure (L4)	0.2297	-0.1786
Quality of communication and power infrastructure (L5)	0.2157	0.1881
Irregular payments and bribes (C1)	0.2186	0.2994
Burden of customs procedure (C2)	0.2404	0.0565
Prevalence of non-tariff barriers (C3)	0.2196	-0.0938
Corruption Perceptions Index (C4)	0.2222	0.2281
Transparency of government policymaking (R1)	0.1996	0.0401
Burden of government regulation (R2)	0.2198	0.0323
Efficiency of legal framework in settling disputes (R3)	0.2321	0.0578
Efficiency of legal framework in challenging regulations (R4)	0.1961	-0.3531
Judicial independence (R5)	0.2259	0.1523
Favouritism in decisions of government officials (R6)	0.2111	0.2128
Availability of financial services (F1)	0.2134	-0.3566
Affordability of financial services (F2)	0.2239	-0.2685
Government online service index (F3)	0.2181	0.1212
E-Participation Index (F4)	0.1988	0.2803
Availability of latest technologies (F5)	0.2233	-0.2325
Firm-level technology absorption (F6)	0.2198	-0.3268
Proportion	0.7931	0.0638

The weight of the first-level indicator is the sum of the weights of the secondary indicators contained in it. The normalized trade facilitation index (TFI) evaluation model of ASEAN countries is as follows:

$$\begin{aligned} TFI = {} & 0.050L_1 + 0.048L_2 + 0.046L_3 + 0.047L_4 + 0.050L_5 \\ & + 0.053C_1 + 0.053C_2 + 0.046C_3 + 0.052C_4 \\ & + 0.044R_1 + 0.049R_2 + 0.052R_3 + 0.037R_4 \\ & + 0.052R_5 + 0.050R_6 + 0.041F_1 + 0.045F_2 \\ & + 0.050F_3 + 0.048F_4 + 0.045F_5 + 0.043F_6 \end{aligned} \quad (2)$$

Formula (2) shows that the contribution weight of each first-level indicator is the L indicator (logistics and infrastructure environment) and has a weight of 0.242, the C indicator (customs environment) has a weight of 0.205, the R indicator (regulatory environment) has a weight of 0.283, while the F indicator (finance and e-commerce) has a weight of 0.271.

Analysis of the measurement results of trade facilitation in ASEAN countries

Putting the standardized data of each secondary indicator into equation (2), we are able to obtain the comprehensive index scores of ASEAN countries' trade facilitation from 2010 to 2017. The higher the score, the higher the level of trade facilitation in the country. Table 6.5 shows the average value of the first-level indicator trade facilitation scores and comprehensive score of each country from 2010 to 2017. This table shows that there are significant differences among ASEAN countries in terms of trade facilitation. Overall, Singapore, as a world-renowned open and free trading port, has significantly better performance in trade facilitation than other countries, ranking first in all indicators. According to the numerical value, the level of trade facilitation is divided into four intervals of 0.8~1, 0.7~0.8, 0.6~0.7, 0~0.6, which respectively represent extremely convenient, relatively convenient, generally convenient, and inconvenient. According to this classification criterion, Singapore is extremely convenient, Malaysia is relatively convenient, and Brunei is generally convenient, while Thailand, Indonesia, Laos, and Cambodia are all classified as being in the inconvenient zone. In this regard, these four developing economies all have significant room for improvement in the areas of logistics and infrastructure environment, customs environment, regulation environment, and finance and e-commerce.

Effects of ASEAN trade facilitation on China's OFDI

With continual development in the field of economics, scholars have sought to use theories of other disciplines in order to explain and study some economic phenomena. The gravity model is a theoretical hypothesis used by economists to analyze the flow of trade between countries by using the law of universal gravitation in classical physics. The first to make outstanding contributions to such applications were Tinbergen (1962) and Poyhonen (1963), who posed a similar view, that the trade flow between two economies is directly proportional to their respective economic scales and inversely proportional to their distances. Since then the model has been shown to have many practical economic applications, with scholars trying to add other variables to explore relevant trade influencing factors, such as tariffs, non-tariff measures, bilateral exchange rates, per capita income, and human capital intensity further expand the traditional gravity model. At present, the extended gravity model is widely used in the literature related to trade facilitation, and is not limited to the analysis of trade flows, but can also be used to analyze the impact of foreign direct investment scale. Since this study examines the impact of ASEAN's trade facilitation level on China's OFDI scale, the extended gravity model can be set as follows:

$$\begin{aligned} \ln OFDI_{ijt} &= \alpha_0 + \alpha_1 \ln Pop_{jt} + \alpha_2 \ln Dist_{ij} + \alpha_3 TWI_{jt} \\ &\quad + \alpha_4 \ln EXP_{ijt} + \alpha_5 MES_{jt} + \varphi Year_t + \varepsilon_{ijt} \end{aligned} \tag{3}$$

Table 6.5 Average trade facilitation index for ASEAN countries

Country	*Logistics and infrastructure environment*		*Customs environment*		*Regulatory environment*		*Finance and e-commerce*		*Comprehensive index*	
	L-TFI	*Rank*	*C-TFI*	*Rank*	*R-TFI*	*Rank*	*F-TFI*	*Rank*	*TFI*	*Rank*
Brunei	0.1306	3	0.1535	4	0.1595	3	0.1577	3	0.6013	3
Cambodia	0.0868	7	0.1198	6	0.1307	7	0.1138	7	0.4512	7
Indonesia	0.1025	5	0.1470	5	0.1585	4	0.1351	5	0.5432	5
Laos	0.0986	6	0.1184	7	0.1538	5	0.1220	6	0.4928	6
Malaysia	0.1313	2	0.1985	2	0.1883	2	0.1908	2	0.7090	2
Singapore	0.1811	1	0.2306	1	0.2301	1	0.2236	1	0.8654	1
Thailand	0.1065	4	0.1580	3	0.1476	6	0.1557	4	0.5678	4

Note: The Philippines, Myanmar, and Vietnam are not measured due to missing data. L-TFI, C-TFI, R-TFI, F-TFI, represents the score for logistics and infrastructure environment, customs environment, regulatory environment, finance and e-commerce, respectively. For comprehensive index-TFI = L-TFI + C-TFI + R-TFI + F-TFI.

where I represents China, j represents the ASEAN countries, t is years 2010–2017. $Year_t$ represents the year fixed effects, ε_{ijt} is the error term.

Dependent and independent variables

In this sub-section, we define and explain the dependent and independent variables used in our empirical analysis.

Dependent variable $\ln OFDI_{ijt}$

$\ln OFDI_{ijt}$ represents China's OFDI on ASEAN country j in year t. We obtained the data from the Annual Statistical Bulletin of China's Outward Foreign Direct Investment.

Figure 6.1 displays the trends of China's outward direct investment in seven ASEAN countries from 2010 to 2017. From the perspective of the major countries that the investments flowed to, Singapore ranked first, with an inflow of USD 6.32 billion in 2017, which was twice that of the same period last year. This accounts for 44.8% of the investment flow to ASEAN, with the majority of this invested in wholesale and retail, leasing, and business services. Malaysia is second, with 1.722 billion USD of investments, accounting for some 12.2% of the total investment volume in ASEAN. In this regard, the investment has focused primarily on the manufacturing, real estate, and construction sectors. Indonesia was ranked third with US$1.682 billion, or 11.9% of the China's OFDI in ASEAN. The key areas of investment include the manufacturing, construction, electricity/heating/gas and water production and supply sectors.

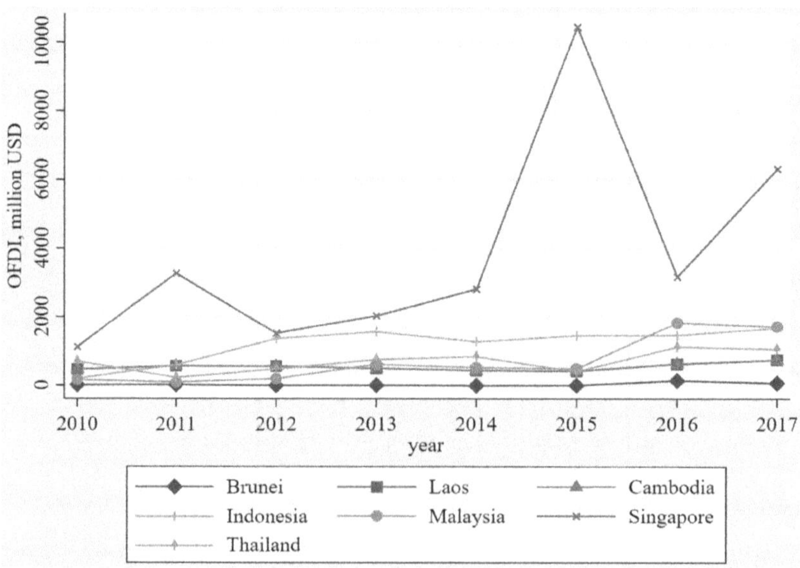

Figure 6.1 China's outward foreign direct investment on ASEAN countries

In 2017, despite the decline in overall investment, China's investment in the ten[5] ASEAN countries performed well, with a flow of USD 14.119 billion, a year-on-year increase of 37.4%, accounting for 8.9% of the total flow, and 12.8% of the investment flow to Asia. Overall, China's total investment in the ASEAN region is USD 89.014 billion, which accounts for 4.9% of Chinese total global OFDIs and 7.8% of its OFDIs throughout Asia as a whole. At the end of 2017, China had established more than 4,700 direct investment enterprises in ASEAN, employing 353,000 foreign employees. In 2017, China's investments in ASEAN mainly flowed to a range of sectors and countries (see Table 6.6).

Independent variables

TWI_{jt} is the main variables of concern in this study. In addition, we also selected $\ln Pop_{jt}$, $\ln Dist_{ij}$, $\ln EXP_{ijt}$ and MES_{jt} as the control variables.

Market size $\ln Pop_{it}$

Using data obtained from the Centre d'Études Prospectives et d'Informations Internationales (CEPII), $\ln Pop_{it}$ is used as a means of measuring the market size and investment demand of the target country, it is assumed that the larger the market size, the more positive the effect would be on OFDI.

Distance $\ln Dist_{ij}$

Using data obtained from the CEPII, $\ln Dist_{ij}$ refers to the distance of most populated cities between China and the ASEAN countries. It is assumed that

Table 6.6 Country and industry recipients of China's OFDI

Industry	*Main recipients of OFDI*	*Amount in millions (USD)*	*Percentage of total*
Manufacturing	Indonesia, Thailand Malaysia, and Vietnam	3,174	22.5
Wholesale and retailing	Singapore and Cambodia	2,449	17.3
Leasing and business service	Singapore	2,142	15.2
Construction	Indonesia, Singapore, Malaysia, Cambodia, and Vietnam	1,896	13.4
Transportation, warehousing, and postal	Laos, Singapore, Cambodia	758	5.4
Financial	Singapore, Malaysia, and Indonesia	739	5.2
Real estate	Malaysia and Thailand	711	5
Electricity/heating/gas	Indonesia, Myanmar, and Laos	633	4.5
Agriculture/forestry/husbandry/fishing	Laos and Singapore	623	4.4

the greater circle distance a target country is from China, the greater the negative effect would be on OFDI.

Trade facilitation level TWI_{jt}

This variable is the level of trade facilitation calculated above and reflects the degree of trade facilitation of ASEAN countries in terms of logistics and infrastructure environment, customs environment, regulation environment, finance, and e-commerce. According to the Melitz's (2003) firm heterogeneity theory, the profit of FDI enterprises is affected by production costs, labour productivity, and also by trade costs. Given the firm productivity, the trade-off between export and investment depends on the level of trade costs. For horizontal investment, firms investing overseas are often to avoid the trade barriers of the host country, and expand the market area to increase the market share. When the host country's trade facilitation level is improved to reduce the trade cost of firms, these investment firms will replace their investments through the production of exports due to the increase of export earnings. On the other hand, for vertical investment, the cost of importing intermediate products and raw materials from the home country in the production process will be reduced due to the influence of trade facilitation, thus increasing such investment. Therefore, the impact of trade facilitation level on OFDI will depend on the comprehensive impact of various parties.

Export $\ln EXP_{ijt}$

Using data obtained from the UN Comtrade, $\ln EXP_{ijt}$ refers to the export value of China to country *j* in year *t*. According to the literature, FDI and foreign trade are the two main ways that multinational firms can increase their overseas market shares and obtain overseas resources. Existing studies have found that they may be complementary or alternative to each other, or the relationship between the two may change due to the heterogeneity of the host country. Therefore, the effect of this variable on OFDI is uncertain.

Share of manufacturing exports MES_{jt}

Using data obtained from the UN Comtrade, $\boldsymbol{MES_{ijt}}$ refers to the share of manufacturing exports of country *j* in year *t*. This variable is added to take into account that China's investment in ASEAN is concentrated in the manufacturing industry, so the share of manufacturing exports may play a promoting role in attracting China's OFDI.

Data

This study analyzes the effect of trade facilitation in the ASEAN countries on China's OFDI. For the purpose of this study, all OFDI data were gathered from the Annual Statistical Bulletin of China's Outward Foreign Direct Investment, while the trade facilitation data were calculated using the PCA method. In regards to the other related variables, export, population, and distance were gathered from UN Comtrade and the CEPII. Table 6.7 details the basic statistics of the variables used in this analysis. Moreover, considering the potential multicollinearity problem that may exist between the explanatory variables, we first examine the correlations among right-hand side variables before conducting the formal analysis. As shown in Table 6.8, we were able to deduce that there is no high correlation between independent variables, so it can be considered that there is no multicollinearity problem in our analysis model.

Analysis of empirical results and discussion

The regression analysis results are shown in Table 6.8. Column (1) shows the comprehensive regression results of trade facilitation (TFI). Columns (2) to (5) are listed as the four first-level indicators of trade facilitation, namely, logistics and infrastructure environment (TFI_L), customs environment (TFI_C), regulation environment (TFI_R), finance and e-commerce (TFI_F). Table 6.9 shows that the signs of regression coefficients of explanatory variables are consistent with theoretical expectations, and the regression coefficients of all variables are statistically significant. First, the estimates on *Pop* are, as expected, positive and statistically significant on all equations. The distance (*Dist*) displays a statistically significant negative effect, confirming that distance is a significant impediment to OFDI. As for the findings for the trade facilitation variables (TFIs), both are

Table 6.7 Descriptive statistics for the variables included in the study

	Unit	*Count*	*Mean*	*SD*	*Min*	*Max*
OFDI	Million USD	55	1118.98	1660.31	0.99	10452.48
Pop	Million people	55	54.95	85.09	0.4	264.65
Dist	Kilometre	55	3913.25	789.42	2778.65	5220.88
TFI	Ratio	55	0.60	0.13	0.42	0.88
EXP	Million USD	55	22005.19	18307.47	367.61	51942.44
MES	Ratio	55	0.9	0.08	0.7	1

Table 6.8 Correlation analysis of independent variables

	Pop	*Dist*	*TFI*	*EXP*	*MES*
Pop	1				
Dist	0.304*	1			
TFI	–0.192	0.525***	1		
EXP	0.513***	0.640***	0.693***	1	
MES	–0.630***	0.15	0.391**	–0.0775	1

Note: * $p < 0.05$, ** $p < 0.01$, *** $p < 0.001$

Table 6.9 Analysis of results

	(1)	*(2)*	*(3)*	*(4)*	*(5)*
	TFI	*TFI_L*	*TFI_C*	*TFI_R*	*TFI_F*
Pop	2.524***	2.952***	1.350***	1.615***	1.719***
	(0.411)	(0.402)	(0.449)	(0.250)	(0.489)
Dist	−4.702***	−5.790***	−3.470***	−4.500***	−2.847***
	(0.941)	(0.900)	(1.044)	(0.946)	(0.968)
TFI	24.945***				
	(4.272)				
TFI_L		122.726***			
		(16.798)			
TFI_F			49.928***		
			(18.295)		
TFI_R				60.335***	
				(9.421)	
TFI_T					59.686***
					(18.019)
EXP	−2.045***	−2.021***	−0.951*	−0.822***	−1.274**
	(0.421)	(0.363)	(0.523)	(0.188)	(0.519)
MES	12.695***	13.268***	4.739**	12.052***	7.258**
	(2.756)	(2.384)	(2.312)	(2.272)	(3.031)
Year fixed effect	Yes	Yes	Yes	Yes	Yes
Constant	28.814***	36.207***	26.821***	24.423***	19.489***
	(6.070)	(6.055)	(7.668)	(5.956)	(7.008)
Observations	55	55	55	55	55
R^2	0.751	0.833	0.582	0.730	0.586

statistically significant with a positive sign; that is, China's OFDI to ASEAN countries will increase with the improvement of their trade facilitation level.

This section examines the economic magnitudes of TFI on OFDI (as shown in column (1)). With TFI reflecting the natural numbers that are used in the regressions (e.g., the mean of TFI is 0.60, as shown in Table 8.8), the coefficient of the TBTF is 24.945. Measuring TFI in percentage points (the TFI mean in the sample is 60 percentage points), the results for a coefficient change to 0.24945, implying that a one percentage point increase in TFI results is a 24.95% increase in OFDI flow. Secondly, from the perspective of the impact of various sub-indices of trade facilitation on OFDI, the improvement of logistics and infrastructure environment (TFI_L) has the greatest impact on OFDI, indicating that the logistics and infrastructure of the host country are important factors in attracting Chinese investment, which is followed by regulation environment (TFI_R), and finance and e-commerce (TFI_F). In terms of the environment and finance and e-commerce, the key factors involved include the transparency of the government's policy formulation, the improvement of financial service affordability, etc., and finally the improvement of the customs environment. That is, the transparency of government policymaking and the improvement of financial service affordability also have an important impact on attracting Chinese investment. In addition, the improvement of the customs environment has also brought considerable positive effects. The host country needs to build a healthier customs environment to attract investment. As for other control variables, the estimates on *EXP* are, as expected, negative and statistically significant on all equations, confirming the substitution relationship between China's exports to ASEAN and OFDI. The coefficients of the *RES* variable are also significant with the expected positive signs in all equations, which demonstrates that countries with a comparative advantage in manufacturing will attract more Chinese investment.

Conclusion

In recent decades, China has undertaken a series of policy initiatives, such as the BRI which have sought to not only grow its political influence and international reach but also provide a policy environment from which Chinese firms' transnational operations can flourish. As part of this and a desire to grow its global reach, the country has greatly increased its level of OFDI, which has had impacts on not only its own domestic economy but also the foreign recipient economies. However, in order to achieve its OFDI investments, the issue of trade facilitation has been very important. As such we sought to assess the impacts on the trade facilitation of China's OFDI in ASEAN economies. In order to measure this effect, we build on the trade facilitation index, developed by Wilson et al. (2003), by incorporating both the indicators of port efficiency (P), customs environment (C), regulatory environment (R), and finance and e-commerce (F), and also a further 21 secondary indicators. The results show that there are significant differences in the level of trade facilitation among different countries, with Singapore being more conducive to FDI from China. While other ASEAN economies receive significant investments from China, our study also showed that these developing economies can improve their levels of trade facilitation by being more transparent in their policymaking, enhancing financial service affordability, as well as providing a clearer, more robust customs environment. Change in these areas will help to attract new FDI from China and in doing so further develop the ASEAN region.

Notes

1 Corresponding author: Department of International Economics and Trade, College of Economics, Zhejiang University of Technology, China; and Adjunct Research Fellow, JCU Singapore Business School, JCU Singapore. Email: wujie91@zjut.edu.cn.
2 JCU Singapore Business School, JCU Singapore, Singapore, and Department of International Trade, Chungnam National University, Daejeon, South Korea.

3 JCU Singapore Business School, JCU Singapore, Singapore.
4 The ASEAN countries are: Brunei, Cambodia, Indonesia, Laos, Malaysia, Singapore, and Thailand.
5 These 10 ASEAN countries included in this calculation are: Brunei, Cambodia, Indonesia, Laos, Malaysia, Myanmar, the Philippines, Singapore, Thailand, and Vietnam.

References

Buckley, P. J., and Munjal, S. (2017). The role of local context in the cross-border acquisitions by emerging economy multinational enterprises. *British Journal of Management, 28*(3), 372–389.

China's Ministry of Commerce (MOFCOM). (2017). *Statistical Bulletin of China's Outward Foreign Direct Investment 2016.* Beijing: Ministry of Commerce.

Cui, L., and Jiang, F. (2009). FDI entry mode choice of Chinese firms: A strategic behavior perspective. *Journal of World Business, 44*, 434–444.

Deng, Z., Yan, J., and van Essen, M. (2018). Heterogeneity of political connections and outward foreign direct investment. *International Business Review, 27*(4), 893–903.

Driffield, N., Love, J. H., and Yang, Y. (2014). Technology sourcing and reverse productivity spillovers in the multinational enterprise: Global or regional phenomenon? *British Journal of Management, 25*(S1), S24–S41.

Fu, X., Buckley, P. J. and Fu, X. (2020). The growth impact of Chinese direct investment on host developing countries. *International Business Review, 29*(2), 101658, https://doi.org/10.1016/j.ibusrev.2019.101658

Gaur, A. S., Ma, X., and Ding, Z. (2018). Home country supportiveness/unfavorableness and outward foreign direct investment from China. *Journal of International Business Studies, 49*(3), 324–345.

Grainger, A. (2011). Trade facilitation: A conceptual review. *Journal of World Trade, 45*(1), 39–62.

Hong, J., Wang, C., and Kafouros, M. (2015). The role of the state in explaining the internationalization of emerging market enterprises. *British Journal of Management, 26*(1), 45–62.

Li, J., Strange, R., Ning, L., and Sutherland, D. (2016). Outward foreign direct investment and domestic innovation performance: Evidence from China. *International Business Review, 25*(5), 1010–1019.

Li, L., Liu, X., Yuan, D., and Yu, M. (2017). Does outward FDI generate higher productivity for emerging economy MNEs?: Micro-level evidence from Chinese manufacturing firms. *International Business Review, 26*(5), 839–854.

Liu, X., and Giroud, A. (2016). International knowledge flows in the context of emerging economy MNEs and increasing global mobility. *International Business Review, 25*(1), 125–129.

Lu, J., Liu, X., Wright, M., and Filatotchev, I. (2014). International experience and FDI location choices of Chinese firms: The moderating effects of home country government support and host country institutions. *Journal of International Business Studies, 45*(4), 428–449.

Luo, Y., and Tung, R. L. (2018). A general theory of springboard MNEs. *Journal of International Business Studies, 49*(2), 129–152.

Melitz, M. J. (2003). The impact on Trade on Intra-Industry Reallocations and Aggregate Industry Productivity. *Econometrica, 71*(6), 1695-1725.

MOFCOM. (2018). *Statistical Bulletin of China's Outward Direct Investment 2018*. Beijing: Ministry of Commerce.

Poyhonen, P. (1963). A tentative model for the volume of trade between countries. *Weltwirtschaftliches Archiv*, *90*(1), 93–99.

Ramasamy, B., and Yeung, M. (2020). China's outward foreign direct investment (OFDI) to developing countries: The case of Central and Eastern Europe (CEE). *Asia Pacific Economy*. https://doi.org/10.1080/13547860.2020.1790182. https://www.tandfonline.com/action/showCitFormats?doi=10.1080%2F13547860.2020.1790182&area=0000000000000001

Shi, J., and Hu, X. (2019). Does the belt and road initiative reshape China's outward foreign direct investment in ASEAN? Shifting motives of state-owned and private-owned enterprises. *Singapore Economic Review*, *66*(1), 161-183 https://doi.org/10.1142/S0217590819500772

Shi, W., Sun, S. L., Yan, D., and Zhu, Z. (2017). Institutional fragility and outward foreign direct investment from China. *Journal of International Business Studies*, *48*(4), 452–476.

Tinbergen, J. (1962). *Shaping the World Economy: Suggestions for an International Economic Policy*. New York: The Twentieth Century Fund.

Wang, C., Hong, J., Kafouros, M., and Boateng, A. (2012). What drives outward FDI of Chinese firms? Testing the explanatory power of three theoretical frameworks. *International Business Review*, *21*(3), 425–438.

Wilson, J. S., Mann, C. L., and Otsuki, T. (2003). *Trade Facilitation and Economic Development: New Approach to Quantifying the Impact*. Washington, DC: World Bank.

World Trade Organization (WTO). (2021). *Trade Facilitation*. Retrieved online 31 May 2021 from: https://www.wto.org/english/tratop_e/tradfa_e/tradfa_e.htm

Wu, J., Wood, J., and Huang, X. (2021). How does GVC reconstruction affect economic growth and employment? Analysis of USA–China decoupling. *Asian-Pacific Economic Literature, 35*(1), 67–81. https://doi.org/10.1111/apel.12319

7 The linkage between international financial integration and income inequality

New evidence on threshold effects

Sook-Rei Tan[1] *and Wai-Mun Chia*[2]

Introduction

Since the 1980s, the world has embarked on a wave of financial globalization, characterized by a surge in international capital flows and asset holdings. Advances in information technology and digital finance have broken the geographical boundaries for cross-border investments between nations, enabling more and more developing nations to join the bandwagon of financial liberalization by allowing foreign investments to pour into their countries. At first glance, financial globalization may seem like a straightforward solution to tropical underdevelopment, an economic puzzle where the majority of countries located in the tropics are falling behind in economic performance (Sachs, 2001). However, history has shown that financial globalization can be a double-edged sword, as untamed capital flows may invite macroeconomic instability and accentuate the host country's income inequality (Eichengreen et al., 2021).

Indeed, while countries receiving greater capital flows often also enjoyed higher economic growth, the fickleness of foreign inflows and lack of regulation in the financial opening process was blamed for exposing the recipient economies to the risk of Sudden Stop of capital inflows and led to a series of financial crises in emerging market economies during the late 20th century, including the notable Latin American debt crisis in the 1980s and Asian financial crisis in the 1990s (Prasad et al., 2005; Calvo, 1998). Such widespread financial turmoil undoubtedly caused a devastating blow to the emerging market economies, many of which are also situated in tropical areas.[3] Economic growth in the crisis-stricken countries was impeded, and poverty rose sharply as a result.[4] While the linkage between cross-border capital flows and income inequality is less clear ex ante, some empirical studies find evidence that capital account liberalization tends to increase income inequality. For instance, Furceri and Loungani (2018) discover that the impact of financial liberalization on inequality is more substantial when liberalization is followed by a financial crisis. The finding of Das and Mohapatra (2003) suggests the top quintile of the income distribution benefits from capital account openness at the expense of the middle class, while the lowest income share group is least affected in the event of liberalization.

DOI: 10.4324/9781003153580-7

Moreover, financial openness associated with different types of foreign investment flows are likely to exhibit different behaviours and have heterogeneous economic effects. According to the International Monetary Fund's capital flows classification, the types of capital flows can be broadly categorized as direct investment, portfolio investment, and other investment flows. Foreign direct investment (FDI) involves an investment by a foreign investor with an ownership of more than 10% of a local business. Portfolio investment refers to investments made in securities and other financial assets such as shares and bonds. Other investment, sometimes also known as credit flows in the capital flow literature, is mainly related to bank deposits and lending transactions. Due to their different characteristics, these capital flow components differ vastly in their dynamic patterns and impact on the domestic financial and economic systems. Ample evidence in the existing literature indicates that FDI is usually a source of stable long-term capital flows conducive to the country's development and able to reduce extreme poverty through facilitating economic growth and creating jobs in the host countries. In contrast, portfolio and other flows are shorter-term capital flows that are very sensitive to external financial conditions and thus are deemed more volatile and likely to be the main contributor to the Sudden Stop phenomenon (see Sula & Willett, 2009; Ahlquist, 2006). Therefore, it is imperative to consider the composition within the capital flows when analyzing the economic impact of international financial integration.

Clearly, financial globalization comes with both benefits and costs that may be shared unevenly among different income groups within an economy, which has implications for a nation's income inequality. This adds an essential aspect to the debate of whether the tropical economies should adopt a more conservative stance when embracing financial openness as one of the drivers of economic growth. Understanding the income inequality effects of capital flows may help policymakers in these economies design policy measures that allow growth gains from financial liberalization to be more equally distributed among different segments of society and achieve greater social welfare. However, much of the existing research focuses on the impact of financial openness on economic growth (for instances, see Sahoo & Sethi, 2020; Selvarajan & Ab-Rahim, 2020; Yakubu et al., 2020; Estrada et al., 2015; Kim et al., 2012; Bekaert et al., 2011), whereas the studies on the nexus between international financial integration and income inequality remain relatively thin. Among this strand of literature, Lim and McNelis (2016) build a small open economy heterogeneous agent model and conduct simulation exercises which show both trade and financial openness improve income growth and equality once an economy crosses a critical threshold in capital intensity and the use of imported intermediate goods in the production process. This implies that the relationship between economic globalization and income inequality is nonlinear. Erauskin and Turnovsky (2019) employ a stochastic growth model to study the impact of international financial integration on income inequality based on the premise that financial liberalization will reduce costs of investing and borrowing abroad while these activities favour the wealthy and thus tend to increase inequality.

The simulations suggest that financial liberalization during the period 1970–2015 contributed significantly to the increase in income inequality experienced over that period. In terms of empirical evidence, Jaumotte et al. (2013) find that financial globalization (particularly FDI) tends to exacerbate inequality as opposed to the equalizing effect of trade openness. Asteriou et al. (2014) find similar results in that financial globalization through FDI, capital account openness, and stock market capitalization has been driving up inequality in the EU-27 countries over the period 1995–2009. Heimberger (2020) conducted a meta-analysis based on 123 existing studies and concluded that while the effect of trade globalization is small, financial globalization shows a more substantial inequality-increasing impact. In terms of evidence of nonlinear FDI-inequality nexus, Lin et al. (2015) use a smooth transition regression model on a panel of developing and advanced countries from 1976 to 2005. They find that FDI increases income inequality, and the effect becomes more assertive with greater financial sophistication. Jung ad Kim (2021) find that financial market integration and financial depth interact to influence income inequality, in which financial openness worsens income inequality in the countries with underdeveloped financial markets, but the effect is statistically insignificant in the countries with developed financial markets.

Building on the above extant literature, our study aims to reexamine the relationship of a country's degree of international financial integration (IFI) – a proxy for financial openness – with the country's income inequality in the context of tropical economics. In particular, we attempt to contribute to the empirical research on the income distributional effect of financial openness in three respects. First, we explore whether there exists a threshold level of financial openness in the IFI-inequality linkage, i.e., whether the impact of IFI on income inequality varies across different regimes contingent on the country's magnitude of IFI. This is motivated by the pioneering theoretical model on the finance-inequality nexus as developed by Greenwood and Jovanovic (1990), which hypothesizes an inverted U-shaped relationship between income inequality and financial development. According to this hypothesis, financial factors tend to worsen income inequality during the early stage of economic development since only the rich can afford to access the financial market and make gains from financial investments. As the economy develops, stable income distribution across people is attainable under a maturely developed financial structure, allowing less endowed people to participate in financial markets. While the theoretical framework mainly focuses on domestic financial factors, we assume such hump-shaped behaviour may also be present for the international financial market due to the same rationale. This hypothesis also has important implications for the tropical economies, given that most tropical economies are still in the early phase of financial openness relative to their developed counterparts. If this hypothesis is true, the nations may experience rising income inequality when they first integrate into global financial markets, but such a situation may only be transitory.

Second, we employ dynamic panel threshold regression (PTR) as developed by Kremer et al. (2013), which has not been used before in exploring the nonlinear relationship between IFI and income inequality. One of the main appeals of PTR methodology, compared to the ad hoc methods of sample-splitting or linear interaction specification, is that it provides an endogenous estimation of threshold levels. Furthermore, dynamic PTR is a combination of the original static PTR model (Hansen, 1999) with the instrumental variable estimation of the cross-sectional threshold model (Caner & Hansen, 2004). This method allows for the inclusion of instrumented initial values for income inequality as one of our control variables, hence enabling us to capture the dynamic adjustment and persistence of income inequality without running into endogeneity issues.

Third, de facto IFI indicators constructed from different types of capital flows (including FDI vs. non-FDI inflows) are employed in our analysis to capture differences between FDI and non-FDI investments. It is argued that de jure indicators, i.e., capital account restrictions, do not adequately represent the amount of external financing received in developing countries due to the poor enforcement of capital control policies for examples, see Edison et al., 2004; Prasad et al., 2005; Edwards, 2007). Our study analyzes how financial openness influences income inequality; what matters most is the actual integration level between the country's economy and the international capital market. As such, de facto instead of de jure financial openness is what we should consider.

We find evidence of a nonlinear relationship between IFI and income inequality, in which IFI indicators significantly increase inequality in the low financial openness regime, but the impact diminishes in the high financial openness regime. The qualitative outcome of the nonlinear IFI-inequality nexus holds for several robustness checks. Our results also corroborate heterogeneity across various types of capital flows, as different IFI indicators yield different results for the estimated regime-dependent parameter values. Out of four IFI indicators, FDI inflows seem to be associated with a more significant increase in income inequality at the early phase of liberalization, but such correlation becomes insignificant when the ratio of FDI over GDP reaches a certain threshold. These findings provide insights into the financial liberalization process and its accompanying inequality effect on the tropics. Since most of the tropical economies within our sample have passed the FDI openness threshold, this implies that while FDI inflows have a more substantial worsening effect on income distribution than the non-FDI inflows, such an effect only prevails at the early stage of financial integration and will not persist as the country further opens to receiving more FDI investments.

This chapter is organized as follows. The second part gives a brief context of the distinct economic characteristics of the tropics. The third part presents the data and empirical methodology. The fourth part discusses the empirical findings. The fifth part concludes.

Tropical economies

In the field of development economics, many economists have observed a geographical pattern of wealth and poverty. Influential work by Gallup et al. (1999) that set foot in this field uncovered the empirical fact that tropical and landlocked areas are systematically more impoverished and less developed than the other regions. In fact, according to the United Nation's country classifications from the World Economic Situation and Prospects (WESP) report published in 2020 (United Nations, 2020), out of 52 high-income economies (by per capita GNI in June 2019), only 8 are tropical;[5] and none of the 33 developed economies is from the tropical area.

No doubt, the determinants of tropical poverty are incredibly complex, and even within the economic profession, a consensus has yet to be reached. Some of the leading hypotheses aiming to explain tropical poverty include historical reasons (such as colonization) and tropical disease prevalence (Gallup et al., 1999), institutional factors (Easterly & Levine, 2003), agricultural productivity (Gallup & Sachs, 2000), as well as environment and latitude which determine the frequency of natural catastrophe and climatic condition of the regions (Hsiang & Jina, 2014; Hsiang & Meng, 2015).

Compared to the literature on tropical underdevelopment, few studies have examined the tropical income inequality issue. A seminal study by Engerman and Sokoloff (1994) proposed the famous factor endowment hypothesis to explain the association between tropical ecology and income inequality. Under this hypothesis, the production of tropical crops such as tobacco and sugar had significant economies of scale as compared to the production of non-tropical crops such as wheat and barley, hence giving rise to wealth concentration in the hands of a few elites, who had incentives to monopolize human capital resources to entrench their political power. Gavin and Hausmann (1998) adopt this explanation for their empirical finding of Latin America, where countries located near the equator and with large natural resource endowments tend to encounter slower growth and higher income inequality than less resource-intensive economies located in non-tropical climates. Easterly's (2007) empirical exercise further corroborates this hypothesis. Using cross-country data, he confirms that agricultural endowments can predict inequality, and inequality in turn predicts development.

We have briefly discussed the economic traits of the tropics, but what is meant by the tropical region? As noted by Gallup et al. (1999), the tropics can be defined on the basis of geography or ecology. The geographical tropics refer to regions of the Earth that lie between the latitude lines of the Tropic of Cancer (23.5° N) and the Tropic of Capricorn (23.5° S). However, there lacks a fundamental explanation of why physical geography can have economic implications since countries located in the same latitude can be affected by very different climates depending on factors other than latitude.[6] Instead, most of the theories outlined above suggest that the more meaningful definition of the tropics in an economic sense should be based on ecological or climatic attributes which will influence the country's economic activities, especially those heavily reliant on nature. Therefore, we will follow country classification by Hsiang and Meng (2015), who identify tropical countries based on the country's susceptibility to El Niño-Southern Oscillation (ENSO) climate.[7] Specifically, tropical countries are defined as countries whose local temperatures are strongly related to ENSO, whereas temperate countries are those with local temperatures weakly linked to ENSO.

Data and empirical methodology

Data

The data employed in this study comprises a balanced panel of observations from 43 countries covering the 1980–2014 period. To reduce the possible effects of short-term fluctuations and measurement errors, the data are averaged over five-year intervals resulting in seven distinct periods per country (1980–1984, 1985–1989, 1990–1994, 1995–1999, 2000–2004, 2005–2009, and 2010–2014). The selection of countries is restricted by the availability of data on inequality and balance of payment statistics. Following Hsiang and Meng's (2015) country assignment, our sample consists of 20 tropical and 23 temperate countries (see Table A7.2 in the Appendix).

The dependent variable is (log of) Gini coefficient, a standard measure for within-country income inequality. Specifically, we collect Gini indices from the Standardized World Income Inequality Database (SWIID) created by Solt (2009), which provides comparable data of market-income- and disposable-income-based Gini coefficients across an extensive set of countries. Market income Gini coefficient measures inequality of gross income so that this indicator proxies inequality exclusive of fiscal policy effect. On the other hand, the net income Gini coefficient is calculated based on the after-tax income inclusive of taxation and transfer payment effects and may complicate our purpose of studying the IFI-inequality linkage. Hence, we use market income Gini coefficient (*gini_mkt*) as our preferred income distributional measure and dependent variable in our primary analysis, whereas disposable income Gini coefficient (*gini_disp*) is included in the section of robustness check. Figure A7.1(a) and A7.1(b) in the Appendix plot the world map of Gini coefficients by country based on the average values of market income Gini coefficient and disposable income Gini coefficient during the period 2010–2014, respectively. As can be seen from the figure, the top three countries with the highest *gini_mkt* are concentrated in the southern area of Africa, including South Africa (72.3), Namibia (69.8), and Botswana (63.7), all of which belong to the tropical zone. Meanwhile, several temperate countries also have the value of *gini_mkt* greater than 50. For instance, the *gini_mkt* of the United States is 51.9. However, if we consider the disposable income Gini coefficient, due to a more progressive tax system adopted in many developed and temperate nations, the net income in these countries actually results in lower Gini coefficient values in the temperate zone. For example, the *gini_disp* of the United States is 37.3, much lower than its *gini_mkt*. This is further substantiated by the mean and median of the Gini coefficients between tropical and temperate economies as presented in Table 7.1, in which the tropical-temperate difference is more apparent for *gini_disp*.

To indicate the country's degree of financial openness, we construct four de facto international financial integration (IFI) measures used as regime-dependent and threshold variables in the PTR regressions. Following Kose et al. (2011) and Chen and Quang (2014), total flows of capital are measured by summing the absolute inflows (external liabilities) and outflows (external assets) of capital, divided by the country's nominal GDP. As the extant capital flows studies have pointed out, the financial stability of emerging market economies is prone to the Sudden Stop phenomenon mainly caused by foreign inflows, particularly non-FDI inflows, which are more speculative and erratic. Therefore, we also construct IFI indicators based on only the inward component of capital flows and IFI indicators that distinguish between FDI and non-FDI (defined as the sum of portfolio and other investments) inflows. As shown in Table 7.1, generally, temperate countries have higher financial openness than tropical countries, especially in terms of non-FDI inflows. This is unsurprising given that the temperate economies are usually more developed economies with deeper markets for trading in financial securities that can efficiently facilitate cross-border portfolio flows. In terms of direct investment, developed nations are also more likely to be net capital investors than investees when the local enterprises seek a blue ocean market or lower labour costs in less developed markets.

To strengthen our empirical results, control variables are selected similar to previous studies on the linkage between financial openness and income

Table 7.1 Mean, standard deviation, and quantiles of Gini coefficients and IFI indicators for tropical and temperate economies

Variable	*n*	*Mean*	*S.D.*	*Min*	*0.25*	*Mdn*	*0.75*	*Max*
gini_mkt	140	47.49	7.24	35.66	41.94	46.44	52.08	68.22
gini_disp	140	45.14	5.68	31.7	41.08	45.27	49.02	58.5
Inflows	140	9.71	13	0.08	3.75	6.18	9.58	85.18
FDI inflows	140	2.91	3.68	0	0.55	1.57	3.51	21.19
Non-FDI inflows	140	6.8	11.08	0.08	2.2	3.83	6.9	81.56
Total flows	140	15.39	26.95	0.08	4.89	7.87	11.43	172.76
Temperate economies								
Variable	n	Mean	S.D.	Min	0.25	Mdn	0.75	Max
gini_mkt	161	45.7	7.24	30.12	42.78	46.76	49.46	59.96
gini_disp	161	32.12	5.68	20.66	26.62	31.46	34.9	51
Inflows	161	10.65	13	0.7	4.76	7.5	12.76	73
FDI inflows	161	2.85	3.68	0	0.77	1.79	3.44	40.41
Non-FDI inflows	161	7.8	11.08	0.48	3.37	5.58	9.22	45.19
Total flows	161	19.91	26.95	1.5	7.32	13.16	25.89	144.53

inequality. First, growth of GDP per capita is included to capture the income effect on distribution. Following Kuznets (1955), inequality is expected to follow a hump-shaped curve with economic growth over levels of income. Second, (a log of) average years of secondary level schooling compiled by Barro and Lee (2013)[8] is used as a proxy for the impact of human capital on income inequality. Third, (a log of) age dependency ratio controls for the income distributional effect of demographic change through population age distribution. Age dependency ratio is defined as the young and old population as a fraction of the working population. Fourth, the initial Gini coefficient (given by the first annual observation within each five-year interval) enters the dynamic model specification to capture the persistence in income inequality. The persistence of high and, in many economies, rising income inequality over the recent period is a growing concern for policymakers and economists worldwide (Clements et al., 2015; Dabla-Norris et al., 2015). Income inequality is persistent in the long run since low-income families are unable to catch up with the rest of the population due to various reasons such as an imperfect financial market (Mookherjee & Ray, 2003) or the choice of high fertility rate over child educational investment rate (Moav, 2005).

Moreover, we tested the sensitivity of our results by including the (log of) level of trade share, given by the sum of exports and imports as a percentage of nominal GDP, to capture the impact of trade openness on income inequality. Finally, inflation measured by percentage changes in the GDP deflator is also included as a robustness test.

Table 7.2 summarizes the descriptive statistics of all the variables used in this paper. Table A7.3 provides the definitions and sources of data.

Table 7.2 Summary of statistics

Variable	*Mean*	*Std. Dev.*	*Min*	*Max*
gini mkt	3.8303	0.1404	3.4052	4.2227
gini disp	3.6115	0.2519	3.0282	4.0690
IFI variables	10.2153	11.2905	0.0783	85.1808
Inflows				
FDI inflows	2.8771	4.1191	0.0000	40.4090
Non-FDI inflows	7.3382	9.0803	0.0783	81.5577
Total flows	17.8092	23.5334	0.0783	172.7622
Control variables	3.8266	0.1421	3.4078	4.2268
Initial gini mkt				
Initial gini disp	3.6090	0.2552	3.0301	4.0673
Growth	1.9652	2.7382	-20.9885	10.8843
Secondary education	0.7837	0.7039	-1.9661	1.9228
Age dependency ratio	4.0572	0.2301	3.5865	4.6017
Trade openness	4.0347	0.5668	2.5936	6.0157
Inflation	0.2967	1.4425	-0.0135	16.7741

Panel threshold regression

To study the potential nonlinear relationship between IFI and income inequality, we adopt a panel threshold regression which allows for endogenous identification of threshold levels. First proposed by Hansen (1999) in a static setup, the panel threshold regression model for a two-regime case in our study can be represented by the following equation:

$$\begin{aligned} INEQ_{it} &= \mu_i + \beta_1 IFI_{it} I\left(IFI_{it} \leq \lambda\right) + \alpha_1 I\left(IFI_{it} \leq \lambda\right) \\ &\quad + \beta_2 IFI_{it} I\left(IFI_{it} > \lambda\right) + \gamma' Z_{it} + \epsilon_{it} \end{aligned} \tag{1}$$

where *INEQ* is an income inequality indicator, *IFI* is the international financial integration indicator used to split the sample into low or high openness regime, $I(\cdot)$ is the indicator function equals 0 when *IFI* is less than or equal to the threshold parameter λ and 1 otherwise. Z_{it} contains the control variables in which the slope coefficients are constrained to be regime-independent. β_1 is slope terms of IFI under low openness regime. α_1 captures differences in the regime intercept following Bick (2010). β_2 is the slope coefficient of IFI under high openness regime, γ indicates slope coefficients for control variables, μ_i is the country-specific fixed effect. The error term ϵ_{it} is assumed *i.i.d.* of mean 0 and variance σ^2.

Given the dynamic nature of most macroeconomic indicators, we employ dynamic panel threshold regression approach of Kremer et al. (2013), which is an extension based on Hansen's static panel threshold regression model and Caner and Hansen's (2004) cross-sectional threshold regression, where generalized methods of moments (GMM) type estimators are used to deal with possible endogeneity induced by initial values of income inequality as one of the controls. Under such a dynamic setting, Z_{it} in Equation 1 is partitioned into a subset $Z_{1,it}$ of exogenous variables uncorrelated with ϵ_{it}, and a subset of endogenous variables $Z_{2,it}$ (initial Gini coefficient in our case) that is correlated with ϵ_{it}.

Prior to the estimation procedure, one must first eliminate the fixed effects, μ_i, through variable transformation. As suggested by Kremer et al., the endogenous regressor (initial Gini index) in the dynamic model will be correlated with the transformed errors resulted from the within transformation or first differencing methods and thus lead to inconsistent estimates. As such, the forward orthogonal deviations transformation proposed by Arellano and Bover (1995) is used to eliminate individual effects. This method subtracts the average of all available future observations from the contemporaneous one, hence avoiding a serial correlation of the transformed disturbance terms. The error term after the forward orthogonal deviation transformation is as shown below:

$$\epsilon_{it}^{\star} = \sqrt{\frac{T-t}{T-t+1}}\left[\epsilon_{it} - \frac{1}{T-t}\left(\epsilon_{i,t+1} + \ldots + \epsilon_{iT}\right)\right] \tag{2}$$

And the uncorrelatedness of the error terms remains:

$$Var(\epsilon_i) = \sigma^2 I_T \Delta Var(\epsilon_i^\star) = \sigma^2 I_{T-1}$$

Thus, we can proceed to apply the estimation procedure developed by Caner and Hansen to Equation 1.

The estimation of threshold indicator, following Caner and Hansen, consists of three steps. First, a reduced form regression of the endogenous variables, $Z_{2,it}$, is conducted on the set of instruments, X_{it}, together with exogenous variables, $Z_{1,it}$, to obtain the fitted values, $\hat{Z}_{2,it}$. After replacing $Z_{2,it}$ by their predicted values $\hat{Z}_{2,it}$, the sequential least square regressions based on Equation 1 are carried out for a strict subset of the support of the threshold variable *IFI*. Finally, the estimator of the threshold parameter λ is selected as the one that corresponded with the smallest sum of squared residuals (SSR) obtained in the previous step, i.e. $\hat{\lambda} = \text{argmin}\, SSR_n(\lambda)$.

As in Hansen and Caner and Hansen, the critical values for determining the 95% confidence interval of the threshold value are given by:

$$\Gamma = \{\lambda : LR(\lambda) \leq C(\alpha)\}$$

where $C(a)$ is the 95% percentile of the asymptotic distribution of the likelihood ratio $LR(\gamma)$ that has been adjusted to account for the time dimension for each cross-section unit. Once the threshold parameter $\hat{\lambda}$ is determined, the slope coefficients can be estimated by the GMM for the previously used instruments. In line with Kremer et al., we use lags of the endogenous regressor, i.e., lags of initial Gini coefficient, as its own instruments.

Estimation results

As a preliminary inspection before proceeding to PTR analysis, we first run a simple panel regression by including a dummy variable for tropical countries and assuming all slope coefficients are regime-invariant. Table 7.3 reports the regression results for random-effects models (1a to 1d) corresponding to each IFI measure. We find that tropical dummy is significantly associated with higher *gini_mkt*, suggesting tropical economies in our sample tend to have a higher income inequality than their temperate counterparts. Regarding the financial openness indicators, only total flows openness has a significant positive coefficient. Per capita GDP growth is negative across all four specifications, implying an upper Kuznets curve effect where income inequality is lower with higher economic growth. The result also suggests a positive linkage between average secondary schooling and income inequality, consistent with Coady and Dizioli's (2018) finding. This may be attributed to the fact that inequality in educational attainment has further worsened income inequality within the country.

Table 7.3 Random-effects panel regression with tropical dummy

	Model 1a	*Model 1b*	*Model 1c*	*Model 1d*
Constant	3.8870***	3.8440***	3.8872***	3.8971***
	(0.1618)	(0.1598)	(0.1627)	(0.1611)
Growth	-0.0047***	-0.0052***	-0.0047***	-0.0046***
	(0.0014)	(0.0014)	(0.0015)	(0.0014)
Secondary education	0.0524***	0.0557***	0.0547***	0.0504***
	(0.0134)	(0.0134)	(0.0131)	(0.0133)
Age dependency ratio	-0.0325	-0.0213	-0.0328	-0.0349
	(0.0378)	(0.0372)	(0.0380)	(0.0376)
Inflows	0.0007			
	(0.0004)			
FDI inflows		0.0011		
		(0.0010)		
Non-FDI inflows			0.0007	
			(0.0004)	
Total flows				0.0004**
				(0.0002)
Tropical dummy	0.0788*	0.0780*	0.0806**	0.0791*
	(0.0404)	(0.0405)	(0.0404)	(0.0405)
R-squared:				
Within	0.1694	0.1635	0.1678	0.1754
between	0.0581	0.0617	0.0571	0.0528
Overall	0.0730	0.0754	0.0717	0.0688
Observation	301	301	301	301
N	43	43	43	43

Notes: Standard errors in parentheses. Significance at 10%, 5%, and 1% are denoted by *, **, and ***, respectively.

To investigate the potential inverted U-shaped relationship of IFI and inequality, we estimate Equation 1, considering IFI as a threshold variable. Table 7.4 reports the dynamic PTR results. The results suggest evidence of heterogeneity of different capital flows components since the regime-dependent slope coefficients vary significantly across the four indicators of IFI. Our findings highlight the existence of a nonlinear relationship between IFI and income inequality. However, aside from FDI inflows, we do not find evidence of a clear inverted U-shaped IFI-inequality nexus for the other IFI indicators. Based on the results, a country would experience rising income inequality during the early phase of financial openness, but the positive effect either diminishes or turns insignificant as the extent of financial openness passes a certain threshold.

Referring to Model 2a, where the IFI measure is inflows of capital, the point estimate of the threshold value is 4.2966 (% of GDP). In our data set, 225 out of 301 observations have inflows to GDP ratio exceeding this threshold value.

Table 7.4 Results of dynamic panel threshold estimations

	Model 2a *Inflows*	*Model 2b* *FDI inflows*	*Model 2c* *Non-FDI inflows*	*Model 2d* *Total flows*
$\hat{\alpha}_1$	-0.0751***	-0.0647***	-0.0145***	-0.0728***
	(0.0137)	(0.0056)	(0.0046)	(0.0083)
Initial Gini	0.8171***	0.9219***	0.8793***	0.8328***
	(0.0496)	(0.0454)	(0.0484)	(0.0509)
Growth	-0.0013**	-0.0025***	-0.0005	-0.0011*
	(0.0006)	(0.0006)	(0.0006)	(0.0006)
Secondary education	-0.0033	-0.0148***	0.0018	-0.0024
	(0.0042)	(0.0044)	(0.0043)	(0.0043)
Age dependency ratio	0.0019	-0.0022	-0.0091	0.0224*
	(0.0121)	(0.0118)	(0.0127)	(0.0117)
Financial openness	0.0122***	0.1976***	0.0061***	0.0102***
Low regime				
	(0.0038)	(0.0156)	(0.0007)	(0.0012)
High regime	0.0000	-0.0004*	0.0005***	0.0001***
	(0.0001)	(0.0002)	(0.0001)	(0.0000)
Threshold estimate	4.2966	0.4626	9.2314	9.0468
95% confidence interval	[3.572–12.375]	[0.147–3.269]	[7.965–9.256]	[3.073–22.616]
Observations	301	301	301	301
N	43	43	43	43

Notes:
1. Low (high) regime refers to low (high) financial openness state.
2. Standard errors in parentheses. Significance at 10%, 5%, and 1% are denoted by *, **, and ***, respectively.

We then examine the statistical significance of its regime-dependent coefficients and find that the inflows indicator is a positive and statistically significant regressor for income inequality if it is less than the threshold value, but its impact on income inequality turns insignificant beyond the threshold. Model 2b and 2c compare between FDI and non-FDI components of inflows. In our sample, 246 out of 301 observations lie in the high FDI openness regime, while 62 out of 301 observations lie in the high non-FDI openness regime. FDI has the largest positive impact on income inequality out of the four IFI indicators during the low openness state, but its correlation with income inequality becomes negative with a 10% significance level in the high openness state. On the other hand, non-FDI inflows (comprising a portfolio and other investments) have positive and significant effects on inequality in both low and high regimes even though the coefficient value in the latter regime becomes much smaller. This finding confirms the composition effect of capital flows widely recognized in the previous literature, that the distinct behaviours and effects existed between FDI and non-FDI flows (for examples, see Smith & Valderrama, 2009; Aizenman et al., 2013; Kirabaeva & Razin, 2010). Finally, looking at the aggregate IFI variable as indicated by total flows, 169 out of 301 observations are in the high regime in which the threshold is estimated to be 9.0468 (% of GDP). Similar to non-FDI inflows, the magnitude of positive coefficient for IFI reduces in the high openness regime.

Implications of nonlinear IFI-inequality to the tropics

To further shed light on the impact of financial liberalization on income inequality in the context of tropical and temperate economies, Table 7.5 shows the number of countries with IFI exceeding the threshold levels as provided in Table 7.4. Focusing on FDI inflows, by comparing the average value of the country's FDI inflows to GDP ratio across time with the estimated threshold level of 0.4625, we find that most of the tropical countries (18 out of 20) and temperate countries (all 23 countries) have already achieved the high FDI inflows regime. This is not the case if we look at non-FDI inflows when only a few countries (2 out of 20 for the tropical countries and 7 out of 23 for the temperate countries) have fulfilled the threshold as a high non-FDI inflows regime. The outcomes based on median instead of average values are similar, except that fewer temperate countries are detected as high openness regimes in terms of FDI and non-FDI inflows (the numbers are 22 and 4 countries, respectively).

The implications of our research findings are twofold. First, even though our results align with the existing finding on the inequality-increasing effect of financial globalization, such an effect only prevails during the stage of low financial openness. This means the inequality effect of financial integration may not seem as intimidating as the existing literature has suggested. Second, FDI inflows have a more substantial worsening effect on income inequality than non-FDI inflows at the low financial openness regime, but the effect only exists at a very low threshold level of FDI openness. Once the threshold is crossed, FDI inflows will have a negative association (albeit weakly significant) with the nation's *gini_mkt*. This result, together with the above finding that the degrees of FDI openness of most tropical economies in our sample have reached the threshold level, implies FDI flows have a more benign impact than non-FDI flows on income inequality in the long run. This suggests that

Table 7.5 High-financial-openness countries identified by comparing mean or median of IFI to the estimated threshold

	By mean		*By median*	
	Tropic (20)	*Temperate (23)*	*Tropic (20)*	*Temperate (23)*
Inflows	16	21	16	21
FDI inflows	18	23	18	22
Non-FDI inflows	2	7	2	4
Total flows	9	18	8	18

a multifaceted approach to financial liberalization is necessary to deal with heterogeneous impacts across different types of capital inflows. In particular, developing nations should treat non-FDI inflows with extra caution, and a more mature income distribution mechanism should be in place as they further develop their portfolio and credit markets to accept more financial inflows.

Robustness checks

In this section, we conduct several robustness checks to examine the sensitivity of the PTR results to using an alternative measure of Gini coefficient as the dependent variable, adding additional control variables, and using trade openness instead of financial openness as a threshold variable. The results of nonlinear IFI-inequality nexus are consistent throughout all sensitivity tests.

Alternative Gini measure as the dependent variable

Models 3a–3d in Table 7.6 show results using disposable income Gini coefficient (*gini_disp*) as a dependent variable. As aforementioned, *gini_disp* is

Table 7.6 Results of dynamic panel threshold estimations with alternative Gini coefficient

	Model 3a	*Model 3b*	*Model 3c*	*Model 3d*
	Inflows	*FDI inflows*	*Non-FDI inflows*	*Total flows*
$\hat{\alpha}_1$	-0.0288***	0.0856***	0.0079*	-0.0660***
	(0.0067)	(0.0087)	(0.0046)	(0.0111)
Initial Gini	0.8944***	1.0390***	0.8638***	0.9792***
	(0.1162)	(0.0988)	(0.1254)	(0.1074)
Growth	-0.0005	-0.0025***	-0.0004	-0.00002
	(0.0006)	(0.0006)	(0.0006)	(0.0006)
Secondary education	-0.0067	-0.0321***	0.0000	-0.0156***
	(0.0049)	(0.0047)	(0.0052)	(0.0049)
Age dependency ratio	0.0076	0.0094	-0.0051	0.0253
	(0.0169)	(0.0155)	(0.0187)	(0.0154)
Financial openness	0.0078***	0.2615***	0.0038***	0.0101***
Low regime				
	(0.0011)	(0.0251)	(0.0008)	(0.0015)
High regime	0.0007***	0.0010***	0.0009***	0.0004***
	(0.0001)	(0.0004)	(0.0001)	(0.0001)
Threshold estimate	10.0154	0.4626	9.2314	9.2204
95% confidence interval	[3.596–12.639]	[0.147–2.550]	[1.3441–9.2563]	[2.968–22.616]
Observations	301	301	301	301
N	43	43	43	43

Notes:
1. Low (high) regime refers to low (high) financial openness state.
2. Standard errors in parentheses. Significance at 10%, 5%, and 1% are denoted by *, **, and ***, respectively.

calculated using disposable income, which is income after redistribution policies. This may explain why the findings differ from baseline results which use gross income Gini coefficient as the dependent variable.

Nonetheless, even with *gini_disp*, we find some evidence of nonlinear linkage between financial openness and inequality after controlling for the same set of control variables. The coefficients are positive across four IFI measures, but the magnitude significantly reduces the high financial openness regime.

Inclusion of further explanatory variables

We also conducted a robustness check concerning how results are affected by adding additional covariates such as trade openness and price inflation to our baseline model. To save space, we only display regression results for inflows and total flows indicators. As suggested by the Hecksher-Ohlin-Samuelson (HOS) model, trade openness of a nation is linked to the nation's income distribution, and the distributional effect of international trade, in turn, depends on

the relative factor abundance and the extent to which individuals obtain income from labour or capital endowment (Easterly, 2005). Previous empirical studies which focus on the impact

of economic openness on income inequality have found that trade openness exerts an equalizing effect as opposed to that of financial openness (Asteriou et al., 2014). Our results partially support the previous findings in which trade openness has a significant and negative correlation with the Gini coefficient in Model 4b.

The finding from robustness checks may also suggest that high trade openness might moderate the positive impact of financial openness on inequality in the low regime. Jaumotte et al. (2013) investigate the impacts of globalization in trade and finance on income inequality and find the effect insignificant. The authors explain that this is because the inequality-dampening effect of trade liberalization and the inequality-widening effect of financial openness have offset each other.

Inflation is regarded as a cruel tax that hurts the poor more than the rich, given that the rich are likely to have better access to financial instruments that hedge against inflation (Easterly & Fischer, 2001). Our findings in Model 4c and 4d confirm this view with a significant and positive coefficient found for the inflation variable.

In a nutshell, the qualitative results of the nonlinear IFI-inequality relationship still hold across Models 4a to 4d in Table 7.7 with additional control variables.

Trade openness as threshold variable

Previous empirical studies find a complementary effect between trade and financial liberalization. Notably, Aizenman and Noy (2003) discover that de

Table 7.7 Results of dynamic panel threshold estimations with additional control variable

	Model 4a	*Model 4b*	*Model 4c*	*Model 4d*
	Inflows	*Total flows*	*Inflows*	*Total flows*
$\hat{\alpha}_1$	-0.0228***	-0.0533***	-0.0758***	-0.0724***
	(0.0056)	(0.0076)	(0.0135)	(0.0082)
Initial Gini	0.8836***	0.9239***	0.8231***	0.8314***
	(0.0561)	(0.0532)	(0.0482)	(0.0495)
Growth	-0.0013**	-0.0007	-0.0012**	-0.0011*
	(0.0006)	(0.0006)	(0.0006)	(0.0006)
Secondary education	0.0066	-0.0006	-0.0031	-0.0020
	(0.0044)	(0.0042)	(0.0042)	(0.0043)
Age dependency ratio	0.0200*	0.0166	0.0011	0.02136*
	(0.0105)	(0.0104)	(0.0122)	(0.0118)
Trade openness	-0.0012	-0.0125**	-	-
	(0.0068)	(0.0064)	-	-
Inflation	-	-	0.0010***	0.0009***
	-	-	(0.0003)	(0.0003)
Financial openness	0.0059***	0.0078***	0.0125***	0.0100***
Low regime				
	(0.0007)	(0.0011)	(0.0037)	(0.0011)
High regime	0.0001	0.0001***	-0.0001	0.0001***
	(0.0001)	(0.0000)	(0.0001)	(0.0000)
Threshold estimate	10.3637	9.0468	4.2966	9.0468
95% confidence interval	[3.587–12.779]	[3.073–22.568]	[3.571–12.375]	[3.073–22.568]
Observations	301	301	301	301
N	43	43	43	43

Notes:
1. Low (high) regime refers to low (high) financial openness state.
2. Standard errors in parentheses. Significance at 10%, 5%, and 1% are denoted by *, **, and ***, respectively.

facto financial openness depends positively on trade openness. Thus, to further shed light on the nonlinear linkage between IFI and income distribution, we also inspect such linkage conditional on different trade openness regimes.

Table 7.8 reports PTR results with trade openness acting as a threshold variable. Interestingly, there exists evidence of nonlinear IFI-inequality nexus (except under FDI inflows where the low-regime coefficient is insignificant) that even the regime considered is based on trade openness.

The majority of the countries in our sample, both tropical and temperate, have trade openness surpassing the estimated threshold values.[9] This implies that the income inequality effect induced by the financial opening process is weakening as the host economy becomes further globalized, both in cross-border financial flows and international trade.

Table 7.8 Results of dynamic panel threshold estimations with trade openness as threshold variable

	Model 5a *Inflows*	*Model 5b* *FDI inflows*	*Model 5c* *Non-FDI inflows*	*Model 5d* *Total flows*
$\hat{\alpha}_1$	-0.1138***	-0.0757***	-0.1073***	-0.1038***
	(0.0083)	(0.0070)	(0.0064)	(0.0078)
Initial Gini	0.8972***	0.9550***	0.9179***	0.8610***
	(0.0475)	(0.0463)	(0.0454)	(0.0497)
Growth	-0.0022***	-0.0021***	-0.0017***	-0.0024***
	(0.0006)	(0.0005)	(0.0006)	(0.0006)
Secondary education	-0.0015	-0.0013	-0.0007	-0.0023
	(0.0042)	(0.0043)	(0.0041)	(0.0041)
Age dependency ratio	0.0469***	0.0434***	0.0408***	0.0406***
	(0.0110)	(0.0105)	(0.0110)	(0.0109)
Financial openness Low regime (Trade $\leq \gamma$)	0.0096***	0.0032	0.0118***	0.0060***
	(0.0013)	(0.0039)	(0.0012)	(0.0008)
High regime (Trade > γ)	0.0000	-0.0004	0.0001	0.0001***
	(0.0000)	(0.0003)	(0.0001)	(0.0000)
Threshold estimate	3.6177	3.4520	3.6177	3.6177
95% confidence interval	[3.452–3.727]	[3.238–3.702]	[3.238–3.641]	[3.238–3.702]
Observations	301	301	301	301
N	43	43	43	43

Notes:
1. Low (high) regime refers to low (high) trade openness state.
2. Standard errors in parentheses. Significance at 10%, 5%, and 1% are denoted by *, **, and ***, respectively.

Conclusion

Following the volatile capital flows and contagious financial market crashes witnessed from the emerging market crises during the end of the last century, the recent disastrous Global Financial Crisis, and the current ongoing COVID-19 pandemic, there has been controversy as to whether the current economic liberalization is too excessive. While more comprehensive and in-depth research is needed to deal with such a broad topic, this chapter attempts to contribute to the debate by looking at the linkage between financial openness and income inequality.

Our results provide new evidence on the nonlinear relationship between IFI and income inequality using data from 43 countries covering the period from 1980 through 2014. The empirical results indicate that there exists a significant IFI threshold effect in the IFI-inequality linkage. For financial openness below the threshold, IFI indicators exert a positive impact on income inequality. However, once the degree of financial openness exceeds the threshold level, the effect of IFI on inequality will diminish. The qualitative results hold across four measures of IFI indicators and various robustness checks, such as when an alternative Gini coefficient is used as the dependent variable when additional controls variables are included and when trade openness replaces financial openness as the threshold indicator.

Previous empirical studies have suggested that while trade openness improves income distribution, financial openness worsens it. Our result confirms the positive effect of financial openness on income inequality, but the good news is that such an effect is weaker as the economic globalization process continues. The financial openness threshold, especially when the FDI inflows are based on IFI, is not hard to attain, as the majority of the tropical countries within our sample are identified as high FDI inflows regime. FDI inflows can therefore be seen as an important source of capital inflows that can help solve the structural poverty issue facing the tropics without creating too much burden on the country's income gap. As for non-FDI inflows, the tropical countries will need a more sophisticated income distribution policy as their financial market further opens up to accept more non-FDI investment flows.

Our study only establishes the first step of identifying a nonlinear IFI-inequality nexus. Other questions such as which factors lead to such nonlinearity or whether the effect of IFI on growth is permanent or transitory remain to be further explored in the future.

Acknowledgments

We are grateful to Alexander Bick and Siong Hook Law for sharing the panel threshold estimation code.

Notes

1 Lecturer, James Cook University Singapore Business School, James Cook University, Singapore.

2 Corresponding author: Associate Professor, Department of Economics, School of Social Science, Nanyang Technological University, 14 Nanyang Drive Singapore 637332, Singapore. Email: aswmchia@ntu.edu.sg.

3 Such as most Latin American countries hit by the 1980s debt crisis, and Southeast Asian countries affected by the Asian financial crisis.

4 According to Cline (2002), around 40 to 60 million people were forced into poverty by the financial crises originated in the eight emerging economies (Mexico, Thailand, Indonesia, Korea, Russia, Brazil, Argentina, and Turkey), which was a stark figure comparing to the 800 million total population of these countries combined.

5 They are Bahamas, Barbados, Brunei Darussalam, Hong Kong SAR, Panama, Singapore, Taiwan Province of China, and Trinidad and Tobago.

6 Other climatic factors such as ocean current, topography, wind and air masses, and so on, can also determine the regional climate condition.

7 In short, ENSO is a climatic phenomenon periodically fluctuating between three phases which affect the climate of much of the tropics and subtropics. The three phases are El Niño (w. arming of the ocean surface), La Niña (c. ooling of the ocean surface), and Neutral (neither El Niño or La Niña).

8 The data version we use is 2016 updated version.
9 16 tropical and 23 temperate economies are classified as high trade openness regime if we consider the threshold value at 3.6177. And the numbers change to 17 tropical and 21 temperate economies at threshold of 3.4520.

References

Ahlquist, J. S. (2006). Economic policy, institutions, and capital flows: Portfolio and direct investment flows in developing countries. *International Studies Quarterly*, *50*(3), 681–704.

Aizenman, J., & Noy, I. (2003). *Endogenous financial openness: Efficiency and political economy considerations* (Tech. Rep.). National Bureau of Economic Research.

Aizenman, J., Jinjarak, Y., & Park, D. (2013). Capital flows and economic growth in the era of financial integration and crisis, 1990–2010. *Open Economies Review*, *24*(3), 371–396.

Arellano, M., & Bover, O. (1995). Another look at the instrumental variable estimation of error-components models. *Journal of Econometrics*, *68*(1), 29–51.

Asteriou, D., Dimelis, S., & Moudatsou, A. (2014). Globalization and income inequality: A panel data econometric approach for the EU27 countries. *Economic Modelling*, *36*, 592–599.

Barro, R. J., & Lee, J. W. (2013). A new data set of educational attainment in the world, 1950–2010. *Journal of Development Economics*, *104*, 184–198.

Bekaert, G., Harvey, C. R., & Lundblad, C. (2011). Financial openness and productivity. *World Development*, *39*(1), 1–19.

Bick, A. (2010). Threshold effects of inflation on economic growth in developing countries. *Economics Letters*, *108*(2), 126–129.

Calvo, G. A. (1998). Capital flows and capital-market crises: The simple economics of sudden stops. *Journal of Applied Economics*, *1*(1), 35–54.

Caner, M., & Hansen, B. E. (2004). Instrumental variable estimation of a threshold model. *Econometric Theory*, *20*(5), 813–843.

Chen, J., & Quang, T. (2014). The impact of international financial integration on economic growth: New evidence on threshold effects. *Economic Modelling*, *42*, 475–489.

Clements, M. B. J., de Mooij, R. A., Gupta, M. S., & Keen, M. M. (2015). *Inequality and fiscal policy*. International Monetary Fund.

Cline, W. (2002). Financial crises and poverty in emerging market economies. *Center for Global Development Working Paper* (8).

Coady, D., & Dizioli, A. (2018). Income inequality and education revisited: Persistence, endogeneity and heterogeneity. *Applied Economics*, *50*(25), 2747–2761.

Dabla-Norris, M. E., Kochhar, M. K., Suphaphiphat, M. N., Ricka, M. F., & Tsounta, E. (2015). *Causes and consequences of income inequality: A global perspective*. International Monetary Fund.

Das, M., & Mohapatra, S. (2003). Income inequality: The aftermath of stock market liberalization in emerging markets. *Journal of Empirical Finance*, *10*(1–2), 217–248.

Easterly, W. (2005). National policies and economic growth: A reappraisal. *Handbook of Economic Growth*, *1*, 1015–1059.

Easterly, W. (2007). Inequality does cause underdevelopment: Insights from a new instrument. *Journal of Development Economics*, *84*(2), 755–776.

Easterly, W., & Fischer, S. (2001). Inflation and the poor. *Journal of Money, Credit and Banking*, *33*(2), 160–178.

Easterly, W., & Levine, R. (2003). Tropics, germs, and crops: How endowments influence economic development. *Journal of Monetary Economics, 50*(1), 3–39.
Edison, H. J., Klein, M. W., Ricci, L. A., & Sløk, T. (2004). Capital account liberalization and economic performance: Survey and synthesis. *IMF Staff Papers, 51*(2), 220–256.
Edwards, S. (2007). Capital controls, sudden stops, and current account reversals. In *Capital controls and capital flows in emerging economies: Policies, practices and consequences* (pp. 73–120). University of Chicago Press.
Eichengreen, M. B. J., Csonto, M. B., ElGanainy, M. A. A., & Koczan, Z. (2021). *Financial globalization and inequality: Capital flows as a two-edged sword.* International Monetary Fund.
Engerman, S. L., & Sokoloff, K. L. (1994). Factor endowments, institutions, and differential paths of growth among new world economies: A view from economic historians of the united states. *NBER Working Paper* (h0066).
Erauskin, I., & Turnovsky, S. J. (2019). International financial integration and income inequality in a stochastically growing economy. *Journal of International Economics, 119*, 55–74.
Estrada, G. B., Park, D., & Ramayandi, A. (2015). Financial development, financial openness, and economic growth. *Asian Development Bank Economics Working Paper Series, 442*. Available at SSRN: https://ssrn.com/abstract=2707518 or http://dx.doi.org/10.2139/ssrn.2707518
Furceri, D., & Loungani, P. (2018). The distributional effects of capital account liberalization. *Journal of Development Economics, 130*, 127–144.
Gallup, J. L., & Sachs, J. D. (2000). Agriculture, climate, and technology: Why are the tropics falling behind? *American Journal of Agricultural Economics, 82*(3), 731–737.
Gallup, J. L., Sachs, J. D., & Mellinger, A. D. (1999). Geography and economic development. *International Regional Science Review, 22*(2), 179–232.
Gavin, M., & Hausmann, R. (1998). Nature, development and distribution in Latin America: Evidence on the role of geography, climate and natural resources. *IADB, Research Department Working Paper* (378).
Greenwood, J., & Jovanovic, B. (1990). Financial development, growth, and the distribution of income. *Journal of Political Economy, 98*(5, Part 1), 1076–1107.
Hansen, B. E. (1999). Threshold effects in non-dynamic panels: Estimation, testing, and inference. *Journal of Econometrics, 93*(2), 345–368.
Heimberger, P. (2020). Does economic globalisation affect income inequality? A meta-analysis. *The World Economy, 43*(11), 2960–2982.
Hsiang, S. M., & Jina, A. S. (2014). *The causal effect of environmental catastrophe on long-run economic growth: Evidence from 6,700 cyclones* (Tech. Rep.). National Bureau of Economic Research.
Hsiang, S. M., & Meng, K. C. (2015). Tropical economics. *American Economic Review, 105*(5), 257–61.
Jaumotte, F., Lall, S., & Papageorgiou, C. (2013). Rising income inequality: Technology, or trade and financial globalization? *IMF Economic Review, 61*(2), 271–309.
Jung, J. W., & Kim, K. (2021). Financial market integration and income inequality. *East Asian Economic Review, 25*(2), 175–203.
Kim, D.-H., Lin, S.-C., & Suen, Y.-B. (2012). Dynamic effects of financial openness on economic growth and macroeconomic uncertainty. *Emerging Markets Finance and Trade, 48*(1), 25–54.
Kirabaeva, K., & Razin, A. (2010). *Composition of capital flows: A survey* (Tech. Rep.). National Bureau of Economic Research.

Kose, M. A., Prasad, E. S., & Taylor, A. D. (2011). Thresholds in the process of international financial integration. *Journal of International Money and Finance, 30*(1), 147–179.

Kremer, S., Bick, A., & Nautz, D. (2013). Inflation and growth: New evidence from a dynamic panel threshold analysis. *Empirical Economics, 44*(2), 861–878.

Kuznets, S. (1955). Economic growth and income inequality. *The American Economic Review, 45*(1), 1–28.

Lim, G., & McNelis, P. D. (2016). Income growth and inequality: The threshold effects of trade and financial openness. *Economic Modelling, 58*, 403–412.

Lin, S.-C., Kim, D.-H., & Lee, Y.-H. (2015). Financial development and the FDI-inequality nexus. *Contemporary Economic Policy, 33*(3), 513–534.

Moav, O. (2005). Cheap children and the persistence of poverty. *The Economic Journal, 115*(500), 88–110.

Mookherjee, D., & Ray, D. (2003). Persistent inequality. *The Review of Economic Studies, 70*(2), 369–393.

Prasad, E., Rogoff, K., Wei, S.-J., & Kose, M. A. (2005). Effects of financial globalization on developing countries: Some empirical evidence. In *India's and China's recent experience with reform and growth* (pp. 201–228). Springer.

Sachs, J. D. (2001). Tropical underdevelopment. *National Bureau of Economic Research Working Paper Series* (w8119).

Sahoo, M., & Sethi, N. (2020). An empirical insight into the financial globalization–growth nexus via trade openness: Evidence from select south Asian countries. *Global Business Review, 18*(1)

Selvarajan, S. K., & Ab-Rahim, R. (2020). Financial integration and economic growth. *Journal of Economic Integration, 35*(1), 191–213.

Smith, K. A., & Valderrama, D. (2009). The composition of capital inflows when emerging market firms face financing constraints. *Journal of Development Economics, 89*(2), 223–234.

Solt, F. (2009). Standardizing the world income inequality database. *Social Science Quarterly, 90*(2), 231–242.

Sula, O., & Willett, T. D. (2009). The reversibility of different types of capital flows to emerging markets. *Emerging Markets Review, 10*(4), 296–310.

United Nations. (2020). *World economic situation and prospects* (Tech. Rep.). Retrieved from https://www.un.org/development/desa/dpad/wp-content/uploads/sites/45/
WESP2020 Annex.pdf

Yakubu, Z., Loganathan, N., Mursitama, T. N., Mardani, A., Khan, S. A. R., & Hassan, A. A. G. (2020). Financial liberalisation, political stability, and economic determinants of real economic growth in Kenya. *Energies, 13*(13), 3426.

Appendix

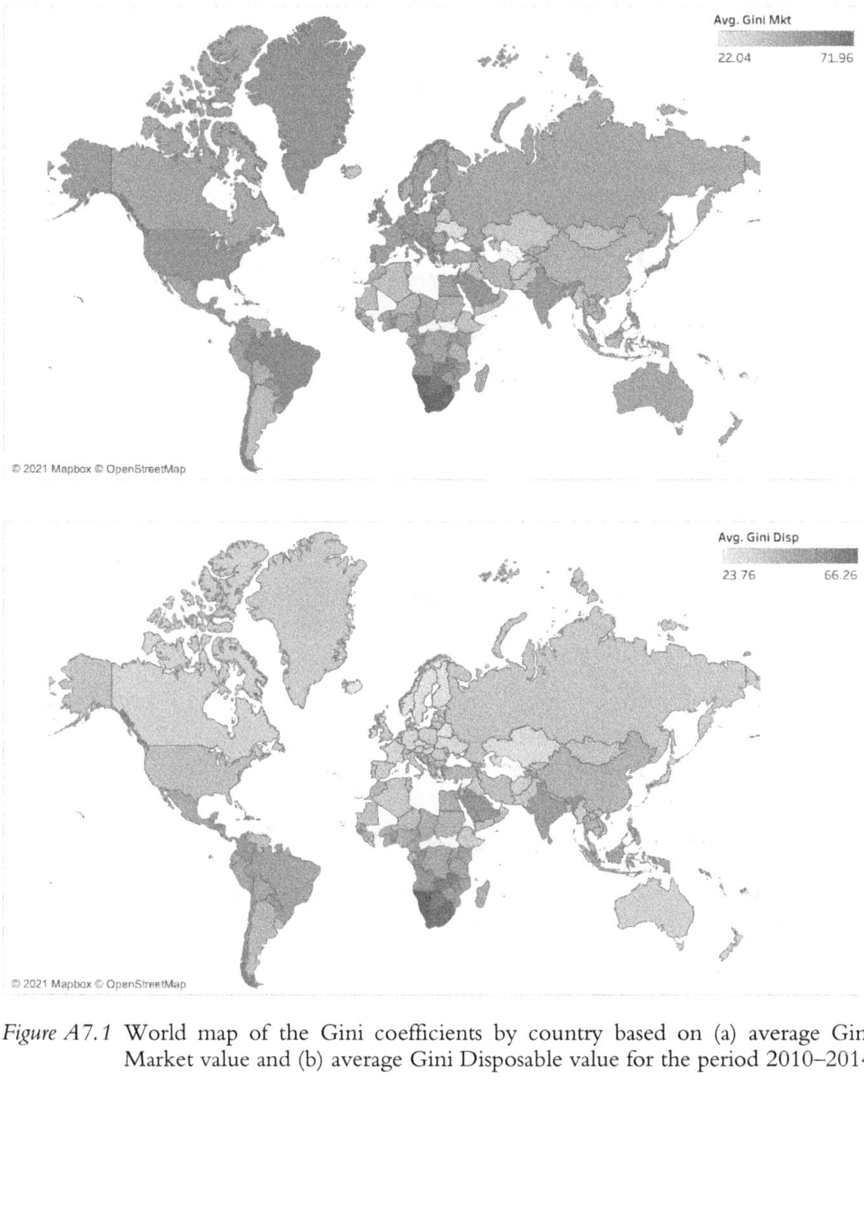

Figure A7.1 World map of the Gini coefficients by country based on (a) average Gini Market value and (b) average Gini Disposable value for the period 2010–2014

Table A7.2 List of countries

Tropical (20)		*Temperate (23)*	
Bangladesh	Philippines	Argentina	Italy
Barbados	Sierra Leone	Canada	Korea, Rep.
Brazil	Singapore	Chile	Netherlands
Colombia	South Africa	China	Norway
Costa Rica	Sri Lanka	Denmark	Pakistan
Fiji	Tanzania	Egypt, Arab Rep.	Portugal
India	Thailand	Finland	Spain
Indonesia	Venezuela, RB	France	Sweden
Malawi		Germany	Switzerland
Mexico		Greece	United Kingdom
Panama		Hungary	United States
Peru		Israel	

Table A7.3 List of variables

Variable	*Definition*	*Sources*
gini_mkt	Logarithm of Gini index calculated from household market (pre-tax, pre-transfer) income	Solt (2009)
gini_disp	Logarithm of Gini index calculated from household disposable (post-tax, post-transfer) income	Solt (2009)
IFI variables		
Inflows	Absolute inflows of capital, divided by GDP	IFS
FDI Inflows	Absolute inflows of FDI investments, divided by GDP	IFS
Non-FDI Inflows	Absolute inflows of portfolio and other investments, divided by GDP	IFS
Total flows	Sum of absolute inflows and outflows of capital, divided by GDP	IFS
Control variables		
Initial gini_mkt	First observation of every five-year interval for gini_mkt	Solt (2009)
Initial gini_disp	First observation of every five-year interval for gini_disp	Solt (2009)
Growth	GDP per capita growth (annual %)	WDI
Secondary education	Logarithm of average years of secondary school education	Barro and Lee (2013)
Age dependency ratio	Logarithm of the ratio of people younger than 15 or older than 64 to people ages 15–64	WDI
Trade openness	Logarithm of the sum of exports and imports to GDP	WDI
Inflation	GDP deflator (annual %)	WDI

8 COVID-19

Its impact on trade and development in the ASEAN region

Jacob Wood[1], *Haejin Jang*[2], *and Benedict Atkinson*[3]

Introduction

Southeast Asia has enjoyed remarkable economic progress in recent decades (Heshmati et al., 2019; Kim and Wood, 2020), with many countries embracing substantially liberalized foreign trade and direct investment (FDI) regimes within the frameworks of, firstly, the General Agreement on Tariffs and Trade (GATT), and then more recently the World Trade Organization (WTO). The significant growth in trade and FDI that has emerged has been at the forefront of economic development in the region. More recently, these trade and FDI developments have been replaced by new forms of industrial organization that have focused on global production networks and supply chains (Baldwin, 2012). However, in early 2020 the positive developments came to a very sudden and abrupt halt with the emergence of the COVID-19 pandemic, which has triggered a severe economic downturn across the region with almost all ASEAN (the Association of Southeast Asian Nations)[4] economies experiencing negative GDP performance in 2020 (see Table 8.1).

Despite the significant economic and health-based heartache caused by the global COVID-19 pandemic, many ASEAN nations have moved rapidly by utilizing, in many instances, locally developed technologies to contact tracing platforms and mapping interfaces to quickly contain possible spreads. Nonetheless, such offerings are relatively minor in the scheme of things, with some of the key underlying trade and supply chain problems further exacerbated by the pandemic. Of particular concern, are the broad-based export restrictions that exist on many essential products by economies in the region, such as vital medicines, medical supplies, and food (see Appendix A8.1) (Chandra et al., 2020). While these measures were implemented as a temporary adjustment, there are concerns such restrictions might have over the long term if they remain in place. Recognizing these potential implications, many policymakers agree that international trade policy can play a very influential role in overcoming the economic issues associated with the COVID-19 pandemic. As a key mechanism of not only reducing the costs and improving access to essential goods and services, trade policy, when properly managed, can stimulate

DOI: 10.4324/9781003153580-8

Table 8.1 Real GDP growth in ASEAN, China, and India, 2019–21

ASEAN	*2019*	*2020*	*2021**
Indonesia	5.0	-2.4	4.0
Malaysia	4.3	–5.2	7.0
Philippines	6.0	–9.0	5.9
Thailand	2.4	–6.4	4.5
Vietnam	7.0	2.6	7.0
Brunei Darussalam	3.9	1.8	3.1
Singapore	0.7	–5.5	5.0
Cambodia	7.1	–2.9	5.4
Lao PDR	5.5	0.6	5.0
Myanmar	6.8	1.7	5.0
Average of ASEAN 10	4.7	–3.4	5.1

* Estimated
Source: OECD Development Centre.

economic growth and the development of a more resilient economy in the face of future crises.

This study documents key trade policy responses in the ASEAN region as well as where other important international trade developments may lie. It also outlines economic development opportunities and the key implications for growth and development across Southeast Asia. With the pandemic continuing to evolve, this research provides an important guide for policymakers and practitioners operating in the fields of international business and trade. Key research questions (RQ) addressed include:

RQ1: What are the impediments to ASEAN-wide recovery from the effects of the pandemic?
RQ2: What are key risks to recovery from the pandemic?
RQ3: What are the positive actions that can be taken to ensure recovery?
RQ4: Which countries can lead recovery and how?

A roadmap for the paper consists of observations about economic growth trends and prospects in ASEAN, the long-term effects of the pandemic on the region, and the primary necessity for ASEAN countries to successfully roll out vaccination programmes to ensure suppression of the virus and a return to normal or a 'new normal'.

Economic development in Southeast Asia

While much of the region's recent growth has been generated by an expanding labour force and developments in both its manufacturing and service sectors (Kim and Wood, 2020; Park and Shin, 2012), it is important that the region looks to address its low levels of productivity to achieve more sustainable means of economic growth. International trade and the negotiation of new trade agreements have the potential to further develop the region (Wood, 2017), and while deeper participation in international trade can herald new forms of competitive pressures, which are beneficial from a productivity standpoint, they have the potential to disrupt the growth trajectories of current corporate leaders. Nonetheless, the biggest potential for Southeast Asia in the near term is capturing a larger share of the world's trade in goods and services.

From an international trade perspective, previous empirical works involving the Asian region have focused on a wide range of areas, including the implementation and impact of various neo-protectionist trade policies (Cheong and Tongzon, 2018; Wood et al., 2017a, b; Wood et al., 2020a, b), others have also examined the domestic factors that influence trade negotiations (Wood, 2017), intra-industry trade flows (Wood et al., 2021), the WTO dispute settlement mechanism (Sally, 2004; Wood and Wu, 2020), and the impact that Brexit (Wood and Jang, 2017) and the US–China trade war (Wood et al., 2020a) may have on the region. This research differs from previous efforts by providing an examination of how the Southeast Asian region can capture economic growth opportunities from the development of new trade connections. In order to provide such an assessment, relevant trade and economic policy decisions will be examined as well as empirical works that focus on the development of the region.

In recent times, much of the research has focused on COVID-19 and its impact on trade and investment, and these ramifications for the wider society (Asian Development Bank (ADB), 2021). From an ASEAN perspective, there are fears that the reductions in these areas could threaten to reverse the region's progress in poverty reduction and food security. While specific forecasts are not yet available, initial findings from a broader study on East Asia and the Pacific suggest that poverty headcount rates (calculated at USD 3.20 per day) may increase for the first time since 1990, rising from 7.6% in 2018 to 10.2%, which implies an increase in the absolute number of poor in the region by 54 million in 2020 (Sumner et al., 2020). Exacerbating this problem is the fact that large percentages of the population (see Table 8.2) are part of the informal labour market and as such, lack the protections, insurance, and rights that are usually mandated in formal labour (International Labour Organization, 2020a, b). This means that these workers have little, or any protection from sudden loss of income or unexpected health costs.

Economic development work must now turn to the implementation of relevant policy initiatives that balance public health concerns and economic costs. The severity of the pandemic's impact varies across ASEAN economies, with impacts, largely dependent on public health system capacity, informal sector size, initial government containment measures, and economic stimulus responses (ASEAN Secretariat, 2020b). Social distancing, quarantine measures, and travel restrictions will continue to play an important role in containing the spread of the virus; however, such measures create significant economic costs,

Table 8.2 ASEAN Informal employment rate and poverty incidence

ASEAN member	*Informal employment rate*	*Year*	*Poverty incidence*	*Year*
Brunei	46.6	2017	N.A	N.A
Cambodia	90.3	2012	13.5	2014
Indonesia	44.1	2018	9.8	2018
Lao PDR	75.4	2017	23.2	2013
Myanmar	10.6	2017	0.4	2015
Malaysia	84.1	2017	32.1	2015
Philippines	N.A	N.A	16.6	2018
Singapore	N.A	N.A	N.A	N.A
Thailand	37.1	2018	8.6	2016
Vietnam	57.2	2016	9.8	2016

Sources: ASEAN Secretariat (2019).

particularly in countries that rely heavily on the incomes generated from tourism and international trade.

The longer-term effect of the pandemic on ASEAN countries

It should be noted that Table 8.1 optimistically projects ASEAN growth rates for 2021 presumably on the presumption that negative exogenous factors, principally the COVID-19 pandemic but also including continuing political trade and political tension between China and the United States and others, will weaken in their influence on production and trade patterns. This presumption is yet to be validated. In particular, the COVID-19 pandemic may cast a long shadow over the region (ADB, 2021). While the development in different countries of various vaccines to inoculate against the COVID-19 virus and variants will potentially lead to effective suppression of the virus in the worldwide population, vaccine rollout across the world is expected to proceed at a relatively slow pace. ASEAN growth rates may be constrained by continuation of the pandemic.

Worldwide – as opposed to country by country – suppression of the COVID-19 virus is likely to be delayed by vaccine production and supply costs, argument over distribution agreements, and so-called 'vaccine nationalism'. To the extent that the growth of ASEAN countries is predicated on international trade and commerce, any delayed worldwide rollout of vaccines is likely to continue to adversely affect domestic production and international supply chains (Brookings, 2021).

Endogenous factors are also pertinent to consideration of ASEAN growth prospects. Myanmar is mired in extreme domestic political turmoil engendered by the military's cancellation of democratic election results, and Thailand is also affected by disputes over its military-dominated government. Malaysian politics is experiencing a 'mid-life crisis' which could result in Islamic domination of politics (Chin, 2021). The Malaysian government instituted a state of emergency, supposedly to enable it to grapple more effectively with COVID-19. Its critics argue, however, that the emergency is a pretext for maintaining the government in power and exerting control over political discourse (Teoh, 2021). The emergency ended on 1 August 2021.

Meanwhile, Singapore's role as a trade and investment facilitator is likely to continue to be adversely affected by continued disruption of global supply chains. Vietnam, which has apparently successfully avoided pandemic contagion, also continues to grow economically. Indonesia suffered economic contraction in 2020 but, like Vietnam, can expect positive growth provided that it successfully contains spread of the COVID-19 virus.

The extraordinary irruption of the pandemic in the Indian subcontinent has also contributed to regional trade disruption and tightening of border closures. One consequence of the pandemic in some countries has been the voluntary repatriation of guest workers and reduction in the size and flow of remittances. The political-economic outlook for ASEAN countries is thus difficult to predict. Ostensibly, world economies – fuelled by enormous monetary stimulus injected into the economies of advanced countries – are projected to grow in coming years and the green shoots of economic recovery have been discerned in some of these economies (De Wiljder, 2021).

However, 'recovery' is predicated on continued unprecedented fiscal and monetary stimulus in advanced countries and the outcome of debt-fuelled recovery is uncertain. The OECD has argued (OECD, 2020) that expenditure in advanced economies could stimulate capital flows throughout the world leading to a debt trap. If the global financial system is characterized by low interest rates, high liquidity, and rapid debt accumulation the effect of rapid capital inflow on ASEAN markets could be disruptive.

As the OECD reported,

> From the production perspective, goods exports, particularly manufactured goods, tend to use substantial service inputs. These include logistics, finance, business facilitation and communication services. This linkage makes the service sector sensitive to external market developments akin to the industry sector.

ASEAN economies dependent on trade flow for increasing prosperity are thus exposed to supply chain disruption in the advanced economies. Another disrupting factor is the continued geopolitical assertiveness of China. China's rivalry with the United States is becoming crystallized in latent and increasingly explicit hostility arising in relation to China's territory claiming (or island-building) activities in the South China Sea. Chinese aircraft incursions into Taiwan's airspace have raised troubling questions about China's intentions – in both the short and long term – with regard to Taiwan's security and sovereignty.

Geopolitically and economically, ASEAN is an organization confronting very substantial challenges with no clear way out of its predicament.

Low trade earnings and above all the collapse in tourism have imperilled the service sectors of the ASEAN economies. The political-economic outlook for ASEAN countries is thus difficult to predict. Ostensibly, developed world economies – fuelled by enormous monetary stimulus injected into the economies of advanced countries – are projected to grow from 2021, and in theory, recovery among developed nations will lead to recovery of ASEAN trade.

However, such a theory is simplistic. The loss of tourism, the danger of geopolitics spiralling into outright hostility between the Five Eyes nations[5] and China, the continued ravaging effect of the pandemic in India, and the slow pace of inoculation in ASEAN countries portend danger for those countries. In the northern summer of 2021, European countries which are implementing successful vaccination programmes anticipate some resumption of tourist activity. But ASEAN countries are a long way from benefitting from an increased demand in tourism. Until populations are effectively inoculated countries are not in a position to open borders to tourists. The Australian government, for instance, has stated that Australia's borders may not be open to international traffic until the second half of 2022 (Whitley and Scott, 2021).

The absence of tourism for the foreseeable future is not the only significant stress factor confronting ASEAN nations. Recovery in the developed nations is largely supply-driven rather than demand-driven. In this sense, a trade recovery is likely to be confined by a paucity of international as opposed to domestic demand. The International Monetary Fund has predicted growth in the global economy based on the premise that vaccination rollouts will lead recovery (IMF, 2021). However, the IMF also cautions that tourism-dependent countries with slower vaccine rollouts are likely to emerge more slowly from economic doldrums.

Moving forward, what does the future hold for ASEAN?

Worst-case scenario

The best case for ASEAN recovery from the global pandemic is easily outlined. It would involve steady supply and uptake of vaccines worldwide, with ASEAN countries at the forefront of inoculation efforts. In turn, widespread vaccination as well as maintenance of appropriate safety measures (for instance the wearing of face masks) could permit something like a return to normal cross-border interaction. The worst case, however, bears more careful analysis and foresight is advisable when considering appropriate responses to crises of any description.

A worst case assumes that ASEAN nations as a whole are unable to organize effective vaccine rollout and the pandemic continues to impose a very considerable burden on the health services and economies of different countries. According to Dezan Shira and Associates (2021), Brunei had sourced enough supplies to cover 50% of the population. Cambodia was expecting to import vaccines from both China and Russia. Indonesia had administered over nine million doses of vaccine. Laos had been trialling the Russian Sputnik V vaccine and was also in discussions with China about acquiring supplies. Malaysia had signed a deal with Pfizer to acquire 12.8 million doses. Myanmar was seeking assistance from the Gavi and Covax programmes to acquire vaccines. The government aimed to treat 20% of the 'most at risk' in the country with vaccines. However, the government was struggling economically and logistically and with the effects of US sanctions. The Philippines aimed to inoculate 25% of its population during 2021. Singapore aimed to give all adults a least one dose of vaccine by August 2021 (Sim, 2021). Thailand planned to inoculate 13 million people (in a population of 69 million) from the middle of 2021. Vietnam's had signed an agreement with Medigen Vaccine, a Taiwan-based vaccine company to secure the supply of three million to ten million COVID-19 vaccine doses in 2021. Vietnam is also working on producing its own vaccine.

The figures on inoculation rollout in ASEAN countries speak for themselves. Given that the total population of ASEAN countries is over 665 million people it can be seen that the slow-moving pace of inoculation throughout ASEAN countries (with the exception of Singapore) is more likely to lead to a worst-case rather than best-case outcome. This fact in turn points to problem of interconnectedness. Health and economic recovery in jurisdictions are interconnected. One jurisdiction cannot open its borders to another jurisdiction if the latter has not contained the spread of the COVID-19 virus. To do so would invite renewed outbreaks in the first jurisdiction. Thus until all ASEAN countries – and the countries with which they trade and co-operate – inoculate their populations against the COVID-19 virus it is predictable that the interconnection necessary for productive trade and commerce will be stymied.

Thus a worst-case can be readily identified: ASEAN countries (with the exception of Singapore) fail collectively to inoculate their populations for the foreseeable future, meaning that they are unable to resume output, trade, and tourism in the same way (or to the same degree) as pertained before the outbreak of the pandemic. In this weakened state, they may also be ineffectual in responding to a security crisis that might erupt proximate to one or more ASEAN nations. Specifically, if a dispute arose between the United States and China and/or North Korea, the ASEAN states might find themselves in the position of helpless bystanders (*The Economist*, 2020).

The likely future case

Extreme prognostications are not usually vindicated by subsequent events. The effluxion of time creates its own normative logic which renders predictions only partly true. In the case of ASEAN and its relations with the rest of the world it is probably unlikely that in the near future China will invade Taiwan or North Korea loose atomic weapons. It is also unlikely that ASEAN nations will fail to inoculate, over time, at least a majority of their populations. But so far as recovery and flourishing are concerned, time may be of the essence (Reuters, 2021). The longer that nations take to effectively implement vaccination programmes the longer that a normativity based on flourishing international trade can be established. The longer that ASEAN countries are unable to welcome tourists the more distant they will become from economic certitudes that prevailed in the past. The likely case, then, is a slow and patchy recovery underpinned by gradual vaccination of populations (Goh, 2021). From a policy perspective, while countries in the region will need to work together in a coordinated manner, however, the unique dynamics of individual natures dictate that the paths travelled will be particularly different. For example, in Singapore, as the leading developed nation in ASEAN, its vaccine roll-out is such that things may return to levels of normality sooner that the likes of Malaysia or Indonesia. Nonetheless, it is important countries work to find the right balance between addressing both the healthcare and economic necessities of the pandemic. Moving forward, one would also expect to see a continuation of high-level meetings, joint declarations, and commitments. However, in specific terms, what can be done to maximize the recovery efforts?

How can the ASEAN region engender maximal recovery?

In 2020, the ASEAN Secretariat published a 'Comprehensive Recovery Framework' (CRF), which outlined five broad recovery strategies. These were: enhancing health systems, strengthening human security, maximizing the potential of the intra-ASEAN market and broader economic integration, accelerating inclusive digital transformation, and advancing towards a more sustainable and resilient future (ASEAN Secretariat, 2020a). The document placed in perspective the relative virulence of the pandemic in ASEAN countries.

The CRF charts the significant downturn in ASEAN's in trade in raw and intermediate goods (32% of total ASEAN trade): '[b]y end of first semester 2020, based on preliminary data, ASEAN's trade fell by 12.4% and FDI inflows by 32.9% compared to the previous year'. The CRF explained that amelioration/recovery measures fell into three broad categories: fiscal stimulus packages; monetary policy and financial measures; and sector-specific measures and interventions. The CRF announced a combined USD 397.4 billion stimulus by September 2020 or 12.5% of the region's 2019 GDP (ASEAN Secretariat, 2020a, p. 13). A key issue facing the region is the high level of economic and social interconnectedness that exists across ASEAN. Such a situation means that COVID-19 recovery cannot be pursued and contained within national boundaries. The region can only truly recover once all economies are able to overcome the virus and mitigate its socioeconomic impact.

Published before general rollout of vaccine programmes, the CDF is largely rhetorical in content, outlining ways for ASEAN nations to act and co-operate in virus suppression and enhancing trading relations. Once rhetoric is put to one side it can be seen to make a number of key assertions. Firstly, ASEAN is now at an inflexion point, unless the region is fully immune to the disease to blunt the transmission, the economy and the social fabric that holds it together will be seriously undermined until such a time that a vaccine is rolled out. Secondly, the post-pandemic recovery will not be a return to business as usual for ASEAN. Since COVID-19 has irreversibly transformed economies and societies in the region, equally transformative responses are needed. This means that there can be no going back to the old way of doing things. As such, the next steps for the ASEAN region should be to review the development of post-2025 vision, in a manner that would make the integration outcomes not only better in the future but also more inclusive and resilient. For this to happen, it is important that all ASEAN members continue to uphold the core principle of open regionalism (ASEAN Secretariat, 2020a).

As ASEAN lies at an inflexion point, how effectively it will respond to that inflection point is moot. The vaccine rollout in 2021 has clarified what seemed less clear in 2020, which is that vaccination offers the only reliable method – at least in the next few years – to suppress the COVID-19 virus and enable countries to resume trade and tourist links at levels comparable to those in 2019. At present, ASEAN, with a population of 665 million people, is lagging in its rate of inoculation, and sluggishness in vaccination rates predicts prolonged economic and social uncertainty and enervation (*Financial Times* Editorial Board, 2021). To a large extent, laggardness is explained by a limited supply of vaccines as the United States, United Kingdom, and Economic Union prioritize vaccine delivery to their own populations. This is not to say that ASEAN cannot better implement policy identified in the CDF, chiefly the encouragement of intra-regional trade, albeit that political volatility in some jurisdictions makes meaningful trade difficult.

One potentially important way for ASEAN to successfully negotiate the pitfalls of vaccine delivery is for those member states, namely Singapore and Brunei, that have most successfully implemented vaccination programmes, to offer expert advice to other ASEAN nations on procurement and programme-design-and-implementation. Singapore in particular has proved especially effective in procuring supplies of the Pfizer vaccine and rolling out delivery in an efficient phased way. The Singapore government has encouraged citizens and foreign nationals to register for vaccines and provided well-organized vaccination hubs to process vaccinations. By late May 2021, 26% of the population had been fully vaccinated and 35% had received one vaccination dose. If rollout continues at the current pace, about 75% of the population will have been fully vaccinated by year's end (Ministry of Health Singapore). Singapore is therefore an exemplar within ASEAN of efficient vaccine procurement and rollout (Pazos, R. and Adeline, S., 2021). It could provide invaluable advice to other ASEAN nations about effective virus suppression.

In addition to the management of the vaccine rollout is the important role that trade can play in driving economic development. The highly bureaucratic nature of many ASEAN economies must change moving forward. Greater transparency in policymaking, improved customs procedures, export and import documentation, and the freeing up of trade in general as well will make it easy for important new overseas foreign direct investment opportunities.

Such developments will encourage countries like the US and China to make stronger commitments in the region. These investments would lead to the creation of not only new jobs but also a strong signal to the rest of the world that the ASEAN region has a fresh perspective and is open for business for again.

Conclusion

The COVID-19 pandemic has, as discussed, adversely affected the societies and economies of the ASEAN countries. The effect of economic contraction in 2020 is expected to be mitigated by some demand-based rebound growth in 2021 but the severity of the COVID-19-induced downturn, compounded by political turmoil in some member countries, predicts very unsettled socioeconomic conditions for at least the near future. The slow and variable pace of vaccine rollout in most ASEAN countries suggests that a swift return to pre-COVID normalcy is unlikely. As is the case in other parts of the world, trade underpins economic recovery but the corollary of disrupted economies and societies is disrupted trade, the consequence of which is more and continued social disruption. Political uncertainty in several ASEAN countries is another disruptive factor, the effect of which is uncertain. ASEAN is a trade-based organization and the logic of trade is to break down barriers obstructing the flow of goods and services – and people. COVID-19 creates barriers to trade circumscribing the flow of goods, services, and people. ASEAN is therefore certainly at an inflexion point (Balakrishnan, 2020). Effective vaccine rollout in ASEAN countries (and countries around the world) is a precondition for return to productive trading relations. ASEAN countries need to respond to the inflexion point by continuing to co-operate politically to ensure effective vaccine rollout and normalize trade relations.

Notes

1 JCU Singapore Business School, JCU Singapore, Singapore, and Department of International Trade, Chungnam National University, Daejeon, South Korea.
2 Corresponding author: JCU Singapore Business School, JCU Singapore, Singapore. Email: Haejin.jang@jcu.edu.au.
3 JCU Singapore Business School, JCU Singapore, Singapore.
4 ASEAN member nations include: Brunei, Cambodia, Indonesia, Laos, Malaysia, Myanmar, the Philippines, Singapore, Thailand, and Vietnam.
5 The intelligence alliance comprises Australia, Canada, New Zealand, the United Kingdom, and the United States.

References

ASEAN Secretariat (2020a). *ASEAN Comprehensive Recovery Framework*. The ASEAN Secretariat Community Relations Division (CRD), Jakarta. https://asean.org/storage/ASEAN-Comprehensive-Recovery-Framework_Pub_2020_1.pdf

ASEAN Secretariat (2020b). *ASEAN Rapid Assessment: The Impact of COVID-19 on Livelihoods across ASEAN*. Jakarta. https://asean.org/storage/ASEAN-Rapid-Assessment_Final-23112020.pdf

Asian Development Bank (2021). *Latest Publications on Covid-19.* https://www.adb.org/publications/spotlight.

Balakrishnan, V. (June 22 2020). *Remarks by Minister for Foreign Affairs Dr Vivian Balakrishnan on 'Diplomacy in a Post-COVID-19 World'*, https://www.mfa.gov.sg/Newsroom/Press-Statements-Transcripts-and-Photos/2020/06/20200622---MFATownHall

Baldwin, R. (2012). *WTO 2.0: Global Governance of Supply-Chain Trade.* CEPR Policy Insight No. 64. London: London Center for Economic Policy Research.

Brookings (2021). *Southeast Asia's Post-pandemic Recovery Outlook.* https://www.brookings.edu/blog/order-from-chaos/2021/03/15/southeast-asias-post-pandemic-recovery-outlook/

Chandra, A. C., Mujahid, I. and Mahyassari, R. K. (2020). Trade measures in the time of COVID-19: The case of ASEAN. *ASEAN Policy Brief. No 3*, 1–12.

Cheong, I. and Tongzon, J. (2018). The economic impact of a rise in US trade protectionism on East Asia. *Journal of Korea Trade, 22*(3), p. 265–279. https://doi.org/10.1108/JKT-03-2018-0025

Chin, J. (2021). Malaysian politics is going through a midlife crisis. *Channel News Asia Commentary.* https://www.channelnewsasia.com/news/commentary/commentary-malaysian-politics-is-going-through-a-midlife-crisis-13102196

De Wijlder, W. (n.d.). *Eurozone: Green Shoots of Recovery.* BNP Paribas. https://economic-research.bnpparibas.com/ecotvweek/en-US/Eurozone-green-shoots-recovery-4/2/2021,c35002

Dezan Shira and Associates (May 25, 2021). *COVID-19 Vaccine Roll Outs in ASEAN & Asia.* https://www.aseanbriefing.com/news/covid-19-vaccine-roll-outs-in-asean-asia-live-updates-by-country/

Financial Times Editorial Board (May 26 2021). *Asia is Lagging Behind on Vaccinations.* https://www.ft.com/content/ad835704-acfb-4501-b676-5f549ef7496c

Goh, Puay Yeong (June 17, 2021). *Slow Vaccination Pace Weighs on Asia's Growth Recovery.* Neuberger Berman. https://www.nb.com/en/global/insights/nb-blog-slow-vaccination-pace-weighs-on-asia-growth-recovery

Heshmati, A., Kim, J. and Wood, J. (2019). A survey of inclusive growth policy. *Economies.* 7(3), 65, 1–18. https://doi.org/10.3390/economies7030065

International Labour Organization (ILO) (2020a). *As Job Losses Escalate, Nearly Half of Global Workforce at Risk of Losing Livelihoods.* https://www.ilo.org/global/about-the-ilo/newsroom/news/WCMS_743036/lang--en/index.htm

International Labour Organization (ILO) (2020b). *Contagion or Starvation, the Dilemma Facing Informal Workers during the COVID-19 Pandemic.* https://www.ilo.org/global/about-the-ilo/newsroom/news/WCMS_744005/lang--en/index.htm

International Monetary Fund (IMF) (2021). *World Economic Outlook, April 2021: Managing Divergent Recoveries.* https://www.imf.org/en/Publications/WEO

Kim, J.-S. and Wood, J. (2020). Service sector development in Asia: An important instrument of growth. *Asia-Pacific Economic Literature. 34*(1), 12–15.

OECD (2020). *COVID-19 in Emerging Asia: Regional Socio-economic Implications and Policy Priorities.* https://www.oecd.org/coronavirus/policy-responses/covid-19-in-emerging-asia-regional-socio-economic-implications-and-policy-priorities-da08f00f/

Park, D. and Shin, K. (2012). *The Service Sector in Asia: Is It an Engine of Growth?* ADB Economics Working Paper Series, No. 322. Asian Development Bank (ADB), Manila.

Pazos, R and Adeline S (August 8, 2021). Singapore aims to vaccinate 2 in 3 residents against Covid-19 by National Day: Are we on track? *The Straits Times.* https://www

.straitstimes.com/multimedia/graphics/2021/06/singapore-covid-vaccination-tracker/index.html?shell.

Reuters (5 May 2021). *U.S. Trade Chief Tai Says 'Time is of the Essence' in Addressing Vaccine Waiver at WTO.* https://www.reuters.com/business/healthcare-pharmaceuticals/us-trade-chief-tai-says-time-essence-addresssing-vaccine-waiver-wto-2021-05-05/

Sally, R. (2004). *Southeast Asia in the WTO.* ISEAS Publishing. https://doi.org/10.1355/9789812307019

Sim, D. (May 18, 2021). *Singapore Ramps Up Vaccination Drive to Give All Adults One Covid-19 Shot by Early August.* https://www.scmp.com/week-asia/health-environment/article/3133930/singapore-ramps-vaccination-drive-give-all-adults-one

Sumner, A., Hoy, C. and Ortiz-Juarez, E (2020). *Precarity and the Pandemic: COVID-19 and Poverty Incidence, Intensity, and Severity in Developing Countries.* WIDER Working Paper 2020/77. Helsinki: UNU Wider.

Teoh, S (March 3, 2021). *Malaysian Government Criticised for 'Draconian' Use of Emergency Powers to Outlaw Fake News.* The Straits Times Whitley, A. and Scott, J. (May 7, 2021). *Australia May Not Open Border Until Late 2022, Minister Says.* https://www.bloomberg.com/news/articles/2021-05-06/australia-s-borders-may-not-open-until-late-2022-minister-says

The Economist (17 November 2020). South-East Asian countries are trapped between two superpowers. https://www.economist.com/the-world-ahead/2020/11/17/south-east-asian-countries-are-trapped-between-two-superpowers

Wood, J. (2017). An industrial sector analysis of the factors effecting FTA negotiation outcomes. *Global Business Review. 18*(4), 1–16.

Wood, J. and Jang, H. (2017). Brexit: The economic and political implications for Asia. *Social Sciences. 6*(41), 1–11.

Wood, J. and Wu, J. (2020). The sustainability of the WTO dispute settlement system: Does it work for developing countries? *The Journal of World Trade. 54*(4), 531–566.

Wood, J. Wu, J. Li, Y. and Jang, H. (2017a). The economic impact of SPS measures on agricultural exports to China: An empirical analysis using the PPML method. *Social Sciences. 6*(51), 1–18.

Wood, J. Wu, J. Li, Y. and Kim, J. (2017b). TBT and SPS impacts on Korean exports to China: empirical analysis using the PPML method. *Asian-Pacific Economic Literature. 31*(2), 96–114.

Wood, J., Jang, H. and Oh, K. (2020a). The U.S.–China trade war: Is it more pain than gain? *Journal of China Studies. 23*, 61–85.

Wood, J., Wu, J. and Oh, K. (2020b). Do technical barriers to trade restrict exports? Evidence from South Korea. *Korea and the World Economy. 21*(2), 1–26.

Wood, J. Li, Y. and Wu, J. (2021). An analysis of the trends and determinants of intra-industry trade between China and Asia Pacific Economic Cooperation member countries. *The Singapore Economic Review. 66*(3), 743–766.

World Trade Organization (WTO) (2021). COVID-19: Measures affecting trade in goods. Retrieved online: https://www.wto.org/english/tratop_e/covid19_e/trade_related_goods_measure_e.htm

Appendix

Table A8.1 COVID-19: Measures affecting trade in goods (ASEAN-10 countries)

Country	*Measure*	*Status*
Cambodia	Temporary export ban on COVID-19 test kits.	Effective 30 March 2020
Indonesia	Temporary elimination of import certification requirements on imports of onions and garlic	Effective 18 March 2020 to 31 May 2020
	Temporary export ban on antiseptic, raw materials to fabricate masks, PPE, ethyl alcohol, and masks.	Effective 18 March 2020 to 30 June 2020
	Temporary elimination of import certification requirements on imports of certain products, masks, and PPE.	Effective 23 March 2020 to 30 June 2020
	Postponing the payment of excise duties on imports of certain goods.	Effective 9 April 2020
Malaysia	Temporary export ban on face masks.	Effective 20 March 2020
	Temporary elimination of import tariffs on face masks (effective 23 March 2020); on PPE, medical equipment and COVID-19 consumables (effective 23 March 2020); and on raw materials used for the production of hand sanitizers (effective 30 March 2020).	Effective: see individual dates in measure
Philippines	Temporary elimination of import tariffs on qualified manufacturers and suppliers of medicines, medical equipment and devices, PPEs, laboratory equipment and re-agents and their packaging, medical supplies, raw materials, COVID-19 testing kits.	Originally effective from 24 March 2020 to 23 May 2020. Amended on 11 September 2020.
	Temporary increase of import tariffs (from zero to 10%) on crude petroleum oil and refined petroleum products.	Implemented 2 May, stopped 25 June 2020
Thailand	Temporary export ban on surgical masks; face-masks for protection against dust, smoke, or toxic substances used for safety apparatus.	Effective 5 February 2020, for 1 year
	Temporary export ban on bird eggs of fowls of the species *Gallus Domesticus*.	26 March 2020 to 30 April 2020

(*Continued*)

Table A8.1 (Continued)

Country	*Measure*	*Status*
Vietnam	Temporary elimination of import taxes on medical and PPE used in the fight of COVID-19 pandemic.	Effective 7 February 2020
	Temporary export licensing requirements on face masks.	Effective 11 March 2020. Stopped 29 April 2020
	Temporary export ban on drugs used in the COVID-19 treatment.	Effective 15 April 2020. Stopped 5 May 2020
	Temporary elimination of import tariffs on non-woven fabrics for the PPE clothing used in the fight of COVID-19 pandemic.	Effective 27 March 2020
Singapore	Temporary relaxation of import licensing requirements for hand sanitizers, masks, thermometers, and protective gear.	Effective 31 January 2020
	Elimination of import tariffs and all other duties and charges on essential goods including medical, pharmaceutical products, and agricultural products; temporary elimination of tariff on samsu.	Effective 15 April 2020
Laos	Temporary elimination of import tariffs and other duties on medical devices and other products for prevention, control (e.g. masks, sanitizers, medical equipment).	No date given
Myanmar	Temporary restrictions of export of rice, to prevent critical shortage of rice which is an essential foodstuff in the national diet.	No date given
	Temporary elimination of import license fees on medicines and raw materials used in medicines.	Effective 11 April 2020
	Temporary reduction of demurrage charges for all imports and exports.	Effective 9 April 2020

Source: WTO (2021).

9 Trade network and global value chains

Akhmad Bayhaqi[1]

The views expressed in this article reflect the author's personal views and not those of any institution or organization.

Introduction

Trade has been an instrumental policy for economies to develop and expand their economic and business capacity. Globalization has brought opportunities for firms to grow faster and for economies to provide employment and welfare to their citizens.

The significance of trade to growth has long been highlighted. The percentage of global trade as a share of global gross domestic product (GDP) has indeed been rising significantly – to its highest peak in 2008, reaching more than 60% of the global GDP (Figure 9.1). The ratios of trade to GDP between high-income and low-/middle- income economies have shown a significant gap that could indicate that high-income economies are more open to trade compared with their lower-/middle- income counterparts. Dollar and Kraay (2001) use the ratio of trade to GDP to classify economies as 'globalizers': those group of economies that increased their trade share to GDP – from 16% of GDP to 33% of GDP – and managed to catch up with the rich economies while the rest of the developing world was falling behind.

Economies trade for a variety of reasons, some economic, some political, and some cultural. Using bilateral trade flows as the basic unit of analysis, this chapter applies centrality measures to trade networks. Gravity models are often used in analyzing bilateral trade in economics and they have been cited in thousands of research papers and journal articles (Shepherd et. al., 2019). Thus, a social network analysis will expand the applicability and insights of such analysis, which is not currently considered mainstream in trade analysis.

Hilgerdt (1943) may have applied network analysis to international trade for the first time. In a more recent study, De Benedictis and Tajoli (2011) argue that network analysis is done to visualize an economy's relationship with other economies rather than to analyze their individual characteristics. The gravity model, on the other hand, assumes that the size of the economy (GDP) affects

DOI: 10.4324/9781003153580-9

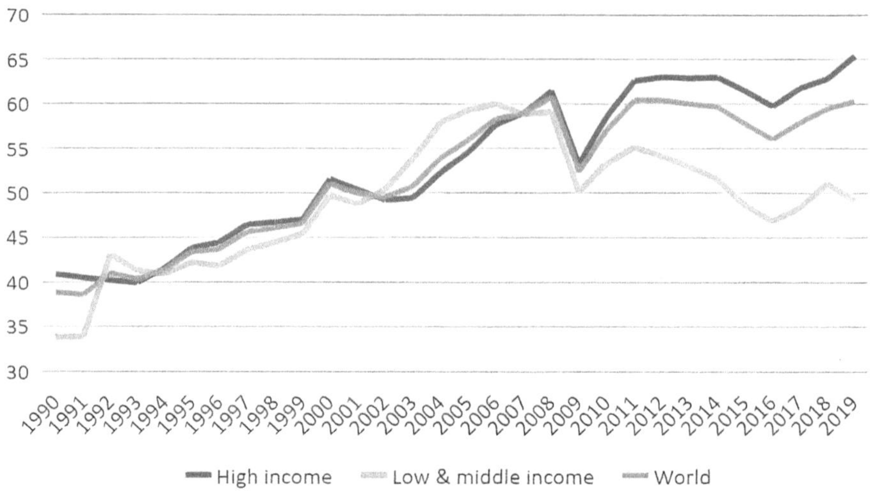

Figure 9.1 Global trade as a percentage of GDP, 1990–2019. Source: calculated by author using data from https://data.worldbank.org/.

trade relations. In their study, De Benedictis and Tajoli (2011) analyzed the structural properties of trade networks using the centrality measures as well. In this chapter, we will examine global bilateral trade networks using (social) network analysis. The purpose is to provide a practical and exploratory analysis of centrality using STATA and Gephi software. In addition, we will discuss the potential role of connectivity in resilience and development. This chapter also illustrates the process of 'catching up' in the stages of import, production, and export under a flying geese pattern framework.

This chapter is organized as follows. After a literature review of global value chains, a brief analysis of global trade and growth follows. We will then explain and analyze several centrality measures. After that, several discussions are included regarding connectedness and how it relates to the tropics, development, and resilience; this section ends with a concluding statement.

Literature review: the rise of global value chains

Global value chains (GVCs), a network of connected firms forming a hub and spoke network of production and distribution, have flourished forming new economic centres across the globe, particularly in Asia (Baldwin 2012; Baldwin and Lopez-Gonzalez 2013).

Global value chains have been supporting global growth and businesses for a number of decades. The term 'Factory Asia' has a long history which started with the East Asian Miracle report published by the World Bank in 1993. Leipziger and Thomas (1997) quoted in Quibria (2002) highlighted three attributes of the miracle: outward orientation, macroeconomic stability, and investment in people. The emerging East Asian economies in the 1990s also indicated strong growth supported by productivity and abundant labour, particularly in manufacturing. Factory Asia represents an extensive regional production network with Korea and Japan as major outsourcing economies, and China and Southeast Asian economies as assemblers of parts and components into final products (Choi and Rhee, 2014).

In 1990, Asia produced 26.5% of global manufacturing output, steadily increasing to 46.5% by 2013. At the same time, trade in intermediate goods increased from 14% in 2000 to 50% in 2012.[2] The flourishing of global trade has opened opportunities for manufacturing firms (both large and small), workers, logistics businesses, as well as governments in opening up their economies to foreign investment. Consumers also benefited by having more options and being given a more competitive price for the products they needed to purchase.

The successful negotiation for the WTO (World Trade Organization) Trade Facilitation Agreement has further supported and facilitated the global operation of supply chain and production networks. Governments are improving their customs operation by going paperless and digital, strengthening structural reform efforts, and improving regulatory reforms. Successful bilateral trade agreements have also been negotiated, covering issues such as non-tariff barriers, investment facilitation, and competition.[3] A study has also suggested that 'deeper' trade agreements help to facilitate access and integration of firms into global value chains and high-value added industries.[4] Business hubs are emerging across Asia and the developing economies with global flows shifting toward Asia on seven dimensions: trade, capital, people, knowledge, transport, culture, and resources.[5]

This economic network phenomenon is actually not new, as a similar framework was coined in the 1930s by Akamatsu (1962) using the term 'flying geese pattern' of economic development. Akamatsu's flying geese model illustrates the process of 'catching up' in the following stages of import, domestic production, and export:

(1) Stage one: manufactured goods are imported from developed economies in return for export from less-advanced economies. This process starts the process of labour transformation or movement to export-oriented industries.
(2) Stage two: domestic production of previously imported goods starts to develop, entailing the import of capital goods. The key prerequisite in this stage is that the domestic industry must be competitive enough (to have the same quality and price) to compete with the imported products.
(3) Stage three: as the domestic industry becomes more competitive and has fully captured the domestic market, it starts to expand to the export market to further exploit the economies of scale opportunities.

Akamatsu's model brings forward the importance of trade networks for emerging economies to attain the developmental status of advanced economies which was later confirmed by the Dollar and Kraay study. Additionally, Ozawa (2006) emphasized the importance of the catching-up concept of the flying geese model for economies to first capitalize their abundant asset of unskilled labour in developing labour-intensive manufacturing for export at the beginning of their development path. Ozawa also suggested the sequencing of industrial upgrading (Figure 9.2).

Global trade and growth

In recent years, though, some have observed some degree of 'disentanglement' between global trade and growth – particularly after the Global Financial Crisis of 2008/09. While the growth of global GDP and imports generally move in the same direction (Figure 9.3), during the recession global trade seemed to be much

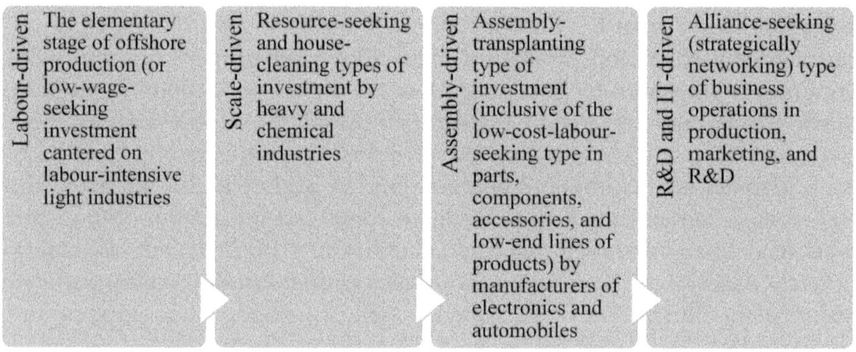

Figure 9.2 Evolutionary sequence of industrial upgrading. Source: Adapted from Ozawa (2006).

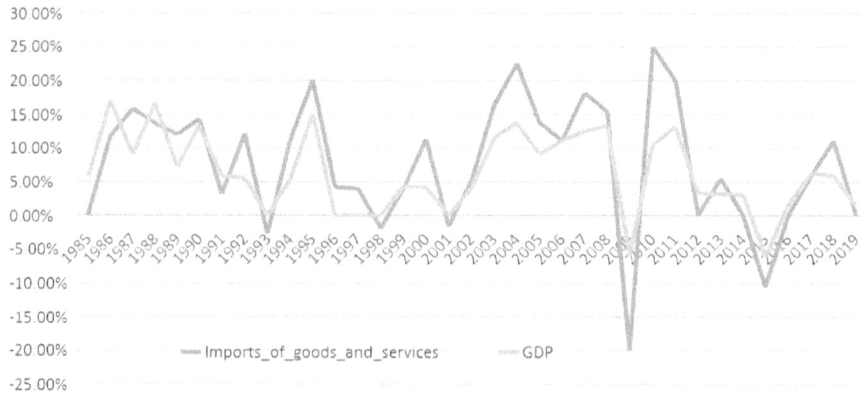

Figure 9.3 Global GDP and Import Growth. Source: calculated by author using data from https://data.worldbank.org/.

more severely affected compared with global GDP. During the Great Recession, the decline in trade (20%) was much more pronounced than the decline in global output (6%). Subsequently, trade recovered and grew at over 12% in 2010, well above global GDP growth. The 2008/09 crisis and subsequent rebound between 2009 and 2011 were marked by significant changes in trade relative to GDP pattern (Table 9.1). For 2012–2016, the yearly average of trade elasticity fell to less than 1 (inelastic). Possible factors determining the global trade elasticities may include cyclical factors and shifts in demand composition, particularly weaker business investment. Structural factors such as weaker global value chain trade may have a more lasting impact on trade-to-income elasticity (ECB, 2014).

GVC trade rose significantly starting in the 1990s and reached its peak of 61% in 2008 and has been somewhat stagnated ever since (Figure 9.4). Lamy (2013) noted the following:[6]

> Twenty years ago, 60% of world trade was between developed countries (North–North), 30% was between developed and developing countries (North–South) and 10% was South–South. By 2020, we are expecting it to be split equally three ways, so the relative weight of North–North trade will have been halved in just 30 years or so. Interestingly, almost 60% of trade in goods is now in intermediates, i.e. goods used as inputs in the production process.

Analysis of the trade network

The earlier discussion has highlighted how trade is now dominated by GVC trade, in which several emerging economies such as China and Vietnam have been actively participating in global trade and hold significant positions in the trade network.

This section will try to apply the social network analysis to analyze the pattern of bilateral trade among economies. The objective here is to provide a

Table 9.1 Income elasticity of global trade (ratios of global trade to output growth)

Period	*Ratio**	*Trade Variable*	*Output Variable*	*Notes*
1982–1986	1.13 (1.38)	Average growth rate of imports of goods and services (constant 2010 USD)	Average growth rate of GDP (constant 2010 USD)	Aggregate values. Based on averages from annual growth data.
1987–1991	1.80 (1.17)			
1992–1996	2.36 (1.53)			
1997–2001	2.13 (1.13)			
2002–2006	2.02 (1.42)			
2007–2011	1.47 (1.61)			
2012–2016	0.99 (1.25)			
2017–2019	1.37 (0.94)			

Note: * The number in brackets is trade elasticity ratio obtained from fixed-effect regression, using the following equation: Ln (Import) = a * Ln (GDP); with a=trade elasticity to income; using panel data at an individual economy level. Similar equation was adopted by Houthakker, Hendrik and Magee, Stephen P., (1969).

Source: calculated by author using data from https://data.worldbank.org/

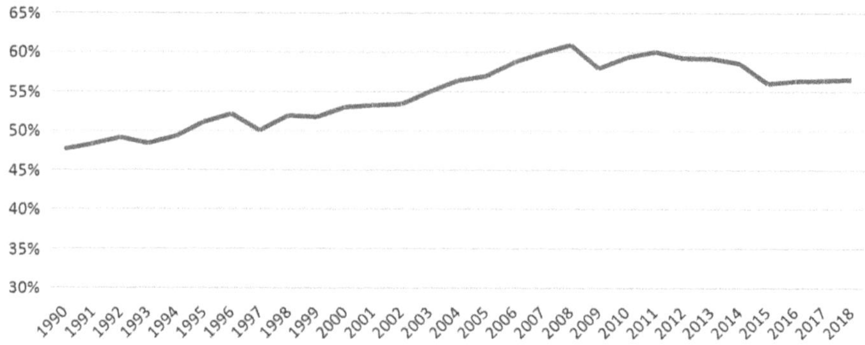

Figure 9.4 Trade in intermediate goods: GVC participation rate, 1990–2018. Source: calculated by author using data from https://worldmrio.com/unctadgvc/.

practical and exploratory analysis using the common centrality measures provided by the network analysis using STATA and Gephi software. We will start first by discussing the concept of 'centrality' as commonly understood by Social Network Analysis. Following this, the chapter will use bilateral trade data to yield several centrality measures and the relevant economic analysis. Discussions on how centrality or connectedness is linked with development and resilience will also be conducted followed by a conclusion section.

Centrality

The concept of centrality holds an important meaning in (social) network analysis. Holding a 'central' position holds several benefits such as being able to control and understand the flow of information; a position of centrality may determine urban patterns and centrality may affect the pattern of diffusion of technological innovation (see Freeman (1979) and Krackhardt (1990)).

Bilateral trade network involves not only the flows of goods and services but also flows of information and business relations reflecting numerous micro-decisions and considerations among the actors involved in the network. GVCs relations may encourage knowledge, productivity, skills transfer, or spillovers benefiting domestic firms; these spillovers may also benefit marginal groups World Bank (2019).

The three most common measures of centrality could be best described using the kite structure in Figure 9.5 as adopted by Krackhardt (1990). The focus is more on having a pragmatic understanding of the concept of centrality rather than embracing the technical concept. A more formal and technical definition for these measures of centrality is discussed in Hage and Harary (1996).

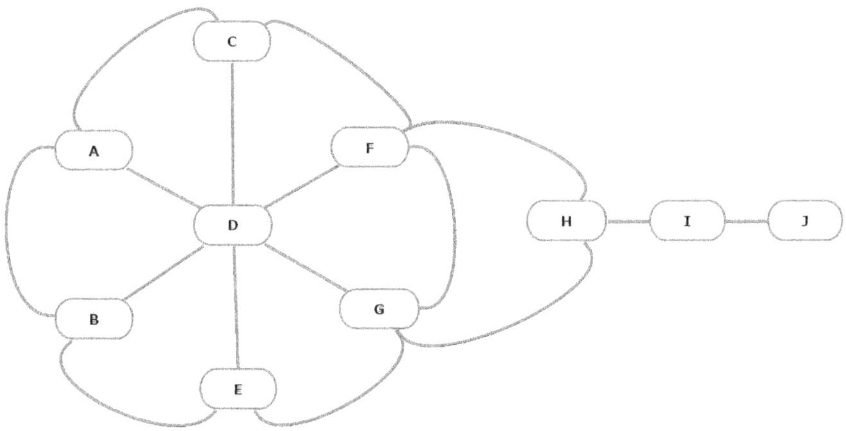

Figure 9.5 Kite Network Structure. Source: Adapted from Figure 2 in Krackhardt (1990).

Degree centrality

Degree centrality is the most straightforward definition of centrality. Basically, a point (such as point D) is the most 'central' in the network since it has the most number of links (six edges) connected to itself, basically the more connections you have the better or the more popular you can be. It is basically the number of 'edges' being connected to a 'node', or the number of ties a node has. The more 'edges' a 'node' has, the more centralized the node is.

Betweenness centrality

While point D has the highest number of connections than point H, point H is the 'key bridge' that connects point I and J to the rest of the nodes, thus controlling the flow of information between the two clusters. In this sense, point H is the central node in the network and holds a powerful position. Formally, 'the betweenness centrality of a node is defined as the number of shortest paths among all other nodes that pass through this node' (Grund, 2015). Hage and Harary (1996) labelled betweenness centrality as an index of the 'potential for control of communication'.

Closeness centrality

Closeness centrality defines centrality by the optimum efficiency in relaying messages to the whole network: a point that has shorter distances to the rest of the nodes. The centrality position allows shorter times and lower costs in performing the transmission (Freeman 1979). Grund (2015) explained that: 'Nodes with high closeness centrality are close to all other nodes, that is, they can reach all other nodes in only a few steps'. In Figure 9.5, point F and G have the highest level of closeness centrality.

Eigenvector centrality

Eigenvector centrality measures the level of influence of a node within a network in which connections to high-scoring nodes will increase the influence of a particular node compared to connections to low-scoring nodes.[7] A common example of the application of eigenvector centrality concept is the web page-rank system.

Visualization of the trade network

There are several pieces of software that could perform the above centrality measures like STATA (NWcommands), Pajek,[8] and Gephi. Gephi has the most friendly interface and platform in visualizing networks while STATA seems to have the most powerful computing power in handling large datasets. In the next sections, we will be using Gephi software for simplicity of purpose in conducting our analysis.

Data source for network analysis

The data used in the network analysis is the 2019 bilateral trade data (export) which were downloaded from the UN Comtrade Database (https://comtrade.un.org/). The data is collected at the total export level as well as at the product categories' level to obtain the intermediate (global value chain) trade data. The calculation of intermediate trade is based on the Broad Economic Categories (BEC) classification which includes the following goods as specified in Table 9.2. The total of bilateral trade pairs (or 'edges') being used in the analysis are 20,261 (for gross export values) and 17,939 (for intermediate goods trade). The centrality measures being calculated in this paper do not take the value of trade into consideration (non-weighted).

Table 9.2 Intermediate goods based on BEC classification

BEC code	*Category of goods*
111*	Food and beverages, primary, mainly for industry
121*	Food and beverages, processed, mainly for industry
21*	Industrial supplies not elsewhere specified, primary
22*	Industrial supplies not elsewhere specified, processed
31*	Fuels and lubricants, primary
322*	Fuels and lubricants, processed (other than motor spirit)
42*	Parts and accessories of capital goods (except transport equipment)
53*	Parts and accessories of transport equipment

Source: https://unstats.un.org/unsd/tradekb/Knowledgebase/50090/Intermediate-Goods-in-Trade-Statistics

Analysis of the trade network using export and intermediate trade data

The concept of 'centrality' described earlier highlighted how a 'central' position of certain actors (or economies in our case) are being measured. Being central means that an economy holds the 'hub' position in the trade network in a way that an economy has a higher number of (bilateral trade) connections, being often used as transit points in trade routes, or to have shorter trade paths with other economies. In this context, being 'central' means being 'connected'.[9] In the remainder of this paper, we will try to explore the relationship of how having a more connected, or a more 'central' position within trade networks will impact an economy's development and resiliency level.

Using Gephi software (available free at https://gephi.org/), simplified global trade network charts are presented in Figure 9.6 using trade and intermediate trade data for 2019. The Gephi software is also able to calculate the centrality measures as mentioned in the earlier section. To allow for simpler visualization, only 19 Asia-Pacific Economic Cooperation (APEC) member economies are displayed in Figure 9.6. APEC membership allows a good combination of developed and developing economies as well including several major trading and manufacturing hubs.

Please note that there is not any single visualization image of network analysis. Using Gephi, you could end up with unlimited numbers of visualizations using the same data set. This is the reason analysis using network visualization is categorized as exploratory data analysis. Venturini et al. (2019) argued that 'the very ambiguity that makes graph drawings unfit for hypothesis confirmation, makes them extremely useful for exploratory data analysis'.

The two charts in figure 9.6 showed similar network structure, in which there are two major hubs: China and the United States. The USA seems to be closely connected with their key neighbouring trading partners: Canada and Mexico. Meanwhile China has become the central hub for most of the remaining economies, in particular with Hong Kong, Korea, and Malaysia. Japan seems to be closer to the USA than to China in both of the trade networks.

Using three centrality measures calculated using STATA (closeness centrality, betweenness centrality, and eigen centrality), the economies are ranked, and the top 20 economies are provided in Appendix A9.1 and A9.2 (for both the bilateral trade based on gross exports and intermediate/GVC trades). The centrality measures based on gross export data covering well-known economic and trade hubs such as the Netherlands, the USA, Germany, the UK, and France in the top ten. Other emerging economies like Thailand, India, Brazil, and China also appear in the top ten list. The three measures of centrality correlated rather strongly, with correlation scores ranging from 0.7 to 0.9 (Table 9.3).

The descriptive statistics for the centrality measures based on the export network data are provided in Table 9.4 and the histograms in Figure 9.7. Based on the histograms it is apparent that the three measures of centrality have a different skewness or distribution. For instance, for betweenness centrality,

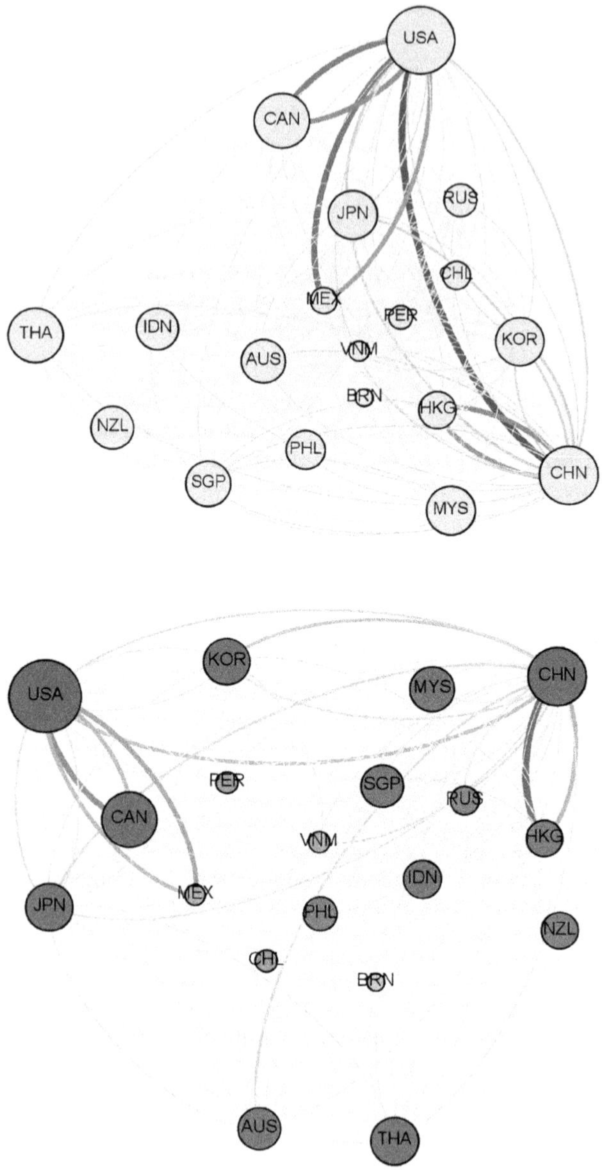

Figure 9.6 Trade network for 19 APEC economies, 2019. Source: Drawn using Gephi software. Note: the economies included in the figure are: Australia (AUS); Brunei (BRN); Canada (CAN); China (CHN); Chile (CHL); Hong Kong, China (HKG); Indonesia (IDN); Japan (JPN); Korea (KOR), Malaysia (MYS); Mexico (MEX); New Zealand (NZL); Peru (PER); Philippines (PHL); Russia (RUS); Singapore (SGP); Thailand (THA); United States (USA); Vietnam (VNM). Notes: The sizes of circle reflects the betweenness centrality scored; the color shades reflect closeness centrality; the color and density of edges (lines) reflect trade flows (export values). The upper chart is constructed using export data, while the lower chart is using intermediate (GVC) export data.

Table 9.3 Matrix of correlations between centrality measures, trade networks, 2019

Variables	*-1*	*-2*	*-3*	*-4*	*-5*	*-6*
(1) between (export)	1					
(2) closeness (export)	0.878	1				
(3) eigenvector (export)	0.711	0.946	1			
(4) between (gvc)	0.983	0.823	0.653	1		
(5) closeness (gvc)	0.908	0.99	0.915	0.865	1	
(6) evcent (gvc)	0.747	0.957	0.991	0.694	0.943	1

Source: calculated by author using STATA.

Table 9.4 Descriptive statistics for centrality measures, export network, 2019

	N	*Mean*	*Std. Dev.*	*min*	*max*	*Median*	*p75*
between	231	47.797	79.409	0	372.724	8.737	54.568
closeness	231	.705	.139	.511	.996	.659	.807
evcent	231	.615	.278	0	1	.606	.881

Source: calculated by author using STATA.

74% of nodes have a value below 46.6. While for closeness centrality, 59% of observations have a value below 0.7. Lastly, 22% of nodes have a value of eigen-centrality (normalized) above 0.9.

Using intermediate trade data, similar results were obtained, with correlations between the two data sets for the same centrality measures ranging around 0.9. A quick comparison using gross export values in 1995 (see Appendix A9.3), the list of top economies are rather similar, with the exception of Japan and Denmark being part of the top ten economies in terms of centrality measures. As export trade data tend to be more reliable than intermediate trade data, we will be using export data to calculate the centrality measures in the following sections.

Connectedness in the tropics

Some economies in the tropics are among the top 20 economies with high scores on connectedness measures. One would notice economies like India, Brazil, Thailand, Singapore, and Malaysia consistently have high scores for the centrality measures. The top 20 tropical economies (based on betweenness centrality scores) are listed in Table 9.5. Seven of these tropical economies are members of APEC. A few tropical economies ranked quite high for closeness and eigen-centrality values, like Thailand, India, and Brazil.

Streeten (1972, p.78) noted that 'Perhaps the most striking fact is that most underdeveloped countries lie in the tropical and semi-tropical zones, between the Tropic of Cancer and Tropic of Capricorn'. Additionally, Sachs (2000) in

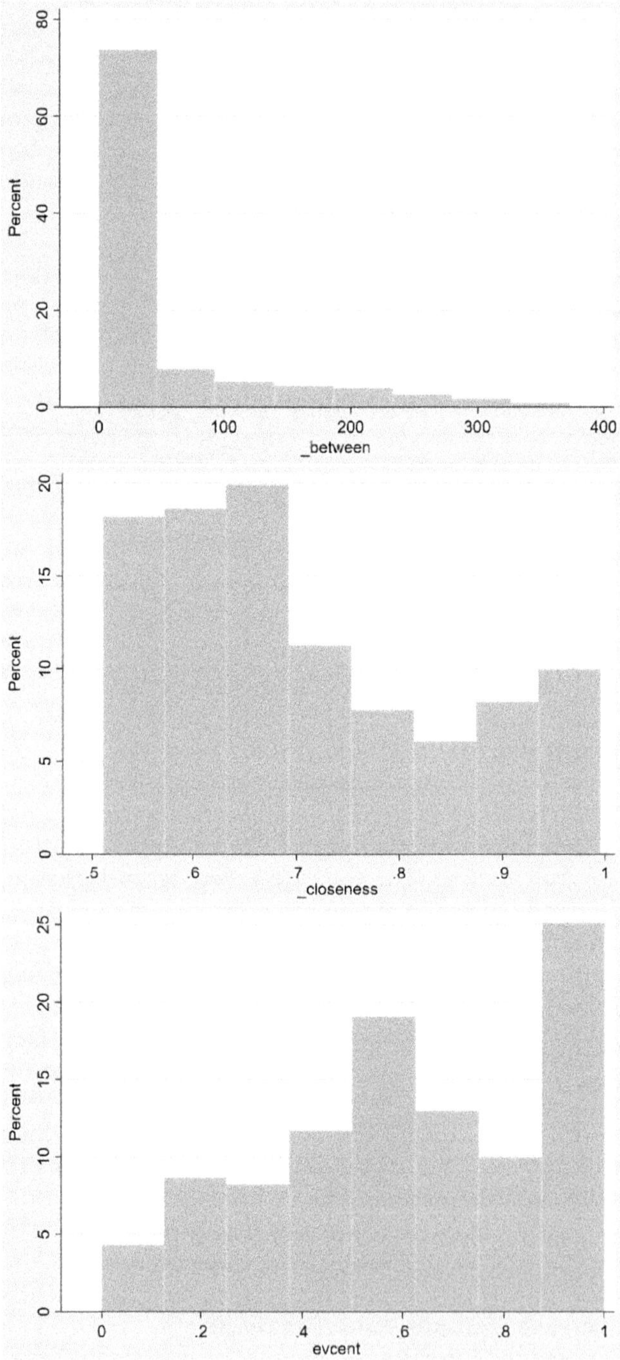

Figure 9.7 Histogram, centrality measures, export network, 2019. Source: calculated by author using STATA.

Table 9.5 Centrality measures for 20 tropical economies (ranking from a total of 231 economies)

Economy	*Between*	*Closeness*	*Eigenvector*	*Rank between*	*Rank close*	*Rank eigenvector*
Thailand	251.86	0.970	0.992	11	7.5	12
India	248.94	0.970	0.994	12	7.5	7
Malaysia	213.17	0.939	0.977	16	22	27
Brazil	208.64	0.970	0.994	19	7.5	6
Singapore	192.32	0.954	0.986	21	15.5	17
Indonesia	168.05	0.935	0.982	28	25	22
Philippines	150.59	0.920	0.962	31	30.5	35
Colombia	108.45	0.842	0.920	39	50	50
Mexico	68.92	0.788	0.852	51	61.5	62
Kenya	66.32	0.821	0.898	53	54.5	53
Peru	50.40	0.804	0.864	60	59.5	60
Mauritius	44.07	0.759	0.804	63	73	73
Nigeria	40.80	0.740	0.785	66	79	77
Ivory Coast	38.83	0.764	0.815	68	71	70
Cambodia	37.83	0.767	0.812	71	69.5	71
Costa Rica	36.92	0.752	0.789	72	75	76
Ecuador	34.79	0.762	0.800	73	72	74
Senegal	34.79	0.767	0.823	74	69.5	69
Myanmar	33.77	0.749	0.785	76	76	78
Madagascar	31.00	0.730	0.750	79	81	82

Lopez-Claros and Perotti (2014) observed that 28 of the 30 richest economies are located in temperate climates.

Intermediate goods or GVC trade for the tropical economies[10] increased more than 12 times in 2018, compared with 1990; from USD 118 billion to USD 1,459 billion. The GVC participation rate also increased from 0.45 (in 1990) to 0.52 (in 2018). In 2018, the following economies contributed the most to GVC trade in the tropical economies: Singapore, Malaysia, Mexico, India, Indonesia, Thailand, Brazil, Philippines, Venezuela, and Vietnam (Table 9.6).

Connectedness in specific product categories

To further link the network analysis with the flying geese concept, this chapter implements a calculation of centrality measures (betweenness and closeness centrality) to specific product categories that could reflect the distinct stages of industrial upgrading, particularly separation of products into: (i) labour-intensive and resource-intensive manufactures; (ii) low-skill and technology-intensive manufactures; (iii) medium-skill and technology-intensive manufactures (electronics and parts/components); (iv) high-skill and technology-intensive manufactures (electronics and parts/components). Please refer to Appendix B9.4 for the list of goods. The results for Brazil, China, India, Indonesia, Japan,

Table 9.6 Largest GVC trades, ten tropical economies (USD 000)

Economies	*GVC value*	*GVC share*
Singapore	292,900,000	20.08%
Malaysia	218,200,000	14.96%
Mexico	165,700,000	11.36%
India	150,600,000	10.32%
Indonesia	141,100,000	9.67%
Thailand	137,200,000	9.41%
Brazil	98,083,280	6.72%
Philippines	84,825,040	5.81%
Venezuela	36,760,180	2.52%
Vietnam	20,394,190	1.40%

Note: The percentage share is based on the share of contribution to a total of 65 tropical economies.
Source: calculated by author using data from https://worldmrio.com/unctadgvc/

Malaysia, Singapore, Thailand, and the USA are discussed in the next section by using betweenness and closeness centrality measures. These economies are selected to draw simple comparisons between tropical economies and the global hubs (China and the USA).

Betweenness centrality

For advanced economies like the USA, their scores for medium- and high-skill manufacturing goods (electronics) are relatively higher than other economies. China also scores very high for these two product categories. High-skill products cover items such as office machines, automatic data processing machines (n.e.s.), and television receivers; while medium-skill includes household type equipment and apparatus for electrical circuits.

Interestingly, Japan's score is relatively high in low-skill and technology-intensive products which cover items such as ships or boats and flat-rolled iron or steel. Japan's connectedness score for labour-intensive and resource-intensive products is also quite high, slightly higher than the score for medium-skill products. High-income economies like Singapore also score relatively high on medium-skill products.

Emerging tropical economies such as Brazil, India, and Indonesia have relatively high scores in labour-intensive and resource-intensive products. Brazil actually scores rather high in medium-skill products (electronics and parts/components); in fact, Brazil scores the highest in this category relative to the other three category of products. India's score for labour-intensive products is the highest compared with the other product categories' scores. Indonesia scores very low for the high-skill product category.

The USA and China seem to hold the 'hub' position in the trade network. The USA and China score the highest (rank #1 and #2, respectively) betweenness centrality scores for all manufactured goods in the four categories, based on the data for 205 economies. Tropical economies ranked somewhat relatively high in low-skill and labour-intensive products: India is ranked #9 (out of 205 economies) in low-skill products and ranked #7 (out of 205 economies) in labour-intensive products; Thailand is ranked #16 (out of 205 economies) for labour-intensive products; while Brazil is ranked #14 and #15 (out of 205 economies) for medium-skill and labour-intensive product trade networks (Table 9.7).

In general, lower-middle income economies are more relatively connected in labour-intensive and resource-intensive product trade than in high-skill product trade. In contrast, high-income economies are more closely connected in the trade of high-skilled or medium-skilled products. Low-income economies have poor connectivity in all manufacturing products, with only two to four shortest paths that go through these economies. Meanwhile, high-income economies have higher trade connectedness for the four categories of manufacturing products as listed in Table 9.8.

Table 9.7 Betweenness centrality scores for manufactured goods by degree of manufacturing groups, selected economies

	BRA	*CHN*	*IDN*	*IND*	*JPN*	*MYS*	*SGP*	*THA*	*USA*
Labour-intensive and resource-intensive	365	722	264	560	289	184	254	347	865
Low-skill and technology-intensive	316	988	236	485	450	201	304	302	1279
Medium-skill: electronics and parts /components	439	1182	184	351	404	130	431	248	1595
High-skill: electronics and parts /components	251	1189	84	465	294	220	349	211	1410

Source: calculated by author using STATA. Note: BRA=Brazil; CHN=China; IND=India; JPN=Japan; MYS=Malaysia; SGP=Singapore; THA=Thailand; USA=United States.

Table 9.8 Betweenness centrality scores for manufactured goods by degree of manufacturing groups, based on income classification

	High-income	*Upper middle-income*	*Lower middle-income*	*Low-income*
Labour-intensive and resource-intensive	151.46	62.59	39.66	3.68
Low-skill and technology-intensive	171.05	65.60	29.81	2.88
Medium-skill: electronics and parts / components	205.10	69.90	26.23	2.08
High-skill: electronics and parts / components	199.82	58.33	28.66	2.59

Source: calculated by author using STATA.

Closeness centrality

For the closeness centrality scores, the USA scores the highest for high-skill products, higher than China. China recorded the highest scores in medium-skill and low-skill products. Meanwhile, India scores the highest for labour-intensive products.

Among the four product categories, Indonesia scores very low for the high-skill product category. It is actually the lowest compared with other economies as shown in Table 9.9. Other economies which also have a relatively low score for high-skill products (compared with other product categories) are Brazil and Thailand. In contrast, Indonesia's score for labour-intensive products is relatively high compared with other product categories. Malaysia, Thailand, India, and Brazil also have relatively high scores for labour-intensive product categories compared with other product categories.

Compared with high-skill products, lower-middle income economies tend to be more relatively connected in labour-intensive and resource-intensive products trade. In high-income economies, the opposite is true; they are more connected in high-skill or medium-skill products trade. Low-income economies have poor trade connectivity for all manufacturing products, while high-income economies have a stronger trade network for the four types of manufacturing products listed in Table 9.10.

Connectedness and development

In general, high-income economies are more connected than other income categories – based on the three measures of centrality. Based on a between-centrality measure, high-income economies are twice more connected than upper-/middle-income economies, and 25 times more connected with low-income economies (Table 9.11).

Further analysis using correlation ratio between the three centrality measures and economic indicators such as GDP and export value show that the strength of correlation varies from positive 0.28 to 0.77. The strongest link is among betweenness centrality scores to exports (0.77), followed by closeness centrality

Table 9.9 Closeness centrality scores for manufactured goods by degree of manufacturing groups, selected economies

	BRA	*CHN*	*IDN*	*IND*	*JPN*	*MYS*	*SGP*	*THA*	*USA*
Labour-intensive and resource-intensive	0.913	0.927	0.885	0.950	0.849	0.868	0.868	0.913	0.924
Low-skill and technology-intensive	0.895	0.927	0.855	0.909	0.888	0.824	0.858	0.888	0.924
Medium-skill: electronics and parts/components	0.806	0.931	0.734	0.861	0.809	0.746	0.842	0.845	0.895
High-skill: electronics and parts/components	0.764	0.927	0.697	0.895	0.842	0.827	0.875	0.833	0.954

Source: calculated by author using STATA.

Table 9.10 Closeness centrality scores for manufactured goods by degree of manufacturing groups, based on income classification

	High income	*Upper middle income*	*Lower middle income*	*Low income*
Labour-intensive and resource-intensive	0.723	0.650	0.631	0.581
Low-skill and technology-intensive	0.712	0.639	0.610	0.570
Medium-skill: Electronics and parts / components	0.679	0.607	0.578	0.551
High-skill: Electronics and parts / components	0.703	0.613	0.591	0.562

Source: calculated by author using STATA.

Table 9.11 Centrality measures based on income level, export trade network, 2019

Income level	*Betweenness*	*Closeness*	*Eigenvector*
High income	97.584	0.792	0.759
Upper middle income	46.802	0.719	0.672
Lower middle income	28.287	0.691	0.630
Low income	3.926	0.635	0.534

Source: calculated by author using STATA.

Table 9.12 Correlations among centrality measures and economic indicators, 2019

Variables	*Betweenness*	*Closeness*	*Eigenvector*
Exports of goods and services	0.766	0.585	0.478
GDP	0.522	0.355	0.284

Source: calculated by author using STATA. Original data in constant 2010 USD, from https://data.worldbank.org/

to GDP (0.59) and betweenness centrality to GDP (0.52). Eigenvector centrality seems to have the weakest link to exports and GDP (Table 9.12).

Connectedness and resiliency

Due to the current global pandemic, trade connectedness has brought about additional concern about the lack of resilience in business operations resulting in slow economic recovery after the global pandemic.

Interconnected and integrated world markets lead to more sophisticated and extensive supply chains to serve those markets. For a lead firm in a supply chain, it can be challenging to be fully in control or have complete visibility of all of its suppliers. The majority of these lead firms or MNCs will only have clear visibility of their second or third suppliers. Around 85% of chief procurement officers (CPOs) admitted they have no visibility beyond their tier one suppliers, according to a survey by Deloitte in 2021.[11]

Coordination across supply chain stakeholders is therefore a challenge. A characteristic of supply chains known as the 'bullwhip effect' makes it even more challenging to maintain a stable and efficient supply chain across different suppliers. Procter & Gamble (P&G) coined the term 'bullwhip effect' in the 1990s to describe the variance amplification phenomenon between the company and its suppliers: even a simple change in customer demand can have severe consequences on inventories – disrupting normal supply chain operations (Xun and Disney, 2016).

Hidden risks also expose firms to vulnerabilities. Even though most firms are quite capable of managing day-to-day risks, as well as implementing a Business Continuity Plan in case of common disaster and disruption, unavoidable uncertainties are always lurking in the background. In recent years, these so-called 'systemic risks' (Benoît et. al., 2017) have become increasingly evident starting with the global financial crisis of 2008–2009 and more recently with the onset of the global pandemic.

Using the IMF data that measures trade uncertainty, a correlation analysis is done using the three centrality measures and the World Trade Uncertainty[12] (WTU) index (data for the year 2019). The strongest positive correlation is among WTU and betweenness centrality (0.599), followed by closeness centrality (0.509), and lastly eigenvector centrality (0.439). Around 36% of variation in WTU index could be explained by the variation in betweenness centrality scores (Figure 9.8).

While highly connected economies are also more vulnerable to economic shocks, they are able to recover more quickly as recovery starts to begin anywhere else in their network (Shepherd and Archanskaia, 2014). While goods trade in the current global pandemic fell more rapidly than it did in the global

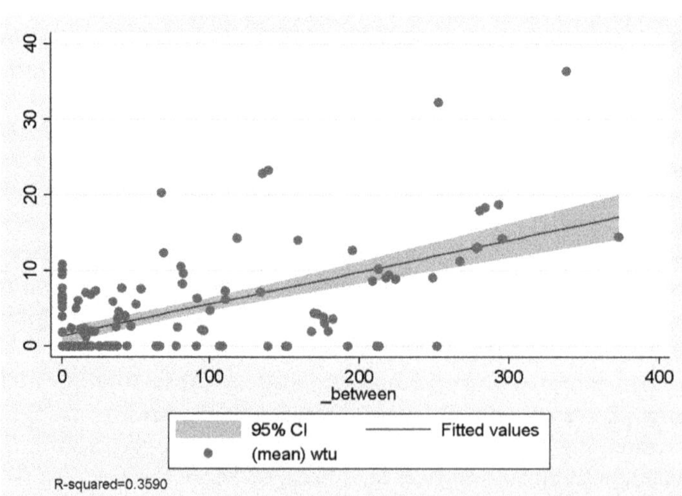

Figure 9.8 Connectedness and trade uncertainty, 2019. Source: calculated by author using STATA, using data from Ahir, H., N. Bloom, and D. Furceri (2018), 'World Uncertainty Index', Stanford mimeo.

financial crisis, a quicker recovery was likely a result of improved GVC resilience (World Bank, 2021). To build resilience, connectivity is essential. Through being connected, firms have more alternatives to suppliers, resulting in greater flexibility. The better the logistics connectivity, the more agile firms will be, and the swifter their recovery and return to normal operations will be. Governments can achieve more effective solutions with stronger networks that will enable faster and more comprehensive cooperation between economies.

Conclusion and way forward

In social network analysis, there are several centrality measures that measure the power of a node based on its position within a network. Application of these centrality measures to bilateral trade data offers interesting insights and findings that can supplement contemporary economic analysis.

Some findings point to a rather significant relationship of the centrality position of an economy in their trade network to their development levels and progress. Being 'globalizers' certainly opens up opportunities for development through trade channels, something that tropical economies may wish to consider in pursuing their development strategy.

There is some indication that being connected may increase vulnerability to economic shocks. On the other hand, connected economies may be able to recover more quickly as part of their network is starting to recover.

Appendix A9.1: Top 20 economies based on centrality measures, export trade network, 2019

	Betweenness centrality		*Closeness centrality*		*Eigen-centrality*	
1	Netherlands	373	Netherlands	0.996	Italy	1.000
2	United States	338	Germany	0.991	Germany	1.000
3	Spain	295	Italy	0.991	Netherlands	1.000
4	Germany	293	Spain	0.975	Spain	0.996
5	Italy	284	Belgium	0.975	Belgium	0.995
6	France	280	United Kingdom	0.970	Brazil	0.994
7	United Kingdom	279	Thailand	0.970	India	0.994
8	China	278	India	0.970	United Kingdom	0.994
9	Belgium	267	Brazil	0.970	France	0.992
10	Canada	253	United States	0.966	Sweden	0.992
11	Thailand	252	France	0.966	Poland	0.992
12	India	249	Poland	0.962	Thailand	0.992
13	Turkey	224	Sweden	0.962	Switzerland	0.990
14	Switzerland	220	Switzerland	0.958	Denmark	0.989
15	South Africa	218	Singapore	0.954	United States	0.987
16	Malaysia	213	Denmark	0.954	South Korea	0.986
17	Japan	212	Canada	0.950	Singapore	0.986
18	South Korea	212	South Africa	0.950	South Africa	0.985
19	Brazil	209	Turkey	0.947	Turkey	0.984
20	Portugal	195	South Korea	0.947	Austria	0.983

Source: calculated by author using STATA.

Appendix A9.2: Top 20 economies based on centrality measures, intermediate (GVC) trade network, 2019

	Betweenness centrality		*Closeness centrality*		*Eigen-centrality*	
1	Netherlands	576	Netherlands	0.979	Netherlands	1.000
2	United States	553	Germany	0.970	Germany	1.000
3	France	475	United States	0.966	Spain	0.997
4	China	409	United Kingdom	0.962	Italy	0.996
5	United Kingdom	383	Italy	0.958	United Kingdom	0.996
6	Canada	382	Spain	0.958	Sweden	0.995
7	Belgium	351	Sweden	0.958	Belgium	0.995
8	Germany	342	France	0.954	India	0.995
9	Italy	339	Belgium	0.954	France	0.994
10	India	336	India	0.954	Switzerland	0.993
11	Switzerland	332	Switzerland	0.950	United States	0.992
12	Spain	321	Canada	0.943	South Korea	0.992
13	Thailand	309	South Korea	0.943	Brazil	0.987
14	Japan	303	Brazil	0.943	Poland	0.986
15	South Korea	293	Thailand	0.935	Denmark	0.986
16	Malaysia	278	Denmark	0.935	Thailand	0.985
17	Sweden	260	Japan	0.931	China	0.984
18	United Arab Emirates	257	Poland	0.931	Canada	0.984
19	Denmark	257	China	0.927	Turkey	0.983
20	Australia	256	Singapore/Turkey	0.924	Japan	0.983

Source: calculated by author using STATA.

Appendix A9.3: Top 20 economies based on centrality measures, export trade network, 1995

	Betweenness centrality		*Closeness centrality*		*Eigen-centrality*	
1	United States	650	United States	0.986	United Kingdom	1.000
2	United Kingdom	556	United Kingdom	0.968	United States	0.998
3	Germany	517	Japan	0.968	Germany	0.997
4	Japan	508	Germany	0.960	Netherlands	0.997
5	France	489	Netherlands	0.960	Italy	0.996
6	Canada	452	France	0.956	Japan	0.995
7	Netherlands	432	Italy	0.956	Belgium	0.993
8	Italy	383	Belgium	0.947	France	0.992
9	Belgium	348	Malaysia	0.943	Denmark	0.988
10	Denmark	335	Denmark	0.939	Sweden	0.986
11	Spain	316	Sweden	0.935	China	0.982
12	Switzerland	308	Canada	0.931	Spain	0.980
13	Australia	277	China	0.931	Canada	0.980
14	India	272	Spain	0.927	Malaysia	0.980
15	China	257	India	0.927	Ireland	0.979
16	Sweden	252	South Korea	0.927	Switzerland	0.977
17	Portugal	248	Ireland	0.927	India	0.975
18	South Africa	245	Thailand	0.927	Thailand	0.974
19	Norway	244	Australia	0.923	Norway	0.970
20	South Korea	229	Switzerland/Czech Republic	0.915	Czech Republic	0.967

Source: calculated by author using STATA.

Appendix B9.4: Manufactured goods by degree of manufacturing groups

Labour-intensive and resource-intensive manufactures			
611	Leather	661	Lime, cement, fabrica. constr. mat. (excluding glass, clay)
612	Manufactures of leather, n.e.s.; saddlery & harness	662	Clay construction, refracto. construction materials
613	Furskins, tanned or dressed, excluding those of 8483	663	Mineral manufactures, n.e.s.
633	Cork manufactures	664	Glass
634	Veneers, plywood, and other wood, worked, n.e.s.	665	Glassware
635	Wood manufacture, n.e.s.	666	Pottery
641	Paper and paperboard	821	Furniture & parts
642	Paper & paperboard, cut to shape or size, articles	831	Travel goods, handbags & similar containers
651	Textile yarn	841	Men's clothing of textile fabrics, not knitted
652	Cotton fabrics, woven	842	Women's clothing, of textile fabrics
653	Fabrics, woven, of man-made fabrics	843	Men's or boy's clothing, of textile, knitted or crocheted
654	Other textile fabrics, woven	844	Women's clothing, of textile, knitted or crocheted
655	Knitted or crocheted fabrics, n.e.s.	845	Articles of apparel, of textile fabrics, n.e.s.
656	Tulles, trimmings, lace, ribbons & other small wares	846	Clothing accessories, of textile fabrics
657	Special yarn, special textile fabrics & related	848	Articles of apparel, clothing access., excluding textile
658	Made-up articles, of textile materials, n.e.s.	851	Footwear
659	Floor coverings, etc.		
Low-skill and technology-intensive manufactures			
671	Pig iron & spiegeleisen, sponge iron, powder & granu	693	Wire products (excluding electrical) and fencing grills
672	Ingots, primary forms, of iron or steel; semi-finis.	694	Nails, screws, nuts, bolts, rivets & the like, of metal
673	Flat-rolled prod., iron, non-alloy steel, not coated	695	Tools for use in the hand or in machine
674	Flat-rolled prod., iron, non-alloy steel, coated, clad	696	Cutlery
675	Flat-rolled products of alloy steel	697	Household equipment of base metal, n.e.s.
676	Iron & steel bars, rods, angles, shapes & sections	699	Manufactures of base metal, n.e.s.
677	Rails & railway track construction mat., iron, steel	785	Motorcycles & cycles

678	Wire of iron or steel	786	Trailers & semi-trailers
679	Tubes, pipes & hollow profiles, fittings, iron, steel	791	Railway vehicles & associated equipment
691	Structures & parts, n.e.s., of iron, steel, aluminium	793	Ships, boats & floating structures
692	Metal containers for storage or transport	895	Office & stationery supplies, n.e.s.
		899	Miscellaneous manufactured articles, n.e.s.
Medium-skill: electronics (excluding parts and components) (SITC 775)			
775	Household type equipment, electrical or not, n.e.s.		
Medium-skill: parts and components for electrical and electronic goods (SITC 772)			
772	Apparatus for electrical circuits; board, panels		
High-skill: electronics (excluding parts and components) (SITC 751 + 752 + 761 + 762 + 763)			
751	Office machines	762	Radio-broadcast receivers, whether or not combined
752	Automatic data processing machines, n.e.s.	763	Sound recorders or reproducers
761	Television receivers, whether or not combined		
High-skill: parts and components for electrical and electronic goods (SITC 759 + 764 + 776)			
759	Parts, accessories for machines of groups 751, 752	764	Telecommunication equipment, n.e.s.; & parts, n.e.s.
		776	Cathode valves & tubes

Source: https://unctadstat.unctad.org/en/Classifications.html

Notes

1 Senior Analyst, APEC Secretariat's Policy Support Unit (PSU). Email: ab@apec.org.
2 'A Tightening Grip', *The Economist*, March 2015. *The Economist*, https://www.economist.com/briefing/2015/03/12/a-tightening-grip.
3 'Modern Free Trade Agreements Are Not About Free Trade', Centre for International Governance Innovation, 11 April 2017, https://www.cigionline.org/articles/modern-free-trade-agreements-are-not-about-free-trade/
4 "This Is How Trade Agreements Affect Global Production." World Economic Forum, https://www.weforum.org/agenda/2018/07/trade-agreements-and-global-production/. Accessed 29 June 2021.
5 O. Tonby, J. Woetzel, W. Choi, K. Eloot, R. Dhawan, J. Seong, and P. Wang (2019). "The future of Asia: Asian flows and networks are defining the next phase of globalization," Discussion Paper, September, McKinsey Global Institute.
6 Lamy, Pascal. 'Global Value Chains, Interdependence, and the Future of Trade', VoxEU.Org, 18 December 2013, https://voxeu.org/article/global-value-chains-interdependence-and-future-trade.
7 For a practical application of this concept in the field of history, see Rosenthal et. al. (1987).
8 More information about Pajek software: http://mrvar.fdv.uni-lj.si/pajek/.

9 Similar approach was also adopted by Minoiu et al. (2013) and Errico and Massara (2011).
10 Using the initial list of 96 tropical economies provided in https://worldpopulationreview.com/country-rankings/tropical-countries [last accessed: 21 August 2021].
11 Source: https://www2.deloitte.com/us/en/insights/topics/operations/chief-procurement-officer-cpo-survey.html
12 For the description of the WTU data and methodology, please refer to: https://worlduncertaintyindex.com/data/

References

Akamatsu, K. (1962). A historical pattern of economic growth in developing countries. *The Developing Economies*, *1*, 3–25.

Baldwin, R. (2012). *WTO 2.0: Global Governance of Supply-chain Trade*. CEPR Policy Insight No.64. London: Centre for Economic Policy Research.

Baldwin, R. and J. Lopez-Gonzalez (2013). *Supply-chain Trade: A Portrait of Global Patterns and Several Testable Hypotheses*. No. 18957, NBER Working Papers. National Bureau of Economic Research, Cambridge MA.

Benoît, Sylvain, Jean-Édouard Colliard, Christophe Hurlin, and Christophe Pérignon. (2015). Where the Risks Lie: A Survey on Systemic Risk. *Review of Finance*, *21*, 1, 109–152.

Choi, Byung-il and Rhee, Changyong. (2014). *Future of Factory Asia*. © Asian Development Bank and Korea Economic Research Institute (KERI). http://hdl.handle.net/11540/52. License: CC BY 3.0 IGO.

De Benedictis, Luca and Tajoli, Lucia. (2011). The world trade network (August 2011). *The World Economy*, 34(8), 1417–1454. Available at SSRN: https://ssrn.com/abstract=1916504 or http://dx.doi.org/10.1111/j.1467-9701.2011.01360.x

Dollar, David and Kraay, Aart (2001), *Trade, Growth, and Poverty*. Available at SSRN: https://ssrn.com/abstract=632684

Errico, L. and A. Massara (2011). *Assessing Systemic Trade Interconnectedness: An Empirical Approach*. Working Paper WP/11/214, International Monetary Fund: Washington, D.C.

European Central Bank. (2014). Monthly bulletin, July 2014. https://www.ecb.europa.eu/pub/pdf/mobu/mb201407en.pdf

Freeman, L. C. (1979). Centrality in social networks: Conceptual clarification. *Social Networks*, *1*, 215–239. doi: 10.1016/0378-8733(78)90021-7

Grund, Thomas U. (2015). *Nwcommands: Network Analysis in Stata*. Manuscript 28 July 2015. https://nwcommands.wordpress.com/tutorials-and-slides/

Hage, P. and Harary, F. (1996). *Island Networks: Communication, Kinship, and Classification Structures in Oceania (Structural Analysis in the Social Sciences)*. Cambridge: Cambridge University Press. doi:10.1017/CBO9780511759130

Hilgerdt, F. (1943). The case for multilateral trade. *The American Economic Review*, *33*(1), 393–407.

Houthakker, Hendrik and Magee, Stephen P. (1969). Income and price elasticities in world trade. *The Review of Economics and Statistics*, *51*(2), 111–25. https://EconPapers.repec.org/RePEc:tpr:restat:v:51:y:1969:i:2:p:111-25

Krackhardt, D. (1990). Assessing the political landscape: Structure, cognition, and power in organizations. *Administrative Science Quarterly*, *35*(2), 342–369. doi:10.2307/2393394

Leipziger, D., & Thomas, V., (1997). An overview of east asian experience. In D. Leipziger (Ed.), *Lessons from East Asia*. University of Michigan Press.

Lopez-Claros, Augusto and Perotti, Valeria (2014). *Does Culture Matter for Development?* Policy Research Working Paper No. 7092. Washington, DC: World Bank Group. © World Bank. https://openknowledge.worldbank.org/handle/10986/20624 License: CC BY 3.0 IGO.

Minoiu, C., C. Kang, V. Subrahmanian, and A. Berea (2013). *Does Financial Connectedness Predict Crises?* Working Paper WP/13/267 International Monetary Fund: Washington, D.C.

Ozawa, T. (2006). *Asia's Labour-Driven Economic Development, Flying-Geese Style: An Unprecedented Opportunity for the Poor to Rise?* Research Paper 2006/059. Helsinki: UNU-WIDER.

Quibria, M. G. (2002). *Growth and Poverty: Lessons from the East Asian Miracle Revisited.* © Asian Development Bank Institute. http://hdl.handle.net/11540/4139. License: CC BY 3.0 IGO

Rosenthal, Naomi, Roberta Karantm, Michele Ethier, and Meryl Fingrutd (1987). Centrality analysis for historians, historical methods. *A Journal of Quantitative and Interdisciplinary History*, *20*(2), 53–62. doi: 10.1080/01615440.1987.9955259

Shepherd, B. and Archanskaia, E. (2014). Evaluation of value chain connectedness in the APEC region. *APEC Policy Support Unit publication*, APEC#214-SE-01.28, Singapore.

Shepherd, B., Doytchinova, H. S., and Kravchenko, A. (2019). The gravity model of international trade: A user guide [R version]. Bangkok: United Nations ESCAP. Available at: https://www.unescap.org/resources/gravity-model-international-trade-user-guide-r-version

Streeten, Paul (1972). *The Frontiers of Development Studies*. London: Palgrave Macmillan.

Venturini, Tommaso, Jacomy, Mathieu, and Jensen, Pablo (2019). What do we see when we look at networks. *An Introduction to Visual Network Analysis and Force-Directed Layouts*. Available at SSRN: https://ssrn.com/abstract=3378438 or http://dx.doi.org/10.2139/ssrn.3378438

World Bank (2021). "Global Economic Prospects, January 2021" (Washington, DC: World Bank), doi:10.1596/978-1-4648-1612-3.

World Economic Forum (2014). *Global Risks 2014*. Geneva: WEF.

Xun, Wang and Stephen M. Disney (2016). The bullwhip effect: Progress, trends and directions. *European Journal of Operational Research*, *250*(3), 691–701. ISSN 0377-2217. https://doi.org/10.1016/j.ejor.2015.07.022.

10 Big data applications in accounting: implications for the tropics

Vahid Biglari[1] *and Zahra Pourabedin*[2]

Introduction

Big data is used in almost all human activities. The reason for the growth in big data applications is the enormous amount of data that can be generated by advanced computing and telecommunication technologies, the Internet, and environmental measurements (Vasarhelyi et al., 2015). Companies seeking competitive advantage have an exponentially expanded capacity for their information systems.

The growing importance of big data will significantly affect various accounting practices including data collection and recording, management use of data to achieve organizational goals, and reporting the financial information (Gärtner and Hiebl 2017). In parallel with the changes, organizations are exponentially collecting more data as time goes by (Chaudhary et al., 2015). A huge amount of such data is often unstructured and collected by sensors or social media. Firms that have used such data effectively have achieved 5–6% higher productivity returns (Grover et al., 2018). In other words, big data, like a trademark, is an intangible asset that can generate surplus returns. The accumulation and evaluation of big data is a key factor in creating and maintaining a company's competitive advantage (Lee et al., 2014).

Big data concept varies between different domains. A small audit firm might have a different concept of big data from what a large audit firm has. Big data scale might be completely different from the viewpoint of a large organization such as the National Aeronautics and Space Administration (NASA). The criterion for classifying data into big or small is whether the in-use information processing system can process its scale. As Zhang et al. (2015) state, 'important features of big data is whether it goes beyond the capacity of existing processing systems' in what are known as the five 'V' aspects, including volume, velocity, variety, value, and veracity. Data variety refers to the types of big data and the speed and rate of their production and processing. Veracity of the data indicates how much data can be relied on, which is affected by measurement and reliability of the data sources. Volume of data indicates its amount, and value of the data indicates the monetary value it can create for the organization (Mayer-Schönberger and Cukier, 2013). Whether a data set is bulky or not

DOI: 10.4324/9781003153580-10

depends to the capacity of the organization information system. Such capacities include data storage and processing power.

Although there have been several studies in the area of big data analysis in business, to our knowledge no review study has been done on using big data analysis in accounting and audit (Gepp et al., 2018). Other available works usually focus on financial distress modelling (Kim and Upneja 2014), financial fraud modelling (West and Bhattacharya, 2016), stock market prediction (Nardo et al., 2016), and quantitative modelling (Xiao et al., 2015), which offer limited implications for using big data in accounting and auditing. The objective of this study is to document the current level of understanding of using big data in accounting and to develop a future research agenda for scholars interested in pursuing this area of inquiry. Drawing from the literature review outcomes, the study aims to explore future research areas and issues that require new theoretical and methodological frameworks to further our understanding of using big data in accounting. The study draws some implications for using big data analysis in tropics.

The next section describes the literature review on the use of big data analytics in accounting. After that, the methodological approach explains the article selection process including the search criteria used for the literature review. Next, a discussion on the research background is followed by a review on the impacts of implementing big data analysis, the unique features of big data analysis, along with the benefits of using big data analysis in the accounting and audit industry. This is followed by a section on the use of big data analysis in Singapore. Finally, a general conclusion of the study is presented.

Literature review

As big data revolutionizes businesses, it enables organizations to address concerns and provides insights into the vast amount of available data. Big data affects every aspect of the accounting profession, and it is rapidly becoming a major focus for professional accountants (regardless of their expertise) at an international level (Cokins, 2014; Yeh et al., 2014). As the technological capabilities improve, to improve the quality of auditing and accounting information, the profession has combined new non-financial data sources, such as Twitter and other social media-related sources. It can predict product demand, product returns, or inventory value. Climate-related information can be compared to sales information in geographic areas, or it can predict unexpected spending and profit patterns. The content of electronic documents, such as email, can help companies to identify policy deviations (Cao et al., 2015; Fay and Nagangard, 2017).

Big data in financial accounting

Due to the differences between the generally accepted accounting principles (GAAP) and the international financial reporting standards (IFRS), the Financial

Accounting Standards Board and the International Accounting Standards Board have made many efforts to converge the two standards. There has been a lot of discussion about these efforts. For example, one of the key differences is in the application of fair value accounting in the valuation of property, plant, and equipment (PPE). According to the IFRS, the fair value approach and revaluation of PPE are permitted, but accounting principles require such assets be reported at historical cost and fair value can be used in certain cases (such as the impairment of assets). In the event of an asset's impairment, the accounting principles should revaluate each of the affected assets so that their value is equal to the reduced value due to the loss (Thornton 2013). The fair value enshrined in the international financial reporting standards and accounting principles has helped to create a global and consistent set of accounting standards which requires using software to gather information to value assets through a continuous automated Internet search over time. In accounting for fair value, software searches all the information on the websites to make fair value estimates more objective and visible, and in this case, subjective judgements in fair value accounting estimates are reduced (Warren Jr et al., 2015).

Cockcroft and Russell (2018) explored the studies focusing on application of big data in accounting and finance. They aimed to provide an overview of large-scale scientific research and highlight future research areas in information systems, accounting, and finance. They focused on published papers from 2007 to 2016. Their findings showed the application of big data is making customer credit models in banking and financial industries. On the other hand, trading signals and fraud prevention are among the areas of interest of researchers.

Zhu (2019) studied whether access to alternative data could improve stock price awareness in the capital market and help discipline company executives. Alternative data is in fact the same data that is obtained from channels of information other than reports or financial statements. They used two alternative data sources including customer transaction data obtained from marketing analytics and data search panels, and satellite imagery captured by traffic cameras to customers' parking lots, which can be used to examine customers buying behaviours. Research findings show that price awareness increases when alternative data such as customer transactions and satellite imagery are accessed. This effect relates to informed investors and news that usually try to access alternative databases. As a result, the improvement of price awareness feature is related to companies whose investors have a high tendency to disclose company information.

Big data in management accounting

Management accounting refers to the use of accounting information to assist managers in their decision-making. One of the important management accountants' tasks is to create a system that aligns the predetermined organization goals with management and employee behaviour. This system is known as the 'management control system' (Malmi and Brown 2008). One of the management control systems that aligns criteria with goals is the 'balanced scorecard' which was introduced by Kaplan and Norton in 1996. This system identifies financial and non-financial criteria for management and employee behaviour to align with the business objectives. As a result, balanced scorecard and other management control systems identify positive and negative performance and reward management for implementing positives and avoiding negatives.

In the meantime, big data input can play a role in management control systems by discovering behaviours related to the consequences of specific goals, which leads to responsible performance metrics. For example, balanced scorecard collects data in four areas: finance, customer, internal business process, and learning and growth. In each of these areas, the input seeks to identify new behaviours that affect the results of the relevant objectives. Use of the Internet to enhance workplace knowledge is related to learning and growth goals. Internal e-mails may be related to the effectiveness of internal processes as well as the quality of services. Customer service quality may also be related to audio files obtained from customer phone calls.

Warren Jr et al. (2015) state that big data affects the design and operation of management control systems since it seeks to identify behaviours related to the goals of the organization. On the other hand, they believe that productivity goals in the organization are achieved by adopting big data. Big data sources such as climate projects, foreign websites, census data, and macroeconomic data improve the organization's budgeting process. On the other hand, big data analysis may eliminate differences between local accounting principles and international financial reporting standards and thus accelerate the move towards a global accounting system with the use of fair value accounting being the cornerstone of this convergence.

In general, big data analysis can help to discover the important metrics in management control systems. Big data provides solutions for discovering new motivational criteria and identifying traumatic events. Big data analysis helps us to discover relationships in large data sets such as the relationship between good management performance and various variables. Finally, to use the data, management accountants must first understand the data and then extract, convert, and analyze it. Since it has been proven that the accumulated data can be used in various organizational activities, management can achieve many benefits through using big data resources (Warren Jr et al., 2015).

Big data in auditing

Salijeni et al. (2019) examined the use of big data and data analytics in audit services. In their research, they interviewed people with experience and expertise in developing, implementing, and evaluating the impact of the above tools in an audit to provide a review of the changes made in the audit through using these tools. They discussed three aspects such as the impact of the integration of data analysis and big data on the relationship between auditors and their clients, technological implications in implementation of audit process, and common challenges related to application of data analysis and big data in audit. Big data can generate useful information to be used in audit process and creates a better experience for clients. In consulting services, the database identifies consulting questions, helps to monitor and improve an organization's performance, and creates analytical models to support a diverse set of products and improve the organization's operations.

Big data can also substantiate management claims about financial statements such as 'existence' and 'valuation' and provide further documentation to improve the auditor's confidence in the statements. As the accounting profession moves towards the use of fair value models, managers' valuations may also improve. Since the valuations are subjective and require lots of accurate quantitative and qualitative information, the data can help facilitate the process of proving the valuations to auditors (Warren Jr et al. 2015). Therefore, a large amount of data that is provided to auditors enables them to prepare the audit report which results in a higher audit quality.

Appelbaum et al. (2017) studied opportunities that big data and advanced analysis create for the independent auditor. They showed that big data analytics have dramatically changed the business environment and business process capabilities. With the expansion of using big data in the business environment, organization performance and capabilities have improved. They believe that such changes should also occur in independent audit and accreditation, and audit standards should be developed. Appelbaum (2016) aimed to highlight reliable audit evidence obtained from a big data field. His findings showed that auditors need to assess the reliability of corporate and external data, which are generated outside the company. Therefore, in a client-centric business environment, auditors may need to identify secure data sources.

Cao et al. (2015) defined big data as the process of handling, clearing, converting, and modelling large volumes of data useful for discovering and transmitting information patterns, and reviewed opportunities and challenges that big data can create in accounting. They showed that identifying audit risk and automation of business operations are examples of opportunities created for the accounting profession. Changing the traditional audit pattern, performing massive calculations, and complexity and privacy issues are among the challenges posed by big data.

Although big data would help accounting and auditing to create a completely different approach to understanding and reporting information at an organizational level, big data does not prevent using traditional accounting and auditing procedures. Meanwhile, the question is: what are the threats and opportunities facing the accounting profession due to big data developments? The interpretations presented in different research introduce practical solutions so that by using big data, the accounting profession can better serve companies, stakeholders, and the public. These interpretations are expected to bridge the gap between theory and practice. Highlights of this area of research are presented below.

The use of big data in financial accounting has improved the quality and relevance of accounting information. Vasarhelyi, Kogan et al. (2015) examined the relationship between structured data obtained from enterprise resource planning (ERP) systems and non-structured and semi-structured data from the business environment. They focused on how resources are used, and the challenges that big data creates in audit verification. They concluded that both accounting academics and professionals are aware of big data benefits and the challenges of using it. Accounting students can also improve their future careers by familiarizing themselves with big data-related issues. Vasarhelyi et al. (2015) believe that big data changes people's perception of information. While traditional accounting and auditing relies on structured data and summary reports, big data enables companies to adopt real-time reporting. Although over the past 50 years accounting and audit research have relied on structured data, capital market data over the next 50 years will be significantly different. Unstructured data analysis from sources such as social media, credit card registrations, websites, media and audio streams can be useful in decision-making. Krahel and Titera (2015) believe that current accounting and auditing standards are misdirected with an emphasis on presentation, collection, and sampling. They argue that arbitrary inflexible data collection and presentation is only due to high transfer costs and low data collection speed. They claim that 'event theory' in accounting, which was abandoned about 50 years ago, will be more defensible in a big data environment.

According to Alles (2015), auditors are allowed to use data in proportion to the extent to which the client uses the data. Also, auditors and auditing standards should adopt big data analysis through customer pressure. Cao et al. (2015) provide insights into how big data helps the audit profession. For example, data analysis systems related to capital markets, financial reporting requirements, and auditing procedures are some of the ways in which auditors use big data analysis to evaluate the lawsuit risk which is a key element in determining the audit fee.

Brown-Liburd et al. (2015) discuss big data challenges facing the audit profession and how big data can affect the quality of the auditors' judgement. Since auditors give opinions on the clients' financial statements and internal control system, they must be vigilant in using big data since there is limited knowledge about using it. More research is needed to understand the effects of moving from traditional audit process to big data. Zhang et al. (2015) develop their view on four main characteristics of big data, namely volume, speed, variety, and veracity. In their view, accuracy poses the greatest challenge to auditors. Among the factors that increase the use of coding techniques by auditors are data variety (differences in data from various sources), data accuracy, and data cleaning.

Warren Jr et al. (2015) examined different types of big data such as audio-visual and text-processed data and pointed to improvements in financial and management accounting through using such data. They showed that using big data in management accounting has led to the evolution of effective budgeting and a management control system.

Method

Littell (2008) defines 'systematic review' as identifying and synthesizing research that has been done on a particular subject. A systematic literature review effectively summarizes and analyzes a specific genre of extant literature (Thirumaran et al., 2021). Following the technique used by previous research such as that of Wood et al. (2020), our literature review begins by searching for and choosing relevant articles from the current literature. A systematic review has been used to identify and review interdisciplinary international studies on big data in accounting and auditing. According to Fink's (2019) model, a systematic review consists of four stages. This research uses Fink's model. Databases and websites were searched, and appropriate search terms were selected. Then, the necessary criteria for including or excluding relevant literature was determined. In the next step, the criteria of methodical review were further examined and applied. In the final stage, the research findings were integrated.

A search of databases, excluding Google Scholar, yielded 88 results. Using the set criteria, we excluded 25 cases and considered 53 cases. These included eight duplicates that were removed after review. Google Scholar search results included 45 results. Eighteen of these results were relevant to our subject matter. Of these, 15 were also found in other databases. In total, 48 publications are included in the analysis. The oldest source to be analyzed was published in 1982. Most publications were after 2012. Therefore, it seems that the popularity of this issue is increasing among the research community.

Findings

From an information system viewpoint, it is becoming increasingly difficult to discern how to use big data. The reasons lie in various types of computational tasks that accounting and audit systems face. More complex tasks such as analyzing the structural relationships between accounts and transactions to estimate the market value of a group of rarely used financial instruments, require a huge amount of computation that exponentially grows with the size of the data set (Vasarhelyi et al., 2015). Therefore, what is considered big from a processing point of view is determined by the processing capacity of the system (Moffitt and Vasarhelyi, 2013).

A set of data is considered big if more complex accounting or auditing calculations are required. The most complex accounting and audit modelling and estimation tasks might require several years to process several hundred megabytes of data. From a traditional processing point of view, such a data source is large. For example, De Spiegeleer et al. (2018) have shown that there are some specific problems with pricing financial derivatives as computations are non-traceable (such as proving valuation estimates) and it requires a lot of time. Although in the case of large data volume, sampling is a reliable historical method, it creates fewer benefits than using all data.

Data storage capacity

Storage capacity of modern information systems covers a wide range. In personal computers, the main data storage medium is a hard drive, which may store up to several terabytes of data. Other devices are faster and more reliable but are also more expensive. According to the information processing system, the concept of big data varies from the point of view of medium to large organizations from several terabytes to several hundreds of terabytes of storage capacity. In addition, accounting and audit systems use large volume external data sources that are connected to internal data sources (Vasarhelyi et al., 2015).

Types of big data to be used in accounting systems

Big data supplement to existing accounting records, consists of structured data, unstructured data (about 50%), and soft information such as e-mails, social media (such as Facebook, blogs, Twitter), telephone conversations, data sent and received by websites, and video transmission data. With the proliferation of big data technology, companies use all sorts of computational techniques to extract information from a data set and make it useful for their decisions. The data can be unstructured audio and video files. The next section describes the information that can be generated from this data and how it strengthens financial information.

Video data

With the advent of video and image capture tools, visual data has become increasingly common. As storage and processing techniques are maturing, using visual data in accounting becomes a current reality to complement accounting records.

The evolution in producing objective information from video files increases the possibility of using video files in producing accounting records. A meta-analysis presented by Khan et al., 2014 shows an algorithm that detects any entry into a restricted access area, counts things and examines and analyzes senses, monitors vehicles, and detects emotions. This method can add important information to accounting records, including: (1) recorded videos can indicate when and how many times people have entered the restricted access area; (2) workplace videos can be effective in tracking employee efficiency; (3) inventory videos can be used to assess the inventory timeliness; inventory changes can be useful for measuring the variable price and identifying bottlenecks; and (4) videos from property, machinery, and equipment can be useful in identifying the impairment of such assets (Warren et al., 2015). Complex computer algorithms increasingly process and interpret static images. Accurate object detection and interpretive image segmentation enables computers to automatically classify and interpret images (Andrés et al., 2017), scenario and object recognition algorithms (Li et al., 2016), training on object recognition through collectivization (Razdan, 2019), and emotion recognition have led to increased knowledge in such processes.

These methods can extract valuable data from the following sources: (1) images that contain views and objects related to a company and are usually uploaded by customers; (2) images related to a sudden fall of customer numbers in a specific geographic area; (3) images that show the conditions and how to use a company's products. Analysis of such data can provide useful business insights into the tendency to consume a company's products and views about the company (Costa and Jongen, 2006).

Audio data

Audio data related to a company's business activities can improve the accounting records and the quality of financial reporting. Important and potential audio sources include seasonal conference calls, board meetings and stakeholders' telephone calls to company staff, and microphones located in the built-in areas for monitoring, and other audio files from the video sources mentioned in the previous section. Teoh (2018) analyzed audio files related to the announcement of quarterly profits by corporate executives to detect cognitive anomalies in the speech pattern of CEOs. His study showed that there is a positive relationship between cognitive abnormality markers and the possibility of restating financial statements attributable to these anomalies. In other words, if cognitive abnormalities in the speech pattern of corporate executives is high, the likelihood of restatement of financial statements would be high. Other applications of voice analysis include crime detection (Radhakrishnan et al., 2005), identifying events in audio streams, and recognizing people's moods. Warren et al. (2015) mentioned how audio big data can provide corroborating evidence in support of accounting records; for example, audio interviews with construction engineers can provide additional evidence about machinery value. It enables prospective accountants to understand the basis of long-term assets' valuation and to consider any issues related to their potential impairment.

Textual data

Textual data includes non-financial data or soft documentation. Some text data repositories include reports submitted by companies to the Securities and Exchange Commission; for example, the number of Facebook members, Twitter users, and blogs in 2013 was 700 million, 250 million, and 156 million, respectively. Data from these sources can be used to evaluate and improve companies' performance. Email data was used in the United States to reduce any losses due to professional fraud, which amounted to approximately 650 billion

USD in 2006, and the company's dissatisfied employees were the main cause (Holton 2009). Losses from fraud in the United States are declining. The Association of Certified Fraud Examiners can use text mining techniques to reduce fraud attributable to employees to identify and anticipate dissatisfied employees' e-mails, and ultimately reduce or prevent the risk of organizational fraud (Holton 2009).

More importantly, such a technique provides relevant information not found in conventional fraud auditing. Fraud triangle analysis (as a method of detecting fraud) uses the principles of fraud in analyzing email messages to identify the motives and justifications for fraud. This is to the extent that companies extract information from audio, text, and video and integrate with traditional financial data. They can evaluate and predict business (Warren Jr et al., 2015).

Impact of big data on financial accounting

Accounting and financial reporting provide relevant information for external stakeholders. The distinguishing feature of financial accounting from management accounting is providing financial information prepared in accordance with a set of standards for external stakeholders of organization. Big data will significantly affect the future of financial reporting and the evolution of generally accepted accounting principles.

The types of big data discussed in this chapter are complementary to conventional financial information and can improve transparency and usefulness in decision-making. For example, in connection with fixed assets, organizational resource planning systems can record video clips and other multimedia tools. In this way, users get a more general view of the conditions, features, and characteristics of each asset. This improvement in transparency not only helps to meet the needs of stakeholders but also provides benefits in dealing with claims related to fixed assets. For example, audio, video, and textual information complement records of any available asset, such as a fixed asset. Auditors will be less challenged in testing for existence of fixed assets. Also, using big data technologies, data can be collectively analyzed through data mining to detect any outdated data or other anomalies. Therefore, big data technologies would be helpful for auditors, managers, and other stakeholders (Warren Jr et al., 2015).

Reporting off-balance sheet assets

Several important intangible items are excluded from balance sheets since it is difficult to objectively determine their value (Färnemyhr et al., 2013). Some off-balance sheet assets include customer databases, human resources, product quality commitments, and company reputation. Since these assets differentiate an organization from others and show competitive advantage, information about these items is clearly valuable to the organization's stakeholders. Since 2002, US corporate investments in tangible and intangible assets have been comparable. Nevertheless, many countries experience more investment in intangible assets than physical assets, leading to an increase in the ratio of off-balance sheet items compared to in-balance sheet items. Such conditions reduce the relevance of conventional financial statements and thus lose their usefulness for decision-making (Orhangazi 2019).

At the company level, initial efforts can be made to understand the general nature and characteristics of intangible assets. This is exactly where big data can be useful. For example, key indicators related to target asset can be accumulated, processed, and analyzed through data mining algorithms. The resulting information will have immediate potential value and can subsequently be disseminated to stakeholders. In the short term, this information may be largely qualitative and may therefore complement the accompanying notes to the financial statements. In this way, some stakeholders will gradually have significant access to some information about intangible off-balance sheet assets. Finally, when data collection and analytical processing are completed, quantitative valuation methods for intangible assets can be developed and reported on the balance sheet (Warren et al., 2015).

Accounting for fair values

In the current situation, financial reporting is oriented towards fair values. For more than a decade, the Financial Accounting Standards Board and the International Accounting Standards Board have been pushing for the convergence of generally accepted US principles and internationally accepted accounting standards that property, plant, and equipment should be reflected in the historical cost and fair value use is prohibited except in cases of devaluation.

When devaluation occurs, US Generally Accepted Accounting Standards require that the asset in question be revalued and reported at a lower amount (market value). Big data can make a huge difference between fair value accounting under international standards and the US Generally Accepted Accounting Principles and create global accounting standards. One potential way to facilitate this process is through the use of agents. The task of these agents is to gather information for a long period of time to help value assets that could not be valued through other means (Warren et al., 2015).

In the context of fair value accounting estimates, software agents use all relevant Internet resources to maximize level one and level two estimates of fair values, with the use of objective, tangible, and current market data being searched. If the company has unique access methods, software agents can use standard procedures to make fair value estimates. To spread this idea, companies may be formed in the capital market and specialize in providing information related to fair valuation of assets and liabilities.

Similar valuation companies provide appraisal and valuation services. On one side of the spectrum, these firms enter contracts with companies that provide information and normal estimates for all assets and liabilities, and these contracts can provide expert judgement on insurance matters in areas where three levels of fair value estimates are required.

At the other end of the spectrum, these institutions provide information about an asset or a liability on a case-by-case basis. In addition, auditors may use these services to confirm reasonableness of expressed fair values (for example by appraisers), like the way they use foreign experts in valuing the portfolio.

Big data reduces subjective assumptions in fair value accounting estimates (Warren and Marz, 2015; Warren Jr et al., 2015). For example, consider the fair value of a depreciable asset. The depreciation chart reflects the overtime change in the value of asset based on its projected useful life and the trend in which these resources generate revenue. Nevertheless, different depreciation methods are available, and their choice is an optional accounting decision that can vary from one company to another. Although the straight-line method is the most common, it does not normally show a change in the value of an asset during its useful life (Barth, 2014). Vehicles owned by a company may be replaced based on years used, or distance travelled; in either case the straight-line method is used to determine depreciation cost over their useful lives. However, this method does not normally show a change in the vehicles' value during their useful life. Fair value accounting can address this problem by eliminating the need to use depreciation charts, which are often optional. Using fair value accounting, the value of the vehicles in each reporting period changes very simply in response to the relevant market variables.

Valuation of data assets

Using big data to value data assets creates two opportunities. First, big data allows companies to properly value their data assets which will add to the company value. Second, big data improves data monitoring and increases data quality which can enhance data value (Liu et al., 2016). However, the challenge with data valuation is that since new data is constantly available, data value decreases rapidly.

It might be challenging for accountants to adapt to ongoing changes. In addition, data may be transformed to make it suitable for application. Ultimately, widespread use of big data requires a complete set of rules and regulations in this area, including global governance, data valuation, and privacy.

Decision-making

With respect to data analysis tools, there are two opportunities that relate to reporting and decision-making. Data analysis tools provide opportunities to develop an appropriate approach to support real-time decision-making. Data analysis also enables big data sharing with internal and external stakeholders.

Data analysis tools also creates two challenges. Through automation and self-service, it helps to tailor internal reporting based on the departmental needs within a company. This might restrict information sharing between the departments of an organization. Organizational culture might also restrict data sharing, especially when we are dealing with independent units in all parts of an organization.

The next section discusses application of big data in wholesale. In wholesale trade, goods are bought and stored in large quantities, and then sold in batches to a limited number of resellers, professional users, or non-end users. Big data can be used to examine the limitations of traders, identify trading patterns, and identify exceptions of trading systems. Data analysis tools can also be used to recover capital expenditures in compliance with contracts. By analyzing recoverable costs, part or all the costs can be recovered.

Risk management

Big data creates three basic opportunities in risk management. They are risk forecasting, risk identification, and predictive analysis.

Risk forecasting helps with creating a comprehensive picture of the future. Data analysis also provides the basis for improving risk forecasts. The second opportunity is risk identification. In this regard, a data analysis tool provides an opportunity to immediately identify risk, which will improve the fraud detection process and forensic accounting.

Finally, by testing the risk of long-term investment in new markets and products, data analysis tools make it possible to use predictive analytics. However, data analysis use in risk management poses three challenges (Moşteanu and Faccia, 2020).

The challenges are of particular importance in areas such as correlation, budgeting, and rapid experimentation. Use of data analysis tools in correlation ensures that there will be no ambiguity about a causal relationship, especially when the risk identification process involves use of different data sources in the big data analysis. The next point is that with the increasing use of advanced methods of predictive analysis, the budgeting process and calculating investment return will change. Finally, with the advent of big data, challenges have arisen in applying rapid tests in budgeting processes and capital allocation (Moşteanu and Faccia, 2020).

Data analysis and internal audit

Data analysis provides great opportunities in an internal audit. Internal auditors use big data to identify business risks and dysfunctional internal controls. This section focuses on internal audit units of public organizations. In such units, big data is used to process important accounting items such as expenses, salaries, and accounts payable.

Other important processes in auditing include customer invoicing, analysis and selection of investment plans, and the job order process. There are also potential benefits in these processes to save costs or other opportunities to increase revenue. If internal auditors have a set of information systems skills, they will be able to mine clients' billing data to identify various operations, procedures, and processes such as customer credits, invalidated or adjusted invoices, errors in the billing process, and customer incentive schemes. Thus, data analysis applications are innumerable.

Since auditing units are frequently analyzing data, it is possible to find new investment opportunities. In addition, due to increasing data analysis applications, audit risk assessment has already become an analysis-oriented process. Data analysis can also be used to analyze risky processes, transactions, and datasets. Data in an independent audit is not as common as in internal auditing. However, data analysis can potentially make significant changes in this area.

Data analysis application in independent auditing

Data analysis is important in the auditing profession. Recent advances in data analytics' software enables auditors to better understand their clients than before (Tysiac, 2015). Tysiac (2015) believes that auditors need to have a good understanding of their clients' business and industry. Data analysis enables auditors to gain a better understanding of their clients' business.

Thus, data analysis helps independent auditors to improve their service in three ways. First, auditors can test complete sets of data, instead of testing a sample of a client's transactions. Second, the data analysis assists independent auditors in assessing the risk of potential anomalies in trends. Finally, auditors can focus their audits on specific areas by comparing customer data with industry data. According to Tysiac (2015), independent auditors can provide the necessary audit evidence through a comprehensive systematic analysis of their client's systems. This allows auditors to better understand the client's business.

Tysiac (2015) believes that to understand big data application in continuous auditing, we should refer to the auditing standards. They emphasize that big data application would significantly increase the auditor's confidence.

Big data in the tropics

Sustainable farming is an important issue for the subsistence agriculture of the tropics. Big data technology must address the issues and constraints faced by the farming community, e.g., labour shortage during peak periods, and basic requirements of an urban lifestyle (Lal Ragland, 1993). Big data also could help to improve sustainability accounting in tropics such as reforestation methods (Olschewski and Benitez, 2005), carbon accounting (Preece, Crowley et al., 2012), and accounting for intangible benefits of pastoral farming (Kosgey, Van Arendonk et al., 2004). Other research suggests using big data to support biodiversity (Zizka, 2019), rehabilitation of mangrove forests (Worthington, Andradi-Brown et al., 2020), and agricultural and environmental analysis in the tropics (Weersink, Fraser et al., 2018).

As a world-leading tropical country, Singapore's journey on digitalization started in the early 1980s with some modest efforts to computerize government databases and some government functions. Transforming government to be more efficient and effective in serving the population has been a key priority for the Singapore government; hence the adoption of digital technologies across the whole government.

Meanwhile, industries, especially telecommunications companies and banks, also invested in a similar infrastructure, recognizing that an efficient Internet highway would allow them to do business more efficiently. This infrastructure plays a vital role in Singapore's ambition to be a smart nation. As the economy and society adopt more digital solutions and remain connected to the Internet highway, a new challenge emerged requiring the government and society response.

Thus, Singapore considers AI an essential and fundamental technology for the digital economy, with AI-powered products offering a level of personalized service at a previously unimaginable scale. In the global discourse on AI ethics and governance, Singapore believes that its balanced approach can facilitate innovation, safeguard consumer and other societal interests, and serve as a common global reference point.

The Singapore vision is to become an AI hub where companies see the value in locating to Singapore and conducting their R&D. There is a need for an enabling environment, with a set of rules and regulations that does not inhibit but allows companies to grow and innovate while preserving and protecting the public interest. The end-user should feel that AI helps to improve his or her quality of life.

The purpose of deploying AI solutions must be to improve the quality of life for Singaporeans. For example, Internet banking has removed the need for bank users to queue up, thereby improving their quality of life. It has made it easier for all cross-sections of society and industry to use banking services for their specific needs. Hence, using big data in an accounting system helps Singapore to do business more efficiently, helping Singapore to lead the move towards digital economy in the tropics.

Technology must, therefore, serve a higher purpose. While technological solutions can be disruptive, it is up to governments and industries to soften the effects of the disruption as much as possible. Job displacement through automation and digitalization has created much anxiety among workers.

Hence there is a need to account for this anxiety in how digital solutions are deployed. Digital readiness for those affected and where there are specific alternatives for them should be one key consideration. Timing is essential, and technology should be deployed in a humane way that improves the quality of life of the society at large.

Discussion

Advances in technology has meant the business world has had to deal with ever-increasing amounts of data and information. The complex nature of the data can provide businesses with valuable opportunities to grow and gain competitive advantages in multiple markets. There is no doubt that access to constantly updated big data, which includes non-traditional information, will further leverage upon the accounting information. However, as there are different types of unstructured data, it is increasingly becoming difficult to discern how to use them in accounting. The challenges of big data in accounting mainly lie in computational the complexity of big data analysis and the processing capacity of accounting systems. It is not appropriate to use traditional tools for big data analysis as both volume and type of data change continuously.

The proliferation of big data technology enables companies to use all sorts of computational techniques to extract information from a data set, making it useful for decision-making. For example, using visual data in accounting is going to become common in complementing accounting records. Analysis of video data can provide useful insights regarding customers' perception about the company as well as their purchase intention (Costa and Jongen, 2006). Audio and textual data can improve the quality of accounting records and financial reporting. Such data can also be used to reduce fraud and provide relevant information which cannot be found in conventional fraud auditing. To the extent that companies integrate the extracted data from audio, text, and video with traditional financial data, they can evaluate and predict business performance (Warren Jr et al., 2015).

Big data will significantly affect the future of financial reporting and the evolution of accounting principles. This can improve transparency which results in better decision-making. Big data would also help auditors, managers, and other stakeholders to better understand the nature and characteristics of intangible assets (Warren Jr et al., 2015). Although in the short term such information would be largely qualitative and may complement the accompanying notes to the financial statements, when data collection and analytical process are completed, quantitative valuation methods for intangible assets can be developed and reported on the balance sheet (Warren et al., 2015). Big data can bridge the gap between fair value accounting under international standards and the US Generally Accepted Accounting Principles, converging global accounting standards through reducing subjective assumptions in fair value accounting estimates (Warren et al., 2015; Warren Jr et al., 2015).

Big data also allows companies to properly value their data assets through data monitoring which results in improved data quality, leading to an increase in company value (Liu et al., 2016). However, as data is being updated constantly, it becomes challenging for accountants to adapt to ongoing changes. Ultimately, widespread use of big data requires a complete set of rules and regulations including global governance, data valuation, and privacy.

Although data analysis tools provide opportunities to develop a real-time decision-making approach, it might restrict information sharing between departments of organizations. Big data can be used to examine the limitations of traders, identifying trading patterns and exceptions of trading systems. Moreover, big data creates three basic opportunities in risk management, including risk forecasting, risk identification, and predictive analysis (Moşteanu and Faccia 2020). Internal auditors use big data analysis to identify business risks and dysfunctional internal controls, analyzing risky processes, transactions, and datasets. Although independent auditing is not using data as much as internal auditing, data analysis can potentially make significant changes in this area. Recent advances in data analytics' software enable auditors to better understand their clients (Tysiac, 2015). Tysiac (2015) believes that big data application would significantly increase an auditor's confidence. Big data could help to improve sustainability accounting issues in the tropics such as reforestation methods (Olschewski and Benitez 2005), carbon accounting (Preece et al., 2012), and accounting for the intangible benefits of pastoral farming (Kosgey et al., 2004).

Although the value of big data analysis in accounting has been proven, insufficient investment has been made in the use of data technologies. The use of such technologies by accounting firms requires high infrastructure costs to scrap old systems. Due to the high costs associated with using big data technologies, accounting firms may not be willing to accept such costs, because these technologies are still immature, and accountants do not have the necessary understanding of the value of investing in such technologies. Another reason for the backwardness of the accounting profession's technologies is that not many accountants have the required information technology skills. This is due to the lack of technology education for accounting students in universities. It is necessary to make investments in information technology education at a university level.

The findings imply that big data helps providing extensive information and improves accuracy of financial reporting. Despite creating opportunities, big data can make several challenges for accountants and auditors such as changing the traditional pattern of financial statements, performing complex and excessive calculations, as well as the confidentiality of big data. This study helps academics and the accounting profession to better understand the tools of big data analysis, the benefits of using that, and the challenges associated with overcoming barriers when using big data analytics in the accounting profession.

Conclusion

This chapter addresses how textual, video, and audio data can change accounting, especially in areas such as supporting documents and evidence, to justify the values for recording transactions. In addition, such data can provide a strong historical perspective on the decision-making processes used to measure the value of assets.

Big data can improve accounting in several ways including, challenges and opportunities in the areas of data asset valuation, decision-making, risk management, and internal and independent auditing. The most important finding of this chapter is that big data will soon be an important part of accounting. As was discussed in this chapter, big data can be used in what is known as 'continuous auditing'. The auditing standards should be modified to include big data applications. This will significantly increase the auditors' assurance level.

It is argued that big data can complement managers claims with respect to financial statements. Claims such as 'existence' and 'valuation' can be supported by non-accounting and complementary data. This data can improve the data collection process and increase accountants' confidence in the reliability of these claims. As accounting principles move towards fair value models, the 'valuation' claim can be improved by the data.

The findings imply that big data helps provide extensive information and an improved accuracy of financial reporting. On the other hand, big data creates gaps between traditional data analysis in current accounting and the analysis required for using big data in accounting, which creates problems for accountants such as collecting and handling large, heterogeneous, and erratic data. The insights gained from this study can be used by academics and the auditing profession to better understand the tools of big data analytics, the social benefits of using it, and the challenges associated with it, so that these groups can plan to adopt big data analytics in the accounting profession.

The convergence between generally accepted accounting principles (GAAP) and international financial reporting standards is helping to create an integrated accounting regime around the world, in which fair value accounting is a cornerstone. By using intelligent information agents that are active in the cloud, all data related to liabilities and assets can be collected, processed, and published globally. The accounting process for financial reporting advances along with advances in technology. Accounting records have evolved over time from manual records in physical accounting offices to electronic accounting machines and to current systems such as enterprise resource planning systems. Big data is yet another technology paradigm that will change the way financial transactions are supported. Through a new form of evidence, big data supports financial accounting and transaction management and will improve the measurement process.

Since Singapore is seeking to become an AI hub in the region, early adoption of big data in accounting would be necessary. Since big data can be used to prepare large-scale real-time personalized reports, using big data in the accounting system helps Singapore to do business more efficiently, helping Singapore to lead the move towards digital economies in the tropics. Meanwhile, there is a need to account for the anxiety and disruption that results from the adoption of such technology.

Notes

1 Corresponding author: Newcastle Business School, University of Newcastle, Singapore. Email: vahid.biglari@newcastle.edu.au.
2 JCU Singapore Business School, JCU Singapore, Singapore, and Department of International Trade.

References

Alles, M. G. (2015). 'Drivers of the use and facilitators and obstacles of the evolution of big data by the audit profession'. *Accounting Horizons* 29(2):439–449.

Andrés, S., D. Arvor, I. Mougenot, T. Libourel, and L. Durieux (2017). 'Ontology-based classification of remote sensing images using spectral rules'. *Computers & Geosciences* 102:158–166.

Appelbaum, D. (2016). 'Securing Big Data provenance for auditors: The Big Data provenance black box as reliable evidence'. *Journal of Emerging Technologies in Accounting* 13(1):17–36.

Appelbaum, D., A. Kogan, and M. A. Vasarhelyi (2017). 'Big Data and analytics in the modern audit engagement: Research needs'. *Auditing: A Journal of Practice & Theory* 36(4):1–27.

Barth, M. E. (2014). 'Measurement in financial reporting: The need for concepts'. *Accounting Horizons* 28(2): 331–352.

Brown-Liburd, H., H. Issa and D. Lombardi (2015). 'Behavioral implications of Big Data's impact on audit judgment and decision making and future research directions'. *Accounting Horizons* 29(2):451–468.

Cao, M., R. Chychyla and T. Stewart (2015). 'Big Data analytics in financial statement audits'. *Accounting Horizons* 29(2):423–429.

Chaudhary, R., J. R. Pandey, and P. Pandey (2015). Business model innovation through big data. In 2015 International Conference on Green Computing and Internet of Things (ICGCIoT), IEEE.

Cockcroft, S. and M. Russell (2018). 'Big data opportunities for accounting and finance practice and research'. *Australian Accounting Review* 28(3):323–333.

Cokins, G. (2014). 'Top 7 trends in management accounting, Part 2'. *Strategic Finance* 95(7):41–48.

Costa, A. and W. Jongen (2006). 'New insights into consumer-led food product development'. *Trends in Food Science & Technology* 17(8):457–465.

De Spiegeleer, J., D. B. Madan, S. Reyners, and W. Schoutens (2018). 'Machine learning for quantitative finance: fast derivative pricing, hedging and fitting'. *Quantitative Finance* 18(10):1635–1643.

Färnemyhr, J., A. Gustavsson, L. Hederberg, and J. Norrman (2013). 'Core and Complexity of Goodwill'. *IFRS Accounting in Progress* 202–204.

Fay, R. and E. M. Negangard (2017). 'Manual journal entry testing: Data analytics and the risk of fraud'. *Journal of Accounting Education* 38:37–49.

Fink, A. (2019). *Conducting research literature reviews: From the internet to paper*, Sage publications.

Gärtner, B. and M. R. Hiebl (2017). *Issues with big data. The Routledge companion to accounting information systems*, Routledge:161–172.

Gepp, A., M. K. Linnenluecke, T. J. O'Neill, and T. Smith (2018). 'Big data techniques in auditing research and practice: Current trends and future opportunities'. *Journal of Accounting Literature* 40:102–115.

Grover, V., R. H. Chiang, T.-P. Liang, and D. Zhang (2018). 'Creating strategic business value from big data analytics: A research framework'. *Journal of Management Information Systems* 35(2):388–423.

Holton, R. J. (2009). *Cosmopolitanisms: New thinking and new directions*, Macmillan International Higher Education.

Khan, N., I. Yaqoob, I. A. T. Hashem, Z. Inayat, W. K. Mahmoud Ali, M. Alam, M. Shiraz, and A. Gani (2014). 'Big data: survey, technologies, opportunities, and challenges'. *The Scientific World Journal* 2014:1–19.

Kim, S. Y. and A. Upneja (2014). 'Predicting restaurant financial distress using decision tree and AdaBoosted decision tree models'. *Economic Modelling* 36:354–362.

Kosgey, I. S., J. A. Van Arendonk, and R. L. Baker (2004). Economic values for traits in breeding objectives for sheep in the tropics: impact of tangible and intangible benefits. *Livestock Production Science*, 88(1–2):143–160.

Krahel, J. P. and W. R. Titera (2015). 'Consequences of Big Data and formalization on accounting and auditing standards'. *Accounting Horizons* 29(2):409–422.

Lal, R. and J. Ragland (1993). 'Agricultural sustainability in the tropics'. *Technologies for Sustainable Agriculture in the Tropics* 56:1–6.

Lee, J., H.-A. Kao, and S. Yang (2014). 'Service innovation and smart analytics for industry 4.0 and big data environment'. *Procedia Cirp* 16:3–8.

Li, D., T. Salonidis, N. V. Desai, and M. C. Chuah (2016). Deepcham: Collaborative edge-mediated adaptive deep learning for mobile object recognition. In 2016 IEEE/ACM Symposium on Edge Computing (SEC), IEEE.

Littell, J. H., J. Corcoran and V. Pillai (2008). *Systematic reviews and meta-analysis*, Oxford University Press.

Liu, J., J. Li, W. Li, and J. Wu (2016). 'Rethinking big data: A review on the data quality and usage issues'. *ISPRS Journal of Photogrammetry and Remote Sensing* 115:134–142.

Malmi, T. and D. A. Brown (2008). 'Management control systems as a package: Opportunities, challenges and research directions'. *Management Accounting Research* 19(4): 287–300.

Mayer-Schönberger, V. and K. Cukier (2013). *Big data: A revolution that will transform how we live, work, and think*, Houghton Mifflin Harcourt.

Moffitt, K. C. and M. A. Vasarhelyi (2013). 'AIS in an age of Big Data'. *Journal of Information Systems* 27(2):1–19.

Moşteanu, N. and A. Faccia (2020). 'Digital systems and new challenges of financial management–FinTech, XBRL, blockchain and cryptocurrencies'. *Quality-Access to Success Journal* 21(174):159–166.

Nardo, M., M. Petracco-Giudici, and M. Naltsidis (2016). 'Walking down Wall Street with a tablet: A survey of stock market predictions using the web'. *Journal of Economic Surveys* 30(2):356–369.

Olschewski, R., and P. C. Benitez (2005). Secondary forests as temporary carbon sinks? The economic impact of accounting methods on reforestation projects in the tropics. *Ecological Economics*, 55(3):380–394.

Orhangazi, Ö. (2019). 'The role of intangible assets in explaining the investment–profit puzzle'. *Cambridge Journal of Economics* 43(5):1251–1286.

Preece, N. D., G. M. Crowley, M. J. Lawes, and P. Van Oosterzee (2012). Comparing above-ground biomass among forest types in the Wet Tropics: Small stems and plantation types matter in carbon accounting. *Forest Ecology and Management*, 264, 228–237.

Radhakrishnan, R., A. Divakaran, and A. Smaragdis (2005). Audio analysis for surveillance applications. IEEE Workshop on Applications of Signal Processing to Audio and Acoustics, 2005, IEEE.

Razdan, R. (2019). *Unsettled technology areas in autonomous vehicle test and validation*, SAE Technical Paper.

Salijeni, G., A. Samsonova-Taddei and S. Turley (2019). 'Big Data and changes in audit technology: contemplating a research agenda'. *Accounting and Business Research* 49(1):95–119.

Teoh, S. H. (2018). 'The promise and challenges of new datasets for accounting research'. *Accounting, Organizations and Society* 68:109–117.

Thirumaran, K., H. Jang, Z. Pourabedin, and J. Wood (2021). 'The role of social media in the luxury tourism business: a research review and trajectory assessment'. *Sustainability* 13(3):1216.

Thornton, G. (2013). *Grant Thornton.* http://www.sibliquidation.com/images/Third_Liquidators_Report_-_Sealed.pdf

Tysiac, K. (2015). 'Data analytics helps auditors gain deep insight'. *Journal of Accountancy* 219(4):52.

Vasarhelyi, M. A., A. Kogan, and B. M. Tuttle (2015). 'Big Data in accounting: An overview'. *Accounting Horizons* 29(2):381–396.

Warren, J. and N. Marz (2015). *Big Data: Principles and best practices of scalable realtime data systems*, Simon and Schuster.

Warren Jr, J. D., K. C. Moffitt, and P. Byrnes (2015). 'How big data will change accounting'. *Accounting Horizons* 29(2):397–407.

Weersink, A., E. Fraser, D. Pannell, E. Duncan, and S. Rotz (2018). Opportunities and challenges for big data in agricultural and environmental analysis. *Annual Review of Resource Economics*, 10:19–37.

West, J. and M. Bhattacharya (2016). 'Intelligent financial fraud detection: a comprehensive review'. *Computers & Security* 57:47–66.

Wood, J., J. Oh, J. Park, and W. Kim (2020). 'The relationship between work engagement and work–life balance in organizations: A review of the empirical research'. *Human Resource Development Review* 19(3):240–262.

Worthington, T. A., D. A. Andradi-Brown, R. Bhargava, C. Buelow, P. Bunting, C. Duncan, ... and Spalding, M. (2020). Harnessing big data to support the conservation and rehabilitation of mangrove forests globally. *One Earth*, 2(5):429–443.

Xiao, S., S.-H. Ma, G. Li, and S. K. Mukhopadhyay (2015). 'European option pricing with a fast fourier transform algorithm for big data analysis'. *IEEE Transactions on Industrial Informatics* 12(3):1219–1231.

Yeh, C.-C., D.-J. Chi, and Y.-R. Lin (2014). 'Going-concern prediction using hybrid random forests and rough set approach'. *Information Sciences* 254:98–110.

Zhang, J., X. Yang, and D. Appelbaum (2015). 'Toward effective big data analysis in continuous auditing'. *Accounting Horizons* 29(2):469–476.

Zhu, C. (2019). 'Big data as a governance mechanism'. *The Review of Financial Studies* 32(5):2021–2061.

Zizka, A. (2019). Big data suggest migration and bioregion connectivity as crucial for the evolution of Neotropical biodiversity. *Frontiers of Biogeography*, 11(2).

11 Financial literacy among Ethiopian high school teenagers

Yohannes Workeaferahu Elifneh[1]

Introduction

Background

Financial literacy, which is an ever-emerging field (Goyal & Kumar, 2020), has become an important research subject in recent years in both developing and developed countries (Hizgilov & Silber, 2020). It is a notion that is still very much relevant today as it influences individuals to attain a specific financial behaviour (Lajuni et al., 2020). Worthington (2006) has also noted that the field of financial literacy is of great interest for academicians, policymakers, government units, and corporate and consumer groups. According to Noctor et al. (1992), financial literacy is described as the capacity to make informed judgements and to take effective decisions regarding the use and management of money. De Beckker et al. (2020) added that financial literacy plays an important role in individuals' financial decision-making and a rising number of studies associate financial literacy with better personal financial decisions. In addition, Bhabha et al. (2014) noted that financial literacy is a combination of awareness, attitude, and behaviour essential to make sound financial decisions and achieve individual financial well-being. Further, Remund (2010, p. 279) indicated that 'by the most basic definition, financial literacy relates to a person's competency for managing money'.

Lusardi (2019) stated that individuals today are more responsible for their personal finances than ever before due to individuals' challenging financial circumstances affected by several factors such as rising life expectancies and pension and social welfare systems getting strained. Given such reality, financial literacy is believed to provide individuals with the ability to make informed decisions about financial planning, wealth accumulation, debt, and pensions (Watanapongvanich et al., 2020). After all, Hastings et al. (2012) explained that individuals with basic financial literacy have sufficient knowledge of financial products, financial concepts (inflation, interest, interest compounding, and diversification), and the necessary mathematical skills or numeracy for effective financial decisions.

However, the level of financial literacy is deemed discouraging even at a global level, leave alone the developing world, where financial literacy is

DOI: 10.4324/9781003153580-11

a new embrace (Willis, 2008). Hastings and Mitchell (2020, p. 1) also assert that still

> many people lack the knowledge of key economic concepts and skills needed to make financial computations, which may cause them to make suboptimal financial decisions. It is this explanation that motivates the many policymakers who have recently launched campaigns to foster financial literacy around the world.

Klapper and Lusardi (2020) further noted that the lack of basic financial knowledge is real in developing countries and in countries with well-developed financial markets. Similarly, Arceo-Gomez and Villagómez (2017) noted that particularly young people and teenagers are among the least financially literate demographic groups.

This study explored the level of financial literacy among high school teenagers in a developing country context (Ethiopia), where the subject is understudied. Surveying the level of financial literacy among high school students is a modish practice in this field (Amagir et al., 2020; Henager & Cude, 2019; Mandell, 2008; Peng et al., 2007). On top of that, unlike the case in the industrialized world, where the subject of financial literacy is not a new embrace, the issue of financial literacy has come to the fore in the developing world very recently (Willis, 2009) and empirical studies on the status of financial literacy in the developing world are scant (Xu & Zia, 2012). This study attempts to close this gap by examining the level of basic financial literacy among high school students in Ethiopia. It represents the first comprehensive study to examine the level of financial literacy among teenagers/high school students at the national level in the country.

In other words, this study is a contribution to both theory and practice. Its theoretical contribution is by way of extending studies on financial literacy to less explored regions. There is a dearth of studies on financial literacy from the part of the developing world (Ansong & Gyensare, 2012; Eniola & Entebang, 2016; Lajuni et al., 2020; Willis, 2009). In addition, the study will also provide a tangible contribution to practice because understanding financial literacy among young people is vital for developing effective financial education programmes (e.g., Cameron et al., 2014). After all, 'the lack of financial literacy in both developed and developing countries needs to be a particular concern for all parties' (Setiawan, 2020, p. 75).

Statement of the problem

Financial literacy is lacking across all age groups globally, but a worrying amount of only less than one-third of young adults have even basic financial knowledge (Wolla, 2017). Also, financial literacy is one of the understudied topics in the developing world, yet equally not much is known about the level of financial literacy among teenagers from this part of the world (Caplinska, &

Ohotina, 2019; Wentzel, 2016). The OECD encourages countries to conduct surveys to assess the level of financial literacy in their respective territories OECD, INFE (2011). As per this understanding, this study examined the level of financial literacy among high school students in Ethiopia. As only little is known about the level of financial literacy in the developing world, this research envisages narrowing this gap. In other words, in addition to this theoretical contribution of extending studies on financial literacy to less explored territories, such a study will also be a practical contribution for policymakers and educators in order to develop appropriate financial education and other related policy interventions to improve personal financial literacy in the study's context (Refera et al., 2016).

Objectives of the study

Financial literacy deals with empowering individuals with sufficient skills and knowledge to make sound financial decisions and allow them to be more in control of their personal financial circumstances (Kefela, 2011). However, the level of financial literacy is reported to be disappointing and concerning in the global context (Greenspan, 2002; Lusardi & Mitchell, 2011; Willis, 2008). For instance, Robb (2011, p. 692) reported that

> college students (such as in USA) are lacking in financial literacy, findings suggest that they are roughly as knowledgeable as the rest of the adult population and this general lack of financial knowledge prompted a virtual explosion of financial education programs in the USA.

Further, speaking of financial literacy among teenagers, Arceo-Gomez and Villagómez (2017) argued that though there is an expectation that there will usually be a positive correlation between financial literacy and education in general, it is concerning to find low levels of financial literacy even among well-educated individuals, which alerts policymakers about the need to financially educate young people starting in high school.

Despite these discouraging circumstances, Wolla (2017, p. 155) assert that the issue of financial literacy

> has become more important than ever as financial markets have become more complex: there are more financial instruments from which to choose, and the transition from defined-benefit pension plans to defined-contribution plans has placed more financial decision-making responsibility on consumers.

Accordingly, this study investigates the level of financial literacy among high school students in Ethiopia. As little is known about the level of financial literacy in the underdeveloped world, this study contributes to narrow this gap. In addition, the results of such studies are usually considered vital inputs for relevant stakeholders such as policymakers, educators, community groups, businesses, and government agencies that have the interest and the duty to enhance the financial literacy level of their citizens (see Ahmed et al., 2021; Hogarth & Hilgert, 2002).

Research focus

The focus/issue of this study investigates the level of financial literacy among high school teenagers in Ethiopia. Accordingly, the research question of the study is stated as: is the financial literacy level among Ethiopian high school teenagers satisfactory? In order to address this question, a survey was carried out among high school teenagers in the country (see details for school types, location, and the data collection methods and materials section). This is consistent with the fact that policymakers have recognized the importance to financially educate teenagers (young people) starting in high school (FEG, 2012). Loerwald and Stemmann (2016, p. 25) also stated that

> children and young people should be enabled to make the most rational decisions possible, in economic life situations. This particularly relates to financial decision-making situations, because these are often characterized by a high level of complexity, and the consequences of wrong decisions have direct material effects.

Furthermore, surveying the level of financial literacy of diverse segments of a society is a commonly taken practice to identify gaps and take measures to improve people's level of financial literacy (OECD INFE, 2011; Lusardi et al., 2010; Sarigül, 2014; Lucey, 2005). More precisely, scholars noted that 'assessing the financial literacy of the population is a key ingredient of any policy' (Kokkizil et al., 2016, p. 135). Xu and Zia (2012) also added that there is no better time to take stock of the evidence than now by surveying the evidence on financial literacy levels around the world as policymakers in both developed and developing nations are increasingly realizing the importance of financial literacy and are investing resources in financial education programmes.

Literature review – theoretical underpinnings

This section outlines the theoretical underpinnings of financial literacy and financial literacy measurement.

Overview of financial literacy

Financial literacy in industrialized countries or underdeveloped countries is an important topic for discussion (Abubakar, 2015). The need for financial literacy has become increasingly significant with the deregulation of financial markets and easier access to credit; the ready issue of credit cards; the rapid growth in marketing financial products, and the government's encouragement for its citizens to take more self-responsibility for their retirement incomes (Sonia & Abraham, 2006.) However, financial literacy in the global context is still disappointing. Even students in high schools and colleges have low levels of financial literacy, and they are no different from the rest of the adult population (Robb, 2011; Willis, 2008). Yet, educating young people while they are still at high schools is recently considered as crucial by national policymakers and educators (Arceo-Gomez & Villagómez, 2017), and the OECD also strongly promotes the importance of financial literacy among teenagers as financial literacy is steadily considered to be an essential life skill that must be learnt at school as early as possible in peoples' lives (FEG, 2012).

Blue and Grootenboer (2019) also shared that examining the financial literacy level of high school teenagers and educating them about personal finance has been acknowledged as essential by governments around the world and financial literacy is considered a twenty-first-century skill for students and that schools are best placed to develop the required skills and capabilities with this regard. Setiawan (2020) expressed that examining the level of financial literacy among teenagers from high schools and the younger generation is essential, because the younger generation is becoming a national priority in several countries; in order to increase financial literacy and knowledge of students' financial literacy the first step is to create financial habits at a young age that will bring benefits to financial management in the future. Bruhn et al. (2013, p. 2) also added that 'the focus on youth is attractive and relevant for a number of reasons as good financial habits formed at an early age are likely to benefit schooling, employment, and standards of living throughout adulthood'.

Financial literacy: what is it exactly?

According to Huston (2010, p. 296), 'the terms financial literacy, financial knowledge and financial education often are used interchangeably in the literature'. Scholars express that although financial literacy is still an emerging field (Antonietti et al., 2016; Goyal & Kumar, 2020), the term is one that is not new and it is perceived as important and as something to be encouraged in those who are not financially literate (Mason & Wilson, 2000). According to Oseifuah et al. (2018, p. 1),

> financial literacy is an essential life skill that has a significant impact on individual, family well-being, and on the broader economy; and as such over the past two decades, both developed and developing countries have become increasingly concerned about the level of financial literacy of their citizens, particularly among young people.

The OECD (2013) described financial literacy as the ability to make effective decisions across a range of financial contexts/situations. It is more precisely described as 'a combination of awareness, knowledge, skill, attitude and behaviour necessary to make sound financial decisions and ultimately achieve individual financial wellbeing' (OECD, INFE, 2011, p. 3). A similar explanation is also provided by the ASIC (2014, p. 16) stating that financial literacy is 'a combination of financial knowledge, skills, attitudes and behaviours necessary to make sound financial decisions, based on personal circumstances, to improve financial wellbeing'.

Financial literacy measurement

Worthington (2006) stated that financial literacy is expressed in terms of mathematical ability and the understanding of financial terms. And it is 'typically measured at the individual level and then aggregated by groups, such as high school students or low-income adults, to provide a macro view' Remund (2010, p. 279). Klapper and Lusardi (2020) also shared that financial literacy is commonly measured using questions that assess basic knowledge of fundamental financial decision-making concepts: knowledge of interest rates, interest compounding, inflation, and risk diversification.

However, thus far, as the academic literature has given little attention to how financial literacy is measured (Huston, 2010), most financial literacy measurement studies rely on the Lusardi and Mitchell (L&M) approach which is the most widely used financial literacy measurement scheme (Agarwal et al., 2015; Lusardi & Mitchell, 2005). The L&M scheme contains five basic financial literacy questions, which are developed to assess an individual's basic financial knowledge: (1) numeracy question; (2) interest compounding question; (3) inflation question; (4) time value of money question; and (5) money illusion question.

Methodology

This empirical study depended on survey design and a standard questionnaire was used to collect the data to assess the level of basic financial literacy among high school teenagers in Ethiopia. The subject of the study is a recent phenomenon making the utilization of an exploratory, descriptive approach an appropriate choice (Patton, 2002; Thomlison, 2001; Yin, 2003). In other words, this exploratory, descriptive approach is useful to 'gain familiarity with this contemporary phenomenon and portray the characteristics of a particular individual, situation or a group' (Kothari, 2004, p. 2) accurately. The data collection instrument (a five-item questionnaire) is on the basis of the instrument initially developed by Lusardi and Mitchell (2005), and this research used the slightly modified version by Van Rooij et al. (2011). As indicated in the preceding section, the instrument measures participants' basic level of financial literacy (knowledge) in terms of numeracy, interest compounding, inflation, time value of money, and money illusion. The questionnaire had two categories – the first category relates to demographic and socioeconomic variables, i.e., age, gender, an education level (high school grades – 9th, 10th, 11th, and

12th). The second section comprises the basic financial literacy measurement questions.

The respondents were drawn from high schools (students) that were willing to participate in the study based on the condition of anonymity of school names. Accordingly, 23 high schools from the Amhara region, Oromya region, Tigray region, and Addis Ababa participated in the study. In addition, as far as sample size is concerned, the study managed to gather 1027 questionnaires from high school students (9th–12th grades) in Ethiopia, which meets OECD INFE (2011, p. 6) recommendation of a minimum achieved sample size of 1,000 participants for financial literacy surveys at national level. Analysis of the data was performed using a descriptive approach using crosstabs revealing the levels of basic financial literacy among the high school students based on correct and wrong answers for the five basic financial literacy measurement questions. This is a common analysis approach for studies that examine/measure the level of basic financial literacy (Elifneh, 2021; Lusardi & Mitchell, 2005; Oehler et al., 2018; Van Rooij et al., 2011).

Results and discussion

This section presents the findings of the study. It begins with preliminary statistics involving (a) the educational level of the participants, (b) the age of participants, (c) gender, and (d) school types. This will be followed by the major findings/results of the basic financial literacy measurement: numeracy, interest compounding, inflation, time value of money, and money illusion.

Preliminary statistics

Tables are used in presenting the preliminary statistics involving educational level, age, gender, and school types of the participants.

As shown in Table 11.1, from the total of 1027 students who participated in the study, 26.6% were grade 9 students, 27.6 were grade 10 students, 23.9% were grade 11 students, and 22% were grade 12 students. This distribution shows that almost an equal number of students participated in the study from the four grades in the high schools.

Table 11.2 demonstrates the ages of the students who have participated in the study range from 13 to 25. But as can be seen from the table, the majority

Table 11.1 Education level

		Frequency	*Percent*	*Valid percent*	*Cumulative percent*
Valid	Grade 9	273	26.6	26.6	26.6
	Grade 10	283	27.6	27.6	54.1
	Grade 11	245	23.9	23.9	78.0
	Grade 12	226	22.0	22.0	100.0
	Total	1027	100.0	100.0	

Table 11.2 Age of participants

		Frequency	*Percent*	*Valid percent*	*Cumulative percent*
Valid	13.00	1	.1	.1	.1
	14.00	21	2.0	2.0	2.1
	15.00	114	11.1	11.1	13.2
	16.00	252	24.5	24.5	37.8
	17.00	283	27.6	27.6	65.3
	18.00	233	22.7	22.7	88.0
	19.00	69	6.7	6.7	94.7
	20.00	28	2.7	2.7	97.5
	21.00	13	1.3	1.3	98.7
	22.00	4	.4	.4	99.1
	23.00	5	.5	.5	99.6
	24.00	2	.2	.2	99.8
	25.00	2	.2	.2	100.0
	Total	1027	100.0	100.0	

Table 11.3 Gender

		Frequency	*Percent*	*Valid percent*	*Cumulative percent*
Valid	Male	481	46.8	46.8	46.8
	Female	546	53.2	53.2	100.0
	Total	1027	100.0	100.0	

Table 11.4 School type

		Frequency	*Percent*	*Valid percent*	*Cumulative percent*
Valid	Public	705	68.6	68.6	68.6
	Private	322	31.4	31.4	100.0
	Total	1027	100.0	100.0	

of the students fall within the range of ages 15 to 18. A total of 54 students fall outside the age range of teenagers but they are still in high school. Such is common in Ethiopian high schools as not everyone has the opportunity to go to school at an earlier age. These students are also included in the study – they are still high school students.

Table 11.3 displays the gender distribution of the participants. Accordingly, 46.8% and 53.2% of the participants were males and females, respectively. This indicates that the number of female students who participated in the study is greater than that of male students.

Table 11.4 displays that while 68.6% of the participants were drawn from public high schools, the remaining 31.4% were from private high schools. It makes better sense to include more of the public high school students in this study as the majority of the high schools in the country are public/government owned.

Major findings

Aggregate findings

This section presents the major findings of the study that measures the basic financial literacy of high school students.

Table 11.5 contains the result of the numeracy assessment question, and the question asked was 'Suppose you had €100 in a savings account and the interest rate was 2% per year. After 5 years, how much do you think you would have in the account if you left the money to grow?'; the result shows that only 68% of the respondents get it right. The rest, i.e., 32% of the respondents (= 398 students) did not get it right. A numeracy measurement is the easiest understanding in the field of financial literacy, but still, 32% of the participants failed to get the correct answer, and this is a worrying amount as it means that those who failed to get the correct answer did not have the basic understanding that money that is kept in a bank gains interest or even some might think that their money in their bank account gets smaller by the day without even withdrawing their money; for example, 101 participants stated a similar notion to the latter idea.

Table 11.6 comprises of the interest compounding question and the question asked was: 'Suppose you had €100 in a savings account and the interest

Table 11.5 Numeracy

		Frequency	*Percent*	*Valid percent*	*Cumulative percent*
Valid	More than $102	698	68.0	68.0	68.0
	Exactly $102	81	7.9	7.9	75.9
	Less than $102	101	9.8	9.8	85.7
	Do not know	121	11.8	11.8	97.5
	Refusal	26	2.5	2.5	100.0
	Total	1027	100.0	100.0	

Table 11.6 Interest compounding

		Frequency	*Percent*	*Valid percent*	*Cumulative percent*
Valid	More than 200	361	35.2	35.2	35.2
	Exactly 200	375	36.5	36.5	71.7
	Less than 200	162	15.8	15.8	87.4
	Do not know	101	9.8	9.8	97.3
	Refusal	28	2.7	2.7	100.0
	Total	1027	100.0	100.0	

rate is 20% per year and you never withdraw money or interest payments. After 5 years, how much would you have on this account in total?' This aspect of the basic financial literacy assessment investigates participants' understanding/knowledge of whether interest itself earns interest income while the money is kept in a bank and started to earn an interest already, and a very concerning result is found out. Only 35.2% (= 361 students) of the participants have this knowledge. A total of 64.8% (= 666 students) of the participants did not get the correct answer. This is a very concerning finding.

Table 11.7 displays the result of the financial literacy assessment result with respect to the participants' understanding of inflation. The question asked was: 'Imagine that the interest rate on your savings account was 1% per year and inflation was 2% per year. After 1 year, how much would you be able to buy with the money in this account?' This question specifically explores whether or not the participants were aware that when inflation is higher (than the saving rate) the value of their money gets weaker. This time 43.1% of the respondents get the correct answer by stating the correct answer. However, we should note that a greater proportion, 56.9% of the respondents (= 584 students), failed to answer the question correctly. What is more worrying is that 25.1% of the participants believed that their money will keep appreciating in the face of inflation, which is quite the contrary to reality. And yet, 13.4% of the respondents think that inflation will have no impact on the purchasing power of their money. Such results are terrifying.

Table 11.8 demonstrates the respondents' knowledge of the time value of money, which means it assessed whether they are aware that money earned sooner is better than money earned later as interest income can be earned if one has it sooner than later. The question asked was: 'Assume a friend inherits €10,000 today and his sibling inherits €10,000 3 years from now. Who is richer because of the inheritance?' Obviously, based on the notion of the time value of money, the one who has it sooner (a friend) is better off than the one who will have it later (his sibling). Again, a shocking amount – 67.4% (= 692 students) – did not get it right. There were a large number of students (16%) who said they are equally rich, and worse, 35.1% claimed the sibling is richer. Such are the concerning results.

Table 11.9 contains the result of the last item in the basic financial literacy measurement – money illusion. The question asked was: 'Suppose that in the

Table 11.7 Inflation

		Frequency	*Percent*	*Valid percent*	*Cumulative percent*
Valid	More than today	258	25.1	25.1	25.1
	Exactly the same	138	13.4	13.4	38.6
	Less than today	443	43.1	43.1	81.7
	Do not know	152	14.8	14.8	96.5
	Refusal	36	3.5	3.5	100.0
	Total	1027	100.0	100.0	

Table 11.8 Time value of money

		Frequency	*Percent*	*Valid percent*	*Cumulative percent*
Valid	My friend	335	32.6	32.6	32.6
	His sibling	360	35.1	35.1	67.7
	They are equally rich	164	16.0	16.0	83.6
	Do not know	131	12.8	12.8	96.4
	Refusal	37	3.6	3.6	100.0
	Total	1027	100.0	100.0	

Table 11.9 Money illusion

		Frequency	*Percent*	*Valid percent*	*Cumulative percent*
Valid	More than today	252	24.5	24.5	24.5
	The same	534	52.0	52.0	76.5
	Less than today	87	8.5	8.5	85.0
	Do not know	95	9.3	9.3	94.3
	Refusal	59	5.7	5.7	100.0
	Total	1027	100.0	100.0	

year 2019, your income has doubled and prices of all goods have doubled too. In 2019, how much will you be able to buy with your income?' Obviously, in such a situation, one will be able to buy less. We can see that 24.5% stated quite the contrary and said they would be able to buy even more, and a monumental proportion of 52% stated it would be the same. Only 8.5% of the respondents got this question correct. Again, another concerning result as when put together, 91.5% of the participants gave the wrong answer.

Results by school types: public vs. private

Notwithstanding the fact that the overall result is poor for all aspects of the basic financial literacy assessments, it will still be interesting to look into comparative results by comparing the responses from the public school students and the private school students. These findings are shown next.

Table 11.10 demonstrates the numeracy assessment result by school type. Accordingly, 61.7% (= 435 students) of the public school students properly answered the numeracy question, and 81.68% (= 263 students) of the private school students correctly answered the numeracy question. Based on this sample-based finding, the students from the private schools have a better understanding of numeracy.

When it comes to interest compounding dimension, as seen in Table 11.11, the public school students (39.3%) exhibited a better performance than the private schools students (26%). But this is an unusual finding to note as it leads

Table 11.10 School type * numeracy

Count						
School type	*Numeracy: Suppose you had €100 in a savings account and the interest rate was 2% per year. After 5 years, how much do you think you would have in the account if you left the money to grow?*					*Total*
	More than $102	exactly $102	Less than $102	do not know	Refusal	
Public	435	67	84	101	18	705
Private	263	14	17	20	8	322
Total	698	81	101	121	26	1027

Table 11.11 School type * interest compounding

Count						
School type	*Interest compounding: Suppose you had €100 in a savings account and the interest rate is 20% per year and you never withdraw money or interest payments. After 5 years, how much would you have on this account in total?*					*Total*
	more than 200	*Exactly 200*	*less than 200*	*do not know*	*Refusal*	
Public	277	194	127	85	22	705
Private	84	181	35	16	6	322
Total	361	375	162	101	28	1027

Table 11.12 School type * Inflation

Count						
School type	*Inflation: Imagine that the interest rate on your savings account was 1% per year and inflation was 2% per year. After 1 year, how much would you be able to buy with the money in this account?*					*Total*
	more than today	*exactly the same*	*less than today*	*do not know*	*Refusal*	
Public	189	116	276	100	24	705
Private	69	22	167	52	12	322
Total	258	138	443	152	36	1027

on to how student groups who performed less in numeracy competence score better in interest compounding.

With regards to the inflation question, Table 11.12 shows that public high school students (39.15%) performed less than private high school students

Table 11.13 School type ⋆ time value of money

Count						
School type	*Time value of money: Assume a friend inherits €10,000 today and his sibling inherits €10,000 3 years from now. Who is richer because of the inheritance?*					*Total*
	my friend	*his sibling*	*they are equally rich*	*do not know*	*refusal*	
Public	178	268	130	102	27	705
Private	157	92	34	29	10	322
Total	335	360	164	131	37	1027

Table 11.14 School type ⋆ money illusion

Count						
School type	*Money illusion: Suppose that in the year 2019, your income has doubled and prices of all goods have doubled too. In 2019, how much will you be able to buy with your income?*					*Total*
	more than today	*the same*	*less than today*	*do not know*	*refusal*	
Public	210	306	69	71	49	705
Private	42	228	18	24	10	322
Total	252	534	87	95	59	1027

(51.86%). So, as per this study the private school students have a better understanding of inflation.

Concerning the issue of time value of money, Table 11.13 indicates that the public school students (25.24%) performed less than the private school students (48.76 %). This implies that though overall rating for both groups is low, the private high school students have a better understanding of the time value of money.

Table 11.14 shows the money illusion result across the two school types. Accordingly, public school students scored better (9.79%) than private school students (5.59%). This indicates that relatively the public school students have a better understanding of money illusion.

Discussion

This study attempted to portray the level of financial literacy among Ethiopian high school students. A total of 1027 participants took part in the study from various high schools in the country. Almost a fairly proportional number of students participated in the study from the high school grades – grade 9, 10, 11, and 12. From the total of 1027 participants, 26.6% (273) were grade 9 students, 27.6% (283) were grade 10 students, 23.9% (245) were grade 11 students, and 22% (226) were grade 12 students. The total numbers of students who participated in the study meet the OECD's recommendation of taking > 1000 participants as a sample in a study conducted inwho have participated in the study meet the OECD's recommendation of taking > 1000 participants as a sample in a sample study conducted at the national level.

The study result showed that the level of financial literacy among the high school students is disappointing. The numbers clearly speak for themselves and confirm that the high school students' basic financial literacy level is at a worrying level. A total of 32% of the participants failed to correctly answer the numeracy question. A total of 64.8% students failed in the interest compounding question; 56.9% failed in the inflation question; 67.4% failed the time value of money question; and a massive proportion of 91.5% failed the money illusion question.

In other words, as noted in the preceding paragraph, even in the assessment with the easiest question, i.e., numeracy, 32% or 329 students are totally oblivious to that fact that money kept in a bank earns interest. With respect to the interest compounding question, an alarming 64.8% or 666 students did not have the idea that interest itself earns interest income while the money is kept in a bank and once started, it is already earning interest. Regarding the inflation question that assessed the respondents' knowledge of whether inflation makes the purchasing power of their money weaker, 56.9% (584), which is more than half of the entire participants are not aware that inflation indeed erodes the buying power of money. Again, the measurement of the participants' knowledge of time value of money produced a daunting result as 67.4% or 692 students failed to give the right answer. Finally, with regards to the money illusion question, 91.5% or 940 respondents gave the wrong answer.

Conclusion

This study was initiated to answer the central research question – is the financial literacy level among Ethiopian high school teenagers fairly good? Such a research question is part of the global initiatives such as by the OECD requesting scholars to show the level of financial literacy among young people in different contexts. As such this study concludes that the level of financial literacy is not fairly good among Ethiopian high school students. The high school students are not well versed with basic financial literacy dimensions/measurements, especially with the questions of interest compounding, inflation, time value of money, and money illusion. Suppose we try to develop some kind of pattern here. In that case, the worst score is with the money illusion question (91.5 % failure), that is followed by the time value of money question (67.4% failure), this is followed by the interest compounding question (64.8% failure), this in turn is followed by the inflation question (56.9% failure), and lastly numeracy question (32% failure). To conclude, these findings indicate that the high school students in Ethiopia are behind the curve with regards to basic financial literacy. They lag in understanding basic financial literacy knowledge and skills.

In sum, this study was conducted assuming that a contribution could be made by extending studies on financial literacy to less charted territories such as in this part of the world where this study was conducted. The study also aspired to provide input to policymakers to fine-tune the curriculum at high school level to improve the level of financial literacy among the youth. Accordingly, this study shows strongly that the level of financial literacy among the high school students in the study context is highly daunting. Policymakers and educators are expected to seriously note this devastating deficiency in basic financial literacy among the high school students in the country and educate the youth this basic life skill at a young age while still at school. One of the approaches that the researcher recommends is to incorporate a robust curriculum that educates the youth about the importance of financial literacy and the application of the knowledge and skills that one needs to make sound financial decisions. The studied high school students have a profound deficiency in financial literacy knowledge and skills, which are considered to be vital life skills.

Note

1 Department of Management, Addis Ababa University. Email: yohannes.workeaferahu@aau.edu.et.

References

Abubakar, H. A. (2015). Entrepreneurship development and financial literacy in Africa. *World Journal of Entrepreneurship, Management and Sustainable Development, 11*(4), 281–294. https://doi.org/10.1108/WJEMSD-04-2015-0020

Agarwal, S., Amromin, G., Ben-David, I., Chomsisengphet, S., & Evanoff, D. D. (2015). Financial literacy and financial planning: Evidence from India. *Journal of Housing Economics, 27*, 4–21. https://doi.org/10.1016/j.jhe.2015.02.003

Ahmed, Z., Noreen, U., Ramakrishnan, S. A., & Abdullah, D. F. B. (2021). What explains the investment decision-making behaviour? The role of financial literacy and financial risk tolerance. *Afro-Asian Journal of Finance and Accounting, 11*(1), 1–19. https://doi.org/10.1504/AAJFA.2021.111814

Amagir, A., Groot, W., van den Brink, H. M., & Wilschut, A. (2020). Financial literacy of high school students in the Netherlands: knowledge, attitudes, self-efficacy, and behavior. *International Review of Economics Education, 34*, 100185. https://doi.org/10.1016/j.iree.2020.100185

Ansong, A., & Gyensare, M. A. (2012). Determinants of university working-students' financial literacy at the University of Cape Coast, Ghana. *International Journal of Business and Management*, 7(9), 126–133. https://doi.org/10.5539/ijbm.v7n9p126

Antonietti A., Borsetto A., & Iannello P. (2016) A metacognitive approach to financial literacy. In Aprea C. et al. (eds.) *International Handbook of Financial Literacy*. Singapore: Springer. https://doi.org/10.1007/978-981-10-0360-8_5

Arceo-Gomez, E. O., & Villagómez, F. A. (2017). Financial literacy among Mexican high school teenagers. *International Review of Economics Education, 24*, 1–17. https://doi.org/10.1016/j.iree.2016.10.001

ASIC (Australian Securities & Investments Commission). (2014). National financial literacy strategy 2014–2017. Retrieved from http://www.financialliteracy.gov.au/media/546585/report-403_national-financial-literacy-strategy-2014–17.pdf

Bhabha, J. I., Khan, S., Qureshi, Q. A., Naeem, A., & Khan, I. (2014). Impact of financial literacy on saving-investment behavior of working women in the developing countries. *Research Journal of Finance and Accounting, 13*(5), 118–122.

Blue, L. E., & Grootenboer, P. (2019). A praxis approach to financial literacy education. *Journal of Curriculum Studies, 51*(5), 755–770. https://doi.org/10.1080/00220272.2019.1650115

Bruhn, M., de Souza Leão, L., Legovini, A., Marchetti, R., & Zia, B. (2013). *The impact of high school financial education: Experimental evidence from Brazil*. The World Bank.

Cameron, M. P., Calderwood, R., Cox, A., Lim, S., & Yamaoka, M. (2014). Factors associated with financial literacy among high school students in New Zealand. *International Review of Economics Education, 16*, 12–21. https://doi.org/10.1016/j.iree.2014.07.006

Caplinska, A., & Ohotina, A. (2019). Analysis of financial literacy tendencies with young people. *Entrepreneurship and Sustainability Issues, 6*(4), 6. https://doi.org/10.9770/jesi.2019.6.4(13)

De Beckker, K., De Witte, K., & Van Campenhout, G. (2020). The role of national culture in financial literacy: Cross-country evidence. *Journal of Consumer Affairs, 54*(3), 912–930. https://doi.org/10.2139/ssrn.3698656

Elifneh, Y. W. (2021) financial literacy among high school teenagers in a developing country context: An empirical study with reference to high school students in Addis Ababa, Ethiopia, *Independent Journal of Management & Production, 12*(5), 1436–1452. https://doi.org/10.14807/ijmp.v12i5.1402

Eniola, A. A., & Entebang, H. (2016). Financial literacy and SME firm performance. *International Journal of Research Studies in Management, 5*(1), 31–43. https://doi.org/10.5861/ijrsm.2015.1304

FEG, PISA. (2012) Financial literacy assessment framework. Doc:FinLit_Frmwrk_PISA12, available at https://www.oecd.org/pisa/pisaproducts/46962580.pdf. accessed on 25 September 2018.

Goyal, K., & Kumar, S. (2020). Financial literacy: A systematic review and bibliometric analysis. *International Journal of Consumer Studies, 45*(1), 80–105. https://doi.org/10.1111/ijcs.12605

Greenspan, A. (2002). Financial literacy: A tool for economic progress. *The Futurist, 36*(4), 37.

Hastings, J., & Mitchell, O. S. (2020). How financial literacy and impatience shape retirement wealth and investment behaviors. *Journal of Pension Economics & Finance, 19*(1), 1–20. https://doi.org/10.3386/w16740

Hastings, J., Madrian, B., & Skimmyhorn, W., (2012). *Financial literacy, financial education and economic outcomes*. NBER Working Paper 18412.

Henager, R., & Cude, B. J. (2019). Financial literacy of high school graduates: Long-and short-term financial behavior by age group. *Journal of Family and Economic Issues, 40*(3), 564–575. https://doi.org/10.1007/s10834-019-09626-2

Hizgilov, A., & Silber, J. (2020). On multidimensional approaches to financial literacy measurement. *Social Indicators Research, 148*, 787–830. https://doi.org/10.1007/s11205-019-02227-4

Hogarth, J. M., & Hilgert, M. A. (2002). Financial knowledge, experience and learning preferences: Preliminary results from a new survey on financial literacy. *Consumer Interest Annual*, 48(1), 1–7.

Huston, S. J. (2010). Measuring financial literacy. *Journal of Consumer Affairs, 44*(2), 296–316. https://doi.org/10.1111/j.1745-6606.2010.01170.x

Kefela, G. (2011). Implications of financial literacy in developing countries. *African Journal of Business Management, 5*(9), 3699–3705.

Klapper, L., & Lusardi, A. (2020). Financial literacy and financial resilience: Evidence from around the world. *Financial Management, 49*(3), 589–614. https://doi.org/10.1111/fima.12283

Kokkizil, M., Karakurum-Özdemir, K., & Uysal, G. (2016). *Financial literacy in developing countries.* BETAM Working Paper, 18.

Kothari, C. R. (2004). *Research methodology: Methods and techniques.* New Age International.

Lajuni, N., Kasuma, J., Yacob, Y., Azali, N. H., Emang, W., & Ismail, M. B. (2020). Islamic financial products/services and the intention to use. *Malaysian Journal of Consumer and Family Economics, 24*(1), 153–172.

Loerwald, D., & Stemmann, A. (2016). Behavioral finance and financial literacy: Educational implications of biases in financial decision making. In Aprea C. et al. (eds.) *International handbook of financial literacy.* Singapore: Springer. https://doi.org/10.1007/978-981-10-0360-8_3

Lucey, T. (2205). Assessing the reliability and validity of the jumpstart survey of financial literacy. *Journal of Family Economic Issues, 26*(2), 283–294. https://doi.org/10.1007/s10834-005-3526-8

Lusardi, A. (2019). Financial literacy and the need for financial education: Evidence and implications. *Swiss Journal of Economics and Statistics, 155*(1), 1. https://doi.org/10.1186/s41937-019-0027-5

Lusardi, A., & Mitchell, O. S. (2011). Financial literacy around the world: An overview. *Journal of pension economics & finance, 10*(4), 497–508.

Lusardi, A., & Mitchell, O. S. (2005). *Financial literacy and planning: Implications for retirement wellbeing.* Ann Arbor, MI: Michigan Retirement Research Center. https://doi.org/10.3386/w17078

Lusardi, A., Mitchell, O. S., & Curto, V. (2010). Financial literacy among the young. *Journal of Consumer Affairs, 44*(2), 358–380. https://doi.org/10.1111/j.1745-6606.2010.01173.x

Mandell, L. (2008). Financial literacy of high school students *Handbook of consumer finance research* (pp. 163–183): Singaopre: Springer. https://doi.org/10.1007/978-0-387-75734-6_10

Mason, C. L. J., & Wilson, R. M. S. (2000). *Conceptualizing financial literacy.* Business School Research Series Paper, 7. UK, Loughborough: Loughborough University.

Noctor, M., Stoney, S., & Stradling, R. (1992). *Financial literacy.* A report prepared for the National Westminster Bank, London.

OECD. (2013). *PISA 2012 assessment and analytical framework: Mathematics, reading, sciences, problem solving and financial literacy.* Paris: OECD Publishing.

OECD INFE. (2011). *Measuring financial literacy: Core questionnaire in measuring financial literacy: Questionnaire and guidance notes for conducting an internationally comparable survey of financial literacy.* Paris: OECD, available at http://www.oecd.org/daf/fin/financial-education/49319977.pdf, accessed on 25 September 2018.

Oehler, A., Horn, M., Wendt, S., Reisch, L. A., & Walker, T. J. (2018). Young adults and their finances: An international comparative study on applied financial literacy. *Economic Notes: Review of Banking, Finance and Monetary Economics, 47*(2–3), 305–330. https://doi.org/10.1111/ecno.12110

Oseifuah, E., Gyekye, A., & Formadi, P. (2018). Financial literacy among undergraduate students: Empirical evidence from Ghana. *Academy of Accounting and Financial Studies Journal, 22*(6), 1–17.

Patton, M. Q. (2002). *Qualitative evaluation and research methods*. London: Sage Publications.

Peng, T.-C. M., Bartholomae, S., Fox, J. J., & Cravener, G. (2007). The impact of personal finance education delivered in high school and college courses. *Journal of family and Economic Issues*, *28*(2), 265–284. https://doi.org/10.1007/s10834-007-9058-7

Refera, M. K., Dhaliwal, N. K., & Kaur, J. (2016). Financial literacy for developing countries in Africa: A review of concept, significance and research opportunities. *Journal of African Studies and Development*, *8*(1), 1–12. https://doi.org/10.5897/jasd2015.0331

Remund, D. L. (2010). Financial literacy explicated: The case for a clearer definition in an increasingly complex economy. *Journal of Consumer Affairs*, *44*(2), 276–295. https://doi.org/10.1111/j.1745-6606.2010.01169.x

Robb, C. A. (2011). Financial knowledge and credit card behavior of college students. *Journal of Family and Economic Issues*, *32*(4), 690–698. https://doi.org/10.1007/s10834-011-9259-y

Sarigül, H. (2014). A survey of financial literacy among university students. *Journal of Accounting & Finance*, *64*, 207–224.

Setiawan, B. (2020). Descriptive analysis of financial literacy: Evidence from public and private university students in Indonesia. *Sriwijaya International Journal of Dynamic Economics and Business*, *4*(1), 73–86. https://doi.org/10.29259/sijdeb.v4i1.73-86

Sonia, M., & Abraham, A. (2006). *Financial literacy research: Current literature and future opportunities*. University of Wollongong Faculty of Commerce Working Papers, available: http://ro.uow.edu.au/commpapers/223

Thomlison, B. (2001). Descriptive studies. In B. A. Thyer (ed.) *The handbook ofsocialwork research methods* (pp. 309–321). London: Sage Publications Inc. https://doi.org/10.4135/9781412986182.n7

Van Rooij, M. C., Lusardi, A., & Alessie, R. J. (2011). Financial literacy and retirement planning in the Netherlands. *Journal of Economic Psychology*, *32*(4), 593–608. https://doi.org/10.1016/j.joep.2011.02.004

Watanapongvanich, S., Binnagan, P., Putthinun, P., Khan, M. S. R., & Kadoya, Y. (2020). Financial literacy and gambling behavior: Evidence from Japan. *Journal of Gambling Studies*, *37*(2), 1–21. https://doi.org/10.1007/s10899-020-09936-3

Wentzel, A. (2016). Financial literacy in South` Africa. In *International Handbook of Financial Literacy* (pp. 329–339). Singapore: Springer. https://doi.org/10.1007/978-981-10-0360-8_22

Willis, L. E. (2008). Against financial-literacy education. *Iowa Law Review*, *94*, 197.

Willis, L. E. (2009). Evidence and ideology in assessing the effectiveness of financial literacy education. *San Diego Law Review*, *46*, 415.

Wolla, S. (2017). Evaluating the effectiveness of an online module for increasing financial literacy. *Social Studies Research and Practice*, *12*(2), 154–167. https://doi.org/10.1108/ssrp-04-2017-0014

Worthington, A. C. (2006). Predicting financial literacy in Australia. *Financial Services Review*, *15*(1), 59–79.

Xu, L., & Zia, B. (2012). *Financial literacy around the world: An overview of the evidence with practical suggestions for the way forward*. World Bank Policy Research Working Paper No. 6107, available at: http://papers.ssrn.com/abstract=2094887.

Yin, R. K. (2003). *Case studies research: Design and methods* (2nd ed.). Thousand Oaks, CA: Sage. https://doi.org/10.3138/cjpe.30.1.108

12 Exploring the literature for understanding of multisensory experiences in heritage boutique hotels

Zahra Pourabedin[1] *and Josephine Pryce*[2]

Introduction

Heritage tourism is one of the growing segments of the tourism industry. Heritage assets create competitive advantage for tourism destinations (Timothy, 2021). Despite increasing research in the heritage tourism space, there is scant extant literature investigating heritage boutique hotels. This area is an important segment of cultural heritage tourism and worthy of exploring. According to Chang (1997, p. 47), heritage lodging holds tremendous potential as 'a tool to promote civic pride, local identity, and cultural capital'. Heritage boutique hotels are unique because they provide heritage experiences and accommodation simultaneously (Lee & Chhabra, 2015). The importance of creating a memorable hotel experience is highlighted by hospitality scholars (Fitri et al., 2015; Martín-Ruiz et al., 2012; Parolin & Boeing, 2019). The challenge within tourism experience contexts is identifying the sensory dimensions of travellers' experiences that can contribute to visitor satisfaction (Pan & Ryan, 2009). Research is lacking in the specific sensory attributes of heritage boutique hotels that contribute to guest experience. This chapter seeks to fill this gap by investigating the multisensory experiences of travellers to heritage boutique hotels. The first part of the chapter focuses on the concept of 'heritage' and then advances to explore the travel motives of travellers to heritage sites. This section then leads to an overview of heritage boutique hotels (HBHs) and the value of guest experiences to this bourgeoning sector. The focus is on the multisensory experiences of guests as a way to critically analyze measurement scales for assessing visitors' experiences. The second part of the chapter analyzes the e-reviews of two HBHs to identify the main factors linked with multisensory experiences, identifying the most frequent senses mentioned in these online reviews. An examination of these e-reviews provides opportunities for future research, including as a segue for development of a scale that can be used in future HBH studies or associated domains.

DOI: 10.4324/9781003153580-12

Literature review

The concept of heritage

The word 'heritage' is generally associated with the 'inheritance' and its meaning, that is, something transferred from one generation to another (Graham et al., 2000). Owing to its role as 'a carrier' of historical values from the past, heritage is viewed as part of the cultural tradition of a society. Heritage is also linked to the uniqueness of the culture as well as the people and their identity, which coexist within such natural places (Saeedi & Heidarzadeh Hanzaee, 2018). Sharpley (1993) indicated that heritage is literally defined as things that are inherited from the past. However, it has become more broadly applied and now the term is used to describe anything associated with the nation's history, culture, wildlife, and landscape (Sharpley, 1993).

In an attempt to describe the pervasive and intangible nature of heritage, Millar (1989, p. 10) defines heritage as 'part of the fabric of people's lives, consciously or unconsciously accommodating aspirations and providing symbols of continuity, icons of identity and places for pleasure, enjoyment and enlightenment in the fast-changing world of global communications'. Johnson and Thomas (1995) also describe heritage as virtually anything linking with the past, which is axiomatic but an elusive definition (Herbert, 1995).

More recently, researchers have tried to capture the elements of heritage attractions. Garrod and Fyall (2000) developed a criteria for what makes a successful heritage attraction. The study suggested that heritage attractions must be inexpensive, visitor-friendly, and deliver value for money. They must be physically and culturally accessible and they must maintain authenticity and integrity. Ultimately, they noted that successful heritage attractions should balance the needs of visitors and the conservation imperative. Such conservation necessities have meant that organizations such as the United Nations Educational, Scientific and Cultural Organization (UNESCO) have become custodians of heritage sites.

UNESCO is the overarching caretaker of the outstanding value of heritage sites to humanity. They seek to identify, protect, and preserve heritage assets. In this way, UNESCO has selected heritage attractions to be listed in the UNESCO World Heritage list. Being in the UNESCO World Heritage List ensures that the property reflects the world's cultural and natural diversity and is of outstanding universal value. UNESCO (2008) listed ten criteria which sites should have to be included so as to be classified as World Heritage Sites. The criteria include addressing of cultural heritage.

Cultural heritage

The literature presents a myriad of definitions for 'cultural heritage', with none fully capturing the underlying meaning of cultural heritage. Hence, this study adopts the definition developed by the United Nations Educational, Scientific and Cultural Organization (UNESCO, 2000), which categories cultural heritage into separate forms, namely tangible and intangible heritage. Tangible heritage sites are physical assets which have cultural values, and include historical sites, buildings, cultural landscapes, and cultural objects (Bak et al., 2019). These assets are of value to the respective communities. Further examples of tangible heritage sites include historic sites, cultural centres, museums, and art galleries.

The other category, intangible cultural heritage, represents the forms of culture, such as folklore, which are the totality of tradition-based creations of a community, expressed by a group or individuals, and recognized as reflecting the expectations of a community insofar as they reflect its cultural and social identity (Bak et al., 2019). Hence, intangible cultural heritage is human activity in the process of creating tangible culture, as well as any social, continuing, and representative activity aiming at satisfying the spiritual needs of a given human community, which in that particular region and community is understood as a manifestation of traditional culture, learning, and techniques. It comprises legends, performances, social customs, ceremonies and festivals, traditional arts, music, dance, literature, handicrafts, and games (Bak et al., 2019).

Heritage tourism

Among the different kinds of attractions, heritage attractions are one of the most important motivators for travel and tourism (Ramires et al., 2018). Those that are known as a World Heritage Site can be a coveted prize, and regarded as a means of increasing tourism. For instance, in 1998 Hall and Piggin conducted a survey of 44 World Heritage Sites, in which over two-thirds of the site managers reported there had been an increase in visitor numbers after their site gained World Heritage status. The result also showed that cultural sites were considered to be more interesting to visit (Hall & Piggin, 2002).

Garrod and Fyall (1998) defined heritage tourism as 'an economic activity that makes use of socio-cultural assets to attract visitors' (p. 199). Based on Hall and McArthur (1998), heritage tourism includes historic and cultural attractions such as national parks, natural supplies, artefacts, ceremonies, building, and landscapes of a nation. Interpretations for what constitutes heritage tourism sites around the world varies. For example, visiting historic sites of cities in northern Europe is considered heritage tourism. Meanwhile North Americans believe visiting natural sites, chiefly national parks (such as Anne of Green Gables, and Niagara Falls in Canada) are described as heritage tourism. Likewise, natural places are essential for the Australian and New Zealander (e.g. Ayers Rock in Australia, and Māori culture and national parks in New Zealand) (McCain & Ray, 2003; Timothy & Boyd, 2003). Given all the various interpretations of heritage tourism, de Rojas and Camarero (2008) advance that heritage tourism can be summarized as being a place to spend leisure time and engage in social interactions to learn about the history and culture of the place.

According to Edgell (1990), since heritage tourism development relies on natural uniqueness, culture and history, it can be considered as a highly viable option in the tourism industry. Heritage tourism has become the principal focus of the tourism industry in many developed countries (Herbert, 2001; Timothy & Boyd, 2006). Besides its role in economic development, heritage tourism is widely accepted as an effective way to achieve the educational function of tourism (Ashworth & Tunbridge, 1990; Light & Prentice, 1994; Timothy & Boyd, 2006), by creating a positive destination image (Richter, 1980; Su et al., 2020) and national identity (Pretes, 2003; Soper, 2007), and also by influencing public opinion (Waitt, 2000). Moreever, tourism is a positive force for the protection of the World Heritage Sites, because of its ability to draw world attention to their importance (Li et al., 2008; Shi et al., 2019). So today, resources such as history, culture, and natural ones like coastlines have been seen by many countries as a way to attract tourists and bring money (Chul Oh et al., 1995). Parallel to these economic activities, heritage tourism has been studied from different perspectives such as sustainability (Caserta & Russo, 2002; Garrod & Fyall, 2000; Li et al., 2008; Weaver, 2007; Zhang et al., 2020), management and development (Ho & McKercher, 2004), and marketing (Park, Choi, and Lee 432019, 2Apostolakis, 2003; Chen & Chen, 2010; Misiura, 2006; Nuryanti, 1996; Park et al., 2019, Poria et al., 2003).

Since heritage assets are not renewable, the major challenge in the heritage tourism field is related to creating a balance between protection and serving, because an increased popularity of heritage sites can become a threat for the sustainability of the destination (Li et al., 2008). According to Beeton (2003), tourism managers consider the factors of attracting more visitors and increasing revenue as measures of success, but this short-term focus can have negative impacts on sustainability. For developing and marketing heritage sites, preservation issues should be considered. For instance, Wicks et al. (2004) focused on the sustainability issue and suggested that instead of heritage tourism marketers focusing purely on visitor numbers, they should focus on visitors who spend more money, are educated, and respect the local people of the destinations. De-marketing is another strategy which has been suggested for controlling the population of visitors in sites (Beeton & Benfield, 2002). Examples of de-marketing in the heritage tourism field include increasing the cost of the visit, introducing alternative attractions in the area, or developing some marketing strategies to encourage visitors to come in low season periods.

Marketing is a vital component of the communication process and helps to make heritage accessible and meaningful to more than just the specialist cultural tourist (Fullerton et al., 2010; Napolitano et al., 2018). According to Apostolakis (2003), heritage marketing is repacking the initial product, making it more appealing and accessible to the mass market. In the area of marketing and management of heritage tourism, scholars highlighted the importance of sites, events, cultures, and experience (Buchmann et al., 2010; Kolar & Zabkar, 2010; Qiao et al., 2016) Marketing is vital for making heritage accessible and meaningful for tourists because of the increasing number of heritage tourists on the one hand, and the high pressure of competitiveness resulted from information technologies development and globalization, on the other hand. In the area of heritage tourism marketing, most researchers have focused to study on the role of the trip experience, the personal characteristics of the visitors, and the site attributes that promote tourist behaviours. For instance, Chen and Chen (2010) studied the behavioural intentions of heritage tourists. Their results showed the direct effect of the quality of experience on perceived value and satisfaction. Hence, both perceived value and satisfaction had significantly direct positive effects on behavioural intentions, while the effect of experience quality on behavioural intentions was insignificant. As another example, Poria et al. (2003) revealed that there are differences between tourists based upon their perceptions and that these lead to differences in behaviour. Authors suggested heritage tourists who view a place as bound up with their own heritage are likely to behave significantly differently from others, as evidenced in such behavioural factors as intention to revisit and length of stay. Hence, the effectiveness of tourism marketing depends on understanding customers' motivations (Fodness, 1994). The next section explains the concept of travel motivation and its related issues.

Travel motives of heritage travellers

Travel motives of heritage tourists are significantly different from those of other tourists (Shi et al., 2019). Generally heritage tourists are motivated by learning (Halewood & Hannam, 2001). Poria et al. (2006), identified two categories of motives within heritage tourists. The first category is related to individuals and includes an opportunity to learn, to be involved in a recreational activity, and to be with family. The next category is associated with attributes of the site (e.g., location and proximity to other sites). Moscardo (1996) identified three main motives among heritage travellers: education, entertainment, and building social connections. Shi et al. (2019) divided the heritage tourism market into three segments of culture-focused group, culture attentive group, and culture-appreciative group. In addition, Jansen-Verbeke (1996) recognized learning as the primary motivation for heritage visits. Other researchers have recognized factors were relaxation, being active, and being creative (e.g., Lowenthal, 1985; Confer & Kerstetter, 2001; Trinh & Ryan, 2017). Also, it is important to acknowledge that a heritage tourist can have a multitude of motivations to visit a certain place and that heritage sites can have different meanings to different visitors (Lowenthal, 2015; Shi et al., 2019). Based on the research of Confer and Kerstetter (2001), variables for predicting heritage tourists' visitation are motivation, decision-making time, the length of stay, group size, and visitation status. Hence, studies to date show that travellers to heritage sites are motivated by a myriad of different reasons, such as ranging from a fleeting desire to learn to a serious quest of knowledge, paralleled by an interest in culture, traditions, and history as determinants of visitors' motives. Though many studies explore various aspects relating to heritage tourism, there is scant research that investigates the multisensory experiences of visitors to HBHs. Before embarking on such multisensory visitor experiences, it is important to understand the nature of HBHs.

Heritage boutique hotels

Heritage boutique hotels are an example of places that travellers experience. They provide unique hospitality experiences through accommodation and ancillary services such as food, beverage, leisure facilities, and entertainment that have historic elements and heritage themes. Consequently, HBHs enrich travellers' experiences through 'interactions and observations that engage customers with the hotel in a personal way and lead to positive customer behaviours such as loyalty and word of mouth' (Elsayed, 2019, p. 3) but they do so through tangible and intangible features that respect the history and culture of the hotel and its environment while presenting 'elegance and comfort' and providing 'high quality personalized service' (Aksoy, 2017, p. 56).

Developing and presenting of hospitality in a framework that attends to heritage and boutique features means that basic daily operations of the hotel are linked back to these features wherever possible. Hence, aspects such as the decor, food, uniforms, and personalized service pay homage to the heritage of the hotel. Equally, operational requirements such as security and safety, need to be aligned to contemporary regulations and expectations. Given these factors, boutique hotels fall into two categories: (1) contemporary buildings that are built to deliver unique experiences consistent with the boutique theme; and (2) refunctioning of old buildings that sustain the historical and heritage authenticity while accommodating modern materials and technologies that satisfy contemporary building regulations and attract modern travellers (Aksoy, 2017). The synthesis of contemporary needs with traditional heritage comes together in the HBHs to create harmony between originality and authenticity with contemporary functional and technical necessities.

Boutique hotels are recognized for their focus on 'social, cultural and personal realms' (Chang, 2017, p. 51). They are defined as 'stylish, trendy, and cool and provide an intimate hotel experience … [that ranges] from heritage and historic settings to contemporary modern architecture' (Ghaderi et al., p.698). HBHs capture the focus on guest experiences that includes architecture, design, and cultural heritage. In exploring the characteristics of HBHs, Chang (2017) highlights the various stakeholders as being the hotel workers/owners, the guests and neighbouring residents, and categorizes each of these as 'creation', 'consumptions', and 'contestation', respectively. Chang (2017) argues that each of these stakeholders contribute to creating 'experiencescapes' that magnify 'identity' and 'belonging' for these historical spaces that through restoration and repurposing become places with intangible dimensions that afford meaning to a myriad of experiences.

This adaptive reuse of heritage and/or historical buildings has a dual purpose. In the first instance, it adds to the diversification of accommodation options for travellers and caters to the increasing demand for HBHs (Ghaderi et al., 2020). Secondly, HBHs contribute to the preservation of historical buildings and conservation of cultural heritage. HBHs have been described as 'a source of tangible heritage and intangible values' wherein luxurious settings can create exceptional experiences (ibid., 2021, p. 697). In HBHs, culture, heritage, and history coalesce and bring to life the past in authentic ways for travellers to experience. This upsurge in converting of historical buildings to boutique hotels has sometimes been referred to as 'a commercialization of the past' (ibid., p. 697). Notably, this repurposing of old buildings does bring financial benefits to the owners but it also does create jobs and preserves the essence of hospitality in delivering a personalized, quality service. It is further argued that the commodification of built heritage can prolong the historic fabric of a city or place by sustaining the intrinsic sociocultural values of the built environment (Ghaderi et al., 2020; Rhaman et al., 2018).

With a growing emphasis and demand on heritage tourism and the value of HBHs, it is worthwhile to investigate the experiences of visitors to HBHs. Hence, the chapter proceeds with an examination of extant scales that are used to understand the experiences of hotel guests, as a way to begin understanding multisensory experiences.

Multisensory experiences of HBHs

Building on the work of Pine and Gilmore (2011), experiences have been recognized as a 'distinct economic offering, occupying a central role in society, and holding a premium position on the four-stage-continuum of the progression of economic value, after commodities, goods and services' (Agapito et al., 2012, p. 9). Further to this conceptualization of experiences, there is growing recognition in the literature that the five human senses (i.e., sight, smell, touch, taste, and hearing) play a major role in people's consumption experiences (Dann & Dann, 2011; Hultén et al., 2009; Krishna, 2012; Mitchell & McIntosh, 1999).

Sensory marketing captures the role of the senses in consumer behaviour. It is defined as 'marketing that engages the consumers' senses and affects their perception, judgement and behaviour' (Krishna, 2012, p. 1). So, invariably, tourist experiences have a multisensory nature and the five human senses play an important role in creating memorable experiences for travellers (Ceren, 2016). In addition, sensory experiences influence word of mouth (Norouzi & Darvish, 2019). Mehrabian and Russel (1974) developed a 'Stimulus-Response Model' which shows the relationship between sensory experiences (with all five senses engaged, customers' responses with increased emotional response and memory recall, along with intuitive responses), and customer buying behaviours (with increased customer loyalty).

A few studies within the tourism context have focused on sensory experiences of tourism destinations (Norouzi & Darvish, 2019; Pharino et al., 2018; Szczepańska & Wilkaniec, 2015; van Hoven, 2011); however, the indispensability of senses in the theory of destination marketing has not yet been realized by scholars in this field (Xingyang et al., 2019). Emerging studies include the work of Szczepánska and Wilkaniec (2015) who revealed the influence of other senses rather than sight on the perceived relaxation by travellers in leisure travelling. Van Hoven (2011) also added to the literature when filming for a documentary identified different multisensory experiences and tourist performances in relation to the Great Bear Rainforest. Xiong et al. (2015) investigated the tourists' multisensory image of Phoenix city in China. The results identified vision as the most important contributor to the destination's image. In addition, authors have highlighted the need to develop a multisensory image scale for tourism destinations (Xiong et al., 2015). Santos et al. (2019) investigated the sensory elements of a winery visit experience. The results revealed the importance of visual and taste elements to attract tourists. Hence, there is variability in what researchers discover to be the main sensory elements that reflect visitors' experiences and future research is needed to understand the influence of the senses in the destination marketing space.

Sensory appeal in the hotel offerings has also not been studied extensively, nor has there been an examination of the major potential that sensory marketing can make to the hotel industry's performance (Kim et al., 2017). Guzel and Dortyol (2015) conducted a content analysis of guest reviews on Tripadvisor .com and identified the sensory profile of tourism experiences of guests in a hotel in Turkey.

Their results showed that the visual component was the most prominent sense (209 responses), and taste was second (65 responses), followed by auditory (14 responses), tactual (9 responses), and smell (2 responses). A more recent study by Pourabedin et al. (2021) who also used guest comments from Tripadvisor, also showed that comments relating to 'sight' were mentioned most frequently, with the combination of 'sight' and 'feeling'/emotion was a common occurrence. This suggests that multisensory experiences are connected to affective and cognitive components, as well as behavioural and relational components. One such model is the Orchestra Model as used by Pharino et al. (2018) in the examination of visitors' experiences at paranormal sites. This model can be adapted to capture the complexity of the experiences of guests at HBHs.

The Orchestra Model (Pharino et al., 2018) consists of five components: (1) sensory elements; (2) affective components; (3) cognitive elements; (4) behavioural components; and (5) relationships. It recognizes that it is the interplay of each of these five components that orchestrate visitors' experiences. Such a research approach will allow for the exploration of which senses are involved for guests of HBHs (sensory), investigation of the feelings and emotions of HBHs visitors, understand what guests do onsite at HBHs (behavioural), identify the levels of heritage information and learning that guests engage with at HBHs (cognitive), and profiling with whom guests travel (relationships). Equally, operators can choreograph the various components to meet visitors' expectations and enhance satisfaction.

In order to gain an understanding of the elements of multisensory experiences, this study sought to advance the work of Pourabedin et al. (2021) and adopt an exploratory approach to identifying the characteristics of sensory experiences of travellers to HBHs. This work is part of a broader project that in time seeks to develop a scale that captures the multisensory experiences of travellers to places of heritage significance.

Methodology

This study drew on Tripadvisor guest reviews of the Duxton Reserve hotel in Singapore and the Hotel Windsor in Melbourne, Australia. Manual content analysis was used to explore the multisensory experiences of travellers. A total of 296 reviews were collected, 146 reviews of the Duxton Reserve hotel, and 150 reviews of the Hotel Windsor. The reviews were dated from October 2018 to June 2021. A random, non-probability sampling regime was adopted as reviews were collected as they appeared progressively in the respective Tripadvisor websites (Saunders et al., 2009).

Content analysis was used to code the reviews based on the five senses (smell, hearing, taste, sight, and touch). Content analysis is understood to be a reliable and valid approach for analyzing texts and interpreting meanings from the data using a systematic approach to coding (Pearce et al., 2020; Vaismoradi et al., 2013). It affords a methodical and comparative evaluation of the data. In this study, the authors adopted the three-phase approach described by Elo and Kyngäs (2008): (1) preparation (data collection and unit of analysis); (2) organization (coding and abstraction); and (3) reporting (synthesis of results).

Hence, each author first worked independently on a respective data set (i.e., either the Duxton Reserve or Hotel Windsor data set) to collate and code the data into the five categories. The authors then met to discuss their findings, further to which the data was revisited to capture consistency in coding between the authors. This approach led to an iterative and systematic means of evaluating the reviews and synthesizing the results to identifying the presence of multisensory components in the guests' experiences.

Results and discussion

This study explored the multisensory based experiences of travellers as guests in two hotels – the Duxton Reserve (Singapore) and the Hotel Windsor (Australia). It sought to identify the attributes according to the five sensation categories of smell; sound; touch; taste; and sight. Table 12.1 shows the frequency for each sense.

The results showed that the sight was the most prominent sense (173 and 387) followed by taste (117 and 129). Although more sight attributes were found in the Hotel Windsor, in both hotels, guests captured their hotel experiences through visual attributes. Nearly 50% of recalled attributes of the Duxton Reserve hotel and 70% of recalled attributes of the Hotel Windsor were related to sight. The sense of smell was the least effective sensation recalled and so, determined as being important for creating sensory experiences. In addition, Table 12.1 presents a few examples of guest e-reviews to illustrate the ways in which the sensory experiences impacted on travellers.

Table 12.1 Frequency for each sense as derived from e-reviews from Duxton Reserve and Hotel Windsor

Sense	*Hotel*	*Frequency*	*Percentage (%)*	*Examples of guests' e-reviews*
Smell	Duxton Reserve	4	1	(1) 'The wonderful fragrance emitted from the lobby is always so welcoming'. (2) 'The moment you step in, you have a different feel with the nice fragrance and unique oriental decoration.' (3) 'They would put special sleep and relaxation remedies throughout the room during my stay'.
	Hotel Windsor	2	0.35	(1) 'In the evening I went to the spot bar for a drink. The bad stinky smell was unbearable. I couldn't finish my drink and had to leave'. (2) 'Lovely big old reception area which smelled musty and op-shoppy'.
Sound	Duxton Reserve	26	7.5	(1) 'The singing bowl welcome experience is not to be missed'. (2) 'You are given a free session with a TCM (traditional Chinese medicine) doctor in house'. (3) 'Singing bowl was awesome'.
	Hotel Windsor	21	3.75	(1) 'Street level rooms on Bourke St are subject to noise from the passing trams'. (2) 'We understand the Windsor is old but the noise generated between rooms by other guests just walking across the floor is an issue'. (3) 'Being a very old building, echo and noise carry is a big problem. Floor boards from the rooms above you creak constantly, and if you are road side, there is very little noise insulation between you and the street'.
Touch	Duxton Reserve	29	8	(1) 'The hot shower was amazing:)'. (2) 'The mattress is very comfortable. Good pillows'. (3) 'This hotel emphasizes wellness in every detail and it resonates well with me. I mean, a singing bowl in my room, tiger balm and shopping back for retail therapy:)'. (4) 'Walking into the foyer didn't disappoint, it's slick and beautiful with black lacquer and silks setting the scene. The rooms were pared back but luxurious, an elegant, seamless black bathroom and a glittering mini bar were the design points, with cushy white linen beds to relax from the hustle and bustle of the city outside'. (5) 'Boutique hotel with unique style in a lively neighbourhood. The Pearl Suite of the Duxton Reserve come with a porch rarely seen at other hotels, which leads to the living room decorated mostly in white. The bedroom has a large bed and many storage cabinets. Very special bathtub'.
	Hotel Windsor	20	3.57	(1) 'Water pressure from shower was a slow trickle'. (2) 'Main fault is the Air Con was blazing hot in my room on 3rd floor, but friend staying on 4th floor complained his was freezing cold'. (3) 'the rooms are comfortable and the bar downstairs has a great atmosphere'.

(Continued)

Table 12.1 (Continued)

Sense	*Hotel*	*Frequency*	*Percentage (%)*	*Examples of guests' e-reviews*
Taste	Duxton Reserve	117	33.5	(1) 'Also remember to get the breakfast if you can, it's served at Yellow Pot which is 10/10!'. (2) 'Exceptionally good cocktails at the bar, my favourite was "Date"'. (3) 'I can only describe as the best breakfast we have ever encountered in any hotel, the Ala [sic] carte menu was exciting and exceptional and we enjoyed Singapore chilli crab omelette (a must) dim sum, Asian beef noodle soup and some incredibly fresh fruit'. (4) 'Breakfast was decent, good variety despite choices being watered down due to Covid. The breadbasket was my favorite / followed by the crab omelette. Ginseng chicken Porridge a little too bland, the usual eggs are the standard'.
	Hotel Windsor	129	23	(1) 'The breakfasts at their restaurant are excellent'. (2) 'afternoon tea; bottle of champagne; petit fours; club sandwich'. (3) 'afternoon tea; delightful breakfast; food was of a very good level'.
Sight	Duxton Reserve	173	49.5	(1) 'Recently rebranded, this boutique hotel looked gorgeous from the outside, and stepping into the lobby; it was even lovelier. The black and gold/yellow colour combination in her furniture and fixtures certainly lent an air of opulence to the surroundings'. (2) 'Yes, the decor is certainly on the dark/black side, both in the public areas and in the rooms, but the hotel is full of character and you can clearly see its historic past'. (3) 'The lobby plays it all bold opulence by way of its dramatic gold and bumblebee colour scheme, with striking East Asian flourishes such as large golden fans and fan motifs; Chinese bamboo screens, calligraphy wallpaper and brushes; and brass singing bowls'.
	Hotel Windsor	387	69	(1) 'The suite was particularly spacious with a separate bedroom, lounge area, bathroom and vestibule'. (2) 'The rooms are very large with amazing high ceilings'. (3) 'The room was aesthetically beautiful (with gorgeous curtains and a beautiful vintage dresser)'. (4) 'Elegance of the rooms … Exudes hushed luxury … Beautifully presented … Artworks dotted around the corridors'. (5) 'Grand façade; elegant furnishings; artwork; the staircase, the ballroom; a beautiful dining room; massive [room] with lounge area'.

Generally, Table 12.1 highlights that the historical attributes and interior design of hotels were key aspects of guests' experiences; these aspects were aligned with the sense of sight. Regarding smell, fragrance and aromatic smells as well as unpleasant smells formed the experiences as illustrated by the following comments relating to the Duxton Reserve:

'The wonderful fragrance emitted from the lobby is always so welcoming'
'The bad stinky smell was unbearable. I couldn't finish my drink and had to leave'
'old reception area which smelled musty and op-shoppy'

The reviews also gave valuable information regarding taste impressions. Breakfast is one of the most important contributors to taste impressions in both hotels. The taste finding related to the Duxton Reserve hotel highlighted the importance of traditional foods in HBSs. While the sound of traditional musical instruments and traditional Chinese medicine may lead to positive experiences, while some sound sensory impressions, such as noise, were construed as being negative to guests' experiences at both these HBHs.

Finally, in relation to touch, bedding and pillows were repeatedly mentioned as important touch related attributes in both hotels. In addition, the wellness attributes of Duxton Reserve such as spa, yoga, and traditional oils are notable. At the Hotel Windsor, it was the water pressure that was mentioned frequently as a sensory aspect that impacted negatively on guests' experiences.

Conclusion

This chapter set out to identify the elements of sensory experience of heritage boutique hotels. It began by exploring the concept of heritage and seeking to understand heritage tourism and the motives of heritage travellers. In the process, it identified gaps in the literature relating to HBHs, especially in relation to research that contributes to understanding the multisensory experiences of travellers to HBHs. With the intent of contributing to the dearth of research in this space, the researchers navigated their investigation on the experiences of guests to HBHs by exploring the notion of multisensory experiences of these guests through their e-reviews on Tripadvisor. The analysis of 296 guest reviews from two hotels – the Duxton Reserve (Singapore) and the Hotel Windsor (Australia) – supported the role of all five senses in creating hotel experiences. Based on the findings, the visual component of multisensory experiences was the most prominent and sound was the least notable. The results support the importance of multisensory attributes in creating memorable hotel experience.

In this endeavour to understanding how the senses play a role in travellers' experiences, the chapter has highlighted that to understand the uniqueness sought in heritage encounters, it is essential to understand what the unique attributes of HBHs are and how these are linked to satisfying the needs of contemporary cultural and heritage consumption and the complexities of multisensory experiences. For example, by designing multisensory experiences for guests, through using aspects such as traditional music, local fragrances, traditional foods, and antique furniture, HBHs can promote the hotel and influence guests' experience and satisfaction.

When considering the relationship between hospitality and heritage, a shortage of literature is noticeable, especially regarding multisensory attributes in the context of visitor experiences in heritage places. Hence, while this study adds value to the literature, further empirical research is required to advance understanding in the space of HBHs. One such proposed study is to develop a measurement scale that accommodates the uniqueness of heritage boutique hotels and their sustained contribution to cultural heritage tourism and more broadly, to business operators, the hospitality and tourism industry, and associated communities. Some current scales and models provide a platform to begin this empirical work and here it has been proposed that the Orchestra Model as used by Pharino et al. (2018) to examine visitors' experiences can be adapted to HBHs.

HBHs are important heritage hospitality and tourism resources, with growing global demand for their consumption. Therefore, there is an imperative for hoteliers globally to implement practices that use the multisensory components of cultural heritage assets to enhance marketing strategies and advance the sustained success of HBHs in ways that are holistic and sensitive to the complexities of heritage experiences.

Notes

1 Corresponding author: JCU Singapore Business School, JCU Singapore, Singapore, and Department of International Trade. Email: zahra.pourabedin@jcu.edu.au.
2 College of Business, Law, and Governance, James Cook University, Australia.

References

Agapito, D., Pinto, P., & Mendes, J. (2012). Sensory marketing and tourist experiences. *Spatial and Organizational Dynamics Discussions Papers, 10*, 7–19.

Apostolakis, A. (2003). The convergence process in heritage tourism. *Annals of Tourism Research, 30*(4), 795–812.

Ashworth, G. J., & Tunbridge, J. (1990). *Tourist-historic city*. UK: Belhaven Press.

Bak, S., Min, C.-K., & Roh, T.-S. (2019). Impacts of UNESCO-listed tangible and intangible heritages on tourism. *Journal of Travel & Tourism Marketing, 36*(8), 917–927.

Beeton, S. (2003). Swimming against the tide-integrating marketing with environmental management via demarketing. *Journal of Hospitality and Tourism Management, 10*, 95–107.

Beeton, S., & Benfield, R. (2002). Demand control: The case for demarketing as a visitor and environmental management tool. *Journal of Sustainable Tourism, 10*(6), 497–513.

Buchmann, A., Moore, K., & Fisher, D. (2010). Experiencing film tourism: Authenticity & fellowship. *Annals of Tourism Research, 37*(1), 229–248.

Caserta, S., & Russo, A. P. (2002). More means worse: Asymmetric information, spatial displacement and sustainable heritage tourism. *Journal of Cultural Economics, 26*(4), 245–260.

Ceren, I. (2016). Sensory marketing in tourism. *Global Issues and Trends in Tourism*, 561–568.

Chang, T. C. (1997). Heritage as a tourism commodity: Traversing the tourist–local divide. *Singapore Journal of Tropical Geography, 18*(1), 46–68.

Chul Oh, H., Uysal, M., & Weaver, P. A. (1995). Product bundles and market segments based on travel motivations: A canonical correlation approach. *International Journal of Hospitality Management, 14*(2), 123–137.

Dann, E., & Dann, G. (2011). Sightseeing for the sightless and soundless: Tourism experiences of the dual sensory impaired. *Studies & Reports, Série L.*, Centre International de Recherches et D'Etudes Touristiques,16(2011) 1–36.

Edgell, D. (1990). *International tourism policy*. New York: Van Nostrand Reinhold.

Elo, S., & Kyngäs, H. (2008). The qualitative content analysis process. *Journal of Advanced Nursing, 62*(1), 107–115.

Fitri, I., Ahmad, Y., & Ahmad, F. (2015). Conservation of tangible cultural heritage in Indonesia: A review current national criteria for assessing heritage value. *Procedia-Social and Behavioral Sciences, 184*, 71–78.

Fodness, D. (1994). Measuring tourist motivation. *Annals of Tourism Research, 21*(3), 555–581.

Fullerton, L., McGettigan, K., & Stephens, S. (2010). Integrating management and marketing strategies at heritage sites. *International Journal of Culture, Tourism and Hospitality Research, 4*(2), 108–117.

Garrod, B., & Fyall, A. (2000). Managing heritage tourism. *Annals of Tourism Research, 27*(3), 682–708.

Graham, B. J., Ashworth, G., & Tunbridge, J. (2000). *A geography of heritage: power, culture and economy: London.*

Guzel, O., & Dortyol, I. T. (2015). *Exploring the multi-sensory based memorable tourism experiences: A search on Adam & Eva Hotel in Turkey*. Paper presented at the Proceedings of Annual Paris Business Research Conference, Paris.

Halewood, C., & Hannam, K. (2001). Viking heritage tourism: Authenticity and Commodification. *Annals of Tourism Research, 28*(3), 565–580.

Hall, M. C., & McArthur, S. (1998). *Integrated heritage management: Principles and practice*: Stationery Office.

Hall, C. M., & Piggin, R. (2002). Tourism business knowledge of World Heritage sites: A New Zealand case study. *International Journal of Tourism Research*, 4(5), 401–411

Herbert, D. T. (1995). *Heritage, tourism and society*. Mansell Publishing.

Herbert, D. (2001). Literary places, tourism and the heritage experience. *Annals of Tourism Research, 28*(2), 312–333.

Ho, P. S. Y., & McKercher, B. (2004). Managing heritage resources as tourism products. *Asia Pacific Journal of Tourism Research, 9*(3), 255–266.

Hultén, B., Broweus, N., & Van Dijk, M. (2009). What is sensory marketing? In *Sensory marketing* (pp. 1–23). New York: Springer.

Johnson, P., & Thomas, B. (1995). Heritage as business. In *Heritage, Tourism and Society* (pp. 170–190). New York: Mansell Publishing.

Kim, B., Wang, S., & Heo, C. Y. (2017). Sensory marketing in hotels: Understanding of sensory triggers for hotel operations. In *The Routledge Handbook of Hospitality Marketing* (pp. 245–254). London: Routledge.

Kolar, T., & Zabkar, V. (2010). A consumer-based model of authenticity: An oxymoron or the foundation of cultural heritage marketing? *Tourism Management, 31*(5), 652–664.

Krishna, A. (2012). An integrative review of sensory marketing: Engaging the senses to affect perception, judgment and behavior. *Journal of Consumer Psychology, 22*(3), 332–351.

Lee, W., & Chhabra, D. (2015). *Heritage hotels and historic lodging: Perspectives on experiential marketing and sustainable culture*. Boca Raton, FL: Taylor & Francis.

Li, M., Wu, B., & Cai, L. (2008). Tourism development of World Heritage Sites in China: A geographic perspective. *Tourism Management, 29*(2), 308–319.

Light, D., & Prentice, R. (1994). Market-based product development in heritage tourism. *Tourism Management, 15*(1), 27–36.

Lowenthal, D. (2015). *The past is a foreign country-revisited*: Cambridge: Cambridge University Press.

Martín-Ruiz, D., Barroso-Castro, C., & Rosa-Díaz, I. M. (2012). Creating customer value through service experiences: An empirical study in the hotel industry. *Tourism and Hospitality Management, 18*(1), 37–53.

McCain, G., & Ray, N. M. (2003). Legacy tourism: the search for personal meaning in heritage travel. Tourism Management, 24(6), 713–717.

Millar, S. (1989). Heritage management for heritage tourism. *Tourism Management, 10*(1), 9–14.

Misiura, S. (2006). *Heritage marketing*. Routledge, UK: Butterworth-Heinemann.

Mitchell, R., & McIntosh, R. (1999). *Investigating the sensory and affective nature of the wine tourism experience*. Paper presented at the Tourism and Hospitality: Delighting the Senses 1999 Part Two Proceedings of the Ninth Australian Tourism Hospitality and Tourism Research Conference Council of the Australian University Tourism and Hospitality Education (CAUTHE), Adelaide: University of South Australia.

Moscardo, G. (1996). Mindful visitors: Heritage and tourism. *Annals of Tourism Research, 23*(2), 376–397.

Napolitano, M. R., Riviezzo, A., & Garofano, A. (2018). Heritage Marketing. In *Come aprire lo scrigno e trovare un tesoro*. Napoli: Editoriale Scientifica.

Norouzi, H., & Darvish, F. (2019). The effect of sensory components on positive word-of-mouth advertising by mediating role of destination emotion and brand experience in tourism industry (Case study: Foreign tourists). *Journal of Tourism and Development, 8*(2), 66–82.

Pan, S., & Ryan, C. (2009). Tourism sense-making: The role of the senses and travel journalism. *Journal of Travel & Tourism Marketing, 26*(7), 625–639.

Park, E., Choi, B.-K., & Lee, T. J. (2019). The role and dimensions of authenticity in heritage tourism. *Tourism Management, 74*, 99–109.

Parolin, C., & Boeing, R. (2019). Consumption of boutique hotel experiences as revealed by electronic word-of-mouth. *Tourism & Management Studies, 15*(2), 33–45.

Pearce, T., Maple, M., Shakeshaft, A., Wayland, S., & McKay, K. (2020). What is the co-creation of new knowledge? A content analysis and proposed definition for health interventions. *International Journal of Environmental Research and Public Health, 17*(7), 2229.

Pharino, C., Pearce, P., & Pryce, J. (2018). Paranormal tourism: Assessing tourists' onsite experiences. *Tourism Management Perspectives, 28*, 20–28.

Pine, B. J., & Gilmore, J. H. (1998). The experience economy. Harvard Business Press.

Poria, Y., Reichel, A., & Biran, A. (2006). Heritage site management: Motivations and expectations. *Annals of Tourism Research, 33*(1), 162–178.

Pourabedin, Zahra, Mahony, Tracey, and Pryce, Josephine (2021) Towards developing a multisensory scale to capture attributes of heritage boutique hotels. In: Community Empowerment, Sustainable Cities, and Transformative Economies: proceedings of the 1st International Conference on Business, Economics, Management, and Sustainability., 2–3 July 2021, Cairns, QLD, Australia and Online. (In Press)

Pretes, M. (2003). Tourism and nationalism. *Annals of Tourism Research, 30*(1), 125–142.

Qiao, F., Choi, Y., & Lee, T. J. (2016). Assessing feasibility of film-induced tourism: The case of Singapore. *International Journal of Tourism Sciences, 16*(3), 93–105.

Ramires, A., Brandao, F., & Sousa, A. C. (2018). Motivation-based cluster analysis of international tourists visiting a World Heritage City: The case of Porto, Portugal. *Journal of Destination Marketing & Management, 8*, 49–60.

Richter, L. (1980). The political uses of tourism: A Philippine case study. *The Journal of Developing Areas, 14*(2), 237–257.

Saeedi, H., & Heidarzadeh Hanzaee, K. (2018). The effects of heritage image on destination branding: An Iranian perspective. *Journal of Heritage Tourism, 13*(2), 152–166.

Santos, V., Caldeira, A., Santos, E., Oliveira, S., & Ramos, P. (2019). Wine Tourism Experience in the Tejo Region: The influence of sensory impressions on post-visit behaviour intentions. *International Journal of Marketing, Communication and New Media, 5*, 54–75.

Saunders, M., Lewis, P., & Thornhill, A. (2009). *Research methods for business students*. UK: Pearson education.

Sharpley, R. (1993). *Tourism & leisure in the countryside*. Dublin: Elm Publications.

Shi, X., Day, J., Gordon, S., Cai, L., & Adler, H. (2019). An exploratory study of visitors' motivations at a heritage destination: The case of the South Luogu Alley in China. *Journal of Hospitality and Tourism Insights*.

Soper, A. K. (2007). Developing Mauritianness: National identity, cultural heritage values and tourism. *Journal of Heritage Tourism, 2*(2), 94–109.

Su, D. N., Nguyen, N. A. N., Nguyen, Q. N. T., & Tran, T. P. (2020). The link between travel motivation and satisfaction towards a heritage destination: The role of visitor engagement, visitor experience and heritage destination image. *Tourism Management Perspectives, 34*, 100634.

Szczepańska, M., & Wilkaniec, A. (2015). Attractive multi-sensory landscape of a city as a potential space for tourism and recreation. *Studia Periegetica, 13*, 13–25.

Timothy, D. J. (2021). *Cultural heritage and tourism*. UK: Channel View Publications.

Timothy, D. J., & Boyd, S. W. (2006). Heritage tourism in the 21st century: Valued traditions and new perspectives. *Journal of Heritage Tourism, 1*(1), 1–16.

UNESCO. (2000/2008). https://en.unesco.org.

Vaismoradi, M., Turunen, H., & Bondas, T. (2013). Content analysis and thematic analysis: Implications for conducting a qualitative descriptive study. *Nursing & Health Science, 15*, 398–405.

van Hoven, B. (2011). Multi-sensory tourism in the Great Bear Rainforest. *Journal of the Association of Icelandic Geographers, 25*, 31–49.

Waitt, G. (2000). Consuming heritage: Perceived historical authenticity. *Annals of Tourism Research, 27*(4), 835–862.

Weaver, D. B. (2007). *Sustainable tourism: Theory and practice*. UK: Routledge.

Wicks, B., Do, K., Hsieh, P. C., Komorowski, A., Martin, K., Qiu, X., … & Yu, G. (2004). Direct Marketing of Crafts and Souvenirs to Vladimir Visitors. Retrieved *January, 25*, 2006.

Xingyang, L., Haijun, X., & Huifan, L. (2019). A review of tourism destination marketing from perspective of sensory marketing theory. *Tourism and Hospitality Prospects, 3*(4), 66–92.

Xiong, J., Hashim, N. H., & Murphy, J. (2015). Multisensory image as a component of destination image. *Tourism Management Perspectives, 14*, 34–41.

Zhang, G., Chen, X., Law, R., & Zhang, M. (2020). Sustainability of heritage tourism: A structural perspective from cultural identity and consumption intention. Sustainability, *12*(21), 9199.

13 The influence of technology acceptance model aspects on the adoption of database marketing technology by tour operators in Tanzania

Omary Swallehe[1]

Introduction

Database marketing is a methodical technique for acquiring, consolidating, and analyzing data of both current and potential consumers stored in a company's databases (Blattberg, Kim & Neslin 2008). According to Gandomi and Haider (2015), marketing managers in most organizations use the outputs generated from database marketing to support decision-making so that they can meet objectives such as new product development, selling products to customers, enhancing customer loyalty and patronage, increasing market share, and combating the efforts of competitors. Marketing database systems ensure that databases are integrated into marketing campaigns. Such systems enable several workstations on a computer network to view information simultaneously. Intranet networks can be used to connect marketing database systems, whether within a firm or between a corporation and its geographically scattered subsidiaries (Lycett, 2013; Mithas et al., 2013). Put simply, while databases have long been utilized for customer data in traditional marketing, the database marketing approach differs in that it keeps considerably more data and processes and uses it in new or more advanced ways than in the past (Lycett, 2013; Mithas et al., 2013). According to Yaqoob et al. (2016), the rate of data being processed has increased substantially within a short period of time. This is possible because of technological advancements that enable ease of processing, storing, and synthesizing a huge amount of data that was previously not possible (Gandomi et al., 2016). Big data management has attracted the interest of both researchers and practitioners (see, e.g., Akter et al., 2016; Frizzo-Barker et al., 2016; Gandomi and Haider, 2015). The growing interest in researching big data and analytics can be justified by the number of papers published since 2011. According to Gandomi and Haider (2015), 2011 is considered the year when database management was acknowledged in management science due to the advent of big data initiatives.

Although many businesses realise the importance of big data, it has been claimed that more than half of all big data projects fail (Mithas et al., 2013). Furthermore, it is uncertain how far firms have progressed in their use of big

DOI: 10.4324/9781003153580-13

data (Erevelles et al., 2016). Organizations are oblivious to how big data may influence their operations, and how such changes can benefit them (Lycett, 2013; Mithas et al., 2013). It should be mentioned that all marketing programmes are tailored to their target audiences, which is only feasible if a business has developed effective and relevant database marketing. Following effective market segmentation, target markets will be drawn from proper database marketing (Mithas et al., 2013). The database marketing idea has been quickly adopted/adapted by businesses around the Western world and those in more sophisticated Asian countries, such as China, Singapore, Indonesia, Japan, Malaysia, and North and South Korea, to name a few (Chiang et al., 2018). The existing literature regarding database marketing adoption by tourism industry enterprises is inconsistent and requires a methodological and theoretical review. Furthermore, the theoretical models employed in most of the studies differ significantly and in most case suggest a relationship between database marketing applications and larger corporations (Lycet, 2013; Mithas et al., 2013). The studies are valuable in terms of creating an understanding of database marketing and organizational performance, although more robust theoretical, methodological, and empirical research, especially on adoption of the concept, is paramount. It is undeniable that database marketing techniques vary from one nation to another, as do industries and marketing strategies.

Developing nations including Tanzania also suffer from a lack of attention in social and managerial research, such as in database marketing techniques, because the bulk of studies have been performed in rich economies and advanced Asian countries such as China and Japan (Paas, 2009). Unlike other industries, tourism is known for its reluctance in adopting new marketing innovations (Rosenfield, 1993). However, notable researchers have been studying businesses in the tourism sector that are starting to realise the significance of marketing developments in their day-to-day operations. Companies have started to realise that they can use database marketing as a strategic apparatus to gain competitive advantage by creating barriers for new entrants and gaining insight into new markets that they can tap into (Pass, 2009). In the first place, studies have shown a direct relationship between DBM and organizational performance, but still the concept has never lived up to its potential as very few organizations practise it in their day-to-day operations. (Petrison et al., 1997). The majority of the studies analyzed above focus on the value of database marketing, while little is known regarding the determinants for the adoption of the concept despite its usefulness. The problem here could be both contextual, in the sense that not enough studies have been conducted in developing countries like Tanzania, as well as methodological, as shown above. Many of the studies analyzed above have been conducted in developed economies and focused on the application of DBM and big data analytics for larger organizations (see, e.g., Akter et al., 2016; Frizzo-Barker et al., 2016; Gandomi & Haider, 2015). Again, most research has focused on the usefulness of the concept and ignored the majority of studies that have forgotten to assess the determinants for the adoption of DBM as an engine of competitive advantage in modern business setups. It is from this that this study seeks and identifies an answer to the following question: 'What is the influence of perceived ease of use, perceived usefulness, self-efficacy, and innovativeness on database applications for tour operators in Tanzania?' The current study is organized into four sections, beginning with an introduction, which is the first section and covers aspects such as background, justification, and purpose of conducting the study. The second part presents a critical review of literature in the area of database marketing and aspects of the technology acceptance model such as perceived ease of use, perceived usefulness, self-efficacy, and innovativeness. In the third part, the research methodology is covered and elements such as the area of study, sample, and the sampling techniques employed, as well as how data were collected and analyzed and the ethical consideration for the study, are discussed. The fourth part presents the results, hypotheses testing, discussion, conclusion, limitations, and areas for future study.

Theoretical review of the literature

The technology acceptancy model/theory (TAM), as propounded by Davis (1989), has been in use for many years and been involved in a large number of research studies in the area of technology adoption. According to Chang et al. (2017), the TAM has gained prominence and is regarded as a robust model for informing studies concerning the adoption of new technologies. Furthermore, according to a recent systematic study conducted by Al-Qaysi et al. (2018), the application of the TAM in the area of education has shown great uptake compared to its use in other fields of study. Their findings showed that the aspects of the TAM concerning usefulness and ease of use are normally influenced by external variables in determining one's attitude towards a product. A sizeable number of studies relating to the TAM have been conducted that explain the factors contributing to the adoption of new technologies. The studies conducted by Al-Busaidi (2013) and Al-Emran et al. (2018) found that the TAM has established itself and become regarded as a robust model for predicting the adoption of technology in various situations. Having been developed in the USA, the TAM has since been studied in a number of countries and different empirical investigations (see, e.g., Alshammari et al., 2016; Al-Busaidi, 2013; Tan et al., 2012; Tarhini et al., 2013b). Furthermore, Abdullah and Ward (2016) investigated 107 publications over ten years and found that there were 152 variables relating to the TAM. In their findings, the most obvious external elements used to study the TAM were subjective norms, self-efficacy, anxiety, enjoyment, and experience in working with computer programmes. It was noted, however, that the most commonly used external variables in studying adoption, and the TAM in particular, were the TAM's fundamental beliefs of ease of use and usefulness. Despite the contribution made by the works of Abdullah and Ward (2016) in the literature on adoption of new technologies, their studies lacked contributions made by other researchers in these phenomena. In the current study, we have reviewed the work of Abdullah and Ward

(2016), as well as relevant studies to investigate the effects of the TAM in adopting different technologies. Nonetheless, Huh et al. (2009) contended that the TAM had also been studied in the tourism sector of the economy. The TAM has also been widely employed in many situations within the hospitality industry.

Casaló et al. (2010) also used the TAM to investigate the intentions of customers to participate in online purchases of products and services. The study by Sánchez-Prieto et al. (2016) revealed that the TAM had also been utilized in higher education as a means to better understand instructors' behavioural intentions in the adoption of new methodologies for imparting knowledge. The theory of planned behaviour (TPB) by Ajzen (1991) is one of the widely used models, but past studies have claimed that the TAM should be preferred over the TPB when studying behavioural intentions in a business context. According to Chiang et al. (2009), Zain et al. (2005), and Huh et al. (2009), the TAM, like any other theories, is limited/restricted by differences in humans' level of experience, which has a significant impact on behavioural intention.

The TAM emerged from the theory of reasoned action developed by Ajzen and Fishbein (1980) to describe one's willingness to deploy new technology in different contexts (Davis 1989). Researchers such as Davis (1989) and Yang et al. (2012) revealed that, in this model, usefulness can be defined as one's perception of the utility of using certain technology. Usefulness is regarded as a powerful predictor of a person's willingness to accept new technologies (Wu and Zhang, 2014). Ease of use, on the other hand, relates to a person's perception of how physically and mentally liberated they are towards utilizing a certain invention (Davis, 1989; Suki and Suki, 2011).

Perceived ease of use and perceived usefulness

In the context of technology adoption, ease of use signifies an individual's cognitive efforts towards understanding the technology in question (Yang et al., 2012). Surprisingly, in many previous studies, stated ease of use has been identified as a predicting variable for usefulness (see, e.g., Suki and Suki, 2011). In the context of this investigation, the perceived ease of use of database marketing initiatives by business owners and key managers indicates the cognitive efforts of these individuals towards understanding and applying the concept to achieve competitive advantage in the tourism sector.

Moreover, other researchers have found out that perceived ease of use positively affects both the individual's behaviour as well as perceived usefulness (Wu & Zhang, 2014). In their study conducted on hotel reservation websites, researchers such as Morosan & Jeong (2008) reported that perceived usefulness had only a positive effect on individuals' perceptions towards employing such websites. It can be summarized that both the perceived ease of use and perceived usefulness affect the attitudes of business owners and managers (Davis, 1989; Suki and Suki, 2011). Conversely, attitude has been investigated in the hotel and hospitality industry as one of the predictors of the intentions of performing certain tasks (Park et al., 2012; Yuzhanin and Fisher, 2016). Another notable study conducted by Shin and Kang (2015) found out that attitude is one of the best predictors of technology acceptance using the TAM. Attitude assists in determining managers' perceptions and understanding their beliefs in technological system effectiveness.

Self-efficacy

Self-efficacy refers to an individual's ultimate belief in their capacity to perform a certain activity. Furthermore, Zolait (2014) defined self-efficacy in technology as a person's ability to understand and use computer technology (Garavan et al., 2010; Tagoe and Abakah, 2014). Early tourism scholars such as Reichel et al. (2007) and Dolnicar (2005) argued that people differ in their willingness to take risks and that self-efficacy is a main determinant in explaining people's willingness culture for absorbing risks. As a result, self-efficacy is a driving force behind the adoption of hospitality technology (Huh et al., 2009). Conversely, self-efficacy promotes people's acceptance of tourist products or services and leads to them being extremely enthusiastic about the usefulness of new hospitality technology. It has been proposed that using the TAM increases self-efficacy by enhancing perceptions about perceived usefulness (Zolait, 2014). From the fact that self-efficacy influences both ease of use and usefulness, as articulated in the work of Shin and Kang (2005), it becomes apparent that self-efficacy directly or indirectly predicts attitudes towards a certain task. In this study, it can be hypothesized that business owners and managers who believe in their ability to execute tasks are more likely to take risks and enjoy employing new technologies than those who do not. In this situation, self-efficacy is crucial for the adoption of database marketing by Tanzanian tour operators.

Innovativeness

Innovativeness in the context of this study refers to the willingness of individuals to adapt early-stage database marketing technology before others have implemented it. (Gao et al., 2012). Innovativeness may also be defined as a person's eagerness to experiment with new inventions, products, services, or ideas, or it may be personal willingness to undertake/implement new technology, information, or ideas (Bauer et al., 2005; Gao et al., 2012). In the hospitality industry, innovation is perceived as an impetus to drive consumers to the state of taking up new technology and believing that the technology is easy to utilize (Morosan, 2012). The study conducted by Agarwal & Prasad (1998) found that innovativeness increases people's perceptions and encourages willingness to use technology more, and it directly influences the adoption of technology. In other words, innovativeness influences behavioural intentions to adopt new technology (Yang, 2012).

It can be observed that innovation influences people's attitudes and behaviour towards adopting new technologies (Bauer et al., 2005; Compeau

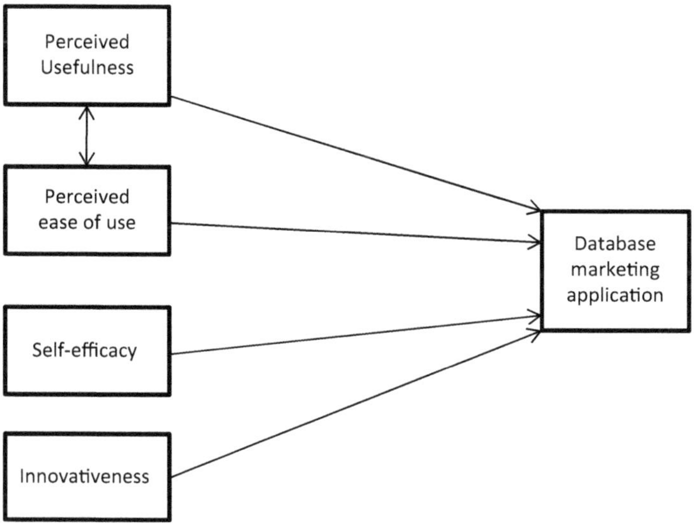

Figure 13.1 The study model

and Higgins, 1995; Gao et al., 2012). The innovativeness variable has been employed as a moderating factor in early studies (Kim and Forsythe, 2008; Lee et al., 2007); however, in technological adoption studies, the impact of IN as a moderating factor has never studied to its fullest (Figure 13.1).

In this study, the application of database marketing initiatives by tour operators in Tanzania depends largely on aspects of the TAM such as perceived ease of use and perceived usefulness, which have five indicators each; self-efficacy, which has three indicators; and innovativeness, which has three indicators. In total, the study model uses 16 variables to measure the influence that these have on the adoption of database marketing by tour operators in Tanzania.

Research methodology

Sample and data collection

The study employed a survey approach, which is a data-gathering tool that has been commonly used in research that predicts attitudes about information technology (Liaw and Huang, 2003; Liaw et al., 2007). Thus, a survey was employed to collect data from tour operators from the two tourist destination regions of Arusha and Kilimanjaro in Tanzania. These regions are widely recognized as popular tourist hubs in the country. The sampling frames were obtained from the Association for Tour Operators (TATO) in order to determine the sample size for the study. By using simple random sampling, the study collected data from 255 tour operators that were obtained by chance. The decision regarding the sample size was largely influenced by the nature of the study. This study investigated the influence of TAM aspects such as perceived ease of use, perceived usefulness, self-efficacy, and innovativeness on the adoption of database marketing initiatives by tour operators in Tanzania. According to Tabachnick and Fidell (1996), researchers should use a sample size that is in line with the rules of thumb of $N \geq 50 + 8m$ in a multivariate data analysis and $N \geq 104 + m$ for individual predictors. In this formula, N is the sample size required and m represents the number of independent variables. The current study has 20 independent variables comprising both the latent and observed variables. In this regard, the appropriate sample size, according to the rules of thumb above, would be $50 + 8 * 20 = 210$. The way a study is designed also plays a significant role in determining elements of the analysis procedure before data is collected. The literature is, however, silent on the issue of adequate sample size, but generally the recommended minimum sample size in quantitative studies is one that has five to ten cases/subjects per variable (Bentler & Chou, 1987; Hancock, 2001). Nevertheless, McQuitty (2004) asserted that it is paramount to decide on a sample size that meets the requirements for robust statistical analysis before data are collected from the unit of enquiry. Despite the fact that there is little agreement on what sample size would be appropriate for inferential research, Hoe et al. (2003), Saunders et al. (2003) argued that it would be prudent to utilize response rates obtained by other similar studies in a particular context because estimating response rates would be challenging. According to Ame (2005), Field (2005), and Hair et al. (1998), previous studies to investigate the adoption of DBM had a non-response rate of less than 30%. The current study was conducted with that assumption in mind. Thus, a sample size of 255 was deemed optimal for this study based on three prerequisites: first, meeting multivariate analysis requirements (Tabachnick and Fidell, 1996); second, the rules of thumb in the quest for minimum sample size requirements (Garver and Mentzer, 1999; Hoe, 2008; Hoelter, 1983); and third, the anticipated response rate. For that matter, a total of 255 questionnaires were administered to the study objects, of which 216 were completed. This suggests a response rate of 84.7%. The tour operators in the regions of Arusha and Kilimanjaro formed the unit of inquiry and analysis. Researchers such as Lumpkin and Dess (1996) contended that using firm level analysis would be in line with classical economics of which individual entrepreneurs are regarded as firms. In this study, the questionnaires were administered to target owners/managers or any responsible person who could respond to the questions on issues relating to the adoption of database marketing.

All participants were told at the start of the exercise that their participation was voluntary and their names and those of their organizations would be kept private. The principal investigator/author was available throughout the data collection to elaborate the purpose of the study and offer personal assistance in completing surveys, as needed. Initially, 255 responses were gathered, from which 23 were eliminated due to excessive missing data, duplicate responses, or the presence of outliers. Based on the exploratory nature of the study and the restricted target group intended for studying database marketing within the tourism sector, the final sample size of 216 was deemed appropriate. Although the literature shows that there is no clear-cut solution to what constitutes an adequate sample size, this study considered the size of the selected sample to be appropriate. For all four hypotheses developed from the independent variables in this case, all data collected from the questionnaires were checked through Pearson correlation analysis for significant correlation and evaluated through multiple regression analysis for linear relations. The use of factor analysis and stepwise multiple regressions also allows sample size flexibility (Ringle et al., 2005). All questionnaire items were adapted from existing research and reviewed by professionals in the tourism sector to ensure clarity, format, and appropriateness. The responses were collected using a five-point Likert scale (1 = strongly disagree, 3 = neutral, 5 = strongly agree). The questions were all written in English, in which the participants had fluency. The survey also included the characteristics of the tour operators to establish business size, industry experience, type of ownership, and much more. Instruments were adapted from similar studies that aimed to determine technology adoption intentions (Jung, 2015). The study utilized five scale items (= 0.816) and other scale items (= 0.963) to assess perceived usefulness and perceived ease of use, respectively. In this study, self-efficacy was used to measure tour operators' self-confidence in computer functions, software, and other associated tasks, whereas innovativeness reflected their inventiveness in obtaining new information. Three scale items were used to measure tour operators' innovativeness (= 0.916) and three scale items were used to assess self-efficacy (= 0.675). Finally, intention to use database marketing was assessed using five scale items (= 0.725).

Ethical considerations

In this study, we have taken into consideration all aspects of ethics for conducting research studies. Due to the fact that the study involved primary data collection, ethical considerations were necessary and paramount. To start with, a letter introduction signed by the University's College Principal to the Tanzania Association of Tour Operators was obtained. This letter served to introduce the researcher, outline the purpose of the study, and assure the respondents that their data would be collected for academic purposes only. It specified the ethical matters that the researcher would consider during the data collection process. Among these were:

1. Voluntary participation: participants/tour operators were free to accept or reject the request to participate in this study.
2. Obtaining the consent of the respondents before they decided to participate in this study. They were told that the aim of the study was to gauge the influence of aspects of the TAM on the adoption of database marketing, and it was not meant to scrutinize the way they run their businesses.
3. The questionnaire for the the study would be clear and comprised simple questions that could be understood by the respondents.

4. Guaranteeing the respondents' privacy and anonymity throughout the research report. We have not mentioned the name of any respondents or attributed the information we have collected from them.
5. Acknowledging the works of other researchers through citations and referencing using the APA system.

Objectivity in the collection, analysis, and discussion was considered throughout the research study, and everything that has been presented comes fully from the field. Given this research context, the following hypotheses for the current study have been proposed:

H1. Perceived usefulness directly and positively influences the attitude of owners/managers towards database marketing utilization in tourism.
H2. Perceived ease of use directly and positively influences the attitude of owners/managers towards database marketing utilization in tourism.
H3. Self-efficacy directly and positively influences the attitude of owners/managers towards database marketing utilization in tourism.
H4. Innovativeness directly and positively influences the adoption of database marketing among tour operators in Tanzania.

Results

The findings on the characteristics of the tour operators in this study reveal that the overwhelming majority of the firms were small (81%), compared to 7.5% of the firms that were in the medium-size category. This is not surprising as previous studies conducted in developing countries have shown that the small business category is predominant across all types of business (Pass 2009).

Apart from that, the findings on the experience of the tour operators indicate that 48.5% of the respondents had 1–5 years of experience, 30% of the respondents had 6–10 years of experience, and 21% had more than 10 years of experience in business. This implies that most of the firms had reasonable experience, which is good for sustainability and performance (Table 13.1).

The relationship between perceived usefulness, perceived ease of use, self-efficacy, and innovativeness was assessed using inferential analysis, including correlation and multiple regressions. This was certain due to the fact that four predicting variables were identified and evaluated based on the adoption of database marketing as the dependent variable. In that case, reliability tests were performed first to determine the level of consistency among the study variables (Table 13.2).

The findings in Table 13.3 describe the results of reliability analysis and show that the variables of the study were reliable with positive consistency. This is attributed by the values of the coefficients of the alpha test that exceeded the 0.7 requirement for reliability verification. This is acknowledged by Saunders et al. (2003), in that the reliability of study variables should be determined when the values of the Cronbach alpha test achieve an 0.7 level or higher.

Table 13.1 Demographic characteristics of respondents

Variables	*Frequencies*	*Percentages*
Size		
Micro-enterprises	25	11.5%
Small	175	81.0%
Medium-sized	16	7.5%
Total	216	100%
Experience		
1–5 years	105	48.5%
6–10 years	65	30.0%
Over 10 years	46	21.5%
Total	216	100%
Form of ownership		
Sole-proprietorship	132	61.0%
Partnership	12	5.5%
Limited companies	72	33.5%
Total	216	100%

Source: field data (2019).

Table 13.2 Cronbach Alpha Test

Study variables	*Cronbach Alpha*
Celebrity attractiveness	0.789
Celebrity expertise	0.842
Celebrity match up	0.825
Customer buying intention	0.757

Source: field data (2019).

Table 13.3 Model summary

Model	*R*	*R square*	*Adjusted R square*	*Standard error of estimate*	*Change statistics*			*Durbin-Watson*
1	.387	.150	.138	.53433	.151	35.765	.000	1.027

Source: field data (2019)
Dependent variable: adoption of database marketing.
Independent variables: perceived ease of use, perceived usefulness, self-efficacy, and innovativeness

Inferential analysis

This was performed to describe the relationship between celebrity endorsements, which was represented by three predicting variables evaluated on consumer buying intention as the dependent variable. Therefore, the overall test of the predicting variables to the dependent variable was performed using a model summary test, with Table 13.4 illustrating the results.

The findings in Table 13.3 describe the influence of all predicting variables on the dependent variable, which was verified through the outcome of the R2 value. In this case, the results depict that the adoption of database marketing was influenced by perceived ease of use, perceived usefulness and self-efficacy by 15% of the respondents. The remaining 85% figure implies that other factors besides the predicting variables attributed to their adoption. Therefore, the results evidently show that the variables as assumptions were positive. Although the influence of the predicting variables is not strong, as suggested in many social science studies, it is significant, as shown in the table. Furthermore, Durbin–Watson is 1.027 greater than the threshold of 1, and shows that the sample was sufficiently adequate to conduct this study. We accept all four hypotheses for the current study at 5% level of significance.

H1. Perceived usefulness directly and positively influences the attitude of owners/managers towards database marketing utilization in tourism.
H2. Perceived ease of use directly and positively influences the attitude of owners/managers towards database marketing utilization in tourism.
H3. Self-efficacy directly and positively influences the attitude of owners/managers towards database marketing utilization in tourism.
H4. Innovativeness directly and positively influences the adoption of database marketing among tour operators in Tanzania.

Correlation analysis

This was performed to show the predicting variable that possesses higher influence on the dependent variable, with findings shown in Table 13.4.

Table 13.4 describes the findings of correlation analysis, from which the highest correlation is between perceived ease of use and perceived usefulness to the adoption of DBM. Since that is the case, perceived ease of use and perceived usefulness have had a stronger influence on the adoption of database marketing by tour operators in the country. This implies that their adoption of database marketing was largely influenced by perceived ease of

Table 13.4 Correlation analysis

	Customer buying intention	*Ease of use*	*Usefulness*	*Self-efficacy*
Adoption of DBM	1.000	1.000	1.000	1.000
Perceived ease of use	.409	.016	.002	
Perceived usefulness	.314	.073		
Self-efficacy	.248			

Source: field data (2019)

use, perceived usefulness, self-efficacy, and innovativeness. Though the correlation was positive, the coefficients were small, with the implication that there was no multicollinearity. This is a problem that has been articulated by multiple regressions.

Multiple regressions

This was conducted to describe the influence of each predicting variable to the dependent variable and correct the multicollinearity problem. Hence, Table 13.5 describes the findings.

The results in Table 13.5 show the findings of multiple regression analysis, which reveal that all predicting variables are positive and possess significant outcomes on the adoption of database marketing ($p < 0.05$). The implication of the results is that the adoption of database marketing by tour operators was positively influenced by perceived ease of use, perceived usefulness, self-efficacy, and innovativeness. The model summary above indicates that these

Table 13.5 Multiple regression

Coefficients[a]

Model		*Unstandardized coefficients*		*Standardized coefficients*	*t*	*Sig.*
		B	*Std. Error*	*Beta*		
1	(Constant)	3.630	.231		15.724	.000
	My company is confident in copying with any changes and development of technology	.187	.053	.236	3.555	.000
2	(Constant)	4.331	.279		15.506	.000
	My company is confident in copying with any changes and development of technology	.219	.051	.276	4.266	.000
	I would find it more useful using this programme	-.206	.050	-.269	-4.154	.000
3	(Constant)	4.124	.289		14.264	.000
	My company is confident in copying with any changes and development of technology	.204	.051	.258	3.999	.000
	I would find it more useful using this programme	-.320	.068	-.418	-4.713	.000
	Using this programme would increase my efficiency and effeciveness	.176	.073	.216	2.426	.016

a. Dependent variable: my company uses DBM to collect and analyze customer information for marketing purposes

Source: field data (2019).

contributed up to 15% of the variance in explaining the adoption of database marketing initiatives by tour operators. The findings further reveal that the remaining 85% of the variance is explained by aspects other than those studied in the current research paper.

Discussion

The results show that perceived ease of use, perceived usefulness, self-efficacy, and innovativeness have positively influenced the adoption of database marketing by tour operators in Tanzania since all predicting variables are positive with significant outcomes on the dependent variable. The implication is that all tour operators who were confident and innovative and who perceived the application of database marketing for collecting and analyzing customers' information to be easy and useful stood a better chance of outshining their counterparts (Wei and Jung, 2017). This is supported by the findings that the TAM is very useful for determining the application and usability of database marketing for attaining competitive advantage. Moreover, the operators who believed in their capability to apply new technologies without hesitation tended be the ones who would adopt the technology faster than their counterparts who did not have confidence in trying new technology (Chin and Lin, 2016; Myung et al., 2017; Wei and Jung, 2017).

The findings of the current study are in line with the work of early tourism researchers such as Dolnicar (2005) and Reichel et al. (2007), who argued that individuals differ in their willingness to commit to risk-taking activities and that self-efficacy is a pre-determining element for identifying those who are willing to engage in risk-taking behaviour. In addition, self-efficacy serves as a driving force for the adoption of tourism- and hospitality-related technologies (Huh et al., 2009). Apart from that, Chin and Lin (2016) suggested that companies that perceive the technology involved/used will generate reasonable outcomes in terms of profitability will automatically adopt the technology. In that case, the results are described by the model, which is illustrated in the manner that:

$$DBM = \beta o + \beta 1PE + \beta 2PU + \beta 3SE + \beta 4IN + e$$

Where DBM refers to database marketing, βo to constant factor, $\beta 1PE$ to perceived ease of use, $\beta 2PU$ to perceived usefulness, $\beta 3SE$ to self-efficacy, and $\beta 4IN$ to innovativeness.

Conclusion and policy implications

Database marketing and information management are two effective strategies used by modern businesses to achieve a competitive advantage over competitors. Customers' information is recorded and utilized by these to predict purchase intentions. Despite the usefulness of the strategies, few companies have invested in such initiatives in either developed or developing countries. Studies conducted in the area of customer information management have shown a direct and positive correlation between investing in the infrastructure of a database marketing application and the competitive advantage of businesses. The current study investigated the influence of perceived ease of use, perceived usefulness, self-efficacy, and innovativeness on the adoption of database marketing initiatives by tour operators in Tanzania. The findings reveal that all the predicting variables, namely perceived ease of use, perceived usefulness, self-efficacy, and innovativeness, play a significant role in influencing the adoption of database marketing when combined, rather than done separately. Although neither the correlation coefficients nor relation coefficients are bigger than those suggested in many social science research studies, they are still significant, at 5%, as shown in the tables above. This is to say that the predicting variables can explain 15% of the adoption of database marketing by tour operators. The findings further suggest that the remaining 85% can be explained by factors other than the predicting variables of the study.

The study recommends that database marketing and customer information management is necessary in modern businesses. Companies should continue to invest in a database marketing infrastructure that will enhance the application of the concept to achieve competitive advantage. Investment in infrastructure should go hand in hand with the entire process of building the capacity of staff at all levels to operate the technologies. Finally, perceived ease of use, perceived usefulness, self-efficacy, and innovativeness are important, but they are not sufficient as predicting variables for the adoption of database marketing by tour operators in Tanzania. Companies should look into other important variables that explain the remaining 85% of the variance for the adoption of database marketing initiatives.

Limitations and areas for further studies

The current study employed a cross-sectional design and collected data from tour operators in Tanzania. It provided valuable insights regarding the effects of predicting variables, namely perceived ease of use, perceived usefulness, self-efficacy, and innovativeness on the adoption of database marketing by tour operators.

We accept that this study, like any other, has limitations. For example, it employed a cross-sectional research design and used a semi-structured questionnaire for data collection from tour operators in Tanzania. It is an uncontested truth that database marketing is a dynamic process that differs significantly in its execution from one country to another and from industry to industry. Thus, various conclusions could be reached if another study were to be conducted using different approaches, such as longitudinal or other methodologies. Thus, the benefits of deploying database marketing are not the same across all countries and industries. Adopting it should be guided by the research conducted; otherwise, the costs incurred would not be justified. Therefore, future studies should look at larger samples and use different methodologies to the one used in this study.

Nevertheless, future studies should be directed towards studying the critical success factors for effective application of database marketing initiatives for small- and medium-sized organizations, especially in developing countries. Moreover, researchers should also investigate the determinants for the adoption of database marketing and customer information management by organizations. It should be noted that the researchers' appetite for investigating this area is almost not-existent as the findings we have reported from many of the studies are too old. Future researchers should try to balance studying other areas such as digital and social media marketing and their applications in different industries. It looks like the literature for database marketing is flimsy and outdated, thus requiring researchers to study it from different angles. We should expect more studies of this nature from developing and emerging economies as contextual issues such as level of technological advancement and speed of taking up new technology differ between countries.

Note

1 Senior Lecturer-Mzumbe University Dar es salaam Campus College. Email: oswalehe@mzumbe.ac.tz.

References

Abdullah, F., & Ward, R. (2016). Developing a general extended technology acceptance model for e-learning (GETAMEL) by analysing commonly used external factors. *Computers in Human Behavior, 56*, 238–256.

Agarwal, R., & Prasad, J. (1998). A conceptual and operational definition of personal innovativeness in the domain of information technology. *Information Systems Research, 9*(2), 204–215.

Ajzen, I. (1991). The theory of planned behavior. *Organizational Behavior and Human Decision Processes, 50*(2), 179–211.

Ajzen, I., & Fishbein, M. (1980). *Understanding attitudes and predicting social behavior.* Prentice-Hall.

Akter, S., Wamba, S. F., Gunasekaran, A., Dubey, R., & Childe, S. J. (2016). How to improve firm performance using big data analytics capability and business strategy alignment. *International Journal of Production Economics, 182*, 113–131.

Al-Busaidi, K. A (2013). An empirical investigation linking learners' adoption of blended learning to their intention of full e-learning. *Behaviour & Information Technology, 32*(11), 1168–1176.

Al-Emran, M., Mezhuyev, V., & Kamaludin, A. (2018). Technology acceptance model in m-learning context: A systematic review. *Computers and Education, 125*, 389–412.

Al-Qaysi, N., Mohamad-Nordin, N., & Al-Emran, M. (2018). A systematic review of social media acceptance from the perspective of educational and information systems theories and models. *Journal of Educational Computing Research, 25*(6), 4961-5002.

Alshammari, S. H., Ali, M. B., & Rosli, M. S. (2016). The influences of technical support, self-efficacy and instructional design on the usage and acceptance of LMS: A comprehensive review. *Turkish Online Journal of Educational Technology, 15*(2), 116–125.

Ame, A. M. (2005). *The effect of quality satisfaction and its consequences on customers' behavioral intentions: A study of selected service firms in Tanzania* (Doctoral dissertation, University of Dar es Salaam).

Bauer, H. H., Barnes, S. J., Reichardt, T., & Neumann, M. M. (2005). Driving consumer acceptance of mobile marketing: A theoretical framework and empirical study. *Journal of Electronic Commerce Research*, *6*(3), 181–192.

Bentler, P. M., & Chou, C. P. (1987). Practical issues in structural modeling. *Sociological Methods & Research*, *16*(1), 78–117.

Blattberg, R. C., Kim, B. D., & Neslin, S. A. (2008). Why database marketing? In *Database marketing* (pp. 13–46). Springer.

Casaló, L. V., Flavián, C., & Guinalíu, M. (2010). Determinants of the intention to participate in firm-hosted online travel communities and effects on consumer behavioral intentions. *Tourism Management*, *31*(6), 898–911.

Chang, C. T., Hajiyev, J., & Su, C. R. (2017). Examining the students' behavioral intention to use e-learning in Azerbaijan? The general extended technology acceptance model for e-learning approach. *Computers & Education*, *111*, 128–143.

Chiang, R. H., Grover, V., Liang, T. P., & Zhang, D. (2018). Strategic value of big data and business analytics.

Compeau, D. R., & Higgins, C. A. (1995). Computer self-efficacy: Development of a measure and initial test. *MIS Quarterly*, *19*(2), 189–211.

Davis, F. D. (1989). Perceived usefulness, perceived ease of use, and user acceptance of information technology. *MIS Quarterly*, *13*(3), 319–340.

Dolnicar, S. (2005). Understanding barriers to leisure travel: Tourist fears as a marketing basis. *Journal of Vacation Marketing*, *11*(3), 197–208.

Erevelles, S., Fukawa, N., & Swayne, L. (2016). Big Data consumer analytics and the transformation of marketing. *Journal of Business Research*, *69*(2), 897–904.

Field, A. P. (2005). Is the meta-analysis of correlation coefficients accurate when population correlations vary? *Psychological Methods*, *10*(4), 444.

Frizzo-Barker, J., Chow-White, P. A., Mozafari, M., & Ha, D. (2016). An empirical study of the rise of big data in business scholarship. *International Journal of Information Management*, *36*(3), 403–413.

Gandomi, A. H., Sajedi, S., Kiani, B., & Huang, Q. (2016). Genetic programming for experimental big data mining: A case study on concrete creep formulation. *Automation in Construction*, *70*, 89–97.

Gandomi, A., & Haider, M. (2015). Beyond the hype: Big data concepts, methods, and analytics. *International Journal of Information Management*, *35*(2), 137–144.

Gao, T., Rohm, A. J., Sultan, F., & Huang, S. (2012). Antecedents of consumer attitudes toward mobile marketing: A comparative study of youth markets in the United States and China. *Thunderbird International Business Review*, *54*(2), 211–224.

Garavan, T. N., Carbery, R., O'Malley, G., & O'Donnell, D. (2010). Understanding participation in e-learning in organizations: A large-scale empirical study of employees. *International Journal of Training and Development*, *14*(3), 155–168.

Garver, M. S., & Mentzer, J. T. (1999). Logistics research methods: Employing structural equation modeling to test for construct validity. *Journal of Business Logistics*, *20*(1), 33.

Hair, J. F., Anderson, R. E., Tatham, R. L., & Black, C. B. (1998). *Multivariate Data Analysis* (5th ed.). Prentice Hall.

Hancock, G. R. (2001). Effect size, power, and sample size determination for structured means modeling and MIMIC approaches to between-groups hypothesis testing of means on a single latent construct. *Psychometrika*, *66*(3), 373–388.

Hoe, S. L. (2008). Issues and procedures in adopting structural equation modelling technique. *Journal of Quantitative Methods*, *3*(1), 76.

Hoelter, J. W. (1983). The analysis of covariance structures: Goodness-of-fit indices. *Sociological Methods & Research*, *11*(3), 325–344.

Huh, H. J., Kim, T. T., & Law, R. (2009). A comparison of competing theoretical models for understanding acceptance behavior of information systems in upscale hotels. *International Journal of Hospitality Management*, *28*(1), 121–134.

Jung, H. (2015). Fostering an English teaching environment: Factors influencing English as a foreign language teacher's adoption of mobile learning. *Informatics in Education*, *14*(2), 219–241.

Kim, J., & Forsythe, S. (2008). Sensory enabling technology acceptance model (SE-TAM): A multiple-group structural model comparison. *Psychology & Marketing*, *25*(9), 901–922.

Lee, H. Y., Qu, H., & Kim, Y. S. (2007). A study of the impact of personal innovativeness on online travel shopping behavior: A case study of Korean travelers. *Tourism Management*, *28*(3), 886–897.

Liaw, S. S., & Huang, H. M. (2003). An investigation of user attitudes toward search engines as an information retrieval tool. *Computers in Human Behavior*, *19*(6), 751–765.

Liaw, S. S., Huang, H. M., & Chen, G. D. (2007). Surveying instructor and learner attitudes toward e-learning. *Computers & Education*, *49*(4), 1066–1080.

Lumpkin, G. T., & Dess, G. G. (1996). Clarifying the entrepreneurial orientation construct and linking it to performance. *Academy of management Review*, *21*(1), 135–172.

Lycett, M. (2013). 'Datafication': Making sense of (big) data in a complex world. *European Journal of Information Systems*, *22*(4), 381–386.

McQuitty, S. (2004). Statistical power and structural equation models in business research. *Journal of Business Research*, *57*(2), 175–183.

Mithas, S., Lee, M. R., Earley, S., Murugesan, S., & Djavanshir, R. (2013). Leveraging big data and business analytics. *IT Professional*, *15*(6), 18–20.

Morosan, C. (2012). Theoretical and empirical considerations of guests' perceptions of biometric systems in hotels: Extending the technology acceptance model. *Journal of Hospitality & Tourism Research*, *36*(1), 52–84.

Morosan, C., & Jeong, M. (2008). Users' perceptions of two types of hotel reservation web sites. *International Journal of Hospitality Management*, *27*(2), 284–292.

Myung, J. K., Choi, Y. H., & Kim, J. D. (2017). Effects of CEOs' negative traits on corporate social responsibility. *Sustainability*, *9*, 543.

Park, S. Y., Nam, M. W., & Cha, S. B. (2012). University students' behavioral intention to use mobile learning: Evaluating the technology acceptance model. *British Journal of Educational Technology*, *43*(4), 592–605.

Pass, L. (2009). Database marketing in newly emerging economies. *Journal of Database Marketing and Customer Strategy Management*, *16*(2), 92–100.

Petrison, L., Blattberg, R., & Wang, P. (1997). Database marketing: Past, present and future. *Journal of Direct Marketing*, *11*(4).

Reichel, A., Fuchs, G., & Uriely, N. (2007). Perceived risk and the non-institutionalized tourist role: The case of Israeli student ex-backpackers. *Journal of Travel Research*, *46*(2), 217–226.

Ringle, C. M., Wende, S., & Will, A. (2005). Smartpls 2.0. Available at: www.smartpls.de

Rosenfield, J. R. (1993). The myth of database marketing. *Direct Marketing*, 28–63.

Sánchez-Prieto, J. C., Olmos-Migueláñez, S., & García-Peñalvo, F. J. (2016). MLearning and pre-service teachers: An assessment of the behavioral intention using an expanded TAM model. *Computers in Human Behavior*, *55*(1), 519–528.

Saunders, M., Lewis, P., & Thornhill, A. (2003). *Research methods for business students*. Prentice Hall: Financial Times.

Shin, W. S., & Kang, M. (2015). The use of a mobile learning management system at an online university and its effect on learning satisfaction and achievement. *International Review of Research in Open and Distributed Learning, 16*(3), 110–130.

Suki, N. M., & Suki, N. M. (2011). Users' behavior towards ubiquitous m-learning. *Turkish Online Journal of Distance Education, 12*(3), 118–129.

Tabachnick, B. G., & Fidell, L. S. (1996). *SPSS for Windows workbook to accompany large sample examples of using multivariate statistics*. HarperCollins.

Tagoe, M., & Abakah, E. (2014). Determining distance education students' readiness for mobile learning at University of Ghana using the theory of planned behavior. *International Journal of Education and Development using Information and Communication Technology, 10*(1), 91–106.

Tan, G. W. H., Ooi, K. B., Sim, J. J., & Phusavat, K. (2012). Determinants of mobile learning adoption: An empirical analysis. *Journal of Computer Information Systems, 52*(3), 82–91.

Tarhini, A. Hone, N., & Liu, X. (2013b). Factors affecting students' acceptance of e-learning environments in developing countries: A structural equation modeling approach. *International Journal of Information and Education Technology, 3*(1), 54–59.

Wu, B., & Zhang, C. (2014). Empirical study on continuance intentions towards E-Learning 2.0 systems. *Behavior & Information Technology, 33*(10), 1027–1038.

Yang, H., Zhou, L., & Liu, H. (2012). Predicting young American and Chinese consumers' mobile viral attitudes, intents, and behaviour. *Journal of International Consumer Marketing, 24*(1/2), 24–42.

Yang, S. H. (2012). Exploring college students' attitudes and self-efficacy of mobile learning. *Turkish Online Journal of Educational Technology, 11*(4), pp. 148–154.

Yaqoob, I., Hashem, I. A. T., Gani, A., Mokhtar, S., Ahmed, E., Anuar, N. B., & Vasilakos, A. V. (2016). Big data: From beginning to future. *International Journal of Information Management, 36*(6), 1231–1247

Yuzhanin, S., & Fisher, D. (2016). The efficacy of the theory of planned behavior for predicting intentions to choose a travel destination: A review. *Tourism Review, 71*(2), 135–147.

Zain, M., Rose, R. C., Abdullah, I., & Masrom, M. (2005). The relationship between information technology acceptance and organizational agility in Malaysia. *Information and Management, 42*(6), 829–839.

Zolait, A. H. S. (2014). The nature and components of perceived behavioural control as an element of theory of planned behaviour. *Behaviour & Information Technology, 33*(1), 65–85.

14 Analysis of challenges in developing and implementing forest policies in Tanzania

Omary Swallehe[1]

Introductions

Policy development and implementation in the area of forestry has been attracting the attention of researchers and stakeholders. Some stakeholders complain that they are not involved in the process, while others speak out about not being given the relevance they deserve. The process of establishing cooperative structures within these entities is frequently organic, top-down, and based on similar structures of values and related interests. For example, makers of charcoal and firewood are also residents of the area where production takes place. According to Dressler et al. (2010), the implementation of participatory forest management (PFM) in some cases prevents people from accessing, using, and controlling valuable forest resources and implies severe inadequacies in terms of social justice. This is to say that even though PFM has been implemented in Tanzania, much is yet to be achieved from it. The study by Ribot et al. (2010) established that in most situations across sub-Saharan Africa, members of local PFM institutions are not representative of the local community. Several studies have found that local elites dominate both decision-making and benefit capture; these works include those of Adhikari et al. (2014), Coulibaly-Lingani et al. (2011), Das (2019), Etongo et al. (2018), Green and Lund (2015), Luintel et al. (2017), and Lund and Saito-Jensen (2013). Jacob and Brockington (2017) explained this further in the Tanzanian context, referring to the lack of accountability and transparency of local institutions that enables favouritism and manipulation by politically powerful and well-connected individuals. Other studies (e.g., Chinangwa et al., 2016) describe how PFM is characterized by partially elected community representatives and their lack of ability, competence (Mohammed et al., 2017), openness in financial management, and accountability to their constituents (Coleman and Fleischman, 2012; Mollick et al., 2018). The high cost of forestry resources (e.g., wood) is also seen as a reason for the poor being excluded from benefiting from PFM (Kumar, 2002). This has exacerbated intra- and inter-community strife (Gross-Camp et al., 2019). In some cases, PFM policies and central governments have delegated limited powers to local communities (Chomba et al., 2015; Das, 2019), leading to devolved authority being

DOI: 10.4324/9781003153580-14

challenged. Active engagement of foresters in PFM may also decrease local people's ownership and authority (Scheba and Mustalahti, 2015). Overall, the efficacy and equity of PFM governance frameworks are fundamental to the shortcomings highlighted (e.g., Chinangwa et al., 2016; Chomba et al., 2015; Das, 2019; Jacob and Brockington, 2017; Maraseni et al., 2019; Mollick et al., 2018).

A country's forest policy is also influenced by the time it is implemented. Information provision increases over time, and the degree to which knowledge is available and utilized by diverse groups of people, such as policymakers, members of a specific class or profession, changes. As a result, a country's forest policy cannot be expected to be static throughout time. Thus, studies have been conducted to investigate how forest policies (development and implementation) impact on people's livelihoods in both developing and developed economies (see, e.g., Adhikari et al., 2014; Chinangwa et al., 2016; Coulibaly-Lingani et al., Das, 2019; Etongo et al., 2018; Green and Lund, 2015; Jacob and Brockington 2017; Luintel et al., 2017; Lund and Saito-Jensen, 2013; Sari, 1995).

However, none of these studies have investigated the challenges of developing and implementing forest policies in developing countries. Although Tanzania developed a new forest policy in 1998, antagonism between the government and other stakeholders such as charcoal and firewood makers remains very high. On the one hand, the government claims that charcoal production destroys the environment through deforestation; on the other, the charcoal makers claim that the government restricts them from accessing trees for making charcoal for their living. These workers make their living by producing charcoal and selling it to users. This study uses stakeholders' analysis/theories to investigate the challenges of developing and implementing forestry policy in Tanzania. The study also uses qualitative focus group discussions to collect data from two sets of respondents – charcoal makers and local government leaders in a district of Tanzania – and thematic analysis to assess the collected data. The local government leaders participated in the study simply to validate the information collected from the charcoal makers. This is somewhat different from the studies in the area conducted and analyzed above.

The objectives of the study

The main objective of conducting this study is to investigate, through focus group discussions (FGDs) and observations, the challenges of developing and implementing forestry policy in Tanzania. Information collected through FGDs was validated by local government leaders in the Mkuranga district. The study investigated an important stakeholder group, charcoal makers, to address the following research questions (RQs):

RQ1: What is the level of understanding of forestry policy, and joint forestry management initiatives in particular, of charcoal makers in the district?

RQ2: What is the level of understanding of environmental issues of the charcoal makers in the district?

RQ3: What is the perception of charcoal makers towards joint forest management and how it is operated in the district?

RQ4: What are the governance issues raised by the focus group discussion participants on the joint forest management initiatives in the district?

RQ5: What are the other challenges in the process of developing and implementing forest policy and joint forest management programmes in the district?

Review of the literature

Historically, Tanzanian forests have been controlled centrally by the Forest and Beekeeping Division (FBD). Since even before Independence in 1961, a fundamental issue has been that authority over forests was fragmented and resources were sparsely distributed to the point at which resource management was difficult. This approach to forestry management has resulted in forest degradation due to unlawful activities and increasing human strain on resources; before Independence, the forest cover was above 50% of the total land, but it gradually dropped to 45% in the late 1970s, around 41% in the late 1990s, and about 36% in the early 2000s. This form of management is currently characterized by excessive state control without local participation. Tanzania has a high deforestation rate on a global scale, ranging from 130,000 to 500,000 hectares per year. Settlement and agricultural growth are direct drivers of deforestation. Overgrazing, uncontrolled fires, shifting cultivation, and illicit logging are all examples of commercial charcoal and fuel wood production. Rapid and unregulated population increase, poverty, market failures, lack of a clear definition of property rights and security of tenure, and general policy failures have been the indirect or underlying causes of deforestation. People in economically disadvantaged nations typically rely on resource extraction from nearby forests for survival, whether for their own consumption, firewood, or a source of revenue. Forest degradation has had an impact on individuals who gather non-timber forest products (NTFPs) in terms of how long they spend seeking and collecting these, how much they consume and their reliance on the market. These changes have an influence on the livelihoods of people as well as on wood supplies in the area. A growing corpus of research has addressed specific aspects of NTFP extraction (Reddy and Chakravarty 1999). These works are, however, non-spatial in nature, rely on cross-sectional data, and pay little regard to the location of resources and related time and distance costs. Villagers' extraction patterns change over time as their access to NTFPs deteriorates due to changing regulations and levels of enforcement. The population itself is changing, as is the time it takes (and therefore the cost) for extraction. The literature on PFM has gained great attention in the way the community accessing resources as per the policies available in various communities (White & Martin, 2002; Wells, 2003). Much of this literature focuses on community-based forest management in South Asia, and specifically on charcoal and fuel wood. The findings from India and Nepal show that when villagers are excluded from accessing forest resources, they may travel to different areas to collect firewood and other non-timber products for making charcoal (Agarwal, 2001). Furthermore, Narain et al. (2005) employed a cross-sectional research study to explain the relationship between dependence on household changes in wealth as a result of changes in natural resources. In another study, Adhikari et al. (2007) revealed how community forestry management has affected the way people live in terms of extracting forest products and the number of livestock they possess.

Nevertheless, Agarwal, (2001)showed how social forestry management in South Asia has been successfully restricting the access of poor people to forest products due to social policy intervention. The policy has made it difficult for poor people to access common pool resources to make their living. This has been the case in many developing countries where the majority of forest policies have been developed to ensure conservation of the environment.

While many developing countries, including Tanzania, have been practising FPM policies, there is still a need for evidence of their effectiveness, and it is difficult to understand if such policies have been successful. In many countries in sub-Saharan Africa, PFM is being practised; for example, Gosalamang et al. (2004) examined the influence of changes in the legal status of a Ugandan forest reserve on household livelihoods, but they lacked quantitative data to back up the research.

In another study, Lokina and Robinson (2008) investigated how PFM in Tanzania has affected PFM forests, adjacent forests, and people's livelihoods, based on villagers' perceptions of changes caused by a shortage of resources. The ecological effectiveness of joint forest management (JFM) efforts is generally measured by the impact on resources within the individual JFM forest. However, as Lewis et al., (2002) noted, shifting extraction from a specific protected region to less protected woods might have a detrimental impact on the number of environmental services supplied for forests as a whole.

Although the effects on nearby forests have been acknowledged in the literature, little actual research has been conducted (Faith et al. 1996). Robinson et al. (2009) provided theoretical models to show the impact of degradation and isolation on neighbouring communities and forest resources (2002, 2005).

Furthermore, Robinson et al. (2002) anticipated how variations in resource density (e.g., degradation) influence how far people will walk into a forest to gather NTFPs, and how intensively they harvest these, given that they have a constant need for a particular resource. Also, the study conducted by Robinson et al. (2002) created a framework for analyzing how exclusion from a specific forest area will affect both villagers and forest resources. Two effects were identified: one of 'displacement', by which villagers will extract more intensively elsewhere, thereby displacing the problems of degradation to other areas, and another of 'replacement', by which villagers will extract more intensively elsewhere, thereby relocating the problems of degradation to other areas.

According to Mohamed et al., (2012); Lund et al., (2018), many independent governments have shown little interest in reviving local-level authority institutions that previous colonial administrations deliberately dismantled. The concept of local political forces questioning the legitimacy of newly independent governments, as happened following colonial administrations, did not sit well with some newly independent governments (see, e.g., Smoke, 1993). Despite other critical issues such as governance, economic growth, self-reliance, and political stability, the Tanzanian state assumed this responsibility. As a result, scarce resources were primarily devoted to address these causes, forest management was not prioritized and forests were allowed to degrade. Much emphasis has been put on reforming the administration of natural resources such as forests, with a focus on either expanding the government's powers, duties, and privatization. Rarely has attention been paid to the management of resources by communities or as common property however. In another development, Ascher (1995) contended that communities might attain this goal through assistance, rather than control. This is the concept advocated by Tanzania's new forest policy: making communities accountable for managing forest resources as common property wherever possible. The former forest policy, which had been in place until recently, was drafted in 1953. This strategy, developed during the colonial era (when Tanganyika was administered by the British), was plainly out of date. Forest policies are influenced by nations' political and economic ideologies and a wide range of shifting socioeconomic situations (Ellefson, 1991; Husch, 1987; King, 1974, 1975). Any advances or changes in a country's general policy should have a corresponding impact on changes to its forest policy (Chinangwa et al., 2016; Kumar et al. 2015).

The stakeholder theory

The theory of stakeholders is interdisciplinary and universal in nature, referring to structural and functional elements of relationships between diverse players in exchange processes. According to Phillips et al. (2003), stakeholders are groupings of entities obliged to collaborate to secure their own activity and development by engaging in relevant production and exchange activities (Phillips et al., 2003). Freeman & McVea (1984) made the following point in their influential book, 'Strategic management: A stakeholder's approach': *stakeholder* refers to an individual or group that may have an impact on, or be affected by, a firm's objectives being attained. As Freeman set the agenda for what we now call 'stakeholder theory', he redrew and mapped the traditional input/output model of firms. This broad definition allows for a wide range of uses, but it also allows for various interpretations (Phillips et al., 2003). It is becoming an increasingly important factor for determining the tactics of entities engaging in interactions and gaining competitive advantage (Harrison et al., 2010). It considers strategic, ethical, and institutional factors (Phillips et al., 2003). Shaping interactions between entities participating in trade activities and producing value in the public space is crucial for the division and redistribution of acquired resources and guaranteeing sustainable growth). According to the general theory of exchange, each exchange subject's needs are met by exchanging values between them according to specific rules (Narain et al., 2005). As a result, they establish various structures for the coordination of exchange processes and the co-creation of values in the form of businesses and organizations to enhance the efficiency of their operations. Transaction costs are the driving force for the creation of businesses and other types of institutions). This brings the stakeholder theory closer to the resource theory (Barney et al., 2001), the value chain concept (Porter and Kramer, 2011), and the concept of co-creation, in which an individual's benefits are achieved through the exchange and co-creation of values with other entities (Lewis et al., 2002). The criteria of value co-creation are components that connect diverse entities with each another around shared values and methods for implementing them. As a result, by building overlapping configurations known as 'multiple stakeholder orientation profiles', each entity can maintain distinct dependencies and network relationships with other entities (Sarin 1995). This results in complex, horizontal, and dynamic dependence structures, and it also leads to substantial issues at the management level as the source of disputes, inefficiencies, and market instability.

An example of this is forest management in Tanzania, where there is a conflict of interest between stakeholders who make and sell charcoal and firewood to the public, who use it as a source of energy, and local authorities that collect revenues from them.

Methodology

The study uses focus group discussions (FCDs) with people who make charcoal for a living in the Mkuranga district of Tanzania. According to Morgan (1996), FCDs are a robust means for collecting data in social science studies. People from different backgrounds are brought together to discuss a topic presented for investigation. Convenience sampling is a form of non-probability or non-random sampling whereby individuals of the target population who satisfy specific practical requirements, such as ease of accessibility, geographical closeness, availability at a certain time, or willingness to participate, are included for the purpose of the research (Dörnyei, 2007). It is also used to refer to population study participants who are freely accessible to researchers (Given & Lisa 2008). Another name for convenience samples is 'accidental samples', since items in the sample may be chosen merely because they are located, geographically, or administratively, close to where the researcher is collecting the data. Ecological data are frequently gathered by convenience sampling, in which data are collected near roads, trails, or utility corridors, and so are not representative (Given & Lisa 2008). The convenience sampling methodology was preferred due to the unwillingness of a majority of people, especially those in developing countries, to be questioned. Studies have indicated that many respondents, in particular in rural areas, do not see the value of research studies; hence, they are reluctant to be included in them. The study used 60 charcoal makers conveniently drawn from a group of unknown population size and five local leaders drawn from the local governments in the district. These respondents were obtained due to the working relationship with the researcher in the area of forests and natural resources.

According to Kumar et al., (2015), FGDs normally take either the form of synchronous discussion, which involves real-time live chat comparable to the conversational interactions of face-to-face focus groups, or asynchronous discussion, using 'static' text-based communication such as through forums or e-mail lists. In this study, we have used FGD participants with charcoal-making experience in the district and who sell their products to local customers and those in nearby regions such as Dar es Salaam and Pwani. After each of the five preliminary conversations were conducted, interactive focus group discussions were held, each lasting 30–60 minutes. The participants discussed the challenges they faced in developing and implementing PFM in Tanzania. First, the participants were asked about their knowledge of PFM in their districts. Second, they were questioned about their understanding of PFM and its use for people's wellbeing in the district. The FGD then focused on the availability of forests reserves in the district. Next, the discussion was directed more generally towards other issues relating to forest management and specifically the business of charcoal making and other NTFPs. This was conducted by asking the participants whether they participated in JFM and understood how it operated. Clearly, the qualitative focus group approach that we applied differs strongly from traditional focus group discussions in a number of ways. Most importantly, the participants were placed in groups of 12 people for the each FGD. We organized a total of five meetings, in addition to a further meeting with the local government leaders. From preliminary discussions with the FGD participants, it became clear that they were unfamiliar with JFM, and forest policy in particular. Therefore, an introduction to the terminology and basic concepts of these was necessary to begin the discussions. This introduction made it possible to assess to what extent the participants were familiar with issues relating to forests and their sustainable management in developing countries.

The focus group transcripts were used to analyze thematically the qualitative data. To carry this out, the researcher coded every five written word lines of participants' conversations to identify the key words. So that the codes had qualitative richness, it was ensured that they were clear, concise, and clearly stated. To ensure the integrity of the codes, code validation was applied. This was done to ensure that the codes were not misinterpreted or biased when reviewed by a person other than the researcher. The researcher double-checked data by reading them more than once to ensure consistency and validation. Through the integration of the codes, a codebook was created, and from this, the researcher identified themes and sub-themes that had emerged from the coded data. These themes emerged from the conversations, frequency of occurrence, and certain other factors. The researcher was able to define each theme sufficiently to make it clear and understandable for others.

The data obtained were read repeatedly until the key concepts were captured. As in the thematic analysis, the codes were sorted into groups depending on their relationships. Since the researcher aimed to examine the challenges encountered across the process of developing and implementing forestry policy in Tanzania, this appeared to be the appropriate method for the current study. We have used charcoal makers as the unit of analysis for this study. The study was conducted in Mkuranga district because it borders Tanzania's largest city, Dar es Salaam. Dar es Salaam is known as the leading user of charcoal for cooking energy. In their study on the economic impact of charcoal production in Dar es Salaam, Msuya et al. (2011) found out that the city would use 150,567 ha of charcoal in a year, which endangered the forests and environment at large. In this regard, Dar es Salaam is the main user of the charcoal, and Mkuranga is the main source of its supply to the city. Further, Mkuranga is a district where a large number of people make their living by making and selling charcoal to various parts of the country. The antagonism between the state organs and charcoal makers is very high in this district, such that they see each other as enemies. Also, the district is conducting a JFM programme through which individuals, the state, and local governments work together to make sure that the forest resource is managed sustainably.

The findings

The previous section examined the research methodologies used in this study. The section further described how data were collected and analyzed. Because the study employs a qualitative design, as identified above, the data collecting methods included FGDs, observation, documentation, and unobtrusive methods. The collected data are presented, analyzed, and interpreted in this section. They have been thematically analyzed from code books created by the researcher. The analysis and interpretation of the collected data was based on the objectives of this study described in the first and second sections.

Demographic characteristics of the respondents

In this sub-section, we present the demographic characteristics of the respondents by highlighting their age, experience in charcoal making, and level of education. This is followed by a brief discussion to compare the individual findings with those from previous studies.

Age of the respondents

Regarding the respondents' ages, those aged 36–45 formed the largest group in the study, accounting for 40% of the respondents. These were closely followed by the group aged 26–35, accounted for 35%, while the respondents aged 18–25 years, and those exceeding 46 years accounted for 15% and 10% of the overall respondents, respectively. This is to say, charcoal making tends to attract people from different age groups. Despite the fact that a majority of the respondents for this study were aged 36–45, the age distribution is an indicator of how the majority of people, especially in rural areas, depend on this type of business to make their living. The age characteristics of the respondents supports the work of other researchers studying areas of natural resources and forest industry. Figure 14.1 below summarizes the age categories of the respondents for the current investigation

Access to forest resources has been changing in Tanzania, as is the case in many other countries, due in part to forest degradation and, more recently, the implementation of PFM, which modifies the quantity of NTFPs that communities can collect from villages and government reserve forests. Forest degradation has influenced where individuals gather certain NTFPs, how long they spend seeking and collecting them, how much they consume, and their reliance on the market (Adhikari 2003).

Experience of the respondents in charcoal making

We put forward the following question: 'How many years have you spent making and selling charcoal?' We found the experience of the respondents went along the lines of their age, such that those who were older had spent more years making and selling charcoal those who were younger. Again, we put a supplementary question to the respondents about how the activity has changed over the years. One participant from Focus Group 3 said:

> Now you need to travel a bit longer to get access to firewood, which is used to make charcoal, unlike a few years ago. The business is not the

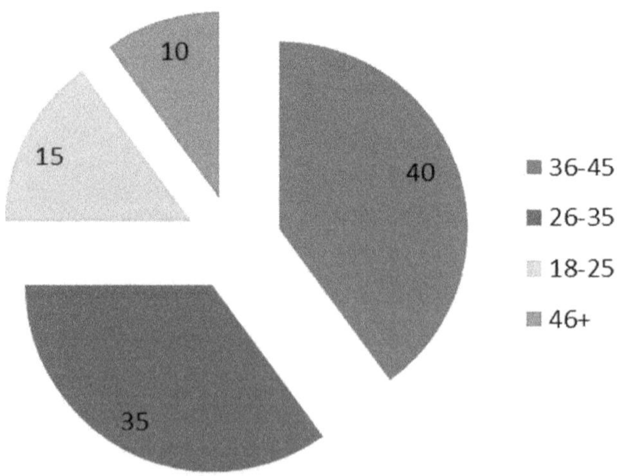

Figure 14.1 Age categories of respondents

> same now, as it is difficult to obtain the materials needed to make charcoal, and there are so many hurdles in selling the charcoal to customers. The business is perceived to be illegal by government officials and local government leaders.

The finding that the charcoal makers travel long distances to find the materials they need to produce charcoal is in line with the work of other researchers, such as Narain et al. (2005), who asserted that households are often forced to make changes when, among other things, policies that affect the accessibility of natural resources are enacted. These people would depend greatly on natural resources for making their living, so any changes to the way that those resources were accessed would certainly change their way of life. Another study conducted by Adhikari et al. (2014) found that the development and implementation of JFM programmes in Nepal had changed the way people lived. People would walk long distances to collect firewood for cooking. The policy might have been good for environmental protection initiatives; however, the poor were significantly affected because they had to access natural resources for their livelihoods. At the same time, Sekhar and Jørgensen (2003) found that JFM had made it nearly impossible for the poor to access resources because of restrictions imposed to protect forests.

Level of education of the respondents

We put forward a question to identify the respondents' level of education and determine how well they understood the forestry policy of 1998. Other factors remain constant: those with a higher level of education tended to understand policy issues better than those with lower levels of education. We wanted to ascertain the relationship between level of education and the type of work the respondents were engaged in. As expected, the overwhelming majority of the respondents (75%) had completed primary education, while just 15% – essentially the younger ones – had finished secondary school education. A further 10% of the respondents were primary school dropouts. A respondent in Focus Group 1, who was one of the oldest in the group, observed the following: Figure 14.2 summarizes the education levels of the respondents for this investigation

> The majority of the kids are dropping out of schools to join this kind of business. Mainly, they are doing so to actually join forces with their parents in making charcoal for their living. This has become a family business for the majority of the people in this district.

The findings in this category signify that charcoal making, like others NTFPs, is conducted largely by people who have a low level of education and who are poor. The findings further support the work of researchers such as Kumar (2002) and Rai et al. (2017), who found that the high cost of forest resources

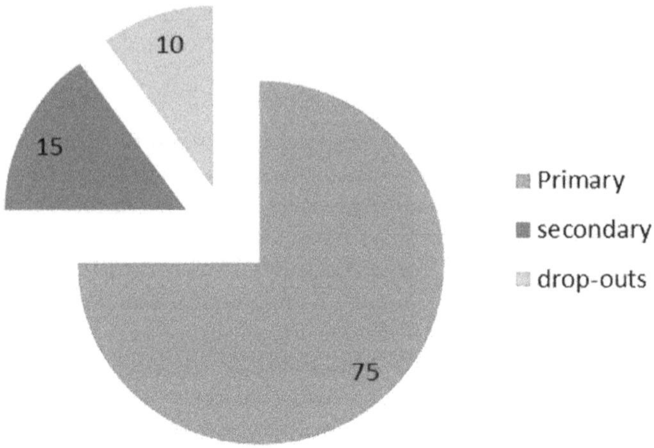

Figure 14.2 Education levels of the respondents

(e.g., wood) would exclude the poorest from benefiting from PFM. This has exacerbated intra- and inter-community strife in many societies (Gross-Camp et al., 2019). Thus, the business conducted by the elite is associated with timber extraction, leaving the poor and less educated to make their livings through NTFPs such as charcoal making. It was noted from the FGDs that this activity was one of the major sources of income for many families in the district.

Challenges in developing and implementing forestry policies in Tanzania

Through the FGDs, it was revealed that development and implementation of the forestry policy of 1998 has faced many hurdles. Despite the implementation of the JFM policy in Tanzania, the majority of respondents commented that they knew nothing about it. Hence, lack of awareness of the development of such policies is regarded as the biggest challenge in many developing countries. We put forward the following question to all five FGDs involving charcoal makers: 'What do you know about joint forest management?' As expected, even the term 'joint forest management' was new to almost everyone in these groups, and we took the time to elaborate that JFM is a programme of the national forest policy of 1998 for certain reserved forests to be jointly owned by the central government and local government in an area. A few of the participants recalled hearing about this from friends; one said:

> I have heard from my friends that we are allowed to purchase some trees from forests reserves areas, this is the justification that, policies are developed without involving the stakeholders at the grassroots level who are going to be affected by these policies either positively or negatively.

The findings about the lack of awareness of the forest policy of 1998 by the majority of respondents corresponds with the work of other researchers, such as Coulibaly-Lingani et al. (2011) and Lund and Saito-Jensen (2013), who asserted that a country's forestry policy is also affected by its place in history. More information is available over time, corresponding with the degree to which such knowledge is available and utilized by diverse groups of people. Coulibaly-Lingani et al. (2011), and Lund and Saito-Jensen (2013) asserted that forest policies in many sub-Saharan countries were developed by placing much emphasis in protecting the environment, but they forgot that other stakeholders would be negatively impacted. As a result, a country's forest policy cannot be expected to be static through time. Thus, studies have been conducted to investigate how the development and implementation of forest policies have impacted the livelihoods of people in both developing and developed economies (see, e.g., Adhikari et al., 2014; Chinangwa et al., 2016; Coulibaly-Lingani et al., 2011; Das, 2019; Etongo et al., 2018; Adejobi et al. 2011; Lambrick et al. 2014; Kumar et al. 2015; Green and Lund, 2015; Jacob and Brockington, 2017; Luintel et al., 2017; Lund and Saito-Jensen, 2013; and Robinson & Kajembe, 2009). In many developing countries, forestry policies were developed without engaging with stakeholders to see how they would be impacted by the projects.

Another challenge observed from the FDGs was lack of knowledge of environmental issues such as deforestation and global warming that result from firewood being cut to make charcoal. We put forward the following question to various groups of participants: 'What environmental issues are caused by charcoal making?' It was noted that such awareness had not spread to many people as the majority thought that environmental issues were the result of acts of God and had nothing to do with their own activity of making charcoal. One participant in Focus Group 4 said:

> I have been in this business for more than 30 years, and the situation is the same with no significant changes to the environment. We are receiving the same amount of rain and we are not short of food to feed our families. Sometimes we receive more rain, despite the claims of authorities that cutting down trees will result in a lack of enough rain for cultivation.

This was supported by a participant in Focus Group 1, who added:

> Cutting down trees to make charcoal and for other activities has been taking place in this areas for many centuries, and we have inherited this activity from our elders.

Another said:

> Every year, farmers clear the bush to open up land for new farms, but we get all the blame for deforestation.

These arguments were in line with the respondent's level of education, as can be seen from the findings above. We can summarize the findings by saying the level of understanding of environment issues and the possible causes of deforestation was very low. People would look at short-term gains for making their living at the expense of the environment. We then asked: 'What will the future hold for your sons, daughters and grandchildren if the land turns into a desert?' It was interesting to hear the following said by one of the respondents:

> The future is always uncertain, as only God the Almighty knows what is in store. Cutting down trees is dangerous for the environment. If such practices continue, the environment will be jeopardized, but we do not have other means to make our living.

We put forward a follow-up question to validate the information above and gauge the participants' understanding of JFM programs in the area: 'Is there a joint forest management project in the district?' It was noted that there were six forests reserves in Mkuranga district, of which only one was owned by 15 villages. In contrast, 15 villages/government forest reserves were jointly owned under JFM, and there were 39027.45 ha of forest land under this arrangement. The respondents agreed that forest officers in the district had been working to prevent them from getting into forests reserves. Asked how a JFM of that size operated, one participant, who asked for anonymity due to reasons of security, said:

> The people do not participate in making decisions about how the reserve operates. Rather, we are told what to do by the forest officers and local government leader ... The business is overshadowed by intimidation from local government leaders and forest officials, such that we sometimes organise camps where we can hide. Actually, it is not known as to what criteria they use to allow access to the reserved forests, as some of the people get access to these forests while others are denied access to the resources.

One participant added that people were not engaged in the business and all of the decisions regarding the management of forests that had been made by local government leaders in collaboration with forest officials. He said the following:

> We have not been consulted nor informed about JFM and how it operates.

Another participant added:

> The only thing that is commonly known by us is that making charcoal is an illegal business in the eyes of government officials and local government leaders.

The findings about the perception of respondents towards JFM practices in the district support the work of researchers such as Dressler et al. (2010), who observed that the implementation of PFM prevents people from accessing, using, and controlling valuable forest resources and implied that there are severe inadequacies in terms of social justice. Nevertheless, a tug of war tends to take place between leaders and their people when the latter are denied access to the resources they use to make their living. According to Ribot et al. (2010), the problem of forest access is taking place in many sub-Saharan countries. This is to say that many local PFM institutions do not represent the people's interests and they are not true representatives of the people for whom the policy was developed.

The above findings were then validated through an FGD between the researcher and five local government leaders of the district. Again, the names of the attendees were kept anonymous for ethical and security reasons.

First, we wanted the leaders to validate the claims that awareness exercises had not been conducted to make the people clear about the district's JFM programme. It was agreed that the ministry concerned had generally tried to raise awareness through radio and TV programming to all Tanzanians, but the level of understanding had been different from one group to another. One political leader said:

> The level of education of the majority is so low that, even if you approach them for awareness and education, they think the government is looking to trap them and take them to court. In essence, you cannot blame them for this as it has been the case for many years.

Regarding the issue of governance of forests and other natural resources, as cited by the participants of all five focus groups, the local government leaders again refuted claims that they had been using their political appointments to benefit from JFM projects in the district. One said:

> We operate this project jointly with the central government under the Ministry of Natural Resources and Tourism. People are also involved through the local government, and everything is undertaken openly with no favouritism at all. The problem we have is historical. Charcoal makers, in most cases, are conducting their activities without following the procedures and guidelines laid down by the authorities. Instead of abiding with the guidelines, the charcoal makers keep on moving from one area to the next. The business is conducted far from the reach of the government, and distribution is always undertaken at night.

We then asked the participants how the project operates, and we came to learn that JFM has been successful in terms of sustainable development and protecting the environment. The meeting agreed that education about the policy was very important as the majority of stakeholders did not speak the same language.

In this meeting, we also came to realize that those who understood these projects and were perhaps participating in them were timber extractors. The level of understanding between timber extractors and charcoal makers would differ significantly. Another important aspect was the level of understanding about environmental issues. While some people understood the negative consequences of cutting down trees, others did not. Clear knowledge would contribute to environmental protection for sustainable development. Another aspect to note was that policy development and implementation involved different groups of people, and those responsible for policy development and those who implemented it were not the same people. This would lead to a great deal of confusion when a policy is implemented.

Based on the researcher's observations and experience of collaborating with people in rural areas of Tanzania, other challenges in developing and implementing the forestry policy of 1998 included a lack of technology and innovation in solving the problems. The availability of affordable means to provide energy for cooking would kill off the business of making and selling charcoal as the main source of power for cooking in most parts of the country. The demand for charcoal derives from its popularity for this purpose in Tanzania. According to an estimate by Kilahama (2005), the charcoal used for cooking in the country exceeds one million tonnes annually, which is equivalent to 109,500 ha of forest loss. The tendency to use charcoal for cooking in preference of either electricity or gas is attributed mainly to its accessibility and the perception that it is cheaper than other fuels. Increasing charcoal consumption has resulted in forest loss, and hence deforestation. Deforestation has caused the degradation of water sources, threatened biodiversity, reduced soil quality, and ultimately had a severe impact on agricultural productivity (TAteDO, 2009). Charcoal making is the livelihood of the majority of people living in rural areas.

Conclusion

Stakeholders' involvement is essential throughout the process of developing and implementing any policy in both developed and developing economies. A successfully developed policy should be one that has involved stakeholders of all levels. Different stakeholders have contrasting ways of looking at different issues. Policymakers should bring on board all potential stakeholders when the policy is at its initial stages. No stakeholder should be left out when policies are developed, which has been a major issue, especially in the developing world. There is a tendency for policymakers to believe that they can develop their policies without engaging those whose lives will be most affected by them.

From the genesis of this study, the main challenge facing the development and implementation of forestry policy in Tanzania is the lack of awareness of the policy itself, which among other things promotes JFM between the people and the central government. JFM operates by setting aside forests reserves within districts that will be used to access resources such as timber, firewood for making charcoal and NTFPs. This arrangement was not known to the majority of the participants of the FGDs. What was known is that cutting down trees to make charcoal is illegal and can lead to penalties for those found to be engaging in it. The severe punishments imposed include, but are not limited to, confiscation of property, such as motorcycles, and monetary fines.

The lack of awareness of the participants in this study of the forests policy of 1998 is attributed largely to their low level of education. The majority had only completed primary education, a few had completed secondary school, and others had dropped out of primary school for various reasons, including engaging in charcoal making as a family business or income-generating activity. Some unscrupulous local leaders appear to have taken advantage of the majority being ignorant of forest policy by penalizing them through fines for a significant amount of money. Despite being fined and forfeiting their properties, these charcoal makers have vowed to continue performing their activity as their main source of income.

Another finding of this study is that the overwhelming majority of participants lack awareness about the environmental damage caused by making charcoal. Demand for charcoal is derived from its use as the main source of fuel for cooking in Tanzania. It is estimated that the charcoal used for cooking in the country exceeds one million tonnes annually, which is equivalent to 109,500 ha of lost forest. The preference for using charcoal for cooking ahead of electricity or gas is mainly attributed to its accessibility and perception that it is cheaper. Increasing charcoal consumption has resulted in forests loss, and hence deforestation. Deforestation has caused degradation of water sources, threatened biodiversity, reduced the quality of soils, and ultimately had a severe impact on agricultural productivity. Whether all the stakeholders are aware of the negative impacts of their activities or not, the general observation was that it would only be easy to tell them to stop charcoal production if were given an alternative source of income. Charcoal making is the livelihood of the majority of people living in rural areas. Therefore, alternative cooking fuels, such as electricity and gas, are perceived as expensive in both rural and urban areas, where charcoal is the leading source of cooking fuel.

Another notable challenge obtained by the study is a lack of good governance in the management of forests resources by local leaders. Favouritism and corruption have been reported, especially on JFM projects in the district. Unscrupulous local leaders would use JFM projects for their own benefits, and the elites have been leaving the people who should be the real benefactors of these projects with no access to forest resources in their district.

Thus, it may be concluded that the development and implementation of forestry in Tanzania should be people-centred and not otherwise. Central and local governments should be speaking the same language while implementing forestry policies and JFM projects in Tanzania. Policymakers should find the best way of managing forest reserves, as lack of awareness by the majority is making the whole process unfruitful. People will continue to engage in cutting down trees so long the business is attractive to them due to demand of their product as the main source of cooking fuel. Other policies such as those for electricity and gas should support the forestry policy as overdependency of charcoal for cooking is causing severe environmental problems.

Note

1 Senior Lecturer-Mzumbe University Dar es salaam Campus College. Email: oswalehe@mzumbe.ac.tz.

References

Adejobi, A. O., Babatunde R. O., & Idowu E. O. (2011, April). Weight and measurement issues in retail marketing of fresh tomatoes: Evidence from Osun state, Nigeria. *Journal of Agricultural and Biological Science, 6*(4), 20–26.

Adhikari, B. (2003). *Property rights and natural resources: Socio-economic heterogeneity and distributional implications of common property resource management* [Working paper]. South Asian Network for Development and Environmental Economics (SANDEE).

Adhikari, B., Williams, F., & Lovett, J. C. (2007). Local benefits from community forests in the Middle Hills of Nepal. *Forest Policy and Economics 9*, 464–78.

Adhikari, S., Kingi, T., & Genesh, S. (2014). Incentives for community participation in the governance and management of common property resources: The case of community forest management in Nepal. *Forest Policy and Economics, 44*, 1–9.

Agarwal, B. (2001). Participatory exclusion, community forestry, and gender: An analysis for South Asia and a conceptual framework. *World Development, 29*(10), 1623–48.

Ahenkan, A., & Boon, E. (2010). Commercialization of non-timber forest products in Ghana: Processing, packaging and marketing. *Journal of Food, Agriculture and Environment, 8*, 962–969.

Ahenkan, A., & Boon, E. (2011). Non-timber forest products (NTFPS): Clearing the confusion in semantics. *Journal of Ecology, 30*(1), 1–9.

Ascher, W. (1995). Communities and sustainable forestry in developing countries.

Chinangwa, L., Sinclair, F., Pullin, A. S., & Hockley, N. (2016). Can co-management of government forest reserves achieve devolution? Evidence from Malawi. *Forests, Trees and Livelihoods, 25*, 41–58. https://doi.org/10.1080/14728028.2015.1087886

Chomba, S. W., Nathan, I., Minang, P. A., & Sinclair, F. (2015). Illusions of empowerment? Questioning policy and practice of community forestry in Kenya. *Ecology and Society*, 20. https://doi.org/10.5751/ES-07741-200302

CIFOR. (2004). *Annual report: Forest for people and the environment*. www.Cifor.org/publications/pdf

Coleman, E. A., & Fleischman, F. D. (2012). Comparing forest decentralisation and local institutional change in Bolivia, Kenya, Mexico, and Uganda. *World Development, 40*, 836–849. https://doi.org/10.1016/j.worlddev.2011.09.008

Coulibaly-Lingani, P., Savadogo, P., Tigabu, M., & Oden, P. C. (2011). Decentralisation and community forest management in Burkina Faso: Constraints and challenges. *International Forestry Review, 13*, 476–486. https://doi.org/10.1505/146554811798811399

Das, B. K. (2019). Denial of rights continues: How legislation for 'democratic decentralisation' of forest governance was subverted in the implementation process of the Forest Rights Act in India. *European Journal of Development Research*, 1–23. https://doi.org/10.1057/s41287-019-0195-2

Dressler, W., Büscher, B., Schoon, M., Brockington, D. A. N., Hayes, T., Kull, C. A., ... & Shrestha, K. (2010). From hope to crisis and back again? A critical history of the global CBNRM narrative. *Environmental Conservation, 37*(1), 5–15.

Etongo, D., Kanninen, M., Epule, T., & Fobissie, K. (2018). Assessing the effectiveness of joint-forest management in southern Burkina Faso: A SWOT-AHP analysis. *Forest Policy and Economics, 90*, 31–38. https://doi.org/10.1016/j.forpol.2018.01.008

Faith, D. P., Walker, P. A., Ive, J., & Belbin, L. (1996). Integrating conservation and forestry production: Exploring tradeoffs between biodiversity and production in regional land use assessment. *Forest Ecology and Management, 85*, 251–260.

Freeman, R. E., & McVea, J. (2001). A stakeholder approach to strategic management. *Available at SSRN 263511.*

Given S. K., & Lisa M. (2008). Convenience sample. In *The SAGE encyclopedia of qualitative research methods*. Sage.

Gosalamang, D., Pal, V., & Gombya-Ssembajjwe, W. (2004). Impact of change of legal status of Mount Elgon Forest Reserve on household livelihoods. *Institutions, Incentives, and Conflicts in Forest Management: A Perspective*, 12–13.

Green, K. E., & Lund, J. F., 2015. The politics of expertise in participatory forestry: A case from Tanzania. *Foreign Policy Economics, 60*, 27–34. https://doi.org/10.1016/j.forpol.2021

Gross-Camp, N., Rodriguez, I., Martin, A., Inturias, M., & Massao, G. (2019). The type of land we want: Exploring the limits of community forestry in Tanzania and Bolivia. *Sustainability, 1*(6), 16–43. https://doi.org/10.3390/su11061643

Jacob, T., & Brockington, D. (2017). Learning from the other: Benefit sharing lessons for REDD+ implementation based on CBFM experience in Northern Tanzania. *Land Use Policy*. https://doi.org/10.1016/j.landusepol.2021

Kilahama, F. (2005). *Impact of increased charcoal consumption to forest and woodlands in Tanzania.* Coastal forests of Kenya and Tanzania. http://www.coastalforests.tfcg.org/pubs/Charcoal&Forests.pdf

Kumar, K., Singh, N. M., & Kerr, J. M. (2015). Decentralisation and democratic forest reforms in India: Moving to a rights-based approach. *Forest Policy and Economics, 51*, 1–8. https://doi.org/10.1016/J.FORPOL.2020

Kumar, S. (2002). Does participation in common pool resource management help the poor? A social cost-benefit analysis of joint forest management in Jharkhand, India. *World Development, 30*, 763–782.

Lambrick, F. H., Brown, N. D., Lawrence, A., & Bebber, D. P. (2014). Effectiveness of community forestry in Prey Long Forest, Cambodia. *Conservation Biology, 28*, 372–381.

Lewis, D. J., Hunt, G. L., & Plantinga, A. J. (2002). Public conservation land and employment growth in the northern forest region. *Land Economics, 78*(2), 245–259.

Lokina, R. B., & Robinson, E. J. (2008). *Determinant of the effectiveness of participatory forest management in Tanzania.* Gothenburg, Sweden: European Association of Environmental and Resource Economists.

Luintel, H., Bluffstone, R. A., Scheller, R. M., & Adhikari, B. (2017). The effect of the Nepal community forestry program on equity in benefit sharing. *Journal of Environmental Development*, 26, 297–321. https://doi.org/10.1177/1070496517707305

Lund, J. F., Rutt, R. L., & Ribot, J. (2018). Trends in research on forestry decentralization policies. *Currrent Opinion in Environmental Sustainability*. https://doi.org/10.1016/j .cosust. 32, 17-22

Lund, J. F., & Saito-Jensen, M. (2013). Revisiting the issue of elite capture of participatory initiatives. *World development, 46*, 104–112.

Maraseni, T. N., Bhattarai, N., Karky, B. S., Cadman, T., Timalsina, N., Bhandari, T. S., ... & Poudel, M. (2019). An assessment of governance quality for community-based forest management systems in Asia: Prioritisation of governance indicators at various scales. *Land Use Policy*, *81*, 750–761.

Mohammed, A. J., & Inoue, M. (2012). Drawbacks of decentralized natural resource management: Experience from Chilimo Participatory Forest Management project, Ethiopia. *Journal of Forest Research*, *17*, 30–36. https://doi.org/10.1007/s10310-011-0270-9

Mohammed, A. J., Inoue, M., & Shivakoti, G. (2017). Moving forward in collaborative forest management: Role of external actors for sustainable Forest socio-ecological systems. *Forest Policy and Economics*, *74*, 13–19. https://doi.org/10.1016/j.forpol.2020

Mollick, S. A., Rahman, K. M., Khan, I. N., & Sadath, N. M. (2018). Evaluation of good governance in a participatory forestry program: A case study in Madhupur Sal forests of Bangladesh. *Forest Policy and Economics*, *95*, 123–137. https://doi.org/10.1016/j.forpol.2020

Msuya, N., Masanya, E., & Temu, A. K. (2011). Environmental burden of charcoal production and use in Dar es Salaam, Tanzania.

Narain, U., Gupta, S., & Van't Veld, K. (2008). Poverty and resource dependence in rural India. *Ecological Economics*, *66*(1), 161–176.

National Population Commission. (2006). Nigeria federal government initiative of individual head count. Spread, state by state, National Population Commission. In *MOFINEWS Jan-Feb, 2007, 6(3): 7.initiative: Money grows on trees Cameroon series 5.* New York: UNDP.

Parmar, B. L., Freeman, R. E., Harrison, J. S., Wicks, A. C., Purnell, L., & De Colle, S. (2010). Stakeholder theory: The state of the art. *Academy of Management Annals*, *4*(1), 403–445.

Phillips, O. L., Martínez, R. V., Vargas, P. N., Monteagudo, A. L., Zans, M. E. C., Sánchez, W. G., ... & Rose, S. (2003). Efficient plot-based floristic assessment of tropical forests. *Journal of tropical ecology*, *19*(6), 629–645.

Ribot, J. C., Lund, J. F., & Treue, T. (2010). Democratic decentralization in sub-Saharan Africa: its contribution to forest management, livelihoods, and enfranchisement. *Environmental Conservation*, *37*(1), 35–44.

Robinson, D. T., & Brown, D. G. (2009). Evaluating the effects of land-use development policies on ex-urban forest cover: An integrated agent-based GIS approach. *International Journal of Geographical Information Science*, *23*(9), 1211–1232.

Robinson, M., Cognard-Plancq, A. L., Cosandey, C., David, J., Durand, P., Führer, H. W., ... & Zollner, A. (2002). Studies of the impact of forests on peak flows and baseflows: A European perspective. *Forest Ecology and Management*, *186*(1–3), 85–97.

Sarin, M. (1995). Regenerating India's forests: Reconciling gender equity with joint forest management. IDS bulletin, *26*(1), 83–91.

Scheba, A., & Mustalahti, I. (2015). Rethinking 'expert' knowledge in community forest management in Tanzania. *Forest Policy Economics*, *60*, 7–18. https://doi.org/10.1016/j.forpol.2020

Smoke, P. (1993). Local government fiscal reform in developing countries: Lessons from Kenya. *World Development*, *21*(6), 901–923.

Southeast Asia. Netherlands Committee for International Union for the Conservation of Nature (IUCN) (n.d.).

TaTEDO. (2009) Charcoal industry in Tanzania with selected TaTEDO experience. *Sustainable Energy and Development Forum*, 7, 8.

Wells, M.P. (2003). Protected area management in the tropics: can we learn from experience? *Journal of Sustainable Forestry*, 17, 67–81.

White, A. & A. Martin. (2002). *Who Owns the World's Forests? Forest Tenure and Public Forests in Transition*. Washington, D.C: Center for International Environmental Law.

15 Tourism in the tropics: emerging themes and keyword analysis

K Thirumaran[1], *Gohar Feroz Khan*[2], *and Jacob Wood*[3]

Introduction

The origins and foundations of tourism scholarship lie in the temperate zones of the world (Pearce, 2009). While tropical destinations and themes have not been ignored in tourism study, a closer focus on the emerging trends of tropical tourism settings is needed. The region itself refers to the lands that lie between the Tropics of Cancer and Capricorn, officially latitudes 23 degrees 30 minutes north and south, respectively, and flanking the equator are commonly referred to as 'the tropics' (Frenkel, 1996). To provide a unique assessment of tourism research, our study utilizes the social network analysis (SNA) technique to analyze and better understand the semantic and knowledge networks that are associated with the field of tourism and more specifically the types of tourism research that are relevant to the tropics region. The SNA approach has yet to be used in any great detail, although it has formed a key mechanism of analyzing trends in information technology management (Khan and Wood, 2015; Khan and Wood, 2017), international trade (Wood and Khan, 2015), human resource management (Wood et al., 2016; Kim et al., 2016), and second language acquisition (Jang et al., 2017).

Any review on trends must acknowledge that tourism studies were very much encapsulated in the direction of key events in the world (Hall et al., 2014). The end of the Cold War and the subsequent economic transformations of some of the economies, political events from Africa to Asia (e.g., Tunisia, Libya, Egypt, Myanmar, Thailand) created new pockets of challenges and opportunities. The Chinese and Indian economies, for example, adopted a capitalistic and global trade framework in the 1980s which is now evidently changing the profile of travellers and bilateral relations in a major way (Putra et al., 2021; Sum, 2019; Wu et al., 2002).

The prolific development of technology has not only impacted the way travellers select destinations, book hotels, and determine their activities – it has also changed their modes of travel and the way they have experienced relevant travel and tourism websites (Štetić et al., 2017). Moreover, governments and industries have too heavily leveraged technology to help shape policy initiatives and their approaches to the tourism economy. More recently, a plethora

DOI: 10.4324/9781003153580-15

of scholarship in the space of epidemics and pandemics have emerged as a result of the disastrous impact on the tourism industry by the COVID-19 infectious virus (Gössling, Scott, & Hall, 2020).

As a consequence, world events have a tremendous impact on global travel, and scholars have been equally busy capturing the contours of those impacts in addition to addressing specific themes in tourism that recur often in different forms that require new concepts and frameworks. This study builds on the research that currently exists in the field of tourism research. This chapter is organized by first outlining some of the key literature that has emerged within the tourism field in recent times. Secondly, a detailed outline of the SNA approach is provided. This is followed by an analytical breakdown of the data that was recovered relating to top journal publications, authors, publication outlets, institutions, countries, and keywords found in the tourism research domain. Finally, the study sheds light on the emerging and fading themes in the domain. In light of the analysis some important implications to tourism studies in the tropics are discussed.

Literature review

At the turn of the 1900s, North Americans and Europeans began to see the tropics as no longer representing 'nature at her most dangerous and came to represent her at her most loving, a change that necessarily had implications for racial and sexual mores' (Cocks, 2013 p.4). Cocks's (2013) historical analysis provides us with a compass on how much the literature has moved away from the tropical south's historical complexities and developed new frameworks in the travel circuit since World War II in particular. A good example is the circulation of women from the tropics migrating to Europe and North America. In the case of Brazilian women participating in the sex trade in Italy once a life partner is found, they leave the sex tourism for a life change (Piscitelli, 2007). The Vietnam War intensified the birth of sex tourism in Southeast Asia with Thailand being in the front line (King, 2017; Trương, 1990) as did the Caribbean yachting industry (Lett Jr, 1983). This sexual theme remains inherently ambiguous as medical tourism (Nelson, 2014) for sex changes and cosmetic surgery (Ackerman, 2010; Piscitelli, 2007; Noree, Hanefeld, & Smith, 2014) have taken precedence in the scholarship focus on the tropics.

As part of the tropics development as an emerging destination, the idea of engaging traditional communities in tourism was another aspect that has had much attention (Kieffer, & Burgos, 2015). Parallel, if not at converging points, community-based tourism (CBT) also involves studies related to sustainable environment and livelihood of the communities affected by climate change and desire to protect their resources as showcased by the example of birdwatching activities in Ethiopia and Costa Rica (SekercioAlu, 2012). The most frequent coverage that is addressed in the context of visitor and community concerns of activities is related to eco-tourism in Mahenye, Zimbabwe

(Mudzengi et al., 2021) and marine life tourism in coastal community areas of Fiji and the Great Barrier Reef, Australia (Tyllianakis et al., 2019; Williamson et al., 2017). These cited examples highlight areas of scholarship that are concerned with the sustainability issues that are often connected to the livelihood of the communities merging with concerns of protecting the natural wildlife found both on land and sea in the tropics.

Following the community-based tourism and eco-tourism, the contours of research on the tropics also take place in the urban context of African and South American cities. Though much has been written in the area of resorts and beaches (Pham, & Thirumaran, 2016; Yasué, & Dearden, 2008), tourism in the cities often are studied in the realm of shopping (Prideaux, & Coghlan, 2006), attractions, museums, and fine dining and luxury tourism (Abidin, Panchal, & Thirumaran, 2017; Daniel, 2015; Silva, & Chapagain, 2013; Thirumaran, & Raghav, 2017; Zhang, 2017). At times, like sustainable tourism focus, city tourism too does not escape the global issue of climate change. For example, the city of Campeche, Mexico experiences wild weather pattern changes impacting tourism (Bertha and Joel, 2019), while other studies have looked at how tourism ventures can be sustained during climatic change (Azzali et al., 2020). Tourism research on the tropics has also looked at the role of social media in luxury tourist settings (Thirumaran et al., 2021). These sub-themes together suggest that the tropics contain a diverse swathe of territories with climate, terrain, and people each unique, and the type of tourism activities is underlined by the specificities of the human and natural geography.

Methodological approach

Data

There are numerous databases such as JSTOR, Proquest, and Scopus that are available to social science researchers. For the purpose of this study, the Web of Science (WoS) database is used due to it being an excellent aggregator of published research material in the tourism field. The ease of navigation and data ontology further adds value to the extraction and analysis of works in an organized manner. Using the keywords 'community-based tourism, sex tourism, urban tourism, tech aided tourism, heritage tourism, one belt economy and tourism, luxury tourism, eco-tourism, back-packer tourism, economic development, and tourism', 584 articles were retrieved from the WoS for this SNA study.

These 584 studies had appeared in 205 sources across the 1997 to 2021 period of assessment. Those documented were authored by 577 institutions, and 1020 authors (Table 15.1). Of the total sample, 412 (70.55 %) were journal articles, 138 (23.63 %) were book reviews, 18 (4.70 %) were early access studies, 12 were editorials, while the remaining 10 were reviews. Table 15.1 further illustrates the breakdown in document types and the percentage based on publications specific to the tropics.

Table 15.1 Tourism scholarship in the tropics

Publication types	*Records*	*% of Sample (n = 584)*
Article	412	70.548
Book review	138	23.63
Early access	18	3.082
Editorial material	12	2.055
Review	10	1.712
Proceedings paper	9	1.541
Meeting abstract	6	1.027
News item	3	0.514
Correction	2	0.342
Letter	1	0.171

A large part of knowledge production on tourism scholarship related to the tropics were contributed in the form of research articles (412), which was followed by book reviews (138). The remaining 6% of works were spread across a wide variety of publication types such as editorial materials, reviews, proceedings papers, abstracts, news items, corrections, and a letter. The variety of sources suggests that Tropics scholars are indeed contributing to a robust discourse in the tourism field.

Properties measured

Based on the level and node properties of the networks, an overview of the keywords 'tropics' and 'tourism' was mapped out. The network analysis was derived from measuring diameter, density, and clustering co-efficient, and the average degree (Hanneman and Riddle, 2005). With the principal and subnetworks connected, the search provides us with a rich data set of information on key topic areas and the oscillating nature of tourism research on the tropics. As part of our approach, we also looked at the relevant authors' collaboration activities as represented by the visual density of nodes (Barabási et al., 2002). The thicker the node, the greater the level of collaboration that has been taking place.

To conceive and present the keyword networks, the VOSviewer was applied (Van Eck and Waltman, 2010). When the keywords co-appear in the title and abstracts, they suggest a relationship such as the prominence of the topic or area of studies (Choi et al. 2011; Yoon and Park 2005). Leydesdorff (2006) supports the deployment of this type of study measure to detect trends in a particular area of study.

Another key tool employed was the Science of Science Tool (Sci2-Team, 2009) to determine emerging and fading themes. Also known as the burst detection tool, it helps to identify the emerging trends (Chen, 2006; Chen et al., 2009; Guo et al., 2011; Mane and Borner, 2004; Swar and Khan, 2014).

Findings

This tourism-focused SNA study unveiled several important results which help to map out the research that is currently being done in the tropics field. From the perspective of a journal, the tropics-focused research, in all of the leading journals including *Tourism Management, Journal of Sustainable Tourism, and the Annals of Tourism Research.* It also features prominently in multidisciplinary outlets such as the *Sustainability Journal* (MDPI), *Urban Studies*, and even the *Journal of Culture, Health, and Sexuality* (see Table 15.2).

Tropics-focused tourism research has grown in appeal significantly over the last 20 years. A key driver of this focus has been the emergence of tourism as a key economic driver for many developing economies that are located in the tropics. Such developments have brought increased interest from scholars. The highest number of publications related to the tropics appear to be in 2020, 2019, and 2016. According to Table 15.3, since 2009, the number of publications on the tropics has been steadily increasing, except for 2021 which will need to be corrected when data is next collected.

Table 15.2 Journal titles' papers published on the tropics

Source titles	*Records*	*% of the sample (n=584)*
Tourism Management	54	9.247
Journal of Sustainable Tourism	40	6.849
Annals of Tourism Research	36	6.164
Sustainability	32	5.479
Current Issues in Tourism	20	3.425
Tourism Geographies	14	2.397
Asia Pacific Journal of Tourism Research	13	2.226
Journal of Tourism and Cultural Change	13	2.226
Tourism Economics	10	1.712
International Journal of Tourism Research	8	1.37
Journal of Travel Research	8	1.37
Culture Health Sexuality	7	1.199
Scandinavian Journal of Hospitality and Tourism	7	1.199
Urban Studies	7	1.199
International Journal of Heritage Studies	6	1.027
Journal of Destination Marketing Management	6	1.027
Cities	5	0.856
Contemporary Sociology: A Journal of Reviews	5	0.856
Development Southern Africa	5	0.856
Tijdschrift Voor Economische En Sociale Geografie	5	0.856
Tourism Management Perspectives	5	0.856
American Behavioral Scientist	4	0.685
Gender Place and Culture	4	0.685
Journal of Travel Tourism Marketing	4	0.685
Sexualities	4	0.685

Table 15.3 Number of publications appearing over years

Years	*Records*	*% of the Sample (n=584)*
2021	1	0.171
2020	68	11.644
2019	67	11.473
2018	37	6.336
2017	36	6.164
2016	40	6.849
2015	33	5.651
2014	23	3.938
2013	26	4.452
2012	22	3.767
2011	26	4.452
2010	16	2.74
2009	20	3.425
2008	16	2.74
2007	7	1.199
2006	16	2.74
2005	9	1.541
2004	8	1.37
2003	11	1.884
2002	15	2.568
2001	11	1.884
2000	2	0.342
1999	7	1.199
1998	5	0.856
1997	10	1.712

Emerging and fading themes (burst detection)

The top 43 latest bursting and disappearing topics in the author-supplied keywords are shown in Table 15.4. In the case when there is no end date noted, the terms are considered as still being active. In the most recent author-prescribed keywords, the areas of enterprises, augment, and reality, as well as satisfaction have emerged as key themes since 2018. These keywords appear in line with studies focused on measuring satisfaction and technology use. One keyword that stands out in this category is CBT which appeared prominently from 2016 to 2018. This result suggests that the keyword 'urban' supplied by authors primarily prominent in the years 1996–2003 has now become less important with the current focus on 'community' involvement in tourism as reflected in the title keywords (2019–) as reflected in Table 15.5. Additionally, the frequency of keywords such as 'sex' (1995–2007), 'prostitution' (1996–2013), 'identity' (1995–2010), 'global' (1996–2010), and 'museum' (1996–2012) all indicate popular topics focused on the tropics but have dissipated since the end years. The title keywords also suggest a strong coherence with abstracts where

Table 15.4 Keywords bursting in the author-supplied keywords

Word	*Weight*	*Length*	*Start*	*End*
Accept	1.9	1	2018	2018
Enterprise	1.7	2	2018	2019
Realities	2.2	2	2018	2019
Satisfaction	2.3	2	2018	2019
Augment	2.2	2	2018	2019
Archaeology	1.8	1	2017	2017
Process	1.8	2	2017	2018
Movement	1.6	3	2017	2019
Indicate	1.6	3	2017	2019
Corporation	1.8	1	2016	2016
Manage	1.7	2	2016	2017
CBT	1.6	3	2016	2018
Develop	1.5	2	2015	2016
Use	1.6	2	2015	2016
Child	1.6	3	2015	2017
Dark	1.8	3	2015	2017
Ecology	2.1	2	2014	2015
Response	2.9	4	2014	2017
Environment	1.6	3	2013	2015
Eco	2.6	3	2013	2015
Territorial	1.8	2	2012	2013
Behaviour	2.0	4	2012	2015
Local	1.6	1	2011	2011
Sociology	1.6	4	2011	2014
Island	1.8	2	2010	2011
Impact	1.8	2	2010	2011
Culture	2.6	2	2009	2010
Economy	1.7	4	2008	2011
Countries	1.6	6	2006	2011
Institution	1.7	11	2003	2013
authentic	1.6	3	2001	2003
Urban	4.1	8	1996	2003
Market	2.2	9	1996	2004
Global	1.9	15	1996	2010
Museum	1.6	17	1996	2012
Prostitution	2.5	18	1996	2013
Sex	2.3	13	1995	2007
Japan	2.2	14	1995	2008
Ident	2.1	16	1995	2010

the emphasis on the 'community' (2018–) and 'social' (2018–) aspects of the tourism scholarships in the tropics appear to continue to matter.

The top 20 latest bursting and disappearing topics in the titles of the articles are shown in Table 15.5. In the case when there is no end date noted, the terms

Table 15.5 Keywords bursting in the titles of the article

Word	*Weight*	*Length*	*Start*	*End*
Social	4.4	3	2019	
Base	5.5	3	2019	
Community	6.1	4	2018	
Culture	7.2	5	2017	
Entangle	3.8	4	2014	2017
Bahia	3.8	4	2014	2017
Ambiguous	4.3	5	2013	2017
American	4.6	7	2005	2011
Historical	4.0	2	2005	2006
Centro	4.0	2	2005	2006
Latin	4.6	2	2005	2006
Plaza	4.6	2	2005	2006
Dominican	4.8	5	2004	2008
Love	4.1	5	2004	2008
Societies	4.9	3	1995	1997
Herbert	5.0	3	1995	1997
Citi	9.7	4	1994	1997
Law	5.6	3	1994	1996
Attract	5.4	3	1994	1996
Visitor	6.3	5	1992	1996

are considered to still be active. Several keywords have interestingly become less important in the context of tourism in the tropics. This is indicated by the disappearance of the words 'visitor' (1992–1996), 'attractions' (1994–1996), 'law' (1994–1996), and 'love' (2004–2008). While 'culture' (2017–) appears to continue to be an issue addressed by scholars, 'community' (2018–) continues to be widely used in titles of articles.

The top 65 latest bursting and disappearing topics that have appeared in the abstracts of the articles are shown in Table 15.6. Again, where there is no end date noted, the terms are considered to still be active. The data in this table provides an important overview of the phenomenon being analyzed in the field over almost the last 30 years. One would think that 'eco-tourism' in the tropics would continue to be on top of the tourism agenda given much of the tropics also covers protected ecology, whether it be marine wildlife or jungle trekking. However, our results showed otherwise, as the theme appears to burst around the late 1990s and completely disappears by 2016. Table 15.6 illustrates the associated words such as 'environment' (2007–2009), 'reserves' (2009–2016), 'eco' (2013–2015), 'protection' (2014– 2015), and 'sustain' (2014–2014). This suggests that scholars may have migrated their focus onto development and urban tourism issues as much of the tropics shifted their focus to non-ecological types of tourism but revisiting some aspects of the 'environment' again in 2018–2019. There is also the idea that tourism works on the tropics might

Table 15.6 Keywords bursting in the abstract

Word	*Weight*	*Length*	*Start*	*End*
Event	2.62265	12	1992	2003
Attract	2.916095	8	1993	2000
Market	5.757924	8	1994	2001
Demand	2.441245	13	1994	2006
Reconstruct	2.360369	15	1996	2010
prostitution	2.461799	11	1996	2006
Impact	3.397687	6	1997	2002
Right	4.305204	11	1997	2007
Reserve	5.958666	12	1997	2008
Product	2.709359	5	1998	2002
History	2.500677	2	1999	2000
Authentic	2.392931	8	2000	2007
Tourist	5.745848	3	2000	2002
Law	2.463325	14	2001	2014
Job	2.431239	10	2002	2011
Island	2.852967	8	2004	2011
Industries	3.291126	4	2004	2007
Village	2.602996	2	2004	2005
Negotiation	2.320996	10	2004	2013
Nation	2.782467	11	2005	2015
Future	2.843798	3	2006	2008
Association	2.307455	4	2006	2009
Nature	4.303936	4	2007	2010
Environment	2.33391	3	2007	2009
Past	2.829401	3	2008	2010
Small	2.575868	4	2008	2011
Resort	2.43037	3	2008	2010
Australia	2.433339	8	2008	2015
Interpret	2.641728	3	2009	2011
South	2.392968	6	2009	2014
Progress	2.550217	7	2010	2016
Visit	3.427589	5	2010	2014
Poverty	2.750768	6	2010	2015
Resource	2.588146	3	2011	2013
Sexual	2.703544	4	2011	2014
Experience	3.247608	2	2011	2012
Service	2.326989	2	2012	2013
Product	2.323938	3	2012	2014
Practical	2.904147	1	2013	2013
Ident	2.331846	1	2013	2013
Quarter	2.294213	3	2013	2015
Eco	2.849007	3	2013	2015
Tour	2.535443	2	2013	2014
Real	2.660452	2	2013	2014
Competition	2.81201	2	2013	2014

(*Continued*)

Table 15.6 (Continued)

Word	*Weight*	*Length*	*Start*	*End*
Emerging	2.331846	1	2013	2013
Reserve	3.128246	3	2014	2016
Interest	2.515859	4	2014	2017
Sustain	2.288067	1	2014	2014
Protect	2.306969	2	2014	2015
Complex	3.310918	1	2014	2014
Promotion	2.456672	1	2014	2014
Planner	2.555189	2	2015	2016
Augment	2.51002	4	2016	2019
Practical	2.32488	2	2017	2018
Distinct	2.547681	2	2017	2018
Engage	2.396554	2	2018	2019
Accord	3.721224	2	2018	2019
Environ	3.401329	2	2018	2019
Change	3.157096	1	2019	2019
Interact	3.339566	1	2019	2019
Quality	2.40216	2	2020	
Mediate	3.632574	2	2020	
Cognition	2.492737	2	2020	

also emphasize 'quality' (2019–2020) tourism. This latter claim may have to be further verified on a longer trend but it is safe to suggest that researchers might want to consider this theme as significant as we know of countries in the tropics such as Singapore and Thailand that are determined to improve service quality (Pongamponkaiwan and Leelasantitham, 2020; Sirilersuang and Pongkijvorasin, 2018; Hamid et al., 2021).

Abstract keywords network

A total of 8373 keywords were extracted from abstracts within the corpus. However, only keyword terms that occurred at least five times (n = 339) are included in our analysis. In Figure 15.1 node size represents the number of occurrences and links represent the co-occurrence relationship. The clustering co-efficient was 0.49 and the diameter was 3. The average degree (i.e., co-occurrence) of the network was 61.69, and the density of the network was 0.18. Based on co-occurrence relationships, words are grouped into eight clusters, as represented by the colours of the nodes. Overall, there were nine clusters of keywords, the largest (the red one) being 76 keywords, and the smallest containing two keywords. The second-largest cluster contained 69 keywords (coloured in green) followed by 53 keywords in the blue cluster. From Figure 15.1, the evidence is clear, community-based tourism has emerged as a major study area along with destination and a smaller number of topics covered such as 'heritage tourism' and 'tourism initiative' largely concerned with tourists' preferences and satisfaction.

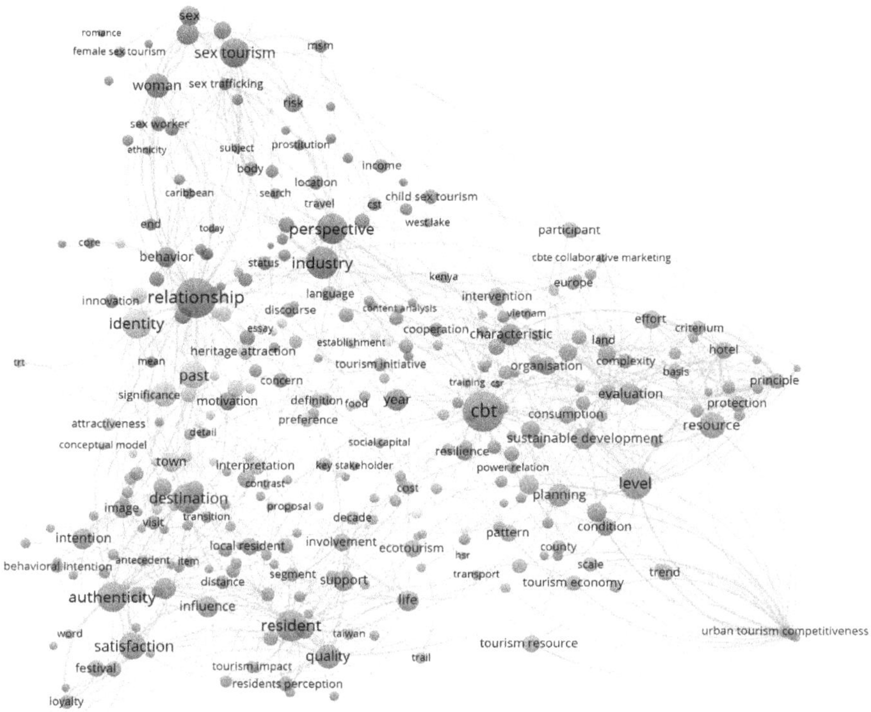

Figure 15.1 Diagram depicting abstract keywords network

Title keywords network

A total of 1420 terms were identified in the titles of the articles: however, only the terms that occurred at least 4 times (n = 92) are included in the analysis. In Figure 15.2, node size represents the number of occurrence and links represent the co-occurrence relationship. The clustering co-efficient was 0.63 and the diameter was 4. Based on co-occurrence relationships, words are grouped into eight clusters as represented by the colours of the nodes. Overall, there were 14 clusters of keywords the largest (the red one) being 14 keywords and the smallest containing two keywords. The second-largest cluster contained 12 keywords (coloured in green) followed by 11 keywords in the blue cluster. The average degree (i.e., co-occurrence) of the network was 8.9, while the density of the network was 0.096. Furthermore, the network properties – such as degree centralities, density, components, and degree distribution – suggest that the title keyword network also exhibits a power-law distribution: a few popular keywords or themes are frequently used by follow-on studies.

Figure 15.2 Diagram depicting title keywords network

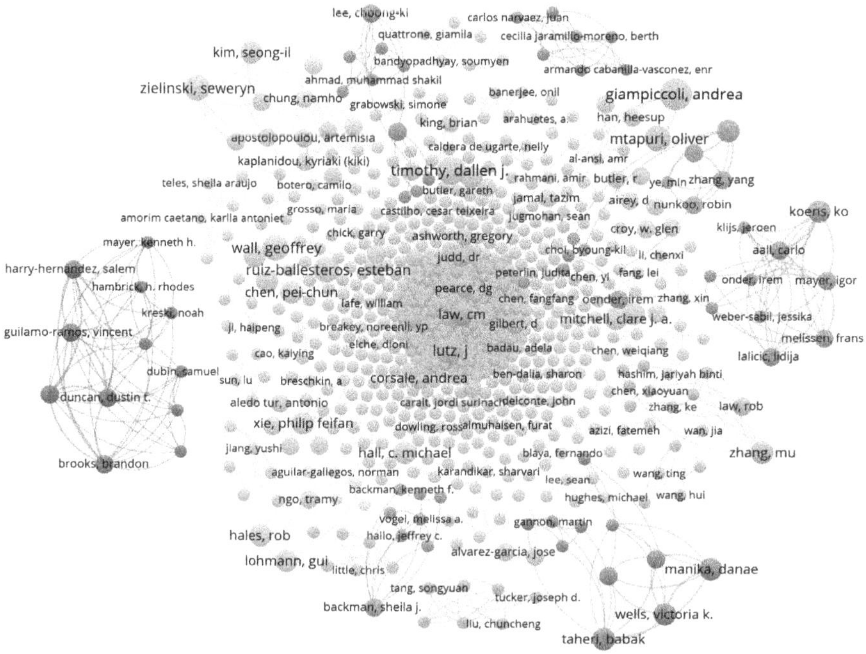

Figure 15.3 Diagram depicting author network

Author network

The authors' network is formed by 1020 authors and 100 co-authorship ties. In Figure 15.3, node size represents the number of collaborations ties an author has, and links represent the co-occurrence relationship. The average degree was 2 collaboration ties and the clustering co-efficient was 0.96 and the diameter was 4. And the graph density was 0.002. There were 463 weakly connected components (e.g., isolated subnetworks as indicated by different colors) in the network. The network properties – such as degree centralities, density, components, and degree distribution – indicate the network is essentially fragmented having several small subnetworks and isolates. There are at least five authors densely connected and similarly a little over seven outlying clusters indicate a network of collaborators on their own. Perhaps, this might also suggest working on similar topics or a network of regular collaborative publications amongst members within the network. The key authors from the SNA include Andrea Giampiccoli, Geoffrey Wall, Dallen Timothy, and Oliver Mtapuri amongst others.

Concluding remarks

There are two limitations to our study. We understand that not all works are captured by the web of science and that when these data were captured in June

2021, not all publications of the year may be included either. However, we are satisfied with the knowledge that the WoS database is used by a significant number of leading international publishing houses such as Springer Nature, and as such it provides a useful means of gauging the significance of a topic or area of study.

Over the last decade or so, tourism research has gradually migrated away from a commodity exchange: souvenir buying and travel to unique destinations for experiences to an academic discipline that is very much focused on urban settings. Given this evolution in focus, researchers might find continued engagement in works related to community-based tourism and destination experiences and satisfaction. As the tropics become a more salient destination for travel in the post-COVID-19 era, academics will be well-placed to assess any changes in the ecological or environment-related tourism sphere.

Our study highlighted several interesting trends. Of particular note, community-based tourism, heritage and cultural tourism, urban and sex tourism continue to be of particular interest, captured and studied by many scholars contributing to knowledge creation on the tropics. The richness of the tropical belt with emerging destinations and a variety of cultural manifestations certainly continues to press for a need to enhance our understanding of people and their heritage to make meaning and reference to the tourism economy. A large part of traditional communities too seek to engage in tourism with their unique natural environment or culture to share with visitors. This latter desire to share as a community through tourism is an enormous contribution to the financial well-being of rural communities. Thus, there is a continuous need to further explore sustainable engagements and preservation of cultures and the environment as much as urban settings become a significant area in the tropics and ground for research.

Notes

1 Corresponding author: Senior Lecturer, JCU Singapore Business School, James Cook University Singapore, Singapore. Email: k.thirumaran@jcu.edu.au.
2 Associate Professor, School of Management and Marketing, The University of Waikato, Hamilton, New Zealand.
3 JCU Singapore Business School, JCU Singapore, Singapore, and Department of International Trade, Chungnam National University, Daejeon, South Korea.

References

Abidin, A., Panchal, J. H., & Thirumaran, K. (2017). Celebrity Chefs and the Enhancement of Culinary Tourism Experiences in Singapore. In Balancing Development and Sustainability in Tourism Destinations: Proceedings of the Tourism Outlook Conference 2015 (pp. 109–115). From: Tourism Outlook Conference 2015, 29-31 July 2015, Lombok, Indonesia.

Ackerman, S. L. (2010). Plastic Paradise: Transforming Bodies and Selves in Costa Rica's Cosmetic Surgery Tourism Industry. *Medical Anthropology*, *29*(4), 403–423. https://doi.org/10.1080/01459740.2010.501316

Azzali, S., Kamble, Z., Wong, C., Wood, J., & Thirumaran, K. (2020). Mitigating Impact from Natural Disasters, Building Resilience in Tourism: The Case of Kerala. In (Eds.) Taha Chaiechi, *Economic Effects of Natural Disasters*. Elsevier Publishing, pp. 119–129.

Barabási, A.-L., Jeong, H., Neda, Z., Ravasz, E., Schubert, A., & Vicsek, T. (2002). Evolution of the social network of scientific collaborations. *Physica A: Statistical Mechanics and its Applications*, 311, 590–614.

Bertha N. C. S, & Joel F. A. (2019). Vulnerable Areas in Tourist Cities of Coastal Zones: Campeche, Mexico. *WIT Transactions on the Built Environment, 188*, 83. https://doi.org/10.2495/CC190081

Chen, C. (2006). Citespace II: Detecting and Visualizing Emerging Trends and Transient Patterns in Scientific Literature. *Journal of American Society for Information Science and Technology*, *57*(3), 359–377.

Chen, C., Chen, Y., Horowitz, M., Hou, H., Liu, Z., & Pellegrino, D. (2009). Towards an explanatory and computational theory of scientific discovery. *Journal of Informetrics*, 3, 191–209.

Choi, J., Yi, S., & Lee, K. C. (2011). Analysis of Keyword Networks in MIS Research and Implications for Predicting Knowledge Evolution. *Information & Management*, *48*(8), 371–381. doi:10.1016/j.im.2011.09.004.

Cocks, C. (2013). *Tropical whites: The rise of the tourist South in the Americas*. University of Pennsylvania Press, Inc.

Daniel, R. (2015). Creative Industries in the Tropics: Reflections on Creativity and Northeastern Australia as Place. *Singapore Journal of Tropical Geography*, *36*(2), 215–230. https://doi.org/10.1111/sjtg.12099

Darma Putra, I. N., Verheijen, B., Ardika, I. W., & Yanthy, P. S. (2021). Affinity Tourism and Exotic Tourism in Bali. The Chinese and Indian Tourist Gaze in the Garuda Wisnu Kencana Park. *Journal of Tourism and Cultural Change*, *19*(4), 427–443. https://doi.org/10.1080/14766825.2020.1797063

Frenkel, S. (1996). Jungle Stories: North American Representations of Tropical Panama. *Geographical Review*, *86*(3): 317–333.

Gössling, S., Scott, D., & Hall, C. M. (2020). Pandemics, Tourism and Global Change: A Rapid Assessment of COVID-19. *Journal of Sustainable Tourism*, *29*(1), 1–20. https://doi.org/10.1080/09669582.2020.1758708

Guo, H., Weingart, S., & Bo¨rner, K. (2011). Mixed-indicators Model for Identifying Emerging Research Areas. *Scientometrics*, *89*(1), 421–435. doi:10.1007/s11192-011-0433-7.

Hall, C. M., Williams, A. M., & Lew, A. A. (2014). Tourism. In *The Wiley Blackwell companion to tourism* (pp. 3–24). Wiley. https://doi.org/10.1002/9781118474648.ch1

Hamid, M. S. B. S., Baxter, G., & Wild, G. (2021). Passenger Perceptions Towards Service Quality of Airlines Based in Singapore. *International Review of Management and Marketing*, *11*(1), 78–91. https://doi.org/10.32479/irmm.9096

Hanneman, R. A., & Riddle, M. (2005). Introduction to social network methods. Riverside, CA: University of California. Published in digital form at http://faculty.ucr.edu/*hanneman/

Jang, H. Wood, J. & Khan, G. F. (2017). A Social Network Analysis of Knowledge Infrastructure in the Second Language Acquisition Domain, *Journal of Linguistic Research*. *34*(Special Edition), 125–160.

Khan, F. G. & Wood, J. (2015). Information Technology Management Domain: Emerging Themes and Keyword Analysis. *Scientometrics*, *105*(2), 959–972.

Khan, F. G & Wood, J. (2017). Semantic and Knowledge Networks of the Information Technology Management Domain: A Social Network Analysis Approach. *Communications of the Association for Information Systems. 39*(1), 367–397.

Kieffer, M., & Burgos, A. (2015). Productive Identities and Community Conditions for Rural Tourism in Mexican Tropical Drylands. *Tourism Geographies, 17*(4), 561–585. https://doi.org/10.1080/14616688.2015.1043576

Kim, W. Khan, F. G. Wood, J. & Mahmood, M. T. (2016). Employee Engagement for Sustainable Organizations: Keyword Analysis Using Social Network Analysis and Burst Detection Approach. *Sustainability, 8*(631), 1–11.

King, R. (2017). An Accidental Bangkok Theme Park. *Tourism Geographies, 19*(5), 717–733. https://doi.org/10.1080/14616688.2017.1320583

Lett Jr, J. W. (1983). Ludic and Liminoid Aspects of Charter Yacht Tourism in the Caribbean. *Annals of Tourism Research, 10*(1), 35–56.

Leydesdorff, L. (2006). *The knowledge-based economy: Modeled, measured, simulated.* Universal Publishers.

Mane, K. K., & Börner, K. (2004). Mapping topics and topic bursts in PNAS. Proceedings of the National Academy of Sciences, *101*(suppl 1), 5287–5290.

Mudzengi, B. K., Gandiwa, E., Muboko, N., & Mutanga, C. N. (2021). Towards Sustainable Community Conservation in Tropical Savanna Ecosystems: A Management Framework for Ecotourism Ventures in a Changing Environment. *Environment, Development and Sustainability, 23*(3), 3028–3047. https://doi.org/10.1007/s10668-020-00772-4

Nelson, R. (2014). Infectious Risks of Medical Tourism. *The Lancet Infectious Diseases, 14*(8), 680–681. https://doi.org/10.1016/S1473-3099(14)70861-8

Noree, T., Hanefeld, J., & Smith, R. (2014). UK Medical Tourists in Thailand: They Are Not Who You Think They Are. *Globalization and Health, 10*(1), 29–29. https://doi.org/10.1186/1744-8603-10-29

Pearce, P. (2009). Tourism Research and the Tropics: Further Horizons, *Tourism Recreation Research, 34*(2), 107–121. DOI: 10.1080/02508281.2009.11081583

Pham, V. P. Q., & Thirumaran, K. (2016). Managing Development of Resort Destinations in Southeast Asia: Emerging and Peripheral Phu Quoc Island. In *Development of tourism and the hospitality industry in Southeast Asia* (pp. 83–95). Springer. https://doi.org/10.1007/978-981-287-606-5_6

Piscitelli, A. (2007). Tropical Sex in a European Country: Brazilian Women's Migration to Italy in the Frame of International Sex Tourism. *Estudos Feministas, 15*(3), 717–744.

Pongamponkaiwan, S., & Leelasantitham, A. (2020). The GAP Model of e-Government Service in Thailand e-Tourism. *ECTI Transactions on Computer and Information Technology, 14*(1), 11–19. https://doi.org/10.37936/ecti-cit.2020141.204409

Prideaux, B. (Bruce), & Coghlan, A. (2006). *Backpacker shopping in the tropics: an overview of the shopping behaviour of backpackers in Cairns.* James Cook University.

Sci2Team. (2009). Science of Science (Sci2) Tool Indiana University and SciTech Strategies. http://sci2.cns.iu.edu.

SekercioAlu, C. H. (2012). Promoting Community-based Bird Monitoring in the Tropics: Conservation, Research, Environmental Education, Capacity-building, and Local Incomes. *Biological Conservation, 151*(1), 69–73. https://doi.org/10.1016/j.biocon.2011.10.024

Silva, K. D., & Chapagain, N. K. (2013). Asian Heritage Management: Contexts, Concerns, and Prospects. In *Asian heritage management* (1st ed.). Taylor & Francis Group. https://doi.org/10.4324/9780203066591

Sirilersuang, P., & Pongkijvorasin, S. (2018). Dynamic Optimal Joint Policies for Tourism Promotion and Environmental Restoration. *Environmental Economics and Policy Studies*, *20*(2), 261–286. https://doi.org/10.1007/s10018-017-0193-6

Štetić, S., Šimičević, D., & Milićević, S. (2017). Information and communication technology as a driving force of changes in tourism. *Quaestus*, (10), 142–161.

Sum, N.-L. (2019). The Intertwined Geopolitics and Geoeconomics of Hopes/Fears: China's Triple Economic Bubbles and the 'One Belt One Road' Imaginary. *Territory, Politics, Governance*, 7(4), 528–552. https://doi.org/10.1080/21622671.2018.1523746

Swar, B., & Khan, G. (2014). Mapping ICT Knowledge Infrastructure in South Asia. *Scientometrics*, *99*(1), 117–137. doi:10.1007/s11192-013-1099-0.

Thirumaran, K., & Raghav, M. (2017) Luxury Tourism, Emerging Destinations: Research Review and Trajectories. *Asian Journal of Tourism Research*, *2*(2): 137–159.

Thirumaran, K., Jang, H., Pourabedin, Z. & Wood, J. (2021). The Role of Social Media in the Luxury Tourism Business: A Research Review and Trajectory Assessment. *Sustainability*, *13*(1216), 1–13.

Trương, T.-M. (1990). *Sex, money, and morality: prostitution and tourism in Southeast Asia*. Zed Books.

Tyllianakis, E., Grilli, G., Gibson, D., Ferrini, S., Conejo-Watt, H., & Luisetti, T. (2019). Policy Options to Achieve Culturally-aware and Environmentally-sustainable Tourism in Fiji. *Marine Pollution Bulletin*, *148*, 107–115. https://doi.org/10.1016/j.marpolbul.2019.07.031

Van Eck, N. J., & Waltman, L. (2010). Software Survey: VOSviewer, a Computer Program for Bibliometric Mapping. *Scientometrics*, *84*(2), 523–538.

Williamson, J. E., Byrnes, E. E., Clark, J. A., Connolly, D. M., Schiller, S. E., Thompson, J. A., Tosetto, L., Martinelli, J. C., & Raoult, V. (2017). Ecological Impacts and Management Implications of Reef Walking on a Tropical Reef Flat Community. *Marine Pollution Bulletin*, *114*(2), 742–750. https://doi.org/10.1016/j.marpolbul.2016.10.069

Wood, J. & Khan, F. G. (2015). International Trade Negotiation Analysis: Network and Semantic Knowledge Infrastructure. *Scientometrics*, *105*(1), 537–556.

Wood, J., Khan, F. G. & Kim, W. (2016). Work Engagement in Organizations: A Social Network Analysis of the Domain. *Scientometrics*, *109*(1), 317–336.

Wu, F., Heng, T. M., Siaw, P. T., Wee, S. K., & Kiat, L. T. (2002). Potential of the Chinese (PRC) and Indian Tourism Markets for ASEAN. *Asia Pacific Journal of Tourism Research*, 7(2), 45–76. https://doi.org/10.1080/10941660208722118

Yasué, M., & Dearden, P. (2008). Methods to Measure and Mitigate the Impacts of Tourism Development on Tropical Beach-Breeding Shorebirds: The Malaysian Plover in Thailand. *Tourism in Marine Environments*, *5*(4), 287–299

Yoon, B., & Park, Y. (2005). A systematic approach for identifying technology opportunities: Keywordbased morphology analysis. *Technological Forecasting and Social Change*, *72*, 145–160.

Zhang, J. (2017). Introduction: Integrated Mega-Casinos and Speculative Urbanism in Southeast Asia. *Pacific Affairs*, *90*(4), 651–674. https://doi.org/10.5509/2017904651lef tbottomInformation Classification: General00Information Classification: General

Index

Note: Page numbers in *italics* indicate figures, **bold** indicate tables in the text, and references following "n" refer endnotes.

For Product Safety Concerns and Information please contact our EU representative GPSR@taylorandfrancis.com
Taylor & Francis Verlag GmbH, Kaufingerstraße 24, 80331 München, Germany

www.ingramcontent.com/pod-product-compliance
Ingram Content Group UK Ltd.
Pitfield, Milton Keynes, MK11 3LW, UK
UKHW020152200926
475702UK00016B/2670

* 9 7 8 0 3 6 7 7 2 1 3 5 0 *